The Aircraft Owner's Handbook

Everything you need to know about buying, operating and selling an aircraft.

Second Edition

Timothy R.V. Foster

VNR **VAN NOSTRAND REINHOLD COMPANY**
NEW YORK   CINCINNATI   TORONTO   LONDON   MELBOURNE

For Mary

Copyright © 1983, 1978 by Van Nostrand Reinhold Company Inc.
Library of Congress Catalog Card Number 82-8507
ISBN 0-442-22579-2 (cloth)
ISBN 0-442-22581-4 (paper)

Printed in the United States of America
Designed by John Wilson of Pellegrini and Kaestle, Inc.

Published by Van Nostrand Reinhold Company Inc.
135 West 50th Street, New York, NY 10020

Van Nostrand Reinhold Publishers
1410 Birchmount Road
Scarborough, Ontario M1P 2E7, Canada

Van Nostrand Reinhold Australia Pty. Ltd.
480 Latrobe Street
Melbourne, Victoria 3000, Australia

Van Nostrand Reinhold Company Limited
Molly Millars Lane
Wokingham, Berkshire, England RG11 2PY

16 15 14 13 12 11 10 9 8 7 6 5 4 3 2 1

Library of Congress Cataloging in Publication Data
Foster, Timothy R. V.
   The aircraft owner's handbook.
   Includes index.
   1. Private flying—Handbooks, manuals etc.   I. Title.
TL721.4.F63   1983   629.133'340422   82-8507
ISBN 0-442-22579-2   AACR 2
ISBN 0-442-22581-4 (pbk.)

Acknowledgments

I would like to acknowledge the help or advice received from many people and firms. In alphabetical order, these are the people: Pappy Agnew, John Alter, Bob Beach, Gerald Berry, Gifford Booth, Karen Borger, George Brewer, David Charlaff, Craig Christie, Leighton Collins, Richard Collins, Keith Connes, Karen Coyle, Bob Dalin, Joe Diblin, Norman Dunn, Roger Elliott, Bob Englander, Don Fairchilds, Dennis Feldman, Mary Foster, Sue Freeman, Bob Garlich, Jim Holohan, Mike Hoffman, Kitty Howser, Chuck Hubbard, Dean Humphrey, Aubrey Johnson, Ray Johnson, David Kaestle, Stancie Lane, Jay Lavenson, Russ Lawton, John Leahy, Ann Lennon, Stu Leventhal, Arnold Lewis, Basil Maile, Hal McClure, Bernie McGowan, Gene Meyer, Gid Miller, Dee Mosteller, Mike Murrell, Ollie O'Mahoney, Bob Pellegrini, Sander Rang des Adrets, Laurie Rice, Steve Rich, Bill Robinson, Ken Ross, Frances Rudulph, Palmer Schade, Mike Schloss, Laurel Smith, Larry Snoddon, Jim Snowden, Bob Stanfield, Marvin Stern, Ed Stimpson, Don Stretch, Ernie Tyler, Mark Weaver, Dick Weeghman, Bob Weingarten, Mike Wilkinson, John Wilson, Betty Wolf, Marilyn Zimmer, John Zimmerman.

And these are the firms and organizations: Adlog Systems, Aerosonic Corporation, Aircraft Appraisal Association of America, Inc., Aircraft Owners and Pilots Association, Air Progress, Airtex Products, Inc., Avco Lycoming, Avemco, The Aviation Consumer, Aviation Convention News, Beech Aircraft Corporation, Bellanca Aircraft Corporation, Bendix Corporation, Cessna Aircraft Corporation, Clear Lake Aviation Services, Davtron, Inc., Federal Aviation Agency, General Aviation Electronics, Inc., General Aviation Manufacturers Association, General Electric Credit Corporation, Great Lakes Aircraft, Inc., Grumman American Aviation Corporation, Jeppesen Sanderson, Inc., King Radio Corporation, Mattituck Airbase, Inc., Mooney Aircraft Corporation, Morgan Stanford Aviation, Narco Avionics, National Aviation Underwriters, National Pilots Association, National Transportation Safety Board, Piper Aircraft Corporation, Robertson Aircraft Corporation, Rockwell International Corporation, Scott Aviation, Seguin Aviation Inc., Taylorcraft Aviation Corporation, Ted Smith Aerostar Corporation, Teledyne Continental Motors, Ziff-Davis Publishing Company.

Much of the material on engines came from the Avco Lycoming Flyer. Many of the photographs were taken by Stu Leventhal. The graphics were created by Gene Soja.

The Aircraft Owner's Handbook was designed by John Wilson of Pellegrini and Kaestle, Inc.

Thank you all.

Timothy R. V. Foster
Yardley, Pennsylvania
March 1982

Table of contents

Table of contents

About the *Plane Profiles*

Throughout this book you will find profiles of currently available aircraft. They appear in random order. A couple of points: the empty weight given is that without optional accessories and the useful load given is that available for passengers, baggage, freight and accessories with full optional fuel on board. Now some aircraft can carry an awful lot of fuel, to the extent that you may be able to carry only two or three people when you fill 'er up. Obviously if you want to fill all the seats, you can't fill all the tanks in such cases. Don't forget that you'll also need to allow for optional accessories (such as avionics, air conditioning and other extras) in the useful load figure. Typical accessories weights amount to 60 to 100 pounds for a single and about 100 to 200 pounds for a twin. Bear in mind also that the range, speed and fuel efficiencies are calculated at 65% power. If you would cruise at a different power setting, all the numbers will change. The range given is an indication of the still-air range calculated by multiplying the maximum endurance at 65% power at optimum altitude, less a one-hour reserve, by the cruising speed at that power setting and altitude. The minimum field length is the longest of either the takeoff or landing distance over a 50-ft obstacle. The Profiles are of some aircraft in current production at the beginning of 1982.

Profile Index
by profile number

Profile Index
alphabetical by manufacturer

Foreword

Profile Index
by configuration

The Aircraft Owner's Handbook is an important addition to aviation literature, as it is the product of a singularly well-ordered mind and is based upon a thoroughly researched need for such a publication. At the same time I have some concern about those critical early months all books go through. In attempting to ease the way, I feel somewhat as if I were in the role of a marriage counselor.

For owning an airplane is a love affair. Many of those who will buy this handbook are those who have their heart set on owning an airplane, and most likely they will have one special one, one above all, constantly in the background of all their thoughts. Which is a good start. But even aircraft ownership is not that simple. No one can pick a mate for someone else, but at least it is possible to try to help the process of natural selection. And that is the role of *The Aircraft Owner's Handbook*. Attuned with a deep desire to be of help and put together by a man who puts his airplane if not first then second.

The handbook is remarkable in many ways. First of all, do not think of it as a book, something you should contemplate sitting down and reading right through and absorbing. It's too comprehensive for that. Instead, think of it as an encyclopedia in which you can find the way to a reasoned answer to almost any problem of buying, operating, or selling an airplane. First you decide what it is you need to know now and then you go to the appropriate section.

As an example, say you have already decided on the airplane you want but would like to know more than you do about its structural history (test flights and test rigs cannot duplicate the entire user environment). You can readily find in the handbook how to go about getting a printout from the FAA covering the last five years' reported service difficulties and how to research the airworthiness-directives history of this particular make and model. Which, of course, would be the starting point for seeing if the aircraft's logs show compliance with these ADs.

On a broader scale I would like to comment on some of the factoring and worksheet pages that might make the handbook seem a bit forbidding. Whatever business you're in, you are likely to find them an intriguing example of the decision-making process in the abstract. Computerlike in a way but clearly marking the path to a happy union. Which, of course, is the way our minds work when they work, which isn't always easy when one is in love.

The purpose of the handbook is to help them work. And I believe the careful research and wealth of data and the analytical approach to picking the right airplane and living happily with it make the handbook a valuable asset. I can't think of a remedy not covered.

by Leighton Collins

Introduction

The purpose of this book

The Aircraft Owner's Handbook is designed to provide current and potential aircraft owners with the information they need to buy, operate, and sell an aircraft. It is intended to be a workbook as well as a source of data.

I have been flying for almost 30 years. I made my first solo in a Miles Hawk Trainer III from Croydon Airport near London at the age of 17, and went on to get my private pilot's license a few months later. I then moved from England to Canada and pursued my flying aspirations by obtaining a commercial license, an instrument rating, a multi-engine rating, and an instructor's rating. I capped it off with an airline transport license. I flew as a primary instructor, as an instrument instructor, and as a charter pilot. I flew all over the United States and Canada, flying over 150 different types of aircraft.

Then I moved to the United States, obtained a U.S. Commercial Certificate, and bought a Piper Comanche 250—my first airplane. Buying the Comanche made me realize something that I hadn't discovered in over two decades of flying: owning an airplane is a very different experience from being a pilot! There are things about owning a plane that a rental pilot or hired hand never get involved with. Like paying the bills, deciding what to buy, filing government use reports and IRS use-tax returns, claiming state fuel-tax rebates, buying insurance, getting an engine overhauled, ordering spare parts, figuring out how to sell a plane, getting warranty work done, complying with ADs, and much more.

This book attempts to put it all together. It starts with a review and needs analysis for those of you who haven't yet made the first move toward buying an airplane. It takes you through budgeting, tax considerations, getting a loan, and buying insurance. It talks about the law and how it affects the owner. It reviews the marketplace and discusses how airplanes are bought and sold. It covers upgrading and modifying your plane and getting it painted. It goes through many operating considerations, such as choosing an FBO, making a survival kit, what to do if you have an accident. It discusses avionics, how to buy them, how to have them maintained, and what they do for you. It gives a quick rundown on basic aircraft systems and then goes into maintenance in some detail—what you can and can't do, what happens at an annual inspection, an engine overhaul, and how to tell if your engine *needs* to be overhauled. And it gives you a troubleshooting guide to help you tell your mechanic what's wrong. Finally the book provides important addresses and a comprehensive index.

The Aircraft Owner's Handbook has been designed for you to *use*. It is not a coffee-table book. It is intended to work for you as hard as you did (or will) to get your airplane.

Feeling the pulse of general aviation

As part of the research I did in preparing this book, I surveyed many aircraft owners and pilots to find out their needs and attitudes. I would like to share with you some of the thoughts expressed. They say better than I can what sort of things are on the minds of general aviation participants today. There were several open-ended questions. Here they are and some of the verbatim answers given:

Q: *What is the single most frustrating thing about general aviation today?*
"High cost of insurance and parts." "Taxes on aviation gas. The taxes are refundable, so why impose them in the first place?" "1. FAA Regulations. 2. Cost of ADs passed on to the owner. 3. Taxation of general aviation and not the airlines." "Cost of flying and maintaining proficiency." "Maintenance: are the FBO and his A&Ps truly reliable? In my case I have an excellent FBO. Many of my friends do not." "The future availability of fuel for pleasure flying." "We need more general aviation airports in metropolitan areas, land to be owned by local or federal government so the FBOs can afford to operate." "Parts costs from airframe and avionics manufacturers (300%-400% markups over original equipment-manufacturer net might work with the auto industry [because of million × efficiencies], but will *kill* general aviation)." "Pilots flying at improper altitudes!" *The high cost*—from the purchase of aircraft, repair of them and inspection of them, to the cost of fuel, use taxes, etc!" "The idle chatter on 122.9 and other frequencies. I don't feel that weather info is current enough. It is hard to find airports with 80/87 fuel."

Q: *Please indicate the best thing about being a pilot:*
"Freedom of movement. The ability to capitalize on precious time." "Flying—it's fun!" "Doing something difficult and challenging—and doing it well." "Only place where you can get a good view without a crowd." "I fly for the pleasure of flight. I keep upgrading my ticket for the challenge." "Better perspective on earthly matters." "It's a many-splendored thing: (a) the beauty and freedom aesthetically, (b) the need to be alert and knowledgeable, (c) the need for study and learning, (d) the emotional quality of its various facets—aerobatics, instrument flying ...—(e) the total dependence of your life on your own skills." "It's what I am and like to do!"

Q: *Please indicate the best thing about owning an airplane:*
"Not having to worry about what works and what doesn't. It's mine and I'm the only one that uses it, so I know." "Having been in a club and a partnership, the plane is always there when I want it, and there is no need to make reservations." "Tre-

Introduction

mendous increase in places to go and things to do." "Ability to travel distances basically without congestion and masses of the road." "Freedom to go where and when I want (subject to weather)—ability to take a trip impossible or expensive otherwise." "Absolute certainty about maintenance and damage history." "Knowing its operating characteristics well, knowing just where all knobs, switches, etc., are. Knowing it hasn't been overstressed by a renter trying to show off." "My leaseback helps to keep the cost of flying down some." "Values appear to be going higher." "Knowing I was in the plane last and its safe condition." "It costs too much, but it's yours." "Despite the great expense, it is the only way to have an airplane 'ready when you are'—further, the condition of the machine is a constantly known quantity." "Use of own plane for travel and ability to fly to small towns and cities." "I feel a lot safer in a plane I alone have responsibility for maintaining."

Q: *In what area of owning an airplane do you feel that you don't know enough?*

"Monitoring and knowing quality of maintenance." "Where to find the best deals on equipment. I currently feel like a captive customer on all my purchases." "Tax write-offs." "Detection of minor mechanical problems before they become major." "How to achieve dollar savings." "Holding costs down." "Flying it." "I like articles about how to get the most out of my plane in the area of performance. How to keep it in good condition for reliable service." "Where to get discount parts." "Insurance—cutting costs—how to make it work financially." "IFR." "I don't know whether to repair or replace in many instances." "I need a continuing review of the basics." "Constant battle to keep thoroughly current in IFR and emergency conditions." "Maintenance." (About half the respondents gave this one-word answer.)

Q: *If you were taking a tour of the plant of an aircraft manufacturer, what question would you ask?*

"Why is everything in and on an airplane so expensive as compared to the manufacturing of automobiles?" "What quality-control procedures are followed and how are the results translated into better, more reliable performance?" "What have you done to make an aircraft truly different and unique in *some aspect* from any of the others?" "Why do you charge so much for your product?" "Why aren't manufacturers interested in developing new techniques which require less 'hand labor' and simpler airframe construction?" "What performance changes or modifications do you see coming up in newer models or types?" "What is being done to control increases in product prices?" "Tell me about the tolerances and backup systems in the aircraft." "What can be done about building in more quality and why is the warranty period so short?" "How do you know what type of plane the normal person desires?" "What documents are available for a complete understanding of the plane and modifications?" "Why can't individual parts be sold for less?" "How could you make the aircraft easier to maintain?" "How do you ensure quality control and what responsibility do you assume?" "What are the quality and safety restraints on manufacturing and how are they maintained?" "With cost of materials and our modern production lines, why does a plane cost so much?" "Since aircraft cost so much and are made to such high standards, why is the guarantee so short as compared to the standard automobile?" "Why do planes cost so much?" "Is your quality-control and inspection program enough?" "Tell me about your research effort for *low-cost, modern* design."

I sent the above questions to Beech, Cessna, and Piper and here are their responses.

Beech replies: "Beech Aircraft has always built handcrafted quality into its products, while employing the latest state-of-the-art trends in avionics, interiors, and so on. Beech is deeply interested in new manufacturing techniques and is a pioneer in metal bonding, a process now being incorporated on many Beechcraft models for nonstructural parts.

"Beech is currently producing 20 distinctly different models, from the single-engine Beech Sport to the turboprop Super King Air, thus offering a wide choice of products for varying tasks and mission requirements.

"Beech parts are priced in accordance with the policy of pricing other Beechcraft products, which simply means that under our free-enterprise system American industry can expect a reasonable profit."

Cessna replies: "At Cessna we anticipate that future performance improvements will concentrate heavily on fuel efficiency. We also expect to continue to make evolutionary changes which will improve the general utility of our aircraft and upgrade payload, takeoff, climb, cruise, and landing performance.

"Cessna has a comprehensive cost-control program. This includes the application of latest technologies in value analysis, make-or-buy analysis, multisource and competitive purchasing, and improved tooling and manufacturing methods. Because of the sizable inflation in the cost of everything that goes into our products—labor, materials, and purchased parts—these efforts in recent years have been successful only to the extent of holding down the rate of increase in our prices. Airplane price increases would be considerably higher without our aggressive cost-control efforts. General aviation aircraft manufacturing is highly competitive and there is a great deal of stimulus for the manufacturers to produce airplanes at minimum cost.

"As a holder of FAA Production Certificates, we maintain a comprehensive quality-control system at each of our manufacturing facilities. The system is operated in accordance with Quality Control Procedures Manuals which are approved by the FAA. Each aircraft model has a large number of quality checks as a part of its fabrication, assembly, and flight-acceptance testing specified for it. These are documented in a product-inspection record prepared for each individual airplane. Quality-control laboratories make numerous accep-

Introduction

tance tests on materials and components. In addition, several hundred skilled quality-control technicians and management personnel continually make a wide variety of checks—dimensional, visual, eddy current, magnaflux, die-penetrant, etc.—using techniques and equipment appropriate for each quality-control task. Operation of the quality-control system is continuously validated by a team which makes audits (spot checks) of the full spectrum of operations affecting aircraft quality. The FAA periodically conducts an extensive audit of each plant's quality-control system. These audits typically take several weeks and involve about a dozen FAA quality-control specialists drawn from various parts of the country. On a continuing basis, both the company and the FAA monitor reports of service difficulties from the field, and corrective action is taken when a potential problem appears.

"Finding out the desires of prospective buyers of any product is a complex subject, one on which most manufacturing companies spend much time and effort. We receive a great deal of input relative to future product desires from dealers, distributors, and other personnel who have close, continued contact with the owners and operators of our current aircraft. We also receive a number of inputs directly from present and prospective owners and operators. Another good source of information is the observance of characteristics and features embodied in those airplanes which are popular in the marketplace."

Piper replies: "With regard to quality control, when field reports indicate that there might be a particular problem with an airplane, the problem is researched, evaluated, and changes are made in design, manufacturing, vendor designs, inspection procedures, or maintenance procedures, and, if necessary, a service bulletin is issued. There are several stages of product refinement at Piper—ranging from simple interpretation of maintenance-manual data for an individual to an all-out,

worldwide campaign to retrofit all aircraft of a certain model.

"Every field report, production-test report, flight-test report, engineering analysis, and suggestion is carefully analyzed and action is taken to provide our customers with the best airplane possible through a continuous process of refinement and improvements.

"With regard to warranties, firstly, an airplane is designed to perform a number of very diverse functions—from crop dusting to airline service, to pleasure flying and student training. Apart from the design intentions, airplanes are put into even more diverse operations by the owners. And, because of the very nature of the industry, an average airplane rarely stays at home or is maintained solely by a single mechanic or flown by a single pilot. Also, an airplane is constantly being flown at the maximum of its performance limits. How often is an automobile run at full power and down roads that test its handling to the limits?

"By the nature of the usage and the design and construction of the airplane, Piper establishes warranty policies to take care of the airplane while we maintain reasonable control over its maintenance and operation. Six months usually results in about 300 hours of service, and enough operational experience to clear up discrepancies attributable to the manufacture of the airplane. The warranty is based on an overall evaluation of the operation of the average airplane and its components, with a careful analysis of our responsibility for workmanship and design involved in manufacturing.

"It would be totally unrealistic to expect a company that is in business to make a profit, to support its product for life, without absolute control over its operation and maintenance.

"Secondly, we, the aircraft manufacturer, are subject to the terms and limitations of the warranties offered by the various component manufacturers whose equipment we install and use.

"The line has to be drawn somewhere, and the time limits and

coverage stated in warranties are carefully analyzed, monitored, and accounted for in order to provide the best service possible while maintaining a reasonable profit margin.

"The price of any aircraft is dictated to a large degree by volume. If aircraft were produced in the same quantities as automobiles, we might see a considerable change in price structure.

"Another view, however, is that a modern, luxury car can cost $10,000 and travel legally at 55 mph and get 15 mpg. A modern aircraft can cost three times as much, travel three times faster, and still get 15 mpg.

"It's a matter of how much your time is worth."

Q: *If you were meeting with the head of the FAA, what would you have to say?*

"Why aren't ATC rules and procedures from your operations manual more publicized to pilots?" "Why can't there be climb and descent corridors instead of TCAs?" "There is a strong need to continue to help promote economically general aviation without excessive federal constraints except where safety can be proven as an issue." "Please don't regulate me any more than necessary." "Continue on your present course, and general aviation will soon be just history." "Test CFIs for teaching skills, not flying skills. Do more research into readily identifying the pilot who won't turn around when he should." "Don't forget the little guy who flies a single-engine plane." "Why are you trying to legislate/price us out of the sky?" "I suggest a thorough housecleaning of deadwood personnel, and the establishment of new goals to *help* general aviation." "There is no easy, low-cost way of keeping up with the regulations." "Take a look at restrictive legislation. The system is tailored to the airlines' needs." "I would encourage persecution of ripoff FBOs, painters, flight schools, and other shady operators." "Your department is relatively insensitive to the largest segment of aviation and too sensitive to the smallest." "Why do your controllers make it so difficult to fly the system?" "We need

Introduction

better, faster weather data dissemination." "The instrument rating should be a universal requirement, and there should be rigid periodic flight checks." "I am a free person living in a free country. Please don't restrict me with needless regulations or force me to purchase more avionics." "FAA costs could be cut—many locations overstaffed—soft jobs/high pay—give *me* a job!" "I am concerned about the costs of the FAA on a per-pilot basis and the constant increase of control over pilots, airspace, and airplanes." "Why not make Parts 2 and 3 of the *Airman's Information Manual* easier to read and understand?" "Thanks for navaids, FSS, Flight Watch, and good basic regulations, but don't lose sight of the rights and value of general aviation and the private pilot." "Thanks for your help!" "Let's ar-

range ATC and FARs to suit pilots, not to serve internal FAA requirements." "Why is it, in the largest regulatory body in existence for aviation, that there is apparently such a lack of knowledge on its part dealing with aviation? If adequate knowledge exists, why are so many regulations arbitrary, indicating otherwise?" "Thank you for the many courtesies shown to me and remember that general aviation carries more people than airlines to places otherwise unreachable conveniently."

I sent these comments to the FAA, and here is their reply:

"One of the major challenges for the FAA in the years ahead is to find ways of providing services that the aviation public truly needs and at a cost it can afford.

"Although the cost of using the national aviation system will continue

to increase, along with everything else, FAA will strive to keep the cost of services it provides at a minimum by making sure operational and equipment requirements are needed, reasonable, and flexible enough to accommodate the various needs of the aviation community.

"FAA recognizes that general aviation is a vital industry that accounts for 98 percent of all civil aircraft in the U.S., and that it is a diverse industry which performs a wide variety of important tasks that could not be handled nearly as efficiently or economically by any other means.

"We will continue to promote the interests of general aviation and see to it that national policy reflects the increasingly vital role that general aviation will inevitably play in the U.S. transportation network of the future."

Plane Profile 1: Piper PA 44-180T Turbo Seminole

Seats	4
Cruise speed, 65% power,	
8,000 feet	154 knots
18,000 feet	169 knots
Range, 65% power, full	
optional fuel, 18,000 feet	625 nm
Maximum endurance	4.7 hours
Gross weight	3,943 pounds
Empty weight	2,430 pounds
Full optional fuel	648 pounds
	108 gallons
Useful load, full fuel	865 pounds
Fuel efficiency, 65%	
power	7.7 nmpg
Stall speed, gear and	
flaps down	56 knots
Rate of climb, sea level	1,290 fpm
	180 fpm s/e
Minimum field length	2,200 feet
Engine type 2 Lycoming	
T0360-E1A6D	180 hp
Engine TBO	1,800 hours
Remarks Turbocharged. Also available without turbocharging.	

Introduction to second edition

It's hard to believe that five years have gone by since I wrote *The Aircraft Owner's Handbook*. In that time, the nature of general aviation has changed substantially. Fuel prices have more than doubled. New aircraft prices have followed suit. Labor rates have gone from about $16 an hour to about $25. Many favorite airplanes are no longer made—Cessna discontinued the old standby, the 180, the Skymaster "push-pull" twin (still being made by their French subsidiary), the Cardinal and Cardinal RG, the Hawk XP, the 310 (once billed as the WBAALT—"world's best all-around light twin"), and the 335. Beech ended production of its Skipper trainer after only a couple of years, although they say they will start the line up again when demand returns. Piper killed off the venerable Aztec and the *Cub!* Is nothing sacred? Grumman American became Gulfstream American and converted exclusively to "big iron," dropping the Trainer, the Tiger and the Cougar. The same company then took over the General Aviation Division of Rockwell International (for-

merly Aero Commander), and put the attractive 112 and 114 high-performance singles to death. They also cut their losses on the oversized, underpowered 700 twin. Bellanca closed down, terminating the Viking, the Aries, the Citabria and Scout. And Wing Aircraft, which ten years ago developed its unique two-seater Derringer Twin, emerged as a production facility, actually selling airplanes!

The atmosphere for general aviation was not affected by higher prices alone. Very high interest rates no doubt made a major contribution to the obituary column above. They reduced sales in the single-engine end, while an increase in sales in the jet and turboprop field was registered.

Another major influence on the aviator's way of life was the 1981 PATCO strike and resultant decrease in air traffic control capacity. Many people found it more difficult to get where they wanted to on any sort of reliable schedule, and it's going to stay that way for the next two years or so.

The general malaise in the world economy has also hit the airline indus-

try very hard. Many airlines are hanging on by a thread as I write. Thousands of airline pilots have been furloughed. There is very little pilot-hiring going on. This has a major trickle-down effect on the flight-training industry. For every airline pilot who gets hired by a major carrier, you can track back to the flight schools and see about 20 student beginners. And every 20 new students translate to perhaps one new trainer on the line. And that is when the general aviation industry is healthy. The reverse is now the case.

The Economic Recovery Tax Act of 1981 will help corporations who need airplanes. Depreciation schedules and investment tax credits have been liberalized, making the acquisition of these expensive business tools more attractive. But the same act killed off the airplane leaseback as a tax shelter for individuals, thus hurting many fixed base operators and flight schools.

Let us hope that the introduction to the *next* issue of *The Aircraft Owner's Handbook* has a more joyful outlook.

Rockwell International Commander 112 TCA

Considering it

Considering it

Why fly?

General aviation in the United States is developed to the highest level of any country in the world. There are more pilots, airplanes, and airports in the U.S. than anywhere else. We have the best facilities for navigation, the best airports, the best aircraft designs—the best aviation *system.*

The freedom a U.S. pilot has would make a pilot from any other country green with envy. Some countries don't even *allow* private airplanes or tax their operation at such punitive rates that no one can afford to use them. Some countries have rules of such complexity and bias against general aviation that the operation of a private airplane is next to impossible.

In the United States you can learn to fly at a place of your choice, in a plane of your choice, over whatever period of time you choose. You can buy an airplane, new or used, in an active marketplace. There is an enormous variety of airplanes to choose from—to suit almost every need. Or you can rent an airplane wherever you go. No matter where you want to go, there is an airport nearby that you can land at, often without payment of any kind. And you don't have to get *permission* to go there. You just go. If the weather's not good, you can, with the proper training and equipment—readily available—still fly just about anywhere. Most towns have an airport with some kind of instrument approach available. The facilities on the ground are designed to suit your needs. You can get a taxi or a rental car or a free courtesy car when you get on the ground. The nearby hotel or motel will pick you up free of charge and bring you back first thing in the morning. When you want to call the Flight Service Station to check weather or file a flight plan, if there isn't one near you, there's probably a local or a toll-free number to call from where you are.

With your own airplane at your disposal you can just about write your own schedule. There are less than 500 towns and cities in the U.S. served by commercial airlines. But there are over 13,000 airports throughout the land. So you go *when* you want to, *where* you want to. *One-third of all intercity air travelers go in non-airline aircraft.*

An airplane can be thought of as a toy for the rich; it can be a relaxation device for the tense and harried, and especially a vital business machine to a corporation. With an airplane, key people can be where they have to be on a schedule that would be impossible to keep any other way. For weekending, if you live in the East, for example, you can be on the Maine shore one weekend, in Montreal the next, and colonial Williamsburg the next. You can fly right across the country in less than two or three days.

Here are some opinions about being a pilot and owning an airplane, expressed by people I surveyed when I was preparing this book.

"Weather allowing, an airplane is a getaway machine to find new clients."

"I get to go longer distances on weekend trips."

"I can go cross-country without waiting on airlines and their schedules."

"An airplane gives me the freedom to go where I please—beautiful scenery—beautiful clouds—saving in time, especially overwater legs."

"I like the freedom of action it gives you."

"Owning your own plane gives you the capability of going or staying without answering to anyone."

"I do it for the sheer enjoyment of flying."

Flying is expensive, there's no denying it. But it can often be justified in terms of time saved, greater opportunity, or flexibility. One of the biggest mistakes you can make is to buy the wrong type of aircraft for the job you want to do. Either it won't perform the tasks you set it or it will cost too much. You will become disillusioned. Maybe its performance and handling characteristics are beyond your level of experience.

Buying an airplane is largely an emotional experience. Most pilots lust in their hearts for a particular type of plane—whether it be a P 51 or a Tiger Moth, a Lear Jet or a Cessna 185 on wheel-floats. That's great if you can afford it. However, when you get down to reality, it makes sense to buy the right kind of plane for the job—or find out that you'd be better off renting one. That's what this section of *The Aircraft Owner's Handbook* is about. In the next few pages you will be able to review in great detail all the considerations you should make when picking an airplane. The first consideration is whether you should buy an airplane at all.

Should you buy, rent, or do what?

This book is called *The Aircraft Owner's Handbook.* However, you should look at all the angles, including not buying. Here are the alternatives.

1. Straight ownership—personal or corporate. This is very straightforward. You have no one to answer to but yourself (or your shareholders) as to what you buy, how you equip it, or where you go. This is also probably the most expensive route to take. It makes sense where you have: (a) legitimate business use for the aircraft, (b) high utilization, (c) the money to afford it. If your utilization is likely to be low (under 150 hours per year), you should consider a less expensive means of getting into an aircraft, such as:
2. Straight ownership with a leaseback arrangement. Here you buy the aircraft, then lease it back to an operator, such as a flight school, who will use the plane and pay you an hourly the rate for its use. This used to be a popular way to buy an airplane.

Considering it

However, under the Economic Recovery Tax Act (ERTA) of 1981, the tax benefits from such an arrangement are not available to individuals unless they are demonstrably in the leasing business. (See page 33 for a more detailed look at this.)

3. Partnership—actually a joint tenancy. This can be a good way of owning an airplane relatively economically. All you need is a partner (or partners) who knows what he or she is doing, whom you can trust, who is financially responsible, and who is not likely to want the airplane when you do and vice versa. This method cuts your fixed costs at least in half and keeps the airplane active, which is good.

4. Flying club. There are many good flying clubs around. This is probably the most economical way to have good, reliable equipment available to you that you can take away for a trip. The best idea here is to pick a club that caters to your level of expertise and needs. Some clubs specialize in IFR, de-iced twins. Others have a Cessna 170 and a Tri-Pacer, with a KX-150 at best for radio. You can match your needs in many instances. According to AOPA, there are about 3,000 flying clubs in existence, operating about 4,500 aircraft. Clubs range from three or four members in size, with one aircraft, up to maybe 200 members using 25 aircraft. You can locate clubs through ads in publications such as *AOPA Pilot* or *Flying*, or ask at the airport.

5. Leasing. There are several ways to lease an aircraft. You can lease them "wet" (with maintenance and insurance), "dry" (without), for a long term (such as five years) or a short term (such as three months). A long-term lease will cost at least as much as ownership, although the tax consequences may differ. (See page 35 for more details.)

Pros.	Cons.
Individual vs multiple ownership	
You call the shots	More expensive
No reservations required to use the airplane	
Lower insurance cost	
You control who flies it	
Multiple vs individual ownership	
Lower cost	Your use of the airplane is subject to the needs of your partners
Greater camaraderie	If one of the other partners damages the airplane, you could be without it for a while, through no fault of your own
	Higher insurance cost
	Airplane may not be equipped exactly according to your taste
	Complex situation regarding changes in partnership or dissolution

Pros.	Cons.
Owning vs leasing	
Ownership is an asset	Capital tied up
Leasing vs owning	
Capital not tied up	Not an asset
Better use of credit lines	Long time liability
Possible tax advantages	Absolute overall cost may be higher
Length of lease can be related to actual need	Lessee is beholden to Lessor
Some leases can be cancelled relatively easily	
Even monthly payments — known costs	
Various lease plans available	

6. Rental. This is the way most of us started. This is what you do when you learn to fly and then keep flying after you get your license. It is the simplest solution for the low-utilization pilot. The biggest problem lies in finding an aircraft equipped as you want it that you can take away for a trip. Hardly any rental outfit wants you to take away its income-producing machine for a long weekend unless you are going to produce a reasonable amount of income for them with it. Rental is probably the best answer for utilization at the 40-to-50-hours-per-year level or lower. To overcome the weekend problem, you may be able to work out a rental arrangement with an individual where you buy a block of time and can use the airplane for reasonably long periods of time when you have it. You will occasionally see "Block time available" ads offering perhaps 50 hours in a Bonanza for a reasonable rate.

Pros.	**Cons.**
Owning vs renting	
Can use airplane at will	Much higher per-hour cost if utilization is low
Can equip airplane according to personal taste	Much more complicated responsibilities
Can select type of airplane ideally suited to type of operation	Aircraft unavailable during maintenance
Greater reliability	Capital tied up
Greater safety due to owner familiarity	Greater liability
Better insurance coverage	
More prestige	
You control who flies it	
Renting vs owning	
Pay for airplane as used	Seldom can get airplane equipped as desired
Lower overall cost unless utilization is high	More prone to mechanical problems due to wide variety of pilots involved
Uncomplicated responsibilities	Lower safety due to lower renter-pilot familiarity
Capital not tied up	Sometimes hard or impossible to get airplane when wanted

Interior of Mooney 201, plush seating for four

Beech Bonanza A 36

Considering it

Considerations and compromises

Picking an aircraft means making a compromise. There is no one ideal airplane. Maybe there are four or five ideal airplanes. I would pick the following for my "dream hangar": something aerobatic—maybe a Pitts Special; something amphibious—maybe a Lake Amphibian or a Lane Riviera if I could find one; a helicopter—probably a Bell Jet Ranger; a Pressurized Centurion for fast short trips and a Lear Jet for fast long trips. I have compromised with a Comanche 250! You too must compromise, if you want to afford one airplane, and select the airplane that does most of the jobs you want it to do most efficiently.

Picking any aircraft involves a series of decisions, and the important thing is to make them in the right order. Where do you start? Some of the decisions will be based on preference; others will be dictated by need. Do you want long range, short-field capability, two engines, six seats, retractable gear, turbocharging, a low wing? Which of these is a preference decision and which is based on need? And what is the first decision you have to make?

To help you I have devised a flow chart that shows the logical sequence of decisions that need to be made. Look at it for a moment and follow the sequence through quickly. Each item shown is covered in this book in greater detail in the following pages. If you follow the routine suggested in this chart, you will find it easy to come up with the best airplane for your needs.

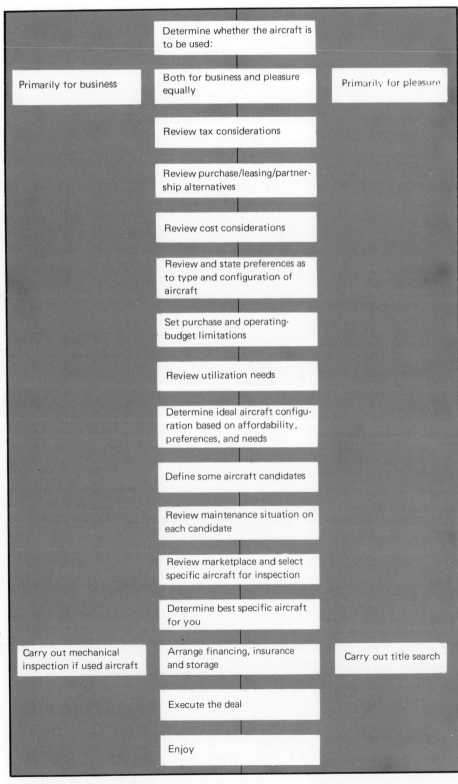

Determine whether the aircraft is to be used:

Primarily for business | Both for business and pleasure equally | Primarily for pleasure

Review tax considerations

Review purchase/leasing/partnership alternatives

Review cost considerations

Review and state preferences as to type and configuration of aircraft

Set purchase and operating-budget limitations

Review utilization needs

Determine ideal aircraft configuration based on affordability, preferences, and needs

Define some aircraft candidates

Review maintenance situation on each candidate

Review marketplace and select specific aircraft for inspection

Determine best specific aircraft for you

Carry out mechanical inspection if used aircraft | Arrange financing, insurance and storage | Carry out title search

Execute the deal

Enjoy

Business, pleasure, or both?

Will you fly your airplane mostly for business trips, mostly for pleasure trips, or both? Your answer is important because it affects the amount of money you can afford to spend on buying and operating the aircraft. Genuine business use of an airplane is a legitimate business expense as much as is use of a computer or a car on business trips. Even occasional use of the aircraft for business can make a contribution to your expenses. However, if you are using the plane strictly for pleasure, you'll be doing it with your own after-tax dollars, and this can be *very* expensive. Whatever your use, review the tax consequences that follow. There *are* tax deductions available even for pure pleasure use.

Should an employee use a privately owned airplane for business purposes?

The following is reproduced, with permission, from a booklet by the Aircraft Owners & Pilots Association.

To fly or not . . . ?

Whether or not an employee should use a private aircraft in the conduct of company business can and should be approached in the same manner as other management decisions; that is, weighing the benefits against the liabilities and making an individual determination as it relates to the particular company.

Unfortunately, the decision is made frequently on emotion without a thorough examination. Some management personnel are unfamiliar with the facts about general aviation. Therefore, it becomes easier to give a flat rejection based on broad generalities of impressions than to examine the proposition in detail. This can—and does—result in adverse decisions whereby companies penalize themselves and miss the many efficient, productive, and competitive advantages of private air transportation.

Similarly, employees seeking to use private aircraft in business can become over-enthusiastic and create genuine problems for management. The fact is, there is no hard and fast rule. What may be right for one company is not necessarily right for another, even in the same category of business.

About 70% of the nation's fleet of 167,000 general aviation aircraft is flown at least partially for business. This number includes those specialized business craft such as agricultural, ambulance, fire-fighting, air taxi, and corporate transport. Owners of about one-fourth of the fleet—in the neighborhood of 40,000 airplanes—list business flying as the primary use of their aircraft.

Private airplanes are being used successfully, safely, and efficiently in many businesses. The number is growing. But, because it is an unfamiliar area for many managements, Aircraft Owners and Pilots Association has prepared this introduction to business flying.

The following information is intended to focus on subjects management should examine and to provide points to consider for developing individual company policies.

Efficiency and Productivity

Distance has never been a factor in conducting business. Time is the consideration. Time is the only thing given equally to all businesses. No company gets more than 24 hours a day.

There are two basic ways in which

a business can make more productive use of time. One is to increase the number of individuals who are working and thus increase the potential manhours. The other is to make hours on the job more productive.

Air travel can assist in making available hours more productive. The difficult question is *what kind of air travel?*

There are no easy answers because no two businesses have the same travel requirements.

Many firms which have their own corporate fleet of general aviation aircraft are also large users of scheduled airlines. Personally flown aircraft meet the requirements for many. There are air taxis, commuter airlines, or a combination of any two or more.

Scheduled airline service in the U.S. is concentrated at major cities. More than one out of every five flights are scheduled into and out of just five population centers. Less than 10% of the airports open to the public have any kind of scheduled service. In total, only about 417 points in the contiguous 48 states receive service from certificated scheduled airlines. Many of these receive only two or three flights a day.

Scheduled service is often the most logical for long distances between selected travel points. However, it frequently requires transfers, layovers, alternate means of transportation over great distances at either or both ends of the trip.

The general aviation airplane, on the other hand, usually can serve an airport of convenience. There are more than 13,000 airports in the U.S. and more than 7,000 of these are open for public use. The general-aviation airplane is available when the traveler needs it, not when a schedule dictates.

The general aviation airplane also provides an alternative to the 55 mile-per-hour speed limit. A typical general aviation airplane will cruise two, three, or more times that speed and save fuel by taking straight-line courses.

In summary, there are many variables in business travel and each busi-

Considering it

ness should examine its own needs and potential. Just as a business has options for communicating by letter, telephone, telegraph, facsimile—so, too, does it have options in travel.

In some instances, a scheduled airline is best; in others, the air taxi, the personally flown airplane, the automobile, the train, the bus. Each has its place. The important point for sound management is to make the method fit the mission.

Safety

The general aviation airplane is basically a safe vehicle. The rarity of accidents is demonstrated by the news attention given to them when they do occur. If the general aviation accident were as common as that of the automobile, there would scarcely be a news medium interested in the incident.

But, accidents do happen.

It is important that safety statistics be put into perspective. General aviation is 98% of all civil aircraft, flown by 95% of the pilots, in the air 84% of the total hours covering 62% of the total aircraft miles, carrying about 50% of the people who travel by air. With this predominance of operations, coupled with flights into much less sophisticated airports than those used by airlines, general aviation can be expected to have a different accident rate.

It is difficult to compare, statistically, one activity with another. This is because the bases are different. General aviation usually prefers to look at safety based on fatalities per 100,000 *aircraft hours flown;* airlines encourage a base of millions of *passenger miles.* The different bases give entirely different impressions. Also, there is a danger for misinterpretation when considering one year's statistics only. One major air disaster in a year can balloon the statistics for either scheduled air carriers or general aviation. If one must use safety statistics, it is advisable to seek a figure balanced over several years. Accident data for general aviation include every type of civil flying other than that of certificated and supplemental airlines.

ACCIDENTS PER 100,000 AIRCRAFT-HOURS					
TOTAL ACCIDENTS	**1971**	**1972**	**1973**	**1974**	**1975**
Pleasure/Personal	30.83	26.45	26.69	23.82	21.05
Aerial Applicator	25.85	21.20	20.54	23.11	19.74
Instructional	15.18	13.69	10.62	11.71	10.51
Business	8.46	8.23	5.11	4.95	4.79
Air Taxi	6.65	5.75	5.32	5.25	5.42
Corporate/Executive	2.64	2.85	2.76	2.15	1.65
Other	3.38	2.42	2.68	2.60	2.41
General Aviation	18.20	15.80	14.20	13.60	12.40
FATAL ACCIDENTS					
Pleasure/Personal	4.76	4.71	4.90	4.49	3.99
Aerial Applicator	2.62	2.14	2.38	1.77	1.56
Instructional	1.17	1.13	0.89	1.11	0.77
Business	1.51	1.84	1.21	1.02	0.96
Air Taxi	1.44	1.64	1.37	1.10	0.95
Corporate/Executive	0.28	0.41	0.71	0.41	0.45
Other	0.54	0.42	0.45	0.47	0.36
General Aviation	2.59	2.57	2.40	2.24	2.00

In one year (1975) approximately 12 percent of the fatalities in general aviation resulted from such activities as aerial application, stunt shows, parachute jumping, glider towing, aircraft testing, forest-fire control, and other types of flights different from routine travel or sport.

The accident rate for all general aviation continues to show marked improvement, and the business pilot has one of the best records.

Cost

When looking at the cost of operating a private airplane, consider more than reimbursement for miles or out-of-pocket expenses. Hidden costs, alternative costs, and benefit/cost ratios should be examined.

An example in a business-communication activity more familiar to most management personnel than the private airplane is the question of telephone vs. letter. Most fiscal experts will keep tight reins over use of long-distance telephone costs suggesting instead the use of a first-class letter. However, the hidden costs of a letter—dictation, transcribing, typing, stationery—run the expense of a typical business letter to at least $2.50. A telephone call may cost 80¢

and save personnel time for other duties. The point is to look at the total picture.

Some of the considerations in preparing a cost analysis would be:

1. Cost per hour of employee's time (usually figured 2.5 to 3.0 times the hourly compensation).
2. Will general-aviation travel provide more productive hours?
3. Will general aviation reduce other expenses such as motels, meals?
4. Will more than one person be traveling in the same airplane, and what would individual fares by other means amount to?

The costs can be applied to alternate means of travel. There are other factors, less tangible, that should be weighed. Will use of a private airplane provide a favorable impression on clients or customers; will use of a private airplane provide a time advantage over competitors; will use of the private airplane improve employee morale by fewer overnights away from home?

The National Business Aircraft Association suggests a different method for determining the value of an employee's time. Simply stated, this is to divide the amount of revenue and/

Considering it

or expense for which the employee is responsible by the number of working hours. A salesman, for example, who produces $500,000 worth of business a year and is on the job 2,000 hours, has a value to the company of $250 an hour.

For most businesses, a simple examination of costs coupled with management judgment is adequate for determining the financial advantages of the use of a general aviation airplane by employees. For those companies wanting a more detailed analysis, there are many resources of additional help. Professional consultants, aircraft companies, or their dealers and distributors will provide personalized consultation.

Liability Protection

Next to safety, liability is the subject of most concern to management investigating use of private aircraft by employees.

A thorough examination with your insurance carrier can resolve many concerns. It is usually advisable to have two or more companies present coverage proposals.

Unless an insurance company deals in aviation coverage as one of its **major** fields, that company may find it easier to simply discourage private flying than to seek out the correct actuary information.

There are considerations as to whether the aircraft is owned, leased, chartered, or borrowed and whether in the corporation's or the individual's name. These factors make it prudent to include at least one aviation-specialty insurance company in your discussions.

A word of caution: do not become emotionally trapped into denying the use of aircraft or contracting for excessive coverage. Most insurance companies have matured beyond the "back the hearse up to the door" sales techniques of years past. But, there still is a tendency to raise the specter of catastrophe as a sales tool.

The in-flight collision is the most frequently stated concern about potentially high liability. The possibility exists. So, too, however, does the possibility that an employee driving an auto on company business will ram a school bus or strike a fuel-tank truck in midtown.

In the 20 years from 1956 to 1975, there were 29 airline-transport aircraft involved in in-flight collisions. Eleven of these were collisions between either two airliners or an airliner and a military craft. Eighteen involved general aviation aircraft. Not all of these accidents caused fatalities or even injuries.

In a substantial number of the accidents, the National Transportation Safety Board official report either exonerated the general aviation pilot or divided the responsibility between the operators of the two aircraft.

During this period, there were well in excess of a billion flights in the United States. (To get one billion in perspective, it was approximately a billion **minutes** ago that Christ was walking on the earth.) The probability of a flight ending in a catastrophic accident, therefore, is extremely remote.

There are four basic categories of flight in general aviation aircraft that require different approaches to liability protection.

1. Flight in an air taxi
2. Flight in a company-owned aircraft
3. Flight in a rented or leased aircraft in which the employee acts as a pilot in command
4. Flight in the employee's own aircraft

In any of these, the employee may also involve passengers, customers, suppliers, consultants, or other individuals. These contingencies should be included in coverage. Some companies limit flight to employees only, which substantially reduces liability potential for passenger bodily injury since employees would be covered by workers' compensation.

For workers' compensation, many states recognize the National Council on compensation insurance. The Council has a code assigned for employees who fly aircraft in the conduct of employer's business. It is Code 7421. The rate is proportional to the amount of time spent flying. For example, suppose a salesman flies a plane on company business two days the first week, none the second, and two days the third week. His payroll for the first and third weeks will be assigned to Code 7421 and his payroll for the second week to the "salesman" Code 8742, providing he maintains records showing the weeks in which he flew on company business. A part of a week will be considered a full week in determining the average weekly payroll. If there are no records of how many flights were made, then the pilot's entire annual salary will be assigned to Code 7421 rather than to the code classification under which it would otherwise apply.

When nonemployees are carried as passengers, some companies find it advisable to have admitted liability coverage. This is an automatic payout of the specified amounts and reduces the prospect of litigation causing adverse publicity in the event of an accident.

Employees who use their own aircraft for their employer's business can, for a small additional premium, add the employer to the owner's policy as a named insured. Management obviously will want to make sure that the limits of the coverage are adequate. For many companies, a million dollars or a million and a half dollars are considered safe limits. The extent of the coverage must be an individual company decision based on many factors. Higher limits can be added for relatively little increase in premiums.

Companies that provide personal travel insurance for their employees occasionally face increased premiums if employees fly for business. To avoid this, employees who fly their own airplanes may agree to carry their own flying accident coverage in the amount of the master company policy for the individual. Such coverage from an aviation-specialty insurance firm is available at a modest rate. This satisfies the employer while not disturbing the master policy.

All companies should have well-defined and -written policies relating to use of private aircraft. (This should apply to use of private autos as well for the same reasons.) These rules will vary with the type of business, the reasons for use of aircraft, even the parts of the country in which flights are made.

Some factors to consider include:

A. Level of management with authority to approve use of aircraft.
B. Proficiency standards.
   1. The number of hours annually an employee must fly for currency.
   2. The license and rating levels needed for different types of business flying.
      a. private or commercial license?
      b. instrument rating?
   3. Types of aircraft and utilization.
      a. single-engine or multi-engine?
      b. night flying—single-engine?
      c. instrument flying—single-engine?
      d. speed requirements vs. trip length.
   4. Reimbursement.
      a. per mile.
      b. out-of-pocket costs plus per-hour usage of aircraft.
      c. equivalent of alternate means.

Rules for flight should be tailored individually. What is appropriate for one company may be entirely wrong for another. Geographic location, weather patterns, availability of alternate means of transportation, types of aircraft, proficiency of pilots, and many other factors affect final decisions. These may seem complex to the person not familiar with flying but can usually be quickly explained by a pilot.

The prototype Bonanza, vintage 1945

Plane Profile 2: Beech Bonanza V 35B

Seats	4/5
Cruise speed, 65% power, 8,000 feet	163 knots
Range, 65% power, full optional fuel, 8,000 feet	701 nm
Maximum endurance	5.3 hours
Gross weight	3,412 pounds
Empty weight	2,110 pounds
Full optional fuel	444 pounds
	74 gallons
Useful load, full fuel	858 pounds
Fuel efficiency, 65% power	12.2 nmpg
Stall speed, gear and flaps down	51 knots
Rate of climb, sea level	1,167 fpm
Minimum field length	1,769 feet
Engine type Continental IO-520-BB	285 hp
Engine TBO	1,700 hours

Remarks Also offered with conventional tail as the Bonanza F 33A.

Considering it

Suggested Company Policy Guidelines for the use of Private Aircraft for Company Business

Because it is in the interest of *(name of company)* for employees to make maximum use of time, the following policy is established to permit use of private aircraft for company business.

1. Authorization
Before using a private aircraft for company business, such use must be authorized by *(authorizing individual or individuals).*

2. Operation
a. The employee using a private aircraft shall in all cases be qualified according to Federal Aviation Administration Regulations for the type of aircraft he/she is piloting and the type of flight *(Visual Flight Rules/Instrument Flight Rules).*
b. The employee shall be current according to FAA regulations regarding recency of experience for the aircraft and type of flight.
c. The employee shall have a current medical certificate appropriate for the level of license and the category of the flight *(third-class, second-class, or first-class medical).*
d. The employee shall operate aircraft properly certificated and inspected according to FAA regulations. The aircraft shall have on board equipment necessary for the category of flight *(instrument flight, visual flight, over water, etc.).*
e. An employee may carry passengers, either other employees of *(name of company)* or clients, customers, vendors, prospects, or others with whom there is a business relationship, but these passengers must not be charged for their passage nor share in the operating expenses. *(Companies may wish to add special requirements based on individual requirements regarding single-engine, multi-engine, night flying,* *speeds required, distances, etc.)*

3. Liability Protection
Employees using personally owned aircraft for company business must:
a. Include *(name of company)* as an additional insured on owner's policy and request a copy of endorsement to the policy and a certificate of insurance be issued by the insurance company and mail both to the attention of *(person of authority)* at the company *(address).* The endorsement and certificate of insurance must be issued by the insurance carrier. Agent binder letters are not acceptable.

Employee renting or borrowing a nonowned aircraft for company business must:
b. Purchase a nonownership liability policy for aircraft to which *(name of company)* is added as an additional insured and provide a certified true copy of the policy to *(person of authority)* at the company *(address).*
c. Minimum insurance will be:

Type of Coverage	Amount of Coverage
Public Liability-Bodily Injury	$000,000/$000,000
Public Liability-Property Damage	$000,000/$000,000
Passenger Liability	$ 00,000 per seat
or	
Single Limit Policy Of	$ 0,000,000

4. Reimbursement
The (name of company) will reimburse employees for the use of private aircraft on the following basis:

Reimbursement policies may be based on any one of many formulas, or a combination:
actual out-of-pocket costs;
x¢ per hour for different categories of aircraft;
equivalent of alternate transportation costs; graduated scale if more than one employee travels in same aircraft. (NOTE: This guideline is only that: a suggestion. Each company should examine its own requirements and establish the policies that will provide proper protection for the employee and the company balanced with the company advantage for use of aircraft.)

Summary

A leading industrialist said: "a company should never be the first to try the new nor the last to discard the old."

Business flying is not a new and untried activity. It has been growing steadily, starting before World War II and accelerating in the sixties and the seventies. Now, more than one-third of the flying hours of general aviation airplanes is for business transportation. These hours in the air are more than double the number of hours all scheduled airline airplanes in the U.S. fly annually.

Business flying presents certain risks. Prudent management recognizes that there are inherent risks merely in being in business. In any endeavor, management seeks to minimize risks and to create cushions for them. It balances the benefits against these risks.

A properly maintained airplane, flown by a pilot who does not try to exceed his or her limitations and those of the aircraft, is a safe, efficient, and effective means of transportation.

The thousands of aircraft, tens of thousands of pilots, and millions of flight hours involved in business flying testify to the satisfactory liability protection available. They testify, also, that somebody's competitor is making use of the speed, efficiency, and effectiveness of business flying.

The business airplane makes business do more because it makes business people do more.

Prepared by AOPA.

Considering it

Reviewing your preferences

When it comes to airplanes, some people swear by high wings; others insist on low wings. Some must have a door on the left. Some pilots won't fly single-engine airplanes at night; others think twins are more dangerous than singles. *Your* preferences may change as you proceed through the book and come to some realizations based on your *needs*, but let's take a first look. To help you, review the accompanying pros and cons of various preference items. If you are interested in a high-performance airplane, a twin, or something to fly off the water, read the following sections, which review these in some detail. Then complete the preliminary preference checklist on page 28.

Pros.	Cons.
Fixed gear vs retractable	
Lower initial cost	Slower due to drag
Much lower maintenance	Not as safe in certain ditching or emergency-landing situations
Simpler operation for pilot	Less prestige
No danger of landing with wheels up	
Cheaper insurance	
Retractable vs fixed gear	
Increased cruising speed	Higher initial cost
Often safer to land with the gear up in a forced landing or ditching in the water	More maintenance required
More prestige	Increases complexity of operation for the pilot
Better-looking in flight	Could cause damage if all wheels don't come down
Can extend gear to use as an air brake	Higher insurance cost if pilot low in experience

Plane Profile 3: Cessna Skylane RG

Seats	4
Cruise speed, 65% power, 8,000 feet	148 knots
Range, 65% power, full optional fuel, 8,000 feet	932 nm
Maximum endurance	7.3 hours
Gross weight	3,112 pounds
Empty weight	1,757 pounds
Full optional fuel	528 pounds 88 gallons
Useful load, full fuel	827 lbs
Fuel efficiency, 75% power	12.5 nmpg
Stall speed, gear and flaps down	50 knots
Rate of climb, sea level	1,140 fmp
Minimum field length	1,570 feet
Engine type Lycoming O-540-J3C5D	235 hp
Engine TBO	2,000 hours

Remarks Also available turbocharged, and in a fixed-gear version, both turboed and non-turboed.

Pros.	**Cons.**
High wing vs low wing	
Better ground clearance for rough field operations	Wing restricts visibility in a turn in most high wing aircraft
Better ground visibility, except in turns	With fuel stored in the wings refueling or checking fuel is awkward
Wing shades cabin for cooler flight in hot weather	Most high wings have a strut, which slows airplane down
Wing provides shelter for boarding in wet weather	High wing has higher center of gravity, giving poor stability on ground
Better in flight stability	More susceptible to the effect of strong winds when taxiing or parked
Fuel stored in wings is fed to the engine by gravity—no fuel pump needed except with fuel injection	Aircraft should be tied down in strong winds—a strong gust can flip a high wing aircraft on its back
Aircraft is lower to ground and thus easier to board	Poorer crash protection
	More complicated gear system required if retractable
Low wing vs high wing	
Better visibility in turns	Fuel pump required
Easier fuel handling	Harder to board airplane
Shorter gear legs needed	More susceptible to damage in rough field operations
Better gear storage if retractable	Poorer visibility of the ground in flight
Wider gear stance possible	Heavier structure needed
Better crash protection	Spar must go through cabin
Not so susceptible to high winds when taxiing or parking	
Lower center of gravity gives better ground stability	

Above Piper Tomahawk

Above Gulfstream American Tiger
Below Cessna Stationair 7

Below Rockwell International Commander 114

Below Bellanca Scout

Below Cessna Pressurized Skymaster with weather radar

Considering it

Above Beech Skipper

Above Cessna 170B
Below Beech Turbo Bonanza

Below Aero Commander 100

Below Piper Comanche 400

Pros.	Cons.
Fixed-pitch prop vs controllable prop (single engine)	
Simple operation	Less flexible performance
Lower initial cost	More noise
Lower maintenance	Less efficient operation if engine is high-powered
Lower weight	
Cheaper to repair if damaged	
Controllable prop vs fixed-pitch prop (single engine)	
Better performance from a higher-powered engine	Higher initial cost
Lower noise	Higher maintenance cost
More prestige	More expensive to repair
	More complex operation

Pros.	Cons.
Carburetor vs fuel injection	
Lower initial cost	Susceptible to carburetor icing and thus possible engine failure or reduced power when flight with carburetor heat is required
Usually easier to start, especially when hot	Less fuel efficiency
Less complex system	
Lower maintenance cost	
Fuel injection vs carburetor	
Carburetor icing threat eliminated	Induction-system icing possible
More efficient use of fuel	Sometimes harder to start, especially when hot
Faster engine response	More complex system
	Higher initial cost
	Higher maintenance cost
	Must be careful when changing fuel tanks in flight to avoid vapor lock and possible engine failure

Considering it

High performance single-engine aircraft

The FAA defines a high-performance single-engine aircraft as one equipped with flaps, a controllable propeller, and retractable gear or an engine of more than 200 hp. If you hold a private or commercial certificate, you may not act as pilot-in-command of such an airplane unless you have either: (a) logged time in such a type prior to November 1, 1973 or (b) received flying instruction in such a type from an authorized flight instructor who has certified in your log book as follows (for example): "Checkout in [specific type of airplane] in accordance with FAA Advisory Circular 61-9B satisfactory, [date], [instructor signature and certificate number]." The referenced Advisory Circular—AC 61-9B—is called "Pilot Transition Courses for Complex Single-Engine and Light Twin-Engine Airplanes" and is available at most airports for about 50¢.

Multi-engine aircraft

To fly a multi-engine aircraft carrying passengers or for hire you must have a *multi-engine rating* on your pilot certificate. The FAA shows a seven-hour syllabus plus a two-hour flight test in its Advisory Circular on the subject, "Pilot Transition Courses for Complex Single-engine and Light Twin-engine Airplanes" (AC61-9B). There is no minimum flying time required for the issuance of the rating. You simply have to present a flying instructor's recommendation that you are ready for the flight test and pass the test. The recommendation should be made on FAA Form 8710-1.

Some pilots won't fly anything with less than two engines. Other pilots merrily fly their high-performance singles all over the place at night, IFR or across the Atlantic Ocean, with every confidence in the safety and utility of their aircraft. If you were to ask some multi-engine-aircraft owners why they fly a twin, you will hear the word *safety* as the prime reason for their choice. Of similar importance will be speed and load-carrying capability. But safety seems to come first. Are twins safer than singles? Not really. The problem is that most light twins don't have very good performance on one engine at certain critical moments of a flight—just after takeoff and in the initial climb stage, during a single-engine overshoot from an aborted landing or at high altitudes, for example. In some such cases it is often safer to treat the airplane as a single if an engine fails. According to the National Transportation Safety Board (NTSB), about 23 percent of accidents caused by an engine failure are fatal in multi-engine aircraft, while in single-engine aircraft just over 5 percent of engine-failure accidents involve a fatality. Part of the problem in the higher twin fatality rate is that when you're flying a twin, you get the idea that if the engine fails you can save it. This is not always the case, as suggested above. Another problem is that there is a fairly high accident rate related to training in light twins. Some cynical single-engine pilots deride the twin as being an aircraft that offers double the chance of an engine failure!

I asked the former head of the NTSB what reasons could be given for using a twin instead of a single, And he suggested that the *redundancy of systems* would be the primary reason. You have two alternators or generators, two vacuum pumps, two hydraulic pumps, and so on. Two engines give you more power if you are pressurized and can handle a heavier electrical load for things such as weather radar, electric propeller de-icers, hot windshields, and so on. Weather radar used to be available only on twins, but there was one twin that couldn't handle it—the Cessna Skymaster. So Cessna and Bendix worked out a wing-mounted radar pod, which promptly made radar a possibility (and now an option) in the Cessna Centurion. The Bonanza has followed with a wing-mounted pod, and undoubtedly other singles will soon be carrying radar.

What it boils down to is still safety but not *complete and utter* safety. I think I would rather be halfway across the Atlantic, flying over the mountains at night, or in heavy IFR with icing or storms, in a twin than a single. But if an engine quit on initial climb out, I think I would rather be in a single, since one decision is immediately eliminated and you can spend your time putting it down somewhere rather than dicing around trying to keep it together and then finding somewhere to put it when you find it's not going to work.

It is easy to *overbuy* if you can afford it. It would be better to start with a fairly simple twin and gradually work up as your experience develops than to go straight into some pressurized, turbocharged super-high-performance airplane as your first venture into owning and flying your own aircraft. Flying a twin *is* different than flying a single, and it requires more finely honed piloting skills at all times. You really ought to have an instrument rating if you want to fly a twin—to do otherwise will severely limit your utilization of the aircraft. Twin flying is a lot more expensive than single—it's not just the higher gas consumption but things like *two* engine overhauls, *24* spark plugs, greater tire wear, and so on. You will also find landing fees and hangarage or parking a lot higher. I was considering a twin at one point and was quoted $175 a month for hangaring a twin vs. $100 a month for a single of the same size.

I like twins and will probably buy one when things look right (affordability and utilization). I guess about half of my flying time has been in twins. Twin flying is very pleasant—it is generally faster and you feel like you are really handling an *airplane* when you have all those throttles and prop controls in your hand. I guess I feel safer at night in a twin. But I have become very accustomed to my own single. I know how it is maintained and how it is flown. I know about its oil changes and the results of its engine-oil analyses. I know how smoothly the engine runs and what the pressures and temperatures look like. So I feel very confident in my airplane. I don't mind flying across Lake Ontario at 1,000 feet or flying from Nantucket to Montauk Point direct. I feel that the airplane can handle it, and if it can't I can handle *that* too! But I'm not quite ready to fly it across the Ocean.

There are a few airplanes around that can be bought as twins *or* singles. The most obvious of these are the Beech Bonanza 36 and the Baron 58, which have basically the same fuselage and wings (see box at right), and the Piper Saratoga and Seneca.

It can be seen that the performance improvements are not paid for at an equitable rate. With the twin you get the same number of seats, 64 percent greater range, 20 percent more speed, and about the same takeoff distance, but a 72 percent greater landing distance and 8 percent less useful load with full fuel for twice the initial cost. So why buy the twin? For an individual, it has to be the subjective safety/redundancy-of-systems argument. And, of course, some air-taxi operations *must* be done in a twin, so for an aircraft operator in the charter business, a twin might be best.

Twins are available both with and without turbocharging. The benefit of turbocharging is that the single-engine ceiling of the twin is much higher with turbos—as is the single-engine rate of climb at altitude. Flying a nonturbo'd twin on a hot day out of an airport with a field elevation of 2,000 feet can be like being at the airplane's single-engine service ceiling on a normal day—in other words, your single-engine rate of climb will be zero or close to it. (See table on the next page.)

How singles and twins compare

	Beech Bonanza A 36 (single)	Beech Baron 58 twin)	Index (single = 100)
Gross weight	3,612 lbs	5,424 lbs	150
Seats	6	6	100
Total power (rated takeoff)	285 hp	570 hp	200
Cruise speed (65% power)	158 kts	190 kts	120
Fuel consumption (at cruise, gph)	13.2 gph	26.8 gph	203
NMPG	12.0 nmpg	7.1 nmpg	59
Rate of climb	1,030 fpm	1,660 fpm	161
Takeoff distance (over 50 feet)	2,040 feet	2,101 feet	103
Landing distance (over 50 feet)	1,450 feet	2,498 feet	172
Useful load	1,417 lbs	2,063 lbs	146
Useful load (with full fuel)	973 lbs	899 lbs	92
Fuel capacity	74 gals	194 gals	262
Range (full fuel, 1-hour reserve)	695 nm	1,140 nm	164
Price (1982 – basic)	$126,650	$253,500	200

Beech Bonanza A 36

Beech Baron 58

How non- and turbocharged twins compare

Model or type					Nonturbo	Turbo	Index (nonturbo = 100)
	Non-TC	Turbocharged					
Aerostar	600	601B	75% cruise	Aerostar	217 kts	247 kts	113
Beech Baron	58	58 TC	best altitude	Beech	200 kts	241 kts	121
Cessna 310	310	Turbo 310		Cessna	194 kts	223 kts	115
Piper Aztec	F	Turbo F		Piper	175 kts	200 kts	114
			Single-engine	Aerostar	6,100 ft	9,100 ft	149
			service ceiling	Beech	7,000 ft	14,400 ft	206
				Cessna	7,400 ft	17,200 ft	232
				Piper	4,950 ft	13,250 ft	268
			Price (1981)	Aerostar	$220,470	$251,480	114
				Beech	$229,950	$259,000	113
				Cessna	$162,000	$188,000	116
				Piper	$165,960	$192,120	116

Plane Profile 4: Cessna Crusader

Seats	6
Cruise speed, 65% power,	
8,000 feet	167 knots
18,000 feet	181 knots
Range, 65% power, full	
optional fuel, 18,000 feet	706 nm
Maximum endurance	4.9 hours
Gross weight	5,175 pounds
Empty weight	3,305 pounds
Full optional fuel	918 pounds
	153 gallons
Useful load, full fuel	952 pounds
Fuel efficiency, 65%	
power, 18,000 feet	7.4 nmpg
Stall speed, gear and	
flaps down	62 knots
Rate of climb, sea level	1,480 fpm
	220 fpm s/e
Minimum field length	1,750 feet
Engine type 2 Continental	
TSIO-520-AE	250 hp
Engine TBO	2,000 hours
Remarks Cabin class, turbocharged twin.	

Above Mooney 201

Below Piper Aerostar 600

Pros.	Cons.
Single vs twin engine	
Cheaper to buy and operate	If it quits, you must find a place to land
Easier to handle	Most singles are slower than most twins
Better miles per gallon	Single systems limitations
Twin vs single	
Greater safety in cruise, night, instrument, or overwater operations	Much more expensive to buy and operate
More prestige	Lower miles per gallon
Most twins are faster than most singles	Almost double the maintenance (time and money)
Generally can carry a greater load	Harder to handle, especially in emergencies
Dual systems redundancy	May have to be operated as a single in certain engine-failure situations (e.g., short fields, high altitudes)
	Requires pilot to have a multiengine rating
	Requires more proficiency maintenance

Plane Profile 5: Piper Seneca III

Seats	6/7
Cruise speed, 65% power,	
8,000 feet	164 knots
18,000 feet	180 knots
Range, 65% power, full optional fuel, 18,000 feet flaps down	864 nm
Maximum endurance	5.8 hours
Gross weight	4,773 pounds
Empty weight	2,875 pounds
Full optional fuel	738 pounds
	123 gallons
Useful load, full fuel	1,160 pounds
Fuel efficiency, 65% power	8.9 nmpg
Stall speed, gear and flaps down	62 knots
Rate of climb, sea level	1,400 fpm
	240 fpm s/e
Minimum field length	2,000 feet
Engine type 2 Continental TSIO-360KB	200 hp
Engine TBO	1,800 hours
Remarks Turbocharged.	

Water flying

Flying an airplane off the water is probably more fun than any other type of flying. It is, of course, a highly specialized activity that requires its own rating if you want to carry passengers or fly for hire, in the same way as you need a multi-engine rating to carry passengers in a twin.

The sea rating is called an *airplane-class rating* and is available as *airplane single-engine sea* (ASES) and as *airplane multi-engine sea* (AMES). To obtain the rating, you must apply to the FAA, using FAA Form 8710-1 and present your log book certified by an authorized flight instructor showing that you have received flight instruction in the class of airplane (i.e., ASES or AMES) for which you are seeking the rating and are considered competent in the pilot operations appropriate to the pilot certificate on which the rating is to be issued (private, commercial, or airline transport). And you must pass a flight test appropriate to your pilot certificate applicable to the airplane (FAR 61.63 [c]). There is no requirement for a written test or for any designated amount of experience. It usually takes between 5 and 10 hours to get a sea rating. The differences are not in *flying* a seaplane—a regular land-plane with floats hanging from it flies quite similarly to one without floats, although it is slower and you may find you need to use more rudder than you are used to in the land-plane version. It's takeoffs, landings (seaings?), and handling on the water that require the practice. The first thing you discover when you get into a seaplane is that the brakes don't work!

The two main varieties of water birds are straight seaplanes and amphibians. Straight seaplanes just fly off the water, while amphibians can be operated off either water or land. Two subdivisions are floats and boats. Floats are pontoons that are mounted partially to the landing-gear attachments of a landplane—

Above Bellanca Scout on Edo floats
Below Cessna 185 Skywagon on Edo 696-3500s

Considering it

floatplanes are almost invariably conversions from landplanes. Some such conversions require additional fins to be mounted on the tail, à la Lockheed Constellation, to give extra directional stability when the floats are installed. And additional bracing may be needed elsewhere. A Cessna 172 seaplane, for example, has a few unfamiliar tubes going back and forth across the windshield area.

Flying boats are *designed* to operate off water, rather than being conversions. The whole airplane sits in the water on the underside of its fuselage, which becomes its *hull* in nautical parlance. Small floats are mounted at or near the wingtips for stability on the water. Flying boats look better and sleeker than floatplanes, and they are faster with equal power, since they offer less drag. Most flying-boat designs are amphibians, while most float designs are not. Amphibious floats are available on some aircraft, making the landing gear *quadricycle*. The main wheels are mounted under the middle of the float, and nose wheels are mounted at the front end of each float. The wheels retract into the float, but some nosewheels flip up and over, out of the water's way, for water landings. Landing any kind of amphibian in the water with the wheels down is guaranteed to flip the airplane upside down. Apart from other considerations this can get you wet!

If you ever had fantasies about flying a 747, get in a Cessna 180 on wheel floats on the ground and taxi around a bit! It's not difficult, but you sure are high. Takeoffs and landings from land on wheel floats are not difficult—just remember to flare a little earlier. Cross winds can be a bit more uncomfortable, due to the higher center of gravity.

Putting a set of floats on a landplane requires a supplemental type certificate (STC). Fortunately, STCs exist for most aircraft that are compatible with floats. Probably the most exotic conversion is the Piper Aztec, which is known as the Nomad when it is converted to a seaplane. If

Above Cessna 150 on floats with a 150 hp engine

Below The Teal Marlin 150 amphibian

Considering it

you have an airplane that could take floats, the best thing to do would be to write to one of the float manufacturers and ask their advice. Here are the addresses of the three major float firms:

Edo-Aire Seaplane Division,
Republic Airport
East Farmingdale, NY 11735

Pee Kay Float Division,
DeVore Aviation Corporation,
6104-B Kircher Blvd NE
Albuquerque, NM 87109

Wipline, Inc.,
South End Doane Trail,
Inver Grove Heights, Minn. 55075

The Aztec conversion is offered by:
Melridge Aviation Company,
Box 1508,
Vancouver, Wash. 98661

I recommend two books if you are interested in exploring the world of water wings. One is *How to Fly Floats* by Jay Frey, published by Edo-Aire and available from the address given above for $2. The other is the *Water Flying Annual*, which is published by the Seaplane Pilot's Association, Box 30091, Washington, DC 20005. It costs $5, or you get it free with membership, which costs $15.

Floats come in various sizes to suit the size of airplane on which they are mounted. They are designated by a number, which approximates their displacement in the water. Edo-Aire, for example, offers 1650 floats for the Super Cub or Champion. They have a displacement of 1650 lbs each. The Super Cub gross weight is 1760 lbs. The FAA requires that floats have buoyancy 80 percent higher than that required to support the maximum weight of the seaplane in fresh water (FAR 23.751). Thus a reasonably good rule of thumb is to say that floats with a designation that approximates the gross weight of the aircraft are the ones for the aircraft.

Edo's current line and some of the aircraft compatible are as follows:

88-1650A	Bellanca 7ECA, Cessna 150, Piper Super Cub
89-2000	Aeronca Sedan, Bellanca Citabria, Cessna 170, Cessna 172, Piper Cherokee 180, Piper Tri Pacer/Pacer, Piper Super Cub
248-2440B	Cessna Hawk XP, Maule M 5 Rocket
597-2790	Cessna 180, Cessna 185
628-2960	Cessna 180 and 185
582-3430	Cessna 185, Cessna 206, Helio Courier, Piper Cherokee Six
679-4930	DHC Beaver, Pilatus Porter, Piper Aztec
Amphibians	
696-3500	Cessna 185, Cessna 206

Plane Profile 6: Lake Buccaneer

Seats	4
Cruise speed, 65% power, 8,000 feet	130 knots
Range, 65% power, full optional fuel, 8,000 feet	598 nm
Maximum endurance	5.6 hours
Gross weight	2,690 pounds
Empty weight	1,555 pounds
Full optional fuel	324 gallons
	54 gallons
Useful load, full fuel	811 lbs
Fuel efficiency, 75% power	13.9 nmpg
Stall speed, gear and flaps down	39 knots
Rate of climb, sea level	1,200 fpm
Minimum field length	775 feet land
	1,450 feet water
Engine type Lycoming IO-360-A1B	200 hp
Engine TBO	1,600 hours
Remarks Amphibian	

Considering it

Here is a comparison of a Cessna Hawk XP as a landplane and as a seaplane:

	Landplane	Seaplane
Maximum speed	133 kts	118 kts
Cruise speed (80% power)	130 kts	116 kts
Rate of climb (sea level)	870 fpm	870 fpm
Gross weight	2,550 lbs	2,550 lbs
Empty weight	1,549 lbs	1,770 lbs
Useful load	1,001 lbs	780 lbs
Takeoff distance (over 50 ft)	1,360 ft	1,850 ft

To get full utilization out of your float-equipped seaplane, you may like to put the wheels back on during the winter. This is fairly easy, especially if the seaplane base is right next to an airport. If not, all is not lost. A floatplane can be landed on grass without too much difficulty and no damage if done carefully. And for taking off from the land on floats you can use a dolly for the roll down the runway.

Floats are not cheap and amphibious floats are downright expensive! I had a friend who had a Cessna 185 and he wanted to put amphibious floats on it so that he could commute from his nearby airport to his summer cottage on a lake, about ten miles from the nearest land airport. He found it would be cheaper to buy a brand-new Cadillac Eldorado and leave it at the cottage airport for local transportation than to put wheel floats on! However, he then realized that he couldn't tow the Caddy around wherever he went, so he put the wheel floats on anyway.

A set of floats for a Cessna 172, for example, costs about $12,000 plus about $1,200 installation. Amphibious floats for a 185 run about $36,000 plus about $2,500 for installation. It costs about $300 to change from wheels to floats or vice versa each season. Insurance rates will go higher, especially if you have little water experience or are flying an amphibian.

You can keep your seaplane in the water or you can beach it, which is preferred. Most seaplane bases have a beaching ramp, which makes this a fairly simple and fast operation.

Some states have fairly stiff regulations as to where you may and may not operate a seaplane. This is something to check if you are considering using a seaplane often.

I find the boat more aesthetically appealing than the float. For one thing, you sit much lower in the water, which gives you a greater sense of intimacy with your surface medium. And since most boats are also amphibians, they are most useful. They are also faster.

Many flying boats have a pusher engine-prop setup. This takes a few moments to get used to, since the nose *rises* when you throttle back and *drops* when you add power.

It is strange that the concept of the small amphibian has never really taken off. The Seabee was produced at the end of World War II and sold for less than $7,000. There are still quite a few around, and they cost quite a bit more than that now! The original Seabee had flying characteristics not unlike those of a Simonized brick when the power was reduced, and it had so much space inside that people tended to overload them and crash. Many Seabees have been modified to have larger engines, longer wings, wingtip endplates, and such, giving better performance. There is even a twin conversion. The Lake Amphibian has very good performance and is a delightful aircraft.

Piper Aztec Nomad on Edo 679-4930 floats

Pros.	Cons.
Boats vs floats	
Less drag, so aircraft can fly faster Usually amphibious	Aircraft sits lower in water, so some docks are too high to use Flying boat is slower than landplane version of floatplane If engine has a pusher prop, aircraft has reverse flying characteristics with application and removal of power
Floats vs boats	
Aircraft can be converted to land or sea configuration each season, as required Aircraft sits higher in water, giving better dock clearance If you get tired of floats, you can sell them and go back to landplane flying	Amphibious versions not available or very costly Aircraft has to be strengthened to take float installation If prop is fixed-pitch, it should be a climb prop, which gives slower cruising speed than a cruise prop Floats slow the airplane down

Preliminary preference check list

Now that you have had a look at the basic considerations, it would be appropriate to take a first look at your preferences. Later, in Chapter 3, we'll be going through some very specific numbers to zero in on exactly the kind of airplane you should have. But first, take a look at what you *think* you want by completing this *preliminary preference check-list.*

Number of engines: One ☐   Two ☐   Either ☐

Number of seats: _____

Ideal cruise speed: _____ knots

Ideal range: _____ nm

Ideal payload: _____ lbs

Configuration preferred:

High wing ☐   Low wing ☐   Mid wing ☐   Any ☐

Fixed gear ☐   Retractable gear ☐   Either ☐

Fixed prop ☐   Controllable prop ☐   Either ☐

New ☐   Used ☐   Either ☐

Price range: $ _____ to $ _____

Manufacturer preferred: _____

Plane Profile 7: Cessna Citation I-SP

Seats	8
Cruise speed, 75% power, optimum altitude	352 knots
Range, 75% power, full optional fuel	1,325 nm
Gross weight	12,000 pounds
Empty weight	6,605 pounds
Full optional fuel	3,807 pounds
	568 gallons
Useful load, full fuel	1,588 pounds
Fuel efficiency, 75% power	2.4 nmpg
Stall speed, gear and flaps down	82 knots
Rate of climb, sea level	2,680 fmp
	800 fmp s/e
Minimum field length	1,946 feet
Balanced field length	2,930 feet
Engine type 2 Pratt & Whitney JT15D-1A	2,200 pounds thrust
Engine TBO	2,400 hours

Remarks   Jet aircraft licensed for single-pilot operation.

Funding it

Funding it

Tax consequences

However you use an aircraft, you can make deductions from your taxable income for the following items:

1. Interest expense on money borrowed to finance the plane and accessories
2. Any state sales tax paid on acquisition of the plane and accessories
3. Any state property tax you must pay because of the plane
4. Any expenses arising from charitable use of the plane
5. Any state avgas tax paid that is not refundable

That's about it as far as strictly pleasure flying is concerned. Business use gives you a whole lot more. What constitutes business use of an airplane?

1. Business travel—travel undertaken for business reasons. The deductible expense here includes "ordinary and necessary" expenses related to a business trip, including the maintenance and operation of an aircraft for the trip (Internal Revenue Code Section 162 [a] [2]).

2. Business entertainment—an aircraft can qualify as a component of an "entertainment facility," which is real or personal property rented, owned or used by a taxpayer in the taxable year, under Regulation 1.274-2 (e) (2) (i). Such an entertainment facility must be primarily used for "ordinary and necessary" business purposes (i.e., more than half the time). "Ordinary" use means that such use is common or accepted in the taxpayer's business. "Necessary" means that the use should be helpful and appropriate in the performance, promotion, or furtherance of the taxpayer's business (Internal Revenue Code Section 162 [a]). Entertainment for business purposes must be "directly related" to business. As a result of the entertainment, the taxpayer must expect to derive income, cost saving, or some other specific business benefit at some point in the future. Business matters must be discussed during or immediately after the entertainment period. The principal purpose for business entertainment must be business (i.e., you wouldn't have done it if it hadn't been for business).

3. Sale and leaseback agreement—the Economic Recovery Tax Act of 1981 has essentially ended this type of tax shelter for *individuals*. Formerly you could buy an airplane and lease it back to the seller, who would operate it for training or charter, paying you a part of the revenue. The IRS will no longer allow deductions for depreciation or the investment tax credit, except to people truly in the leasing business. The lease term must be for less than 50 percent of the useful life of the property (which is now ruled as five years, so the lease has to be for two and one half years or less), and in the first year of the lease, the lessor (you) must provide some significant services with the aircraft equal to at least 15 percent of the rental income produced. The new rules do not allow investment tax credit when the aircraft is rented out on a net-lease basis and the owner is not providing significant services with the aircraft.

4. Specialized uses—if you are going to use the airplane as a means of earning income, as for crop dusting, aerial photography, pipeline patrol, and so on, its expenses are deductible. However, certain types of operations require special certification from the FAA (e.g., an air taxi or flight-training operation), so be aware of these needs before setting up such a business.

FAR Part 135 covers air-taxi, mail-contract transportation, and commercial transportation of people or freight for hire in small aircraft. It does not cover student instruction, nonstop sightseeing flights beginning and ending at the same airport and carried out within a 25-mile radius of that airport, or aerial work such as crop dusting, banner towing, aerial photography or survey, firefighting, rescue operations, or pipeline patrols. Pilot schools are covered under FAR Part 141.

What is deductible for business use?

All related expenses, prorated to the amount of business use vs personal use, are deductible from a taxpayer's income. These include:

1. maintenance
2. fuel and oil
3. storage
4. insurance
5. chart services
6. landing fees
7. auto mileage to and from the airport
8. depreciation
9. investment tax credit

Depreciation

Depreciation is the decrease in value of property due to wear, deterioration, or obsolescence. There are two depreciations to consider in aircraft ownership: the real depreciation (the difference between what you pay for the airplane and what you sell it for) and depreciation for tax purposes, which has meaning if you are using the airplane wholly or partially for business purposes.

Funding it

Real depreciation may not in fact, be depreciation at all. Used airplanes are increasing in value each year at a remarkable rate. What happens is that they depreciate quite fast for the first few years, then they stop depreciating and start to *appreciate* and sometimes even catch up with their original cost.

As an example, consider the average retail selling price for a 1969 Beech V 35A Bonanza over the last few years. The average equipped list price was about $53,000 in 1969. The chart shows the average used prices for the following few years for the same airplane (figures supplied by *Aircraft Price Digest* and used with permission). A 1982 Bonanza V 35B sold for about $172,000 equipped, brand new. (The basic list price was $118,750.) So in the thirteen-year period the airplane dropped to as low as 55 percent of its original value after two years but returned to 83 percent of its value at the end of the period.

Above 1957 Beech Bonanza H35
Below 1967 Beech Bonanza V35

Below 1977 Beech Bonanza V35B, the 10,000th one built

Meanwhile, the new equipped price increased well over three times (a 224-percent rise) in the same period. The thirteen-year-old airplane was selling at about 25 percent of its replacement cost.

This sort of price performance will hold true for efficient airplanes as long as gasoline and new airplane costs continue to increase. Or, to put it another way, *an airplane is not like a car*. It tends to increase in value after a time as it gets older. A properly maintained airplane does not wear out nearly as much as other manufactured items.

Depreciation for tax purposes is something you must discuss with your tax adviser. The way you handle it for your airplane will have to be compatible with the way you handle it for other depreciable property of the same class. The key factor in depreciation for tax purposes is what happens when you dispose of the property. With an airplane, you'll probably sell it for much more than its depreciated value on the books. This profit will be treated as ordinary income in most cases. Your tax adviser will tell you about ways to handle this if you're trading airplanes.

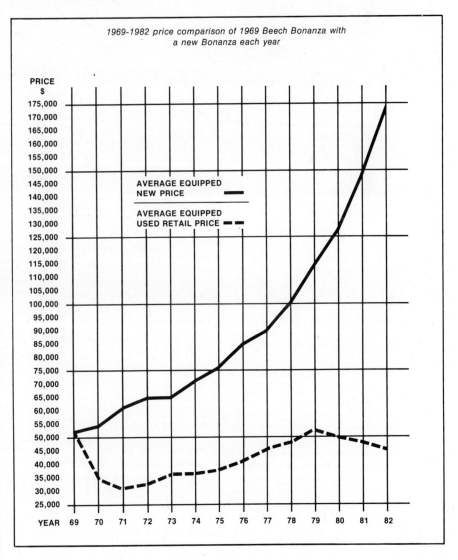

Funding it

Under the 1981 tax act, a new accelerated cost recovery system (ACRS) was introduced, setting the useful life of airplanes at five years. A business can recover the cost of the airplane much faster than before. However, it could make for higher recaptures of income if the airplane is sold at a price above what it has been depreciated to (its *book value*).

Using the manufacturers' resources

Most manufacturers offer to carry out analyses for prospective customers for their aircraft. These can be quite sophisticated. Cessna offers TAP—Transportation Analysis Plan. Piper will do a computerized Cash Flow Analysis and a Travel Cost Analysis. Beech offers a Capital Recovery Guide. I have shown an example of a Piper Cash Flow Analysis on the next page to give you an idea of the kind of information you can get from these services. To obtain one for

1982 Piper Turbo Saratoga

yourself, contact the dealer of your choice and give the necessary information. The analysis will be provided free and quite quickly.

The Investment tax credit

The investment tax credit (ITC) is the most valuable deduction for an aircraft used for business. It is a *credit against tax payable* (not a deduction from taxable income. The rate of credit is 10 percent for aircraft, which now have a useful life of five years under the 1981 tax act. The credit is earned at the rate of 2 percent per year that the property is held, so if you sell the plane after four years, you'd only end up with an 8-percent credit. The credit is available on both new and used aircraft, but a taxpayer is limited to only $125,000 worth of used equipment of all types that are eligible for ITC in any one year (this limit will rise to $150,000 in 1985). The ITC is taken in the first year that the property is acquired, based on the number of years it is expected to be used.

The ITC cannot be used to offset more than the first $25,000 of tax liability, plus 90 percent of any tax liability over $25,000. For example, if your company bought a new $300,000 aircraft in 1982, it would be eligible for $30,000 of ITC. Of this, $25,000 would be taken dollar-for-dollar against its tax liability for the year. The remaining $5,000 of ITC could only be applied on a .9 to 1 basis against the remaining tax liability. Thus to use all of the ITC available, the company would have to have a total tax liability of $30,555. If the tax liability were lower, the ITC can be carried back up to three years and forward for fifteen years, so it is hard to imagine a profitable company not being able to take advantage of the ITC at some point. Needless to say, the advice of a tax expert is strongly recommended!

Typical cash-flow analysis

PIPER AIRCRAFT PURCHASE ANALYSIS

INPUT DATA AND ASSUMPTIONS

SARATOGA SP

CAPITAL COST AND TAX DATA

FINANCE RATE (APR)	VARIABLE	MONEY VALUE RATE	18.00
FEDERAL INCOME TAX RATE	46.00	STATE INCOME TAX RATE	9.00
SALES TAX RATE	5.00	PERSONAL PROPERTY TAX RATE	0.0
YEARS FINANCED	7YRS		
PURCHASE PRICE	150000.00	ESTIMATED RESALE VALUE	105000.00
		DEPRECIATION PERIOD	5YRS
INFLATION FACTOR PERCENT	8.00	DEPRECIATION METHOD IS ACCELERATED COST RECOVERY SYSTEM	

OPERATING COST ESTIMATED IN CURRENT DOLLARS

FUEL AND OIL PER HOUR	29.54	MAINTENANCE PER HOUR	7.95
INSURANCE AND HANGAR RENT	4720.00	RESERVE FOR OVERHAUL PER HOUR	9.01
HOURS FLOWN PER YEAR	300		
TIME BETWEEN OVERHAULS HOURS	2000	CURRENT HOURS ON ENGINES	0

PIPER AIRCRAFT PURCHASE ANALYSIS

DEALER
CUSTOMER TRU FOSTER LTD   1/20/82

SARATOGA SP

*** ESTIMATED ANNUAL CASH FLOW AND EXPENSE SUMMARY ***

INFLATION FACTOR	PURCHASE PRICE	SALES TAX	PURCHASE PAYMENT	AMOUNT FINANCED	TIME FINANCED	MONTHLY PAYMENT	TAX LIFE	DEPRECIATION BASE	GROSS RESALE	TAX DUE ON SALE	PRINCIPAL DUE
8.00	150000.	7500.	15000.	135000.	7.	VARIABLE	5.	157500.	105000.	53403.	55042.

*** ESTIMATED CASH FLOW ANALYSIS ***

YEAR	0	1	2	3	4	5
		12 MO	12 MO	12 MO	12 MO	12 MO
INTEREST RATE		15.00	15.00	17.00	17.00	17.00
MONTHLY PAYMENT		2605.	2605.	2721.	2721.	2721.

ESTIMATED CASH OUTFLOW
BEFORE TAX

PURCHASE PAYMENT	15000.	0.	0.	0.	0.	0.
SALES TAX	7500.	0.	0.	0.	0.	0.
PRINCIPAL		11800.	13697.	15189.	17982.	21289.
INTEREST		19461.	17564.	17468.	14675.	11368.
PERSONAL PROP TAX		0.	0.	0.	0.	0.
FUEL AND OIL		8862.	9571.	10337.	11164.	12057.
INSURANCE & HANGAR RENT		4720.	5098.	5505.	5946.	6421.
MAINTENANCE		2385.	2576.	2782.	3004.	3245.
ENGINE OVERHAUL		0.	0.	0.	0.	0.
PRINCIPAL DUE AT SALE		0.	0.	0.	0.	55042.
TAX DUE AT SALE **		0.	0.	0.	0.	53403.

TOTAL CASH OUTFLOW	22500.	47228.	48506.	51281.	52771.	162825.

ESTIMATED ITEMS THAT
INCREASE CASH DUE TO
TAX EFFECT

DEPRECIATION *		23625.	34650.	33075.	33075.	33075.
OTHER DEDUCTIBLE EXPENSES		35428.	34809.	36092.	34789.	33091.
TOTAL DEDUCTIBLE EXPENSES		59053.	69459.	69167.	67864.	66166.
CASH VALUE OF DEDUCTIBLES AFTER TAX RATE OF 0.5086		30034.	35327.	35178.	34516.	33652.
INVESTMENT TAX CREDIT *		15750.	0.	0.	0.	0.
CASH REC AT SALE		0.	0.	0.	0.	105000.
CASH INFLOW AFTER TAX	0.	45784.	35327.	35178.	34516.	138652.

NET CASH FLOW (-IS CASH OUT)	-22500.	-1444.	-13179.	-16103.	-18255.	-24173.
TOTAL CASH FLOW	-95654.					
COST PER HOUR	63.77					
THE PRESENT VALUE COST IS	-55472.					

* IT IS ASSUMED DISPOSITION OF AIRCRAFT TAKES PLACE 1 DAY AFTER THE END OF LAST YEAR

** IT MAY BE POSSIBLE TO DEFER THE DEPRECIATION RECAPTURE TAX IF THE AIRCRAFT IS TRADED-IN RATHER THAN SOLD

**** JOB TERMINATED - RETURN CODE 00 NORMAL EOJ
*READY

Leasebacks

While the Economic Recovery Tax Act (ERTA) of 1981 gave many good things to taxpayers, such as better depreciation schedules and enhanced ITC, it effectively killed the popular tax shelter of the aircraft sale-and-leaseback. This was a method in which an FBO would offer to take back an aircraft they have sold on a lease for use in their rental or air-taxi operations. For high-tax-bracket individuals, this was an attractive way of buying an airplane.

No more. ERTA has eliminated deductions for depreciation for individuals, partnerships or Subchapter S corporations in such arrangements. In other words, the IRS is trying to limit ITC to those who are conducting a true business operation, and not just leasing an airplane as a tax shelter.

1982 Piper Seneca III

1982 Cessna 152-world's best selling trainer

If your corporation wants to enter into such a deal, bear in mind that leases to government agencies and non-profit organizations also are ineligible for ITC. A professional tax advisor is essential in arranging a leaseback. You have been warned!

Leasing an aircraft

Recent changes in accounting methods (FASB 13, see below) require payment obligations under *capital leases* to be shown as a liability of the balance sheet of a corporation, so one of the main advantages of a lease has been eliminated. Thus having an airplane on lease will have an effect on working-capital figures just as would having the ownership of one with a lien against it.

There are other advantages to leasing an airplane, however.

1. Leasing reduces cash outlays for new equipment. A security deposit of a few months' rent may be required, but this will be less than the 20 percent down payment usually required for a financing deal.
2. Leasing costs on an aircraft used for business purposes are deductible as a direct operating expense.
3. Leasing can remove resale problems. When a lease is over, you can walk away from it.
4. Leases can be drawn for specific periods to suit your needs. If you need a plane for six months, you can lease one for six months.
5. Some leases offer a low-cost purchase option.
6. You can tailor a lease to suit your operational requirements. You can arrange to pay the insurance, or you can lease it insured. You may pay an engine hour allowance or not. You can lease with a crew or not. You can pay for the fuel or not. Whatever is most convenient for you you can usually arrange.

Consult with your tax adviser to see if leasing is better for you than purchasing. It can be a complicated decision, to be based on many aspects of your own financial situation. Leasing is generally more expensive in real dollar terms, but there are often tax advantages that make it the better way.

Some leases pass the investment tax credit on to the lessee; others keep it for the lessor. If the lessor keeps the ITC, your lease rate should be correspondingly lower.

FASB 13

The Financial Accounting Standards Board (FASB) has issued a statement of financial accounting standards (number 13) that establishes standards of financial accounting and reporting for leases. This is known simply as FASB 13. FASB 13 shows two kinds of leases—capital leases and operating leases.

A *capital lease* is one that fulfills one or more of the following criteria:

1. The lease transfers ownership of the property to the lessee by the end of the lease term.
2. The lease contains a "bargain purchase option" that would allow the lessee to buy the leased property at a price so much lower than its fair value that, at the inception of the lease, purchase seems to be reasonably assured.
3. The lease term is equal to 75% or more of the estimated economic life of the leased property (not applicable in certain used-property cases).
4. The present value of the lease payments over the life of the lease equals or exceeds 90% of the fair value of the leased property, less any investment tax credit retained by the lessor.

An *operating lease* is simply defined as any lease that does not fit one of these four criteria.

Piper Cherokee Pathfinder

What you get for your money

Like everything else, airplanes keep getting more expensive. This is not just true of new planes but of used ones as well. Look at the chart on page 31 to see how the price on a 1969 Bonanza has altered in 13 years, for example.

On the adjacent chart you can see the price ranges for various typical light airplanes. Each vertical line represents the price range in 1982 for the type of aircraft indicated—2-place single-engine fixed-gear, for example. The bottom of the line represents a period about 15-20 years ago. The top of the line represents a new fully equipped aircraft. Prices seem to rise about 10 percent each year, so you just mentally move the line up that much for each year beyond 1982. If it's 1985, for example, move the line up about 30 percent in dollars. This should give you an indication of current price ranges.

If you know how much money you have to spend on an aircraft, you can just run your finger across the appropriate price level to see the sorts of airplanes available to you at that price. The box shows various pros and cons of new and used airplanes.

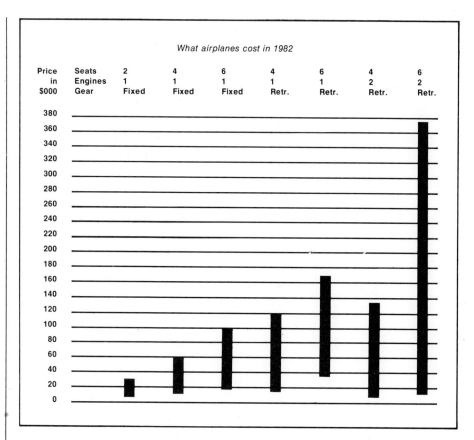

What airplanes cost in 1982

| Price in $000 | Seats / Engines / Gear | 2 / 1 / Fixed | 4 / 1 / Fixed | 6 / 1 / Fixed | 4 / 1 / Retr. | 6 / 1 / Retr. | 4 / 2 / Retr. | 6 / 2 / Retr. |

The most popular airplane in the world—the Cessna 172. This is a 1963 model.

Pros.	Cons.
New vs used airplane	
Full factory warranty	More expensive to buy
Less prone to mechanical failure	Subject to possible bugs
Less maintenance needed	Usually high depreciation in first year or two
"State of the art" technology	Higher insurance cost
Can order exactly as required	
More prestige	
Can get factory training in sophisticated aircraft	
Greater tax benefits	
Better financing arrangements available	
Used vs new airplane	
Lower purchase price	Higher maintenance cost
Lower insurance cost	Reduced or no warranty
Lower depreciation, maybe even appreciation	More prone to mechanical failure
	May have damage history
	Less favorable financing
	Lesser or no tax benefits
	Uncertain history

In 1978, the same basic airplane came as the Hawk XP and the Skyhawk (*top*)

The costs of aircraft ownership

There are certain high fixed costs resulting from owning an airplane that will be incurred whether you fly 1 hour a year or 500. These include items such as storage costs, insurance, financing expense, annual inspection, taxes and fees, chart subscriptions, and depreciation. Once you've decided on a certain type of airplane, there is little you can do to alter these costs. Maybe you can tie the plane down instead of keeping it in a hangar or reduce your insurance coverage, but you can't eliminate the costs entirely and still own an airplane to fly around in.

The variable costs depend on how much you fly the aircraft. These costs include fuel and oil, maintenance, the cost of engine and propeller overhaul, landing fees, spare parts, and your own incidental expenses (tolls on the drive to the airport, taxis and car rentals out of town, telephone calls to the weather office and the airport, and so on).

If your fixed costs come to $3,000 a year and your operating costs come to $20 an hour, here's how your annual utilization affects your true hourly operating costs:

Hours flown per year	Annual fixed costs	Annual operating cost ($20/hour)	Average hourly cost
100	$3,000	$ 2,000	$50
200	$3,000	$ 4,000	$35
300	$3,000	$ 6,000	$30
400	$3,000	$ 8,000	$27.50
500	$3,000	$10,000	$26

At 100 hours of utilization the fixed costs are 60 percent of the total cost. At 500 hours this proportion drops to 23 percent. The more you fly, the cheaper it gets by the hour.

Factors affecting operating costs

Many different factors affect the operating cost of an airplane.

1. The initial cost. The higher the initial cost, the higher will be the cost of financing the airplane. A new $100,000 airplane financed with 20 percent down, the balance over six years, will cost over $1,824 per month for 72 months at 18 percent simple interest—for a total interest cost of over $51,385. A used $50,000 airplane that does about the same as the new one, financed in the same way, would cost about half that in payments and about half that in total interest. The higher the initial cost, the higher will be the cost of insuring the airplane. Assuming a 2 percent hull rate, the annual cost for that insurance would be $2,000 for the new airplane vs $1,000 for the used $50,000 job. The higher the initial cost, especially if it's for a new airplane, the higher the depreciation. The first year's drop in resale value can be as high as 25 percent of the initial cost for a new airplane, whereas a similiar used airplane costing half as much probably won't depreciate much at all and could very likely *appreciate* in value (see page 30). Of course, if you're operating the aircraft for business, a higher initial cost will give you a better depreciation deduction and a better investment-tax-credit situation.

2. New or used airplane. A new airplane costs a lot more than a used one. However, there are some advantages, too. You get a warranty and probably a lesser maintenance problem. You get the knowledge that the aircraft has been operated only by you, so you're not likely to be surprised by some emerging problem you don't know about. But sometimes you get a few minor bugs because the airplane is so new that it is still in its "teething" stage. So in the first 100 hours or so of operation all kinds of little things could happen that will need to be ironed out.

3. The insurability of the airplane. It is harder and more expensive to buy insurance for some types of airplane. An "orphan" (one that is out of production, with the manufacturer out of business) will doubtless cost more than, say, a Cessna 172 to insure, given the same performance characteristics. Likewise, ex-military, highly specialized, and foreign aircraft will take more insurance dollars from your budget. Your own level of experience will also affect the insurance cost. Low-time pilots in high-performance aircraft must pay higher premiums than experienced pilots with lots of "time in type." For a low-time pilot, the simpler the airplane, the lower the insurance cost.

4. The size of the airplane. Larger airplanes cost more to store. Hangar and tiedown rates are based on wingspan, gross weight, and number of engines. Landing fees are usually based on gross weight: the heavier the weight, the higher the cost. Larger airplanes are just generally more expensive. A big aileron costs more than a small aileron. Big tires cost more than small tires. And so on.

5. The efficiency of the airplane. With these days of ever-increasing fuel costs, efficiency is a major consideration in operating costs. This is one reason why the retractable-gear single-engine airplane holds its value so well. You can get mpg efficiencies approaching those of automobiles, with no 55-mph speed limit, in these types of aircraft. Efficiencies vary with the type of plane. The smaller the frontal area and the cleaner the design, the more efficient the aircraft. The Mooney 201 is one of the most efficient four-seat single-engine retractables available. It cruises at 145 knots at 55-percent power, burning 7.8 gph, for a mileage efficiency of 18.6 mpg.

6. Ruggedness of the design. The stronger the airplane, the less likely it is to need extra maintenance due to minor mishaps, such as heavy landings, rough landing strips, flight in turbulence, and so on.

7. Engines. Considering the need for regular overhauls and maintenance, the engine is the most expensive component of the airplane, especially if you have two of them. The things to consider about engines include the size and complexity of the unit—the more the cylinders, the more expensive it is to replace sparkplugs and do overhauls. Turbochargers and gearing systems add to maintenance cost as well as initial cost. A major factor is the engine TBO. This is the manufacturer's recommended time

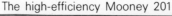

The high-efficiency Mooney 201

between overhauls. An engine with a 2,000-hour TBO, assuming it runs to the limit, should cost less to use than one with a 1,200-hour TBO. A $6,000 overhaul cost runs to $3 per hour on the 2,000-hour engine vs $5 per hour for the 1,200-hour model.

8. Airplane complexity. The more systems there are in an airplane, the more it will cost to run. Things such as retractable gear, electric vs manual flaps, constant-speed propellers, turbochargers, pressurization, de-icing equipment and oxygen systems all make the airplane cost more—not only to buy but to run. Retractable gear means that you have to put the airplane up on jacks when you do a 100-hour or annual inspection so that you can do a retraction test. This brings the labor cost up.

9. Parts availability. An "orphan" may be hard to find parts for. Even an older airplane made by Beech, Piper, or Cessna may have ludicrous parts expenses. Some parts are just out of stock and have to be handmade. A popular aircraft with a long production run, such as the Beech Bonanza, Cessna 172 or Piper Cherokee, presents much less of a problem in this area.

10. Overall maintenance situation. This includes the accessibility of the systems. If it takes four hours to remove and reinstall the engine cowling and if that's the only way you can change the oil or the battery, you've got an expensive-to-maintain airplane. Some airplanes have a history of problems that are well known. Leaking fuel tanks are an example. So are cracked engine crankcases. Check with knowledgeable maintenance people about the maintenance history of the type of airplane you are involved with.

11. The AD story. Some airplanes have a string of airworthiness directives; others have few. Some are costly to perform, and they may have to be repeated at regular intervals, such as every 100 hours. The Piper Comanche has several of these, for example, and you can spend about $400 every 100 hours to get them all fixed. That means you should add $4 per hour to your cost of operation.

Some ADs are really major—maybe a spar repair or a landing-gear rebuild. These can cost in the thousands of dollars. So be aware (see page 71).

12. Avionics complexity. A used Narco Mark 12 and a transponder cost a lot less to buy and maintain than a three-axis autopilot with flight director and couplers, area-navigation, and a slaved gyro-magnetic compass system. As ye equip, so shall ye pay.

13. Utilization. The more you use the airplane, the lower a part of the overall cost will be the high fixed costs. The fixed costs include:
(a) financing charges
(b) storage
(c) insurance
(d) annual inspection
(e) taxes and fees
(f) chart subscriptions
(g) depreciation.

Figuring direct operating costs

Direct operating costs are those costs that are incurred in the hour-by-hour flying of the airplane. The following items are included:

1. Fuel
2. Oil
3. Oxygen
4. Maintenance
5. Spare parts
6. Reserve for regular inspections (such as the 100-hour inspection)
7. Reserve for engine overhaul
8. Reserve for repetitive AD compliance
9. Reserve for any life-limited components
10. Landing and parking fees

Let's discuss these items in detail.

1. Fuel. Fuel is going to cost more and more in the future. An economical aircraft is more important now than it has ever been. Economical operating techniques must be observed. Fuel consumption is directly related to the amount of power being used. Economy cruise settings of 55 to 65 percent of power will save a lot of fuel with little reduction in speed. For example, a Cessna 172 flies at 122 knots at 75 percent power and at 104 knots at 55 percent. That's a 15-percent loss in speed for a 27-percent power reduction. At 75-percent power it burns 8.8 gallons per hour, and at 55 percent it uses only 6.7 gallons per hour. That's a 25-percent reduction in fuel consumption. The table shows a few other aircraft and their speed/fuel relationships. It shows the percentage reduction in speed and the percentage reduction in fuel consumption for a power reduction from 75 to 55 percent, which is a 27-percent reduction in power.

| Aircraft | 27 percent power reduction | |
	Speed reduction	Fuel reduction
Cessna 150	9%	26%
Grumman T-Cat	16%	23%
Grumman Tiger	16%	20%
Cherokee Cruiser	14%	26%
Beech Sundowner	21%	36%
Cessna Cardinal	16%	27%
Cherokee Six	14%	26%
Mooney 201	14%	28%
Cessna Cardinal RG	10%	25%
Rockwell 114	12%	22%
Cessna Centurion	10%	26%
Beech Bonanza	9%	25%
Bellanca Super Viking	10%	21%
Cessna Skymaster	12%	26%
Piper Seneca II	13%	24%
Beech B55 Baron	8%	27%
Piper Aztec F	9%	20%
Cessna 310	9%	24%
Aerostar 600	9%	22%

As can be seen, some of the aircraft have a very small loss in speed—less than 10 percent—for about a 25-percent saving in fuel consumption. One thing's for sure about fuel. The more you fly, the more you're going to use. It is only by using economy power settings that you can get your fuel consumption down. Of course, some aircraft are more efficient than others. This should have a bearing on your own selection of an aircraft.

2. Oil. Oil prices seem to vary all over the place. I've paid anywhere from 80¢ to $1.50 a quart on one trip. The best way to save on oil expense is to buy it by the case and carry some with you. A full-flow oil filter can enable you to run for a longer period between oil changes. If your aircraft does not have this type of filter, you may be able to have one installed. Not only will this reduce your overall oil consumption, but it will reduce engine wear and extend the life of the engine before an over-haul is needed.

3. Oxygen. If you have oxygen, you will need to refill the system from time to time. This can be a very expensive process, depending on where you go. I was recently invited to pay $27 to refill my Scott Executive Mark I bottle (one of the smallest available). This bottle takes 11 cubic feet, supplying two people with oxygen for 1.5 hours. The reason it can be so

costly is that it takes about 20 minutes to do the job, and some FBOs have a one-hour minimum labor charge. So you may be paying $20 labor for a $7 refill. I suggest you shop around wherever you fly, asking for the oxygen-refill price, and make a note of the least expensive places. If you can get it refilled while you are having other maintenance done, you should save on that minimum labor charge. The key factor with oxygen is to use only aviator's breathing oxygen MIL-0-27210D. Medical oxygen can corrode the system's internal hardware, leading to system failure. Oxygen servicing must be done by competent personnel familiar with high-pressure aviation oxygen equipment.

4. Maintenance. The way to cut down on maintenance costs is to have it done properly at regular intervals. The high costs come in when something has been missed and

you're away from base on a trip, it's a Saturday evening, and you need a replacement part delivered and installed by Sunday evening. Overtime labor and air shipment of parts cost a fortune. I recommend that you run a definite scheduled maintenance program, with regular checks every 25, 50, and 100 hours. Check the section on preventive maintenance (page 138) to see what you can do yourself. Try to have as many things as possible done together. Recurrent A.D.s should be combined with other maintenance activities to save on labor costs.

5. Spare parts. Unless you have an "orphan" aircraft or one that's been out of production a long time, you shouldn't have to carry a large stock of spares yourself. Your FBO will probably have the most common items, such as tires and batteries, in stock or readily available through one of the many distributors. Buying

Plane Profile 8: Piper PA 28-161 Warrior II

Seats	4
Cruise speed, 65% power, 8,000 feet	114 knots
Range, 65% power, full optional fuel, 8,000 feet	581 nm
Maximum endurance	6.1 hours
Gross weight	2,325 pounds
Empty weight	1,348 pounds
Full optional fuel	288 pounds
	48 gallons
Useful load, full fuel	689 pounds
Fuel efficiency, 65% power	15.2 nmpg
Stall speed, flaps down	50 knots
Rate of climb, sea level	710 fpm
Minimum field length	1,490 feet
Engine type Lycoming O-320-D3G	160 hp
Engine TBO	2,000 hours
Remarks Current version of the original Piper Cherokee.	

Funding it

the parts yourself and then asking the FBO to install them will cause frowns. The FBO relies on the markup on parts as part of his income, so it would probably be wise to let the FBO get the parts for you. In spite of the high costs of parts and labor, you have a definite interest in keeping your FBO in business! Spare parts can be ludicrously expensive. Some factory-supplied parts are so expensive that you just have to consider an alternative. In buying spares from other than factory dealers and recognized distributors, be very sure that what you are getting is the proper stuff. See the section on spare parts (page 143).

6. Reserve for regular inspections. Many FBOs charge a flat rate for a 100-hour or annual inspection. Check with yours for the local rate. If the rate for a 100-hour is $500, then you should be banking $5.00 for every hour you fly the aircraft to cover this, assuming you have 100-hour inspections performed. You should make provision for the annual inspection as part of your fixed costs (see page 42), so make sure you don't duplicate this item in your direct operating costs.

7. Reserve for engine overhaul. You need to carry a reserve for overhauling the engine when it comes due or be faced with a big bill at some time in the future. Here's how to figure this out. *What is the recommended TBO?* This is the time between overhauls recommended by the engine manufacturer. Let's say your engine has a TBO of 2,000 hours. *How many hours are there on the engine SMOH?* SMOH means since major overhaul. How many hours have been put on the engine since then (or since new, if it hasn't been overhauled yet)? Let's say there are 400 hours SMOH. *What is the cost of bringing the engine back to zero time?* (You can do this by trading in your old engine on a brand-new one or a factory rebuilt one, or you can have your own engine overhauled. See the section on engine overhauls on page 149 for further details.) You can find out this cost by checking with the local en-

gine distributor or with your FBO. Let's say the cost to overhaul is estimated at $10,000, Now you work out the following simple formula:

TBO hours	2000
minus hours SMOH	400
equals hours left	1600
Cost of overhaul divided by hours	$10,000
left on engine	1600
equals cost per hour	$6.25

So you should be banking $6.25 every hour you fly the airplane to pay for your next engine. Bear in mind that the engine may not run to its full TBO, which means that you'll be paying for an overhaul sooner. Or it may run past the TBO, meaning you'll be paying later, and your hourly cost will go down.

8. Reserve for repetitive AD compliance. My Comanche has a number of ADs that need to be complied with at regular intervals. The fuel tanks need to be inspected every 100 hours. This costs about $150 in labor. The fin forward spar must be inspected for

cracks every 100 hours. This costs about $50 in labor. So there's $200 every 100 hours, or $2.00 per hour.

9. Reserve for any life limited components. Certain parts of the aircraft have to be replaced at specific intervals. Propellers have TBOs like engines. Oil filters should be changed at every oil change. Sparkplugs are only good for so many hours. Tires will only last so many landings. Air filters must be replaced regularly. The costs of these items, divided by their expected lives in hours, will give you an hourly figure to set aside for their replacement.

10. Landing and parking fees. These don't account for very much. In 150 hours of flying over 9 months, I paid out $42 in landing fees and $45 for parking. That works out to be 58¢ per hour. Of course, if you go into La Guardia every day at 5 P.M., the $25 fee charged at that time will add up rather fast! So you may or may not want to set aside a figure to cover this cost, depending on the type of flying you're doing.

Piper Tomahawk and its 2000 hour TBO Lycoming O-235

Funding it

Establishing an operating budget

This is kind of a chicken-and-egg proposition However, let us assume that you now have *some* idea of the kind of aircraft you want and an approximate idea of its value. With that in mind, let's proceed.

1. How much cash do you have available to invest in an airplane?

    $ _____ (A)

2. How much cash do you have available per year to allocate to the airplane (this will cover financing, fixed, and operating costs)?

    $ _____

3. Do you want to pay cash for the airplane or finance it?
    a. Pay cash ☐
    b. Finance it ☐

    If you want to pay cash, the amount of cash available in question (1) sets your purchase-price limit. What is your cash-purchase-price limit?

    $ _____

    If you want to finance it, the next question is how much you want to put in as a down payment. Set a low limit of 20 percent.

    How much do you want to put down?

    _____ percent down (20%)
    (minimum)

    $ _____
    (should not exceed the amount of cash available in question 1)

    Now divide the maximum cash-down-payment amount by the percentage down payment you have established. For example, if you decided on a $5,000 down payment and you want to put 20 percent down, divide $5,000 by .2 = $\frac{$5000}{.2}$ = $25,000. The result is the purchase price you are prepared to pay:

    Down payment amount

    $ _____

    Divided by _____ %

    Equals purchase price limit

    $ _____

Now deduct from this figure the amount of down payment to arrive at the amount to be financed (in our example it would be $25,000 − $5,000 = $20,000 to be financed):

Purchase-price limit	$ _____
Minus amount of down payment	$ _____
Equals amount to be financed	$ _____

Now we need to figure a rough idea of what this is going to cost per year. The first question is how many years you want to finance it (a maximum of five years for a used airplane is usual; new airplanes can go higher — say, up to eight years).

Number of years to finance airplane _____

Talk to your banker or other aircraft loan agency and find out what type of interest you would have to pay. If you can't find out immediately, use the prevailing auto-loan rate. See the section on financing your airplane (page 131) for further details. Use this table to figure out your rough annual outlay for your aircraft loan.

In our example we wanted to finance $20,000. Let's say we want to pay this off over five years and we were able to get a loan at 14 percent simple interest. The table shows annual outlay per $1,000. So, referring to the table, we see that a five-year, 14-percent loan would come to $279 per $1,000 per year, or $5,580 per year for five years for $20,000 ($279 × 20 = $5,580).

What is the interest rate you expect to pay?

_____ % simple interest.

What is the number of years you want to repay over? _____ years.

What is the amount to be financed?

$ _____ to be financed

From the table what is the annual outlay for the above?

$ _____ annual outlay. (B)

4. What will be your annual fixed costs? Fixed costs include storage, insurance, the cost of the annual inspection, and any fees or taxes. Depreciation is another fixed cost, but it is not an actual outlay of cash, so we will exclude it from this calculation. Contact your local airport and find out how much it will cost you to store your airplane. Will you keep it in a T-hangar, a regular hangar or a tie-down?

    Annual cost for storage $ _____ (D)

    This is for: T hangar ☐
    Hangar ☐
    Tie-down ☐

    Check with your local fixed-base operator (FBO) and find out what the fee is for an annual inspection for an aircraft of the type you are interested in. They may quote you a flat rate for the inspection, with parts and labor for any fixin's extra. Use the flat-rate figure.

    Cost of annual inspection $ _____ (E)

Annual cost of an aircraft loan of $1,000 (principal and interest — simple interest annualized monthly payments)							
Number of years	**12%**	**13%**	**14%**	**15%**	**16%**	**17%**	**18%**
1	1066	1072	1077	1083	1089	1094	1100
2	568	571	576	582	588	593	599
3	399	404	410	416	421	428	434
4	316	322	328	334	340	346	353
5	267	273	279	286	292	298	305
6	235	241	247	264	200	267	274
7	212	218	225	232	238	245	252
8	195	202	209	215	222	230	237

Funding it

Contact an insurance outlet and get a rough quote on what you need. Tell them you are trying to establish your budget and you need to know what it will cost you to get a proposed airplane covered.

Annual cost for
insurance $ _____ (F)

This is for $ _____ liability

$ _____ hull

$ _____ deductible

Quotation received from:

_____

Figure the cost of any other fixed annual costs. There may be a state licensing fee. Add in the cost of any chart subscription or other fixed annual item. Summarize these here:

State tax $ _____

Charts $ _____

_____ $ _____

_____ $ _____

Total $ _____ (G)

Now let's assemble the annual fixed costs we have worked out:

Storage $ _____ (D)

Annual inspection $ _____ (E)

Insurance $ _____ (F)

Other fixed costs $ _____ (G)

Total annual fixed
costs $ _____ (C)

5. How much money will you have for variable operating costs? Going back over the figures in questions 2, 3, and 4, assemble these figures:

Total annual cash
available $ _____ (A)

Less annual
financing outlay $ _____ (B)

Less annual
fixed costs $ _____ (C)

Equals annual oper-
ating budget $ _____ (H)

This is the amount of money you will have available to fly the airplane. Now refer to the following table to get some idea of the hourly operating costs you can afford vs the annual utilization you can afford.

For example, if you figure that you have $4,000 available for annual direct operating costs, you can see from the chart that you could fly 400 hours a year if your direct operating cost is $10 an hour but only 200 hours a year if the hourly cost if $20. Alternatively, if you know that you will have to fly 300 hours per year, you can afford a direct operating cost of between $10 and $15. You can figure this out exactly by dividing the annual variable cost funds you have available by the number of hours you want to fly. In our example

$4,000 divided by 300 equals $13.33. This is the highest direct operating cost you can afford to pay based on 300 hours of use per year. You can also figure what utilization you can handle if you know your direct operating cost by dividing your annual funds available by the hourly cost figure. If you know that your direct operating cost is $15, then $4,000 divided by $15 equals 266.7 hours. That's all you can afford to fly. Figure yours here:

Annual operating
funds available $ _____ (H)

divided by hourly
cost rate $ _____

equals affordable annual
utilization: _____ hours.

Or:

Annual operating
funds available $ _____ (H)

divided by annual
utilization rate _____ hours

equals affordable
hourly direct
cost $ _____

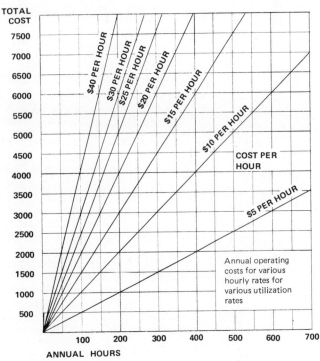

TOTAL COST

$40 PER HOUR
$30 PER HOUR
$25 PER HOUR
$20 PER HOUR
$15 PER HOUR
$10 PER HOUR
$5 PER HOUR

COST PER HOUR

Annual operating costs for various hourly rates for various utilization rates

ANNUAL HOURS

Funding it

Rockwell Commander 700 wide-body twin, now out of production

Financing your airplane

Not all banks are happy about making a loan on a light aircraft. However, there are several banks and finance companies that specialize in aircraft loans, and I recommend that you use one of these. The advantage is that you will be talking to a loan officer who understands airplanes and their equipment. It will be more significant to such a person that your proposed purchase is equipped with an encoding altimeter and TSO'd transponder or that it isn't. Banks that like to make aircraft loans advertise in the national and local aviation publications, and a good way to get a good relationship going is to ask a reliable aircraft dealer to recommend a bank. That's what I did when I bought my first airplane and it worked perfectly. The man I talked to was a pilot and understood my needs. We worked out a very satisfactory arrangement in advance so that I was able to fly away in my new airplane an hour after I first saw it.

Another good source of financing information is to write to:

Aircraft Finance Association
P.O. Box 595
Wichita, Kansas, 67201

They will send you a list of banks and finance companies that specialize in aircraft loans. Beech, Piper, Grumman American, Rockwell International and Cessna have their own finance companies and tend to operate through the local dealer.

The lender wants to know about two items—you and your airplane. As far as you are concerned, the lender will look at your credit record, most likely through one of the local credit-reporting services. Most of your credit references will probably be contacted, and what the lender is looking for is good experience. This means a history of regular, on-time payments. The lender also wants to know about your ability to repay the loan, so you will have to supply a current personal balance sheet (or corporate financial statements, if applicable), and you must show that you will have enough income to comfortably cover the repayments. Don't expect anticipated income from the leaseback of your airplane to a flight school to rate highly as a source in the lender's mind. Aviation businesses are notoriously undercapitalized, and a few weekends of no VFR could seriously affect the school's payment schedule to you. If you have a record of "slow pay," collections, or other bad credit experience, even if you have a high income, the lender may well turn you down. Good credit is essential for an aircraft loan.

Your proposed airplane will require its own investigation. Your lender will require a title search (see page 97). Even with a clean looking title, the FAA does not endorse any information with respect to ownership on a certificate of aircraft registration. However, the person who fills out the application for aircraft registration must sign a declaration of ownership and provide legal evidence of ownership, along with an indication of any encumbrance, and a false statement on this form "may be grounds for punishment by fine and/or imprisonment [U.S. Code, Title 18, Section 1001]". (See page 92.)

The lender may want some evidence of inspection of a used aircraft, which should be carried out by a qualified mechanic. For your own protection you should have this done anyway (see page 83). You will also have to supply evidence of insurance showing the lienholder's interest, including a breach-of-warranty endorsement supplied by the insurer directly to the lender. (See page 99 for the insurance section.)

When I bought my plane, I arranged insurance in advance in anticipation of acceptance (this was done over the phone, with no up-front money required). So when I made the decision to buy, I was able to fly away immediately.

The type of airplane and thus its marketability will have a lot to do with your lender's willingness to lend you money. Expect higher receptivity to your proposal to buy a '71 Bonanza than the North American T-28 you've been hankering to own. The evaluation of the airplane and its equipment will be based on its wholesale value, not on the price you are going to pay. Expect to put at least 20 percent down on the bird. Repayment terms can run over several years—as many as ten years for a new airplane. My loan for a thirteen-year-old airplane called for 20 percent down and the balance over five years. That's 60 months, and

Funding it

there are an awful lot of pages in that repayment book when you first get it!

If you're dealing with a bank, you don't have to be an existing customer to get an airplane loan, so you won't have to change your existing banking arrangements.

Two low-interest loan sources

If you own life insurance that has a cash value, you can borrow money against it at a relatively low rate of interest. If you own marginable securities, such as good-quality common stocks or corporate or government bonds, you might be able to borrow money through your stockbroker at lower interest than you would have to pay for a conventional loan against an airplane. You may like to consider the money-saving aspects of these options.

In both types of loans you can just make interest payments and continue to carry the debt if you prefer.

Interest rates

Bank loans are usually paid off in equal monthly installments. The bank will quote you a rate (called the "annual percentage rate" or APR), which may be calculated in various ways. The various truth-in-lending acts require that all loans show the amount to be financed, the monthly payments, any other charges involved, the total amount to be repaid, and the true annual percentage rate. For example, a $7,500 loan at 9 percent, compounded monthly, repaid in 60 monthly payments over five years, will take $155.69 per month to pay off. The total amount to be repaid is $9,341.40, which gives a total interest cost for the five years of $1,841.40. The annual percentage rate is 9 percent.

The following table will enable you to calculate the monthly payments on a loan for various periods at various interest rates. This table is based on simple interest. Under each interest rate shown is a factor. You simply multiply this factor by the total amount being financed to get your monthly payment (table courtesy of *Aircraft Price Digest*, used with permission).

Rockwell International Commander 114

Monthly Payments for Various Interest Rates

Months	Years	8%	8.5%	9%	9.5%	10%	10.5%	11%	11.5%	12%
12	1	.08699	.08723	.08746	.08769	.08792	.08815	.08839	.08862	.08885
18	1.5	.05915	.05937	.05960	.05983	.06006	.06029	.06052	.06076	.06099
24	2	.04523	.04546	.04569	.04592	.04615	.04638	.04661	.04685	.04708
30	2.5	.03689	.03712	.03735	.03758	.03782	.03805	.03828	.03852	.03875
36	3	.03134	.03157	.03181	.03204	.03227	.03251	.03274	.03298	.03322
48	4	.02442	.02465	.02489	.02513	.02537	.02561	.02585	.02609	.02634
60	5	.02028	.02052	.02076	.02101	.02125	.02150	.02175	.02200	.02225
72	6	.01754	.01778	.01803	.01828	.01853	.01878	.01904	.01930	.01956
84	7	.01559	.01584	.01609	.01635	.01661	.01687	.01713	.01739	.01766

Months	Years	12.5%	13%	13.5%	14%	15%	16%	17%	18%
12	1	.08909	.08932	.08956	.08979	.09026	.09074	.09121	.09169
18	1.5	.06122	.06145	.06169	.06192	.06239	.06286	.06334	.06381
24	2	.04731	.04755	.04778	.04802	.04849	.04897	.04945	.04993
30	2.5	.03899	.03923	.03947	.03970	.04018	.04067	.04115	.04164
36	3	.03346	.03370	.03394	.03418	.03467	.03516	.03566	.03616
48	4	.02659	.02683	.02708	.02733	.02784	.02835	.02886	.02938
60	5	.02250	.02276	.02302	.02327	.02380	.02432	.02486	.02540
72	6	.01982	.02008	.02034	.02061	.02115	.02170	.02225	.02281
84	7	.01793	.01820	.01847	.01875	.01930	.01987	.02044	.02102

Funding it

Following are the action steps I took when I bought my airplane from an individual.

Time	Dealing with the bank	Dealing with the seller	Dealing with others
Day 1	Identified banker by asking aircraft dealer to suggest one.	Identified possible aircraft to buy. Obtained all details.	
Day 2	Discussed proposed purchase with banker on telephone. Bank sent me loan application.		
Day 3			Arranged possible storage of aircraft with FBO
Day 5	Completed and returned loan application.		
Day 6		Arranged inspection of airplane. Arranged to personally view and fly the airplane.	
Day 8	Banker agreed to lend me money to buy an airplane. We agreed on an approximate amount and a 20% down payment.		Contacted insurance company. Arranged tentative insurance.
Day 9	Received copy of retail installment contract from banker which would be the actual execution of the deal. Banker agreed to pay off existing lien and pay difference direct to seller.	Inspected airplane. Checked log books. Flew airplane. Agreed to buy it. Executed retail installment contract. Gave seller check for down payment. Seller to receive check for difference from bank after they paid off existing lien.	Confirmed storage with FBO. Flew away in my new airplane.
Day 10	Advised bank of purchase.		Advised insurance company of purchase. Notified FAA and FCC of change in ownership.

The author in his Comanche

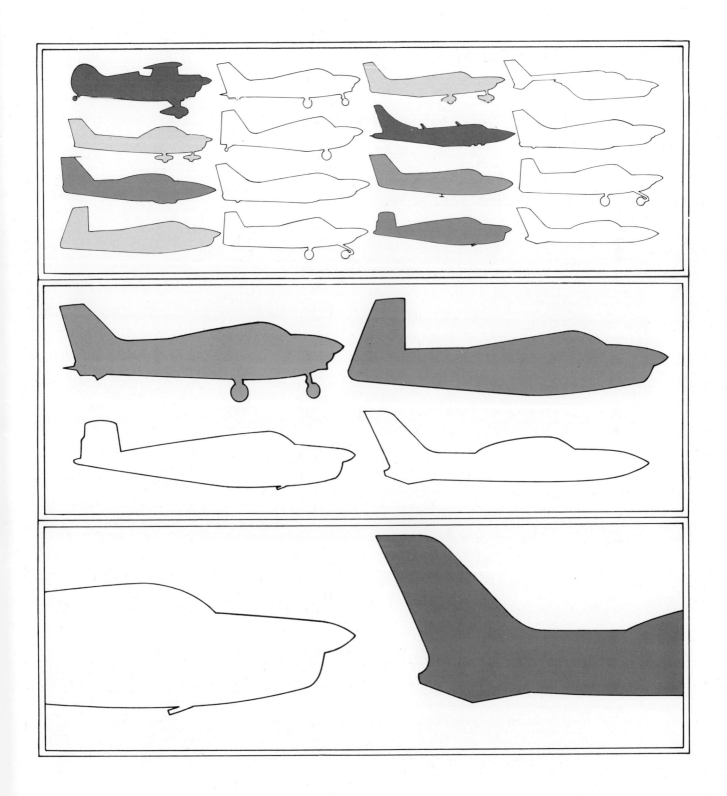

Choosing it

Figuring your needs

Now we get to the fun part—figuring out just what your needs are. Here you will have to consider the types of trips you want to make, their frequency, how many seats you will need, what types of airports you'll use, whether you want to go VFR or IFR and so on. Here is a summary of the action steps laid out on the next few pages. You can summarize your results on here as you go along.

When you have completed your summary on this page, use the results (keys A to R, below) to help you fill out the checklist starting on page 60.

Section	Action	Page	Key	Results	Remarks
1.	Determine the flight rules you will use.	49	(A)	VFR only ☐ VFR/IFR ☐	
2.	Measure your repetitive trips	50	(B)	Total annual distance _____ nm	
			(C)	Total annual landings _____	
3.	Rank your repetitive trips and determine seats needed	51	(D)	Number of seats needed _____	
4.	Estimate your payload	51	(E)	Payload per trip _____ lbs.	
5.	Select ideal cruising speed	52	(F)	Ideal cruising speed _____ kts	
				Power setting _____ % power	
6.	Determine ideal range requirement	54	(G)	VFR range need _____ nm _____ hrs	
			(H)	IFR range need _____ nm _____ hrs	
7.	Determine annual basic utilization	55	(J)	Annual basic use _____ hours	
8.	Determine takeoff, climb, descent allowance	56	(K)	Allowance _____ hours	
9.	Determine expected total annual utilization	56	(M)	Total annual use _____ hours	
10.	Establish target operating cost	56	(N)	Target operating cost $_____	
11.	Determine airport limitations	57	(O)	Shortest runway _____ feet	
			(P)	Under 5,000 feet elev. ☐	
				or highest elevation _____ feet	
			(Q)	Runway length of (P) _____ ft	
12.	Determine ideal cruising altitude	58	(R)	Below 10,000 feet ☐ Between 10,000 ft and FL 200 ☐ Above FL 200 ☐	
13.	Complete aircraft needs and preference checklist	60			
14.	Compare aircraft candidates	64			
15.	Determine avionics needs	66			
16.	Review the maintenance situation	71			
17.	Review the marketplace	73			
18.	Select the right aircraft for you	87			

1. Determine the flight rules you will use.

Step one in figuring your needs is to resolve the VFR — IFR question. The box shows the pros and cons of flight restricted to VFR only vs. flight carried out either under VFR or IFR, whichever is most appropriate. Now, answer these questions:

Do you have an instrument rating?
Yes ☐ No ☐

If not, do you plan to get an instrument rating within the near future?
Yes ☐ No ☐

In your own airplane, will you fly VFR
only ☐ } (A)
Or VFR and/or IFR, as appropriate ☐

Pros.	Cons.
VFR only vs VFR and IFR	
Simpler operation	Liable to weather delays
Easier to stay proficient	Can be very dangerous if you proceed into bad weather
Need less exotically equipped airplane	VFR flight is less disciplined
Do not need expensive current chart service	Delayed search and rescue likely in case of a disappearance
Lower level of competence and experience required	
Reduced delays for simple flights	
VFR and IFR vs VFR only	
Less liable to weather delays	Need to constantly maintain IFR proficiency
Safer operation in bad weather	Need well-equipped airplane
Instrument-rated pilot is better trained and more current than VFR pilot	Need costly chart service
Can go VFR or IFR, whichever is best	Pilot must have instrument rating
	IFR operation more complex
	More likely to become exposed to very bad weather or icing

If your panel looks like this, go VFR! (Beech Staggerwing)

2. Measure your repetitive trips.

Write down all the repetitive trips you make in a year with the one way distance and the frequency whether round-trip or one way, and then calculate the total annual distance for each trip. For example, if you make 10 round trips a year between Des Moines and Kansas City, which is 150 nautical miles, show the one way distance as 150 and the annual frequency as 20 (i.e., you fly the 150 distance 20 times a year, 10 each way). Then show the total annual distance for that trip (20 X 150 = 3,000), and the total number of landings made (20). Finally show the largest number of seats filled for that trip (e.g., 2, 4 etc.)

Some of your repetitive trips might be done in a round-robin pattern, for example, you always fly Kansas City to Wichita to Oklahoma City to Tulsa to St Louis to Kansas City. In such a case multiply out the one-way distance for each leg by the number of times you do the round-robin. To save space, you could show a route like that as one trip, in which case you should show the appropriate number of landings for the trip. In the first example, Des Moines to Kansas City, we would show 20 landings for the 10 round trips. If you do the above round-robin 20 times a year, you would show 100 landings (5 per run) as your total. We need to know the number of landings for some later calculations. A good source of mileage information is the table on the back of the NOS *Flight Case Planning Chart* (see page 118).

From	To	One way distance	Annual frequency	Annual distance	Annual number of landings	Average number of seats
	TOTALS					

Total annual distance _____ (B)

Total annual landings _____ (C)

Beech Duke B 60

3. Rank your repetitive trips and determine seats needed

Now figure out how these trips are distributed by distance — how many of them are under 100 miles, how many are 500 miles, 800 miles, and so on. Also show the largest number of seats needed for each distance segment. Then rank them by frequency of trips — i.e., for the largest number of trips in one mileage group, write in "1" in the rank column, for the next largest number write in "2," etc.

Now we'll find what your range and seating needs are for the majority of your trips. Let's assume that you want your airplane to satisfy at least 80 percent of your missions. Enter the rankings in the lower table, from most frequent to least frequent. For example, if most of your trips were 200-300 miles in length, you would have ranked them number 1, so in the lower table opposite the rank 1, write in 200 to 300 miles, the annual frequency and the largest number of seats needed, etc.

Now we want to find how many of these trips satisfy 80 percent of your missions, so calculate how many trips (the total in the frequency column) represent 80 percent by multiplying the total by .8. Then, starting at the top of the frequency column, add the frequencies vertically until you accumulate to the number representing 80 percent. Make a mark under this rank line. Everything above this mark represents 80 percent of your missions. What is the largest number of seats needed for trips falling above this line?

Number of seats needed for 80% of trips
_____ (D)

Trips (one way distance)	Frequency of trips	Largest number of seats needed	Rank by frequency
Under 100 miles	_____	_____	_____
100-200 miles	_____	_____	_____
200-300 miles	_____	_____	_____
300-400 miles	_____	_____	_____
400-500 miles	_____	_____	_____
500-600 miles	_____	_____	_____
600-700 miles	_____	_____	_____
700-800 miles	_____	_____	_____
800-900 miles	_____	_____	_____
Over 1,000 miles	_____	_____	_____

Rank	Distances involved	Frequency	Largest number of seats
1.	Trips from ____ to ____ miles	____ trips	____ seats
2.	Trips from ____ to ____ miles	____ trips	____ seats
3.	Trips from ____ to ____ miles	____ trips	____ seats
4.	Trips from ____ to ____ miles	____ trips	____ seats
5.	Trips from ____ to ____ miles	____ trips	____ seats
6.	Trips from ____ to ____ miles	____ trips	____ seats
7.	Trips from ____ to ____ miles	____ trips	____ seats
8.	Trips from ____ to ____ miles	____ trips	____ seats
9.	Trips from ____ to ____ miles	____ trips	____ seats
10.	Trips from ____ to ____ miles	____ trips	____ seats

Total number of repetitive trips in year _____ X .8 = _____

4. Estimate your payload

Now express the number of seats (D) as a payload figure. Assume an average weight of 170 pounds per seat plus an allowance for any baggage or freight carried:

Total seats _____ (D) X 170 = _____ pounds

Total baggage allowance _____ pounds

Total freight carried _____ pounds

Total payload, per trip _____ pounds (E)

(Note: this payload figure does not include fuel.)

5. Select an ideal cruising speed

Speed is expensive. It seems that 150 knots at 75-percent power is about as fast as you can go in an airplane with fixed landing gear. And to get that 150 knots in a fixed-gear airplane takes an awful lot of power. It takes about 50 more horsepower to deliver 150 knots with the wheels hanging down as it does with the wheels up. See the box for the main airplane characteristics vs. speed ranges, and the kind of power it takes to get there.

You'll note from the table that there is often a wide spread between horsepower required to deliver various speeds. A 200-hp Mooney 201 cruises faster than the 260-hp Rockwell 114, for example.

The more the drag and the greater the weight to be lifted, the more power is needed to deliver the same cruising speed.

There is a direct relationship between the amount of power being used and fuel consumption. Look at the accompanying chart. It shows the amount of fuel consumed in gallons per hour for the engine's rated take off power at 55- and 75-percent power settings.

For example, a 250-hp engine operated at 55-percent power will burn about 10 gallons per hour. In these days of ever-rising fuel costs economy is important. So your determination of the ideal cruising speed for you is a function of economy and the types of trips you are making. If most of your trips are fairly short, you don't need a fast airplane.

The speed/power/configuration relationship

Speed range (knots)	Power range (hp)	Number of seats	Type of gear Fixed	Type of gear Retr.	Type of propeller Fixed	Type of propeller C/S	Turbocharging	Single engine	Twin engine
(75% power)									
100-109	100-115	2	X		X			X	
110-119	115-180	2-4	X		X			X	
120-129	150-180	4	X		X			X	
130-139	180-260	4-7	Most	Some		X		X	
140-149	180-300	4-7	Some	Most		X		X	
150-159	200-310	4-7		X		X	Some	X	
160-169	200-420	4-6		X		X	Some	Most	Some
170-179	285-500	4-6		X		X		Most	Some
180-189	520	6		X		X			X
190-199	300-570	4-6		X		X	Most	X	X
200-209	450-570	5-6		X		X	Some		X
210-249	570-620	6		X		X	Some		X

How fuel consumption varies by horsepower

This chart shows how fuel consumption at both 55% power and 75% power varies with the size of the engine.

The horsepower shown at the left of the chart is the maximum rated takeoff power at sea level.

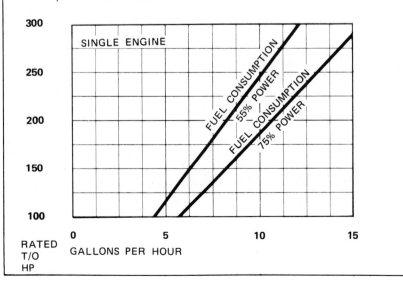

Choosing it

How various cruising speeds work at different distances

(All times shown in hours and minutes. 15 minutes added to all times for take-off, climb and landing allowance)

Speed (knots)	Distance (nautical miles)					
	100	200	400	600	800	1000
100	1.15	2.15	4.15	6.15	8.15	10.15
110	1.10	2.04	3.53	5.43	7.33	9.20
120	1.05	1.55	3.35	5.15	6.55	8.35
130	1.01	1.47	3.20	4.51	6.25	7.57
140	.58	1.41	3.07	4.33	5.57	7.24
150	.55	1.35	2.55	4.15	5.35	6.55
160	.53	1.30	2.45	4.00	5.15	6.31
170	.50	1.26	2.38	3.50	5.01	6.09
180	.49	1.22	2.29	3.35	4.42	5.49
190	.47	1.18	2.21	3.24	4.27	5.31
200	.45	1.15	2.15	3.15	4.15	5.15
210	.44	1.12	2.09	3.06	4.03	5.01
220	.42	1.10	2.05	3.00	3.55	4.48
230	.41	1.07	1.59	2.51	3.43	4.36
240	.40	1.05	1.55	2.45	3.35	4.25
250	.39	1.03	1.51	2.39	3.27	4.15

Look at this table to see how various cruising speeds work over various distances. A 100-knot cruise gets you 100 miles in 1 hour and 15 minutes (allowing 15 minutes for take-off, climb, approach, and landing). A 150-knot speed takes you the same distance in 55 minutes — a saving of 20 minutes, given the same allowances.

Yet you need about double the horse-power (= double the fuel consumption) to get 150 instead of 100 knots. And you probably have to put the wheels up and use a constant speed prop. All these things cost money. So where do *you* come out? What is the ideal speed for you? Decide on an approximate speed range and look at the characteristics of different aircraft that fall within each speed grouping, using the table on page 52.

Ideal cruising speed is _____ knots (F)

Proposed power setting _____ % power

Plane Profile 9: Mooney Turbo 231

Seats	4
Cruise speed, 65% power,	
8,000 feet	157 knots
18,000 feet	170 knots
Range, 65% power, full	
optional fuel, 18,000 feet	1,088 nm
Maximum endurance	7.4 hours
Gross weight	2,900 pounds
Empty weight	1,800 pounds
Full optional fuel	453 pounds
	75.5 gallons
Useful load, full fuel	647 pounds
Fuel efficiency, 65%	17 nmpg
power, 18,000 feet	
Stall speed, gear and	55 knots
flaps down	
Rate of climb, sea level	1,080 fpm
Minimum field length	2,100 feet
Engine type Continental	
TS10-360-GB-1	210 hp
Engine TBO	1,800 hours

Remarks Turbocharged, high-performance aircraft. Prop anti-icing and weather radar available.

6. Determine the ideal range requirement

Now calculate a mileage figure to represent a reserve, using your ideal cruising speed (F). The recommended VFR range requirement is for the aircraft to carry fuel to fly to destination plus 45 minutes at normal cruising speed. The legal IFR requirement is for fuel to complete the flight to the airport of first intended landing, fly from that airport to the alternate airport, and fly for 45 minutes thereafter at normal cruising speed. Under certain circumstances fuel to fly to the alternate is not required (FAR 91.23).

Cruising speed Knots	Still air distance covered in 45 minutes — nm
100	75
110	85
120	90
130	100
140	105
150	115
160	120
170	130
180	135
190	145
200	150
210	160
220	165
230	175
240	180
250	190

Still air range requirement, including reserves, in nautical miles											
Speed knots	*Decimal hours*										
	200	300	400	500	600	700	800	900	1000	1100	1200
100	2.0	3.0	4.0	5.0	6.0	7.0	8.0	9.0	10.0	11.0	12.0
110	1.8	2.7	3.6	4.5	5.5	6.4	7.3	8.2	9.1	10.0	10.9
120	1.7	2.5	3.3	4.2	5.0	5.8	6.7	7.5	8.3	9.2	10.0
130	1.5	2.3	3.1	3.8	4.6	5.4	6.2	6.9	7.7	8.5	9.2
140	1.4	2.1	2.9	3.6	4.3	5.0	5.7	6.4	7.1	7.9	8.6
150	1.3	2.0	2.7	3.3	4.0	4.7	5.3	6.0	6.7	7.3	8.0
160	1.3	1.9	2.5	3.1	3.8	4.4	5.0	5.6	6.3	6.9	7.5
170	1.2	1.8	2.4	2.9	3.5	4.1	4.7	5.3	5.9	6.5	7.1
180	1.1	1.7	2.2	2.8	3.3	3.9	4.4	5.0	5.6	6.1	6.7
190	1.1	1.6	2.1	2.6	3.2	3.7	4.2	4.7	5.3	5.8	6.3
200	1.0	1.5	2.0	2.5	3.0	3.5	4.0	4.5	5.0	5.5	6.0
210	1.0	1.4	1.9	2.4	2.9	3.3	3.8	4.3	4.8	5.2	5.7
220	.9	1.4	1.8	2.3	2.7	3.2	3.6	4.1	4.5	5.0	5.5
230	.9	1.3	1.7	2.2	2.6	3.0	3.5	3.9	4.3	4.8	5.2
240	.8	1.3	1.7	2.1	2.5	2.9	3.3	3.8	4.2	4.6	5.0
250	.8	1.2	1.6	2.0	2.4	2.8	3.2	3.6	4.0	4.4	4.8

Referring to the chart you made in section 3, above, what is the longest distance involved of trips falling **above** the 80 percentile line?

The longest distance of trips satisfying 80

percent of repetitive trips is _____ nautical miles.

VFR mileage figure for 45 minute

reserve: _____ .

To obtain the IFR figure, take the above VFR figure and add 200 miles to it. This will give you a reasonable reserve range for estimating purposes:

IFR mileage figure for legal

reserve: _____ .

Now add this figure to the appropriate reserve requirement, above:

My ideal still air VFR range requirement

is: _____ nm or _____ hours (G)

My ideal still air IFR range requirement

is: _____ nm or _____ hours (H)

7. Determine annual basic utilization

Now we need to figure what your basic annual utilization will be, based on your target cruising speed (F) and your distance requirement (B). Go back to the table in section 2 and obtain these figures:

Total annual distance _____ (B)

Total number of landings _____ (C)

Now take your ideal cruising speed (F) from section 5 and look at the accompanying table to figure your basic annual utilization for repetitive trips.

Basic annual utilization

_____ hours (J)

Or calculate it: Distance _____ (B) ÷

Speed _____ (F) equals basic

annual utilization _____ hours (J)

Cruising speed (knots)	Annual utilization in hours for various cruising speeds						
	Annual mileage — repetitive trips — total nautical miles						
	10,000	20,000	30,000	40,000	50,000	100,000	200,000
	Total flying time — decimal hours — annual rate						
100	100.0	200.0	300.0	400.0	500.0	1000.0	2000.0
110	90.9	181.8	272.7	363.6	454.5	909.1	1818.2
120	83.3	166.7	250.0	333.3	416.7	833.3	1666.7
130	76.9	153.8	230.8	307.7	384.6	769.2	1538.5
140	71.4	142.9	214.3	285.7	357.1	714.3	1428.6
150	66.7	133.3	200.0	266.7	333.3	666.7	1333.3
160	62.5	125.0	187.5	250.0	312.5	625.0	1250.0
170	58.8	117.6	176.5	235.3	294.1	588.2	1176.5
180	55.6	111.1	166.7	222.2	277.8	555.6	1111.1
190	52.6	105.3	157.9	210.5	263.2	526.3	1052.6
200	50.0	100.0	150.0	200.0	250.0	500.0	1000.0
210	47.6	95.2	142.9	190.5	238.1	476.2	952.4
220	45.5	90.9	136.4	181.2	227.3	454.5	909.1
230	43.5	87.0	130.4	173.9	217.4	434.8	869.6
240	41.7	83.3	125.0	166.7	208.3	416.7	833.3
250	40.0	80.0	120.0	160.0	200.0	400.0	800.0

Example: if you fly 30,000 miles per year and you select 160 knots, your annual block utilization would be 187.5 hours (187 hrs 30 mins).

Bellanca Viking touches down

Choosing it

8. Determine takeoff, climb and descent allowance

Now take your total number of landings (C) and multiply it by .25 hours. This will give you an allowance of 15 minutes for each flight for taxiing, takeoff, climb, descent, approach and landing.

Total landings (C) _____ X .25 = _____ hours (K)

9. Determine total expected annual utilization

Now figure how much flying time you'll be spending on training, biennial flight reviews, proficiency maintenance, vacation trips, joyriding, and so on. In this case, figure total flying time (including takeoffs, landings, etc.):

Annual training, proficiency and casual flying hours _____ (L)

Now assemble the figures:

Total flying time for basic annual utilization (J) _____ hours

Plus allowances for takeoffs etc. (K) _____ hours

Plus casual and training flights (L) _____ hours

Equals total annual utilization _____ hours. (M).

See the box for how your proposed utilization will fit into your schedule. A 500-hour-per-year utilization means you'll be flying an average of about 10 hours per week!

Average monthly, weekly, daily hours for various annual utilization rates:
Annual utilization — total flying hours — decimal hours

Year	50.0	100.0	150.0	200.0	250.0	300.0	350.0	400.0	450.0	500.0
Month	4.2	8.3	12.5	16.7	20.8	25.0	29.2	33.3	37.5	41.7
Week	1.0	1.9	2.9	3.8	4.8	5.8	6.7	7.7	8.7	9.6
Day	0.1	0.3	0.4	0.5	0.7	0.8	1.0	1.1	1.2	1.4

10. Establish target operating cost

Now you can relate your proposed annual utilization (M) with the budget you have available to fly the airplane (this is item (H) on page 43 in the *Funding It* chapter preceding this chapter):

Annual budget available [Funding It (H)]

$ _____ divided by annual utilization (M) _____ equals target hourly operating cost $ _____ (N)

11. Determine airport limitations

Now let's look at the types of airports you'll be using to establish a minimum runway length requirement. The considerations here are the shortest field length and the highest field elevation and whether the runway is paved or not.

Write down the longest runway length of any fields you'll be using regularly that have runways shorter than 3000 feet*:

*If you don't know, you can get this information from the *AOPA Airports U.S.A.* or any of the other airport guides available (see page 118).

Airport name	Runway length	Paved	Unpaved
_____	_____	☐	☐
_____	_____	☐	☐
_____	_____	☐	☐
_____	_____	☐	☐
_____	_____	☐	☐
_____	_____	☐	☐
_____	_____	☐	☐
_____	_____	☐	☐
_____	_____	☐	☐
_____	_____	☐	☐

From the above answer the following:

The shortest runway I'll be using regularly is _____ feet and it is paved/unpaved (O).

Now write down the elevation of any airport you'll be using regularly which is *higher than 5000 feet* above sea level

Airport name	Elevation	Longest runway	Paved	Unpaved
_____	_____	_____	☐	☐
_____	_____	_____	☐	☐
_____	_____	_____	☐	☐
_____	_____	_____	☐	☐
_____	_____	_____	☐	☐

From the above answer the following:

The highest airport I'll be using regularly is ☐ under 5,000 feet above mean sea level

or _____ feet above mean sea level (P), with a _____ ft paved/unpaved

runway (Q)*

*Turbocharging is desirable for frequent air port operations above 5,000 feet.

12. Determine ideal cruising altitude:

What is your ideal cruising altitude? If you live in the east, you have a wide choice — from the low altitudes (below 10,000 feet) right on up to FL 510. If you fly mostly in the far west, high-altitude capability is much more important. For any cruising altitudes that will occur frequently above 10,000 feet, you should seriously consider turbocharging and even pressurization. Turbocharging starts to be effective in boosting your cruise speed above 7,000 feet, which is the altitude where most normally aspirated engines reach their maximum potential for cruise power settings. Because of the lower drag at higher altitudes, turbocharging really gets noticed up around FL 180. (Altitudes above 18,000 feet are called *flight levels*, and the last two zeros are left off, so the equivalent of 20,000 feet is called FL 200, etc. Altimeters are set to standard pressure — 29.92" — at FL 180 and above.)

Oxygen is required for the crew for flight above 12,500 feet for flights lasting more than 30 minutes (FAR 91.32). At 14,000 feet and above the flight crew must use oxygen all the time, and above 15,000 feet everyone must have oxygen (See page 200 for more about oxygen systems; see page 179 for more about turbocharging.) The boxes show the pros and cons of various cruising altitudes and of turbocharging.

Pros.	Cons.
Cruising altitudes below 10,000 feet	
Less time spent in climbing to altitude	Often flight is necessary in poor weather precipitation, icing conditions, turbulence
Turbocharging not required	More traffic, greater collision hazard—greater mix of VFR and IFR traffic
Oxygen or pressurization not required	
Lower-altitude winds usually weaker; can avoid strong headwinds	Generally poorer visibility
Less exposure to high-speed aircraft, except in terminal and military-operating areas	More complex IFR routings
	If turbocharged, full advantage of aircraft capability is not taken
Nonturbocharged twins can probably maintain altitude on one engine in an emergency in the lower altitudes	Cannot take advantage of stronger tailwinds if available

Pros.	Cons.
Cruising altitudes above 10,000 feet, below 20,000 feet	
Generally smoother air	More time spent in climbing to altitude
Generally better visibilities	Higher VFR minimums above 10,000 feet (FAR 91.105)
Less exposure to icing conditions at cruising altitude	Oxygen required (FAR 91.32)
Less traffic, reduced collision hazard	Pressurization preferred
Less complex IFR routings; fewer radio contacts with ATC required	Turbocharging desirable
Longer range of navaids	Without turbocharging aircraft performs poorly at higher altitudes; twin can't maintain cruising altitude on one engine without it
If turbocharged, aircraft flies faster and more efficiently	May be exposed to strong headwinds
Can use available strong tailwinds	Flight management more complex
	More exposure to high-speed jet transport and military aircraft
	Transponder and encoding altimeter required for flight in controlled airspace above 12,500 feet, except within 2,500 feet of ground (FAR 91.24)
	Flight above FL 180 must be IFR; pilot must be instrument rated; aircraft must be IFR-equipped (FAR 91.33)

Choosing it

Pros.	Cons.
Cruising altitudes above 20,000 feet	
Generally smoother air and overall better weather conditions	All flights above FL 180 must be IFR; pilot must have instrument rating; aircraft must be IFR-equipped (FAR 91.33)
Much reduced collision hazard, since all flights must be IFR	DME required above FL 240 (FAR 91.33)
Less complex IFR routings; can often go direct; fewer ATC radio contacts required	Transponder and encoding altimeter required (FAR 91.24)
Longer range of navaids	Oxygen required (FAR 91.32); aircraft should be pressurized
Can use available strong tailwinds	Turbocharged or turbine engines required
	May be exposed to strong headwinds
	Weather radar desirable
	More exposure to high-speed jet transport and military aircraft

Pros.	Cons.
Normally aspirated engine vs turbocharging	
Lower initial cost	Poor performance above 7,000 feet
Lower maintenance cost	Poor high-altitude single-engine performance for twins
	Slower speeds for same fuel consumption
	Poorer rate of climb
Turbocharged engine vs normal aspiration	
Much greater efficiency at high altitudes	Higher initial cost
Faster speeds for same fuel consumption above 7,000 feet	Higher maintenance cost
Better rate of climb at altitude	Slightly more complex operation
Better single-engine performance for twins at altitude	Easier to damage engine by careless handling
Better high-altitude takeoff performance	Oxygen required at higher altitudes
Higher service ceiling	

Now that you have reviewed the advantages and disadvantages of the various cruising altitudes and considered your flying environment and desired airplane capabilities, indicate your preferred cruising altitudes:

I want to fly mostly:
Below 10,000 feet ☐ ⎫
Between 10,000 ⎪
and FL 200 ☐* ⎬ (R)
Above FL 200 ☐** ⎭

*Must have oxygen and should have turbocharging above 12,500 feet.

**Must have oxygen, turbine, or turbocharging and should be pressurized.

Choosing it

13. Aircraft needs-and-preference checklist

Now that you have decided whether or not to buy, determined whether your use of an airplane is for business, pleasure, or a combination of these, reviewed the tax consequences, studied the costs of aircraft ownership, established an operating budget, reviewed your personal preferences, and reviewed your utilization needs, you are ready to fill out the aircraft needs-and-preference checklist. This lists most things you have to decide upon in an airplane and lets you check off

what you *need* and what you *want*. A similar checklist for avionics equipment appears shortly.

Using the data you have processed in your earlier preference review (page 28) and your utilization-needs analysis (page 48), indicate on the checklist what you think you might end up buying or operating. From this and the avionics checklist you should be able to be very specific about the type of airplane and equipment you require. (Note: you can

check off more than one item if more than one will do.)

You will notice that there are five boxes to the right of the *need* and *want* boxes, labelled 1, 2, 3, 4 & 5.

These are for you to indicate the actual situation or equipment of each of the five aircraft candidates you are going to be selecting (see page 64), so that you can easily compare these with your established needs or wants.

Aircraft needs and preference checklist

Item	Need	Want	Candidate's actual configuration					Remarks
			1	2	3	4	5	
New aircraft	☐	☐	☐	☐	☐	☐	☐	
Used aircraft	☐	☐	☐	☐	☐	☐	☐	
Single engine	☐	☐	☐	☐	☐	☐	☐	
110-149 hp	☐	☐	☐	☐	☐	☐	☐	
150-199 hp	☐	☐	☐	☐	☐	☐	☐	
200-249 hp	☐	☐	☐	☐	☐	☐	☐	
250-299 hp	☐	☐	☐	☐	☐	☐	☐	
300+ hp	☐	☐	☐	☐	☐	☐	☐	
Twin engine	☐	☐	☐	☐	☐	☐	☐	
150-199 hp each engine	☐	☐	☐	☐	☐	☐	☐	
200-249 hp each engine	☐	☐	☐	☐	☐	☐	☐	
250-299 hp each engine	☐	☐	☐	☐	☐	☐	☐	
300-349 hp each engine	☐	☐	☐	☐	☐	☐	☐	
350+ hp each engine	☐	☐	☐	☐	☐	☐	☐	
Carburetor system	☐	☐	☐	☐	☐	☐	☐	
Fuel-injection	☐	☐	☐	☐	☐	☐	☐	
Turbocharging	☐	☐	☐	☐	☐	☐	☐	
Retractable landing gear	☐	☐	☐	☐	☐	☐	☐	
Fixed landing gear	☐	☐	☐	☐	☐	☐	☐	
Amphibious landing gear	☐	☐	☐	☐	☐	☐	☐	
Float capability	☐	☐	☐	☐	☐	☐	☐	
Ski capability	☐	☐	☐	☐	☐	☐	☐	
Tricycle gear	☐	☐	☐	☐	☐	☐	☐	
Tallwheel gear	☐	☐	☐	☐	☐	☐	☐	

Choosing it

Item	Need	Want	Candidate's actual configuration					Remarks
			1	2	3	4	5	
High wing	☐	☐	☐	☐	☐	☐	☐	
Low wing	☐	☐	☐	☐	☐	☐	☐	
Mid wing	☐	☐	☐	☐	☐	☐	☐	
Pressurization	☐	☐	☐	☐	☐	☐	☐	
One seat	☐	☐	☐	☐	☐	☐	☐	
Two seats	☐	☐	☐	☐	☐	☐	☐	
Three seats	☐	☐	☐	☐	☐	☐	☐	
Four seats	☐	☐	☐	☐	☐	☐	☐	
Five seats	☐	☐	☐	☐	☐	☐	☐	
Six seats	☐	☐	☐	☐	☐	☐	☐	
Over six seats	☐	☐	☐	☐	☐	☐	☐	
One door	☐	☐	☐	☐	☐	☐	☐	
Two doors	☐	☐	☐	☐	☐	☐	☐	
Separate baggage door	☐	☐	☐	☐	☐	☐	☐	
Extra large doors	☐	☐	☐	☐	☐	☐	☐	
Extra large baggage door	☐	☐	☐	☐	☐	☐	☐	
Single controls	☐	☐	☐	☐	☐	☐	☐	
Dual controls	☐	☐	☐	☐	☐	☐	☐	
Strobe lights	☐	☐	☐	☐	☐	☐	☐	
Single, fuselage or tail	☐	☐	☐	☐	☐	☐	☐	
Double, wing tips	☐	☐	☐	☐	☐	☐	☐	
Triple, wing tips and tail	☐	☐	☐	☐	☐	☐	☐	
Instrument post lights	☐	☐	☐	☐	☐	☐	☐	
Integral instrument lights	☐	☐	☐	☐	☐	☐	☐	
Fixed-pitch propeller	☐	☐	☐	☐	☐	☐	☐	
Constant-speed propeller	☐	☐	☐	☐	☐	☐	☐	
Feathering propeller	☐	☐	☐	☐	☐	☐	☐	
Alternator system	☐	☐	☐	☐	☐	☐	☐	
Generator system	☐	☐	☐	☐	☐	☐	☐	
28-volt system	☐	☐	☐	☐	☐	☐	☐	
14-volt system	☐	☐	☐	☐	☐	☐	☐	
External power plug	☐	☐	☐	☐	☐	☐	☐	

Choosing it

Item	Need	Want	Candidate's actual configuration					Remarks
			1	2	3	4	5	
Performance characteristics								
75% power-cruise speed								
Under 100 knots	☐	☐	☐	☐	☐	☐	☐	
100-124 knots	☐	☐	☐	☐	☐	☐	☐	
125-149 knots	☐	☐	☐	☐	☐	☐	☐	
150-174 knots	☐	☐	☐	☐	☐	☐	☐	
175-199 knots	☐	☐	☐	☐	☐	☐	☐	
200-224 knots	☐	☐	☐	☐	☐	☐	☐	
225-249 knots	☐	☐	☐	☐	☐	☐	☐	
250+ knots	☐	☐	☐	☐	☐	☐	☐	
Range with full tanks, 75% power, no reserves								
Under 300 nm	☐	☐	☐	☐	☐	☐	☐	
300-499 nm	☐	☐	☐	☐	☐	☐	☐	
500-699 nm	☐	☐	☐	☐	☐	☐	☐	
700-899 nm	☐	☐	☐	☐	☐	☐	☐	
900-1099 nm	☐	☐	☐	☐	☐	☐	☐	
1100+ nm	☐	☐	☐	☐	☐	☐	☐	
Takeoff distance over 50 feet, sea level								
Under 1000 feet	☐	☐	☐	☐	☐	☐	☐	
1000-1499 feet	☐	☐	☐	☐	☐	☐	☐	
1500-1999 feet	☐	☐	☐	☐	☐	☐	☐	
2000-2499 feet	☐	☐	☐	☐	☐	☐	☐	
2500-2999 feet	☐	☐	☐	☐	☐	☐	☐	
3000-3499 feet	☐	☐	☐	☐	☐	☐	☐	
3500-3999 feet	☐	☐	☐	☐	☐	☐	☐	
4000+ feet	☐	☐	☐	☐	☐	☐	☐	
Rate of climb, sea level								
under 500 fpm	☐	☐	☐	☐	☐	☐	☐	
500-749 fpm	☐	☐	☐	☐	☐	☐	☐	
750-999 fpm	☐	☐	☐	☐	☐	☐	☐	
1000-1249 fpm	☐	☐	☐	☐	☐	☐	☐	
1250-1499 fpm	☐	☐	☐	☐	☐	☐	☐	
1500+ fpm	☐	☐	☐	☐	☐	☐	☐	

Choosing it

Item	Need	Want	Candidate's actual configuration					Remarks
			1	2	3	4	5	
Single-engine rate of climb (twins), sea level								
under 250 fpm	☐	☐	☐	☐	☐	☐	☐	
250-499 fpm	☐	☐	☐	☐	☐	☐	☐	
500-749 fpm	☐	☐	☐	☐	☐	☐	☐	
750-999 fpm	☐	☐	☐	☐	☐	☐	☐	
1000+ fpm	☐	☐	☐	☐	☐	☐	☐	
Service ceiling								
under 15,000 feet	☐	☐	☐	☐	☐	☐	☐	
15,000-17,499 feet	☐	☐	☐	☐	☐	☐	☐	
17,500-19,999 feet	☐	☐	☐	☐	☐	☐	☐	
20,000+ feet	☐	☐	☐	☐	☐	☐	☐	
Single-engine service ceiling (twins)								
Under 5,000 feet	☐	☐	☐	☐	☐	☐	☐	
7,500-9,999 feet	☐	☐	☐	☐	☐	☐	☐	
10,000-12,499 feet	☐	☐	☐	☐	☐	☐	☐	
12,500-14,999 feet	☐	☐	☐	☐	☐	☐	☐	
15,000+ feet	☐	☐	☐	☐	☐	☐	☐	
Useful load (including fuel)								
under 500 lbs	☐	☐	☐	☐	☐	☐	☐	
500-749 lbs	☐	☐	☐	☐	☐	☐	☐	
750-999 lbs	☐	☐	☐	☐	☐	☐	☐	
1000-1249 lbs	☐	☐	☐	☐	☐	☐	☐	
1250-1499 lbs	☐	☐	☐	☐	☐	☐	☐	
1500+ lbs	☐	☐	☐	☐	☐	☐	☐	
Desired price range								
Less than $10,000	☐	☐	☐	☐	☐	☐	☐	
$10-$20,000	☐	☐	☐	☐	☐	☐	☐	
$20-$40,000	☐	☐	☐	☐	☐	☐	☐	
$40-$60,000	☐	☐	☐	☐	☐	☐	☐	
$60-$80,000	☐	☐	☐	☐	☐	☐	☐	
$80-$100,000	☐	☐	☐	☐	☐	☐	☐	
$100-$120,000	☐	☐	☐	☐	☐	☐	☐	
$120-$140,000	☐	☐	☐	☐	☐	☐	☐	
Over $140,000	☐	☐	☐	☐	☐	☐	☐	

14. Compare aircraft candidates

From the data you compiled on the needs-and-preference checklist you have just completed, you are now in a position to define a few specific aircraft candidates. You can get the necessary information from many sources — I recommend *Flying Annual*, which has a good table of currently available aircraft if you are considering a new airplane. For used airplanes a good reference is the aircraft specifications summary to be found in the back of the *Aircraft Price Digest* (see page 79). Another excellent reference on used aircraft is *The Aviation Consumer Used Aircraft Guide*, published by McGraw-Hill.

If you want to read some pilot reports, you can buy reprints from *Flying Magazine* of many of theirs. Write to:

Flying Reprints,
Box 278, Pratt Station,
Brooklyn, N.Y. 11205

and ask for a current list of reprints available. They cost $2.00 each. Or check their ads in *Flying*.

Decide on four or five candidates and enter the appropriate information for ranking and comparison purposes on the accompanying table. Start with the details on each aircraft. Enter this data under the "detail" column for each plane. Then go across the

lines, item by item, and rank each aircraft candidate from highest to lowest. Finally, add the rank columns up vertically so that you have a total for each aircraft. The lowest number will be roughly your highest ranking. This should be the aircraft that suits your needs best.

For a more detailed comparison, enter the actual data for each candidate by checking the appropriate boxes on the preceding needs-and-preference checklist. Check all the data applicable to candidate number one under the '1' column, put number two's data under the '2' column, etc. Then you can see how well each matches your needs and wants.

DESIGNATION	PRICE	WEIGHT AND PERFORMANCE				ENGINE AND FUEL	
PIPER Arrow III	$40,650	Gross	2,570 lbs	75% Cruise	143 kts	Lyc IO-360-C1C6	200 hp
		Empty	1,601 lbs	55% Cruise	130 kts		
		Accessories	NA	Stall w/flaps	55 kts		
		Useful load	NA	Stall clean	60 kts		
		Payload max fuel	NA	1.3 Vso	72 kts		
		Range 75% power	910 nm/6.4 hrs	Climb rate	831 fpm		
		Range 55% power	980 nm/7.5 hrs	Min field length	1,600 ft		
Seats 4		MPG 75% power	14 nmpg			Fuel	432 lbs
Wing loading	16.2 lbs/sq ft	MPG 55% power	16 nmpg			Fuel flow 75% power	61.2 lbs/hr
Power loading	13.7 lbs/hp	Service ceiling	16,200 ft			Fuel flow 55% power	48 lbs/hr
MOONEY 201 M20J	$43,500	Gross	2,740 lbs	75% Cruise	169 kts	Lyc IO-360-A1B6D	200 hp
		Empty	1,640 lbs	55% Cruise	145 kts		
		Accessories	93 lbs	Stall w/flaps	55 kts		
		Useful load	1,007 lbs	Stall clean	63 kts		
		Payload max fuel	623 lbs	1.3 Vso	72 kts		
		Range 75% power	888 nm/5.2 hrs	Climb rate	1,030 fpm		
		Range 55% power	1,080 lbs/7.5 hrs	Min field length	1,610 ft		
Seats 4		MPG 75% power	15.6 nmpg			Fuel	384 lbs
Wing loading	16.4 lbs/sq ft	MPG 55% power	18.6 nmpg			Fuel flow 75% power	64.8 lbs/hr
Power loading	13.7 lbs/hp	Service ceiling	18,800 ft			Fuel flow 55% power	46.8 lbs/hr
BEECH Sierra 200 C24R	$43,850	Gross	2,758 lbs	75% Cruise	137 kts	Lyc IO-360-A1B6	200 hp
		Empty	1,696 lbs	55% Cruise	115 kts		
		Accessories	83 lbs	Stall w/flaps	60 kts		
		Useful load	979 lbs	Stall clean	65 kts		
		Payload max fuel	637 lbs	1.3 Vso	74 kts		
		Range 75% power	646 nm/4.7 hrs	Climb rate	927 fpm		
		Range 55% power	686 nm/6 hrs	Min field length	1,660 ft		
Seats 4/6		MPG 75% power	11.3 nmpg			Fuel	342 lbs
Wing loading	18.8 lbs/sq ft	MPG 55% power	12 nmpg			Fuel flow 75% power	56.1 lbs/hr
Power loading	13.8 lbs/hp	Service ceiling	15,385 ft			Fuel flow 55% power	48.2 lbs/hr

Typical Flying Annual Aircraft Comparisons.
Copyright © 1978 ZIFF-Davis Publishing Company .

Candidate-Aircraft-Type Comparison Chart

Item	Aircraft #1		Aircraft #2		Aircraft #3		Aircraft #4		Aircraft #5	
	Detail	Rank	Detail	Rank	Detail	Rank	Detail	Rank	Detail	Rank
Type										
Price Range										
Engine HP — TBO										
Cruise speed 75% — knots										
Range 75% — nm										
Fuel used 75% — gph										
Fuel efficiency — nmpg										
Useful load — lbs										
# seats										
Takeoff distance over 50 ft — SL										
Rate of climb — SL										
S/E rate of climb (twins)										
Stall speed — knots										
Landing distance over 50 ft — SL										
Gross weight										
Empty weight										
Length										
Span										
Height										
Totals										

Choosing it

15. Determine avionics needs

It is easy to spend as much money as the airplane costs on avionics, particularly if you are retrofitting a used airplane. The technological advances of the last few years have been enormous, particularly in the area of miniaturization. The problem these days is that no sooner do you install some exotic piece of equipment but an improved version comes on the market that costs less, weighs less and does more. The areas of interest for the manufacturers these days seem to lie in the creation of integrated packages that do the jobs of many different units compared to the older models. They take up less space, weigh less, and are less complex. Before you buy any avionics, however, you need to find out what your needs and preferences are. And how much money you have available. Here is a look at how you might fill your needs in order of importance.

For simple VFR-only flying all you will need is a simple NAV/COMM (VOR navigation and VHF communications) and a transponder (transponders are not required for most VFR flight, but I heartily recommend you have one). And, of course, you'll need an ELT (emergency locator transmitter). A brand-new, complete package should cost about $3,800. The communications transceiver should have 360 channels. You won't need 720 channels for VFR flying. Older sets with only 90 or even fewer channels are no longer adequate if you are going to be flying into airports with control towers and approach/departure controllers. The transponder must be TSO'd (it must comply with the requirements specified in the FAA Technical Standard Order for transponders). A lot of older transponders are not TSO'd and are thus now illegal. Some of these can be modified to bring them up to requirements but some can't. They are now just expensive junk. When you are buying a used airplane, make sure that it has a TSO'd

transponder before you pay for the fact that it *has* a transponder (see page 202 for more on the TSO).

As you get into the more advanced types of VFR flying—longer cross-countries, night flying, flights within busy areas, and such—you should add to your basic avionics. Probably the next most useful addition is a DME (distance-measuring equipment). This costs about another $2,500 or more. However, if you will be operating within Class I TCAs (Terminal Control Areas in major metropolitan areas), you will want to add an altitude encoder to your transponder first, since you must have one of these for flying within those control areas. An encoder runs about $650. You can get one built in to an altimeter or you can get a blind encoder, which is not a part of your altimeter.

If you have an instrument rating or plan to get one, I would add radios in the following order of priority (as dollars are available) to the basic 360 nav/comm, transponder, encoder and DME suggested for VFR flight. First, I would make sure that I had at least one 720 channel comm. This will become more necessary for IFR as the years go by, so if you are adding radios, go 720 on one:

1. a second nav/comm (360 or 720 channels) (this will cost about $3,300, including the indicator).
2. an autopilot (about $2,000 to $5,000 or more).
3. an ADF (automatic direction finder) (about $2,000 to $3,000).
4. a marker beacon receiver (about $300).
5. a glideslope receiver (about $1,000, or about $600 if included in a nav/comm).
6. an HSI (horizontal situation indicator) (about $3,500 to $5,500 and more).
7. an audio control panel (about $800. This can include a marker beacon receiver).
8. a digital VOR indicator (about $300).

9. an IVSI (instantaneous vertical speed indicator) (about $700).
10. RNAV (area navigation) (about $3,500 to $7,000. King offers units with built-in nav receivers at considerable savings over the cost of buying individual units).
11. an RMI (radio magnetic indicator) (about $2,500).
12. a radar altimeter (about $1,200 to $3,000).
13. a weather avoidance system (about $3,600 to $8,200 for a Ryan Stormscope and $10,000 to $15,000 and more for radar).
14. a flight director (about $15,000).

When you buy a used airplane, you are automatically buying used avionics, assuming it has some. The general philosophy on avionics seems to be "if it runs well, leave it alone!" So buying avionics that are already installed in an airplane can be a reasonably safe way to buy used radios.

Buying used avionics off the shelf is another matter. I would want to make sure that the unit has been thoroughly inspected and checked out immediately prior to purchase and installation, and I would want a guarantee from the seller that the avionics would be fixed at no charge within a reasonable period of time, say 90 days, if a problem developed. I was shopping for an avionics installation and one very reputable shop offered me a used King KX-175 Nav/Comm at a good price. The unit had been factory-installed in a new Baron, which was flown to the dealer's airport, and held in inventory for a few weeks. Then it was sold and the buyer wanted to go for a custom installation that involved taking out the KX-175. This is the kind of "used" avionics you should buy if possible. The dealer even offered me a new warranty on it. I would avoid buying used avionics through the mail or from an individual unless there was some sort of enforceable guarantee.

The characteristics of avionics components are described starting on

Choosing it

page 202. Some specific considerations for individual radios are given in those descriptions. There are additional considerations in buying avionics, however. These are:

1. Cost
2. Vulnerability to obsolescence
3. Complexity of installation and maintenance
4. Reliability
5. Warranty
6. Compatibility with existing equipment
7. Power drain
8. Weight
9. Size and panel space required
10. Down time required for installation
11. Requirement for additional antennas
12. Weight or power-drain savings caused by replacing existing equipment
13. Aircraft-value enhancement (should insurance coverage be increased?)

Relate the above considerations to your own needs and desires as you determine what you want to buy. Ask people about their experience with the equipment you are thinking about. Ask the radio shop which radios they like to fix best (from an ease-of-servicing point of view).

Avionics needs and preference checklist

Item	Need	Want	Candidate's Actual Configuration					Remarks
			1	2	3	4	5	
Emergency-locator transmitter	☐	☐	☐	☐	☐	☐	☐	
#1 VHF COMM								
360 channels	☐	☐	☐	☐	☐	☐	☐	
720 channels	☐	☐	☐	☐	☐	☐	☐	
Other _____	☐	☐	☐	☐	☐	☐	☐	
#1 VHF NAV								
100 channels	☐	☐	☐	☐	☐	☐	☐	
200 channels	☐	☐	☐	☐	☐	☐	☐	
Separate VOR/ILS indicator	☐	☐	☐	☐	☐	☐	☐	
Integral VOR/ILS indicator	☐	☐	☐	☐	☐	☐	☐	
#2 VHF COMM								
360 channels	☐	☐	☐	☐	☐	☐	☐	
720 channels	☐	☐	☐	☐	☐	☐	☐	
Other _____	☐	☐	☐	☐	☐	☐	☐	
#2 VHF NAV								
100 channels	☐	☐	☐	☐	☐	☐	☐	
200 channels	☐	☐	☐	☐	☐	☐	☐	
Separate VOR/ILS indicator	☐	☐	☐	☐	☐	☐	☐	
Integral VOR/ILS indicator	☐	☐	☐	☐	☐	☐	☐	
Transponder (must be TSO'd)	☐	☐	☐	☐	☐	☐	☐	
Altitude encoder	☐	☐	☐	☐	☐	☐	☐	
Provision to add altitude encoder	☐	☐	☐	☐	☐	☐	☐	
Distance-measuring equipment	☐	☐	☐	☐	☐	☐	☐	
DME remote tuning	☐	☐	☐	☐	☐	☐	☐	
DME groundspeed	☐	☐	☐	☐	☐	☐	☐	
DME time-to-station	☐		☐	☐	☐	☐	☐	

Choosing it

Item	Need	Want	Candidate's actual configuration					Remarks
			1	2	3	4	5	
Automatic direction finder (ADF)	☐	☐	☐	☐	☐	☐	☐	
Rotatable azimuth card	☐	☐	☐	☐	☐	☐	☐	
Crystal tuning	☐	☐	☐	☐	☐	☐	☐	
Digital tuning	☐	☐	☐	☐	☐	☐	☐	
Radio magnetic indicator (RMI)	☐	☐	☐	☐	☐	☐	☐	
ADF only	☐	☐	☐	☐	☐	☐	☐	
ADF and VOR	☐	☐	☐	☐	☐	☐	☐	
Horizontal situation indicator (HSI)	☐	☐	☐	☐	☐	☐	☐	
Slaved	☐	☐	☐	☐	☐	☐	☐	
Unslaved	☐	☐	☐	☐	☐	☐	☐	
Air-driven	☐	☐	☐	☐	☐	☐	☐	
Electric	☐	☐	☐	☐	☐	☐	☐	
Glideslope receiver	☐	☐	☐	☐	☐	☐	☐	
Marker beacon receiver	☐	☐	☐	☐	☐	☐	☐	
Separate unit	☐	☐	☐	☐	☐	☐	☐	
Integral with other radio	☐	☐	☐	☐	☐	☐	☐	
Audio-control panel	☐	☐	☐	☐	☐	☐	☐	
With marker beacon	☐	☐	☐	☐	☐	☐	☐	
Without marker beacon	☐	☐	☐	☐	☐	☐	☐	
Digital VOR indicator	☐	☐	☐	☐	☐	☐	☐	
Integral with existing display	☐	☐	☐	☐	☐	☐	☐	
Separate	☐	☐	☐	☐	☐	☐	☐	
Instantaneous vertical speed (IVSI)	☐	☐	☐	☐	☐	☐	☐	
Area navigation (RNAV)	☐	☐	☐	☐	☐	☐	☐	
1 waypoint	☐	☐	☐	☐	☐	☐	☐	
2 waypoints	☐	☐	☐	☐	☐	☐	☐	
Multi-waypoints	☐	☐	☐	☐	☐	☐	☐	
Vertical navigation (VNAV)	☐	☐	☐	☐	☐	☐	☐	
Radar altimeter	☐	☐	☐	☐	☐	☐	☐	
Weather radar	☐	☐	☐	☐	☐	☐	☐	
Flight Director	☐	☐	☐	☐	☐	☐	☐	
Cross pointer reference	☐	☐	☐	☐	☐	☐	☐	
V-bar reference	☐	☐	☐	☐	☐	☐	☐	
Autopilot	☐	☐	☐	☐	☐	☐	☐	
Single-axis wing leveler	☐	☐	☐	☐	☐	☐	☐	
Single-axis heading select	☐	☐	☐	☐	☐	☐	☐	
Single-axis nav coupler	☐	☐	☐	☐	☐	☐	☐	
Two-axis	☐	☐	☐	☐	☐	☐	☐	

Choosing it

			Candidate's Actual Configuration					
Item	Need	Want	1	2	3	4	5	Remarks
Two-axis with coupler	☐	☐	☐	☐	☐	☐	☐	
Two-axis with flight director	☐	☐	☐	☐	☐	☐	☐	
Three-axis	☐	☐	☐	☐	☐	☐	☐	
Three-axis with coupler	☐	☐	☐	☐	☐	☐	☐	
Three-axis with flight director	☐	☐	☐	☐	☐	☐	☐	
Yaw damper	☐	☐	☐	☐	☐	☐	☐	
Available funds for avionics and autopilot								
Under $2,000	☐	☐	☐	☐	☐	☐	☐	
$2-$4,000	☐	☐	☐	☐	☐	☐	☐	
$4-$6,000	☐	☐	☐	☐	☐	☐	☐	
$6-$8,000	☐	☐	☐	☐	☐	☐	☐	
$8-$10,000	☐	☐	☐	☐	☐	☐	☐	
$10-$15,000	☐	☐	☐	☐	☐	☐	☐	
$15-$20,000	☐	☐	☐	☐	☐	☐	☐	
Over $20,000	☐	☐	☐	☐	☐	☐	☐	

Beech Duke B60 with a custom avionics installation and co-pilot instruments

Factory vs radio-shop installations on new aircraft.

Airframe manufacturers offer to install avionics while the airplane is being built which can make a lot of sense. It is easier to run wiring all over the airplane while it is still being made than after it's all been put together. However, there are some pitfalls. You may be paying a higher price, since most radio shops sell radios at lower than the suggested list price. The installation may not consider future ease of servicing—wiring leads may be too short to pull the radio out of the panel and still have it hooked up so that it can be worked on in the airplane, for example. A radio shop will certainly consider this, since you'll presumably, be going to the same shop for service. And not all manufacturers give you a choice. Cessna has followed in Henry Ford's footsteps and now offers you any type of radio as long as it is Cessna's line. Other manufacturers offer only certain types of radios or brands. Your own requirements may differ from the packages offered by the factories. Installing radios at the factory reduces down time—the airplane is complete and ready to fly when you get it. Field installation immediately takes your pride and joy away from you for a couple of weeks while the radios are put in. The decision should be made in consultation with your local radio shop and the aircraft salesperson. Consider the following:

1. Choice of radios available vs your desires
2. Price
3. Down time
4. Willingness of radio shop to provide service (some shops charge extra for servicing factory-installed radios)
5. Warranty considerations

Pros.	Cons.
Factory-installed avionics vs field installation	
Wiring can be put in while aircraft is being built No down time for installation	May be limited as to what types or brands of radios are available Often installations do not reflect later servicing requirements Avionics dealers will charge more for servicing a factory installation Avionics dealer may be unfamiliar with installation and thus take longer to fix
Field avionics installation vs factory installation	
Can install exactly what you want, where you want Installer can service radios better due to installation familiarity Lower maintenance cost Installation will reflect servicing needs of future	More down time for installation May be harder to install wiring on a finished airplane

Cessna Pressurized Centurion with factory radios

16. Review the maintenance situation

When you have defined three or four aircraft candidates, you need to get a feel for the maintenance situation you're getting into. There are several ways to do this. First, ask around. Talk to owners of the same type of plane to get their input. Talk to mechanics. If the aircraft is operated by a rental outfit or flight school, see how it stands up to heavy use.

Airworthiness directives

Next, review the AD (airworthiness-directive) story on each type. You can go to the local FAA GADO and look at their AD file, or you can ask someone who has a copy of the *Aircraft Price Digest* to show you the AD story. It lists outstanding ADs for each type in its price listings. Your bank, insurance company, or aircraft dealer should be able to help.

Another thing to do is to check with the FAA, which collects a lot of information on aircraft maintenance problems. Two areas of help are the Service Difficulty Program and the book *General Aviation Inspection Aids*.

When an aeronautical product is new, engineers have to rely on past history of similar products or analyses to predict when defects or unsafe conditions will arise. As time in service grows, various problems can come up that create unsafe conditions. Often similar problems could occur in other products of the same design. This happens even though the manufacturers conduct extensive testing under all types of real and simulated conditions. When an unsafe condition is discovered, the owners or operators of the product are notified as to what must be done. The notification is called an airworthiness directive (AD). The AD specifies the aircraft or component found to be unsafe by the FAA and conditions, limitations or inspections, if any, under which the iarcraft may continue to be operated. In setting the requirements of the AD, the FAA considers the effectiveness of restrictions to operation (such as an airspeed or weight limitation), the nature and amount of work involved for repair of the defect, the availability of replacement parts, the recommendations of the manufacturer and operators, and, above all, safety. ADs are issued under FAR part 39. When a condition is discovered that makes the aircraft unsafe, the specified corrective action must be taken.

FAA requires (91.173) that a chronological record be maintained of all ADs extant for the aircraft and its equipment along with an indication of the action taken. This record must include the date, AD number, a brief description of the method of compliance, and the signature and certificate number of the repair station or mechanic who complied with the AD. The best way to meet this requirement is to subscribe to a service called *The Adlog System*. This is a bookkeeping system that may be bought on subscription for most light aircraft. You get a binder and a complete set of ADs on the aircraft since it was certificated plus a comprehensive maintenance log system. You also get pertinent ADs on the aircraft's equipment and a questionnaire for you to list avionics and accessories, which will result in you getting the ADs on this equipment. New ADs are sent to subscribers as they are issued as pertinent. The address for the Adlog System is:

Aerotech Publications, Inc.,
Box 528A,
Old Bridge, NJ 08857
Telephone: 201-679-5151

These same people offer a service called Adlist, which you can order by type of aircraft. You get a complete summary of all ADs for the type and its equipment. Adlist costs $17.95 per aircraft.

A summary of airworthiness directives may be ordered from:

The Superintendent of Documents,
U.S. Government Printing Office,
Washington, D.C. 20402

The summary is divided into two volumes. Volume I includes ADs applicable to aircraft under 12,500 pounds maximum certificated takeoff weight, and volume II covers the rest. The summaries are updated biweekly. Check the GPO for the latest price.

It is the owner's responsibility to assure compliance with all pertinent ADs. This includes those ADs that require recurrent or continuing action, for example, an AD may require a certain inspection every 50 hours, which means that the particular inspection must be accomplished and recorded *every* 50 hours.

ADs are published in the Federal Register as amendments to FAR Part 39. In some instances they are published as a Notice of Proposed Rulemaking, and the public is invited to comment on the contents. In other instances they are published as adopted rules. This is done when immediate compliance is necessary to ensure safety. When any comments are received from the public, they are given consideration. If any changes are considered necessary as a result of this review, they are made. After such changes or if no changes are considered necessary, the AD is again published in the Federal Register as an adopted rule with a compliance date included. Sometimes ADs are withdrawn after this review. ADs are mailed by the FAA to the registered owner.

Emergency ADs are disseminated, in the case of light aircraft, by airmail letter to the registered owner. Large-transport-aircraft emergency ADs are sent by telegram. These ADs come into being when an unsafe condition arises that is so serious as to require immediate action. Often they must be complied with before further flight. This can be a problem in the case of leased aircraft, since the registered owner may be miles away from the actual operator. Since the FAA requires (FAR 91.163) that the owner or operator be responsible for AD compliance and defines "operate" (FAR 1.1) as "use, cause to use, or authorize to use aircraft for air navigation," the lessor is responsible for notifying the lessee of all ADs.

FAA service-difficulty program

The FAA maintains an active recording and analysis program on maintenance and service problems associated with aircraft through its Maintenance Analysis Center. The FAA wants to hear about service difficulties experienced with airframes, engines, propellers, and appliances. These reports provide them with a continuous service record of mechanical difficulties encountered in air-

craft operations. The reports are assembled and computerized so that you can order printouts of data in almost any form you want them. I was told these reports are the "eyes and ears" of the FAA for spotting problems in aircraft-service difficulties. Trends can be spotted and action taken to rectify potentially dangerous situations.

The reports of difficulties are made to the FAA on FAA Form 8330-2, which you can get at any FAA office. Most FBOs will have them in their maintenance areas. See a sample of the form filled out with a typical problem.

You can order the data for any period within the last five years. I ordered a printout of all service difficulties reported on the Piper Comanche. This cost me $5 and arrived within a week of ordering. If you are serious about your airplane or are considering one particular type, I suggest you order a printout for yourself. The charge is $2 for the computer search and $1 per 1000 lines of printout. You order from:

Flight Standards National Field Office,
FAA Aeronautical Center,
AFS-580
Box 25082,
Oklahoma City, Okla. 73125

You can order by type of aircraft, type of problem (all problems relating to landing gear, for example), even by specific airplane serial number. I suggest that you order for the make and model of aircraft you fly or are considering. You'll get a good feel for the types of problems the model has had.

Bear in mind that this reporting procedure is a voluntary one. You are not going to get the picture on *every* problem. But you will get a good insight into the basic situation.

General-aviation inspection aids

Another outcome of the service-difficulty program is an annual publication called *General Aviation Inspection Aids*. This is amended at regular intervals and is sold on a subscription basis through the Government Printing Office. It gives greater detail on the types of service problems that have occurred, with illustrations in some cases. It is organized by aircraft type. Take a look at a copy to see if it would be

1. REGISTRATION NO. N– 123456	DEPARTMENT OF TRANSPORTATION FEDERAL AVIATION ADMINISTRATION MALFUNCTION OR DEFECT REPORT			Form Approved Budget Bureau No. 04–R0003	8. DATE SUB. 3-16-78	FOR FAA USE ONLY CONTROL NO.		
	A. MAKE	B. MODEL	C. SERIAL NO.	7A. COMMENTS *(Describe the malfunction or defect and the circumstances under which it occurred. State probable cause and recommendations to prevent recurrence.)*				
2. AIRCRAFT	Flywell	Flivver	A-101					
3. POWERPLANT	Grinder	O-300 B	1234567890	Pilot's seat won't lock in full forward position. Locking pin won't engage. Pin too large for hole.				
4. PROPELLER	N/A	N/A	N/A					
5. APPLIANCE/COMPONENT *(assy. that includes part)*								
A. NAME	B. MAKE	C. MODEL	D. SERIAL NO.					
Pilot's seat	Flywell	N/A	N/A					
6. SPECIFIC PART *(of component)* CAUSING TROUBLE								
A. NAME	B. NUMBER	C. PART/DEFECT LOCATION		SUBMITTED BY *John Doe*			Continue on reverse	
Locking pin		Pilot's seat						
FAA USE	E. PART TT	F. PART TSO	G. PART CONDITION	B. REP. STA.	C. OPER.	D. MECH.	E. AIR TAXI	F. MFG.	G. FAA	H. OTHER	I.
D. ATA CODE								

Choosing it

17. Review the marketplace

interesting to you. Your FBO repair shop will probably have one.

Most owner-flown light aircraft are sold through franchised dealers in much the same way as are automobiles. The dealers are usually independently owned, although in some cases, notably Beechcraft, some dealers are owned by the factory.

The factories may use distributors (wholesalers) to handle the broad geographic areas and set up individual dealers within their zones, or they may sell directly to the dealer. Cessna and Piper use a distributor-dealer system, while Beechcraft and Mooney deal direct with their dealers. Most other manufacturers have a direct factory-dealer relationship.

The big three assign their dealers specific sales responsibilities. It is not terribly important that you know how these work—just so long as you know that they are set up this way. For example, Beech has three classes of dealer—the Corporate Aviation Center, the Executive Aviation Center, and the Aero Center. The Corporate Aviation Center sells the full Beech line, while the other two operations only sell certain types. However, if you walked into an Aero Center and said you wanted to buy a King Air, you would be taken care of. Cessna uses titles like Full Line Dealer, Multi-Engine, High Performance Single Engine (Cessna calls them "hippsies"), and Light Single Engine Dealer to categorize its outlets. Piper has Corpacs, Full Line, Multi-Engine, Advanced Single Engine, Basic Single Engine, and Agricultural Dealers. Some new aircraft dealers offer more than one line. You often see a dealer offering both Pipers and Cessnas, for example.

Linked to many of the dealers are the flight schools set up by the factories to help develop their future markets. Beech Aero Clubs are part of Beech Aero Centers. Cessna Pilot Centers and Piper Flite Centers are also usually affiliated with dealerships. These schools offer standardized training systems for most pilot ratings and certificates.

Each type of dealer has some kind of quota of aircraft to carry each year. These quotas vary according to the type of dealer and to the area covered in some cases. For example, a Cessna LSE (Light Single Engine) dealer has to buy at least one Cessna 152 and one other aircraft, such as a 172, Hawk, or Cardinal. A Piper Advanced Single Engine Dealer must take at least four aircraft a year, of which at least two must be kept as demonstrators. If a Cessna or Piper dealer wants to show you an aircraft not currently in stock, one can usually be obtained from the distributor, since the distributors keep a selection of demonstrators available almost all the time.

For the dealers to carry an inventory is not a very difficult task. The manufacturers do what they can to help. Cessna, for example, has a plan called STS—Stock to Sell. After buying a minimum number of aircraft in quota the dealer may floor-plan aircraft for no down payment for the first 120 days and no interest expense for the first 90 days. If the dealer makes use of the airplane during these times, it must be insured at dealer expense, and an hourly rate is charged by Cessna. (Floor planning is a system of financing, common in the automobile industry, that enables a dealer to carry an inventory and pay just the interest cost—often at a very favorable rate. It enables the factory to move the airplanes out to the marketplace, and it enables the dealer to carry and offer a good line. Some floor plans are offered through the manufacturer's own finance company, such as Cessna Finance or Beech Acceptance. Others may be run through the dealer's own bank or other credit agency.) In most floor-plan arrangements the aircraft involved are in fact sold to the dealer. They no longer belong to the factory. It's just that the repayment terms are quite favorable. An example of

the advantage of floor planning is the cost of carrying, say, a half-million-dollar inventory for, say, 60 days at, say, 10 percent. It works out to an interest expense of $8,335. This may be a lot easier to handle than laying out a 20-percent down payment of $100,000, plus interest on the remaining $400,000, even at a lower rate. Both Beech and Piper offer similar programs to their dealers.

The dealer as fixed-base operator

Most aircraft dealers are also FBOs. The FBO provides all or part of the following functions:

1. New and used aircraft sales
2. Avionics sales
3. Maintenance and service
4. Storage
5. Fuel
6. Flight training
7. Aircraft rentals
8. Air-taxi and charter services

Some FBOs are a delight to visit. They have clean, modern hangars and excellent customer facilities, such as comfortable lounges and well-equipped flight-planning centers, and they are staffed by competent, helpful people. And then, some FBOs are not . . .

The FBO is an unusual business. Who ever heard of a car dealer who pumped gas, garaged your car, and taught your kids to drive? The FBO has to carve out a market, and the starting point lies in two key areas—flight training and charters. These are the areas where the lay public will first become involved with general aviation in most cases. There is tremendous brand loyalty among pilots. Chances are a pilot who learns to fly in a Cessna 152 will buy a Sky-hawk or Skylane and then move on to a Centurion. This explains the prolif-eration of the Cessna Pilot Centers, Piper Flite Centers, and Beech Aero Clubs just mentioned. They offer first-class training materials and courses, and they are all aimed at the ultimate goal of moving the newly licensed pi-lot into one of their airplanes as an owner and then graduating the pilot through the product line as experience increases.

Beech has found that the average student pilot is 29 years old, while the average age of the first-time air-craft buyer (generally a used plane) is 35. To keep in the circuit for those six years, Beech offers the Beech Aero Club. About three-quarters of all light aircraft made in the U.S.A. are sold to FBOs, who operate them, depreciate them a bit, and then sell them as used aircraft. So the flying-school/rental outlet is a very impor-tant part of the aircraft manufac-turer's marketing organization. There are between 120,000 and 170,000 stu-dent-pilot starts each year, depend-ing on economic conditions. How-ever, about half of these drop out be-fore getting a private certificate. The factories are doing a lot to try to improve this ratio. The Beech Aero Club is one such approach.

How to deal with the aircraft salesman

Aircraft salespeople make their living selling airplanes, so the first thing to remember in talking to them is that they will do everything possible to sell you an aircraft. That is, if they're any good. When I was shopping for my airplane, I spoke to three sales-men. One of them was obviously far too busy selling airplanes to talk to me. I got a very cursory brushoff to my casual enquiry about what types of airplanes he had for sale. I gave him my phone number and told him what I was looking for and I never heard from him again! And these people are in the airplane *sales* busi-ness! I spoke to another one on the phone and he didn't have anything quite in my price range. And I never heard from him either! Undaunted by the attempts of the aviation in-dustry to keep me from buying an airplane, I met another one, who called me because I had circled a reader-service-card number in *Flying* magazine requesting data on the new Cessna 150. Now I was certainly not interested in buying a 150. But I was interested in seeing what they had done to the airplane I spent several hundred hours instructing in. And this salesman had never sold a 150 in his life. He actually found some air-planes that looked interesting and we went to look at a couple. In fact, I made an offer on one, gave a deposit, and agreed to buy it subject to a sat-isfactory inspection. It flunked the in-spection, so the deal fell through when the seller refused to bring it up to snuff within the agreed price.

The point is that this man was in-terested in selling me an airplane. And this is the type of person to deal with. If you get the brushoff or a baleful look when you express inter-est in laying out the price of a mod-est house for something with wings and four seats but no kitchen and no bathroom, take *step one*, which is right out the door! "Sales" people like this deserve to go back to the bakery route they are more suited to. Do not patronize them.

Another sales type to watch out for is the one who tries desperately to sell you what he *has* rather than what you *want*. The thing to remem-ber is that *every* airplane has some-thing knockable! If you talk Barons to a Cessna salesman, he'll deride the single control wheel or the dual wheel hassle or the fact that the prop and throttle controls are reversed. If you talk Aerostar, he'll talk about noise and small space. If you talk Aztec, he'll say slow. And if you talk Cessna 310 to a Beech salesman, he'll complain about all that fuel on the wingtips making it unstable and hard to handle or the fact that you have to be very careful about the way you use the aux tanks or you'll be pumping fuel overboard. This goes right up the line. The new Falcon 50 tri-jet is sometimes de-rided by the competition as being the one with the "spare engine."

A good salesman will try to find what you want. "I think we've got one just coming in on trade" *could* mean, "As soon as you get out of here, I'm going to call around and see what's available." There is a lot of phoning back and forth between dealers as they try to match custom-ers to airplanes and vice versa. This is done quite openly and is really to your advantage.

Russell Baker, the *New York Times* columnist, wrote a beautiful column about life on one of the eastern-sea-board resort islands (it sounded like Nantucket to me). He pointed out that everybody there looked down on everybody else. The people who were born there look down on the people who only moved there a few years ago. The permanent residents look down on the people who just live there for the summer. They look down on the people who only go there for two weeks' vacation. The two-week vacationers look down on the people who go there for a week-end, who look down on the day-trip-pers. And, of course, *they* look down on the people who never go there at all. Aviation is precisely like that. The executive-jet pilot looks down on the prop pilot, but he is looked down on by the airline pilot, who in turn is looked down on by the airline pilot with more seniority. The twin owner looks down on the single owner. The new owner looks down on the used owner. The instrument-rated pilot looks down on the VFR private pilot. The private pilot looks down on the student, who looks down on everyone who doesn't fly an airplane.

Why all this stuff? Because the salesman looks down on *you*! He gets to fly more exotic airplanes than you do, more often, to more interesting places! You are too often an interruption to his true role of flying only the very latest, radar-equipped, pressurized, top-of-the-line model. He knows more about the business than you do. Thus you will be dangled before him as sport. Until it becomes very clear that you mean *business* and that there is an amount of *cash money* involved!

What you have to resolve is letting the salesman get away with looking down on you because you don't fly as nice equipment as he *usually* does, while, in turn, looking down on him because you've got the money and he wants it! The more knowledgeable you are, the better off you will be in your negotiations. Don't be a smart-ass, however. Better to appear a little more stupid than you really are than to try to be smarter than you really are! Be a little humble rather than brash. Ask intelligent questions that show you know something about the airplane and want to know more. Be positive and be businesslike. For example, insist on a bill of sale when you make the deal. You must have

this to register the airplane and you can't fly it unless it's registered. There is more than one unhappy story about the wide-eyed customer paying cash for his plane and going to the factory to pick it up, only to be told that the factory has not been paid by the dealer. With no bill of sale you're in trouble.

Chances are, if you can handle other normal negotiations effectively, such as buying a house or a car, you should be able to deal with the salesman effectively. Don't expect to pay list price for anything except high-demand, limited production types (list prices are illegal, anyway). New airplane markups are about 15 to 20 percent, with avionics markups going up to 35 or 40 percent. Bear in mind that the dealer's financing arrangements may occasionally make it imperative that they sell a certain airplane by a certain date or they have to start paying some serious money to the banker (see page 73). If you are close to this date, you might get a better deal on the air-

plane. Ask the dealer if he has had anything in inventory for more than a few weeks—three to four months is where the airplane starts to look a real nuisance to the dealer. If the dealer is really desperate, bear in mind that you want to be able to get service in the future. He may not be around to give it to you. Everybody needs to make *some* profit.

Beware of your trade-in allowance being adjusted after you've agreed on a price for a replacement airplane. Let's say that you've just traded in a ten-year-old airplane on a brand-new one. You're getting $20,000 for the old one and paying $40,000 for the new one—a $20,000 difference. Make sure that the $20,000 allowance is made on your airplane *after* the dealer has inspected it. Otherwise it would be easy for the dealer to find something wrong with your trade and it will cost $2000 to fix. Suddenly it's a $22,000 difference, and yet you've already made the deal. Get the trade-in allowance written into the original agreement.

Plane Profile 10: Cessna Pressurized Centurion

Seats	6
Cruise speed, 65% power,	
8,000 feet	154 knots
18,000 feet	166 knots
Range, 65% power, full optional fuel, 18,000 feet	
Maximum endurance	5.7 hours
Gross weight	4,016 pounds
Empty weight	2,426 pounds
Full optional fuel	522 pounds
	87 gallons
Useful load, full fuel	1,068 lbs
Fuel efficiency, 75% power	11.3 nmpg
Stall speed, gear and flaps down	58 knots
Rate of climb, sea level	945 fpm
Minimum field length	2,160 feet
Engine type Continental TSIO-520-AF	310 hp
Engine TBO	1,600 hours
Remarks Also available non-pressurized and turbocharged, and non-turbocharged.	

What to look for in a demonstration flight

The demonstration flight is the most likely place for your emotions to make the buy decision. You may have figured everything out to the nth point, using all the tables in *The Aircraft Owner's Handbook*, have your budget set and everything, and then you get your hands on the aircraft, you like the way it feels, Walter Mitty takes over, and you say "I do!"

Let's take a look at what the salesperson has been trained to do in demonstrating the aircraft to you.

First, the aircraft should be shiny and clean. When you first see it, it should be parked in the position that gives you the most attractive view. A general walk around should follow, in which the salient points of the aircraft will be pointed out. Ease of access to preflight items will be stressed if they are easy. You should ask to see how the fuel and oil are checked if these are not shown to you. What about draining the fuel strainers? Is this awkward or easy? If you aren't shown how easy it is, maybe it's because it isn't. Where is the battery? Is it easy to get access to? I once spent an hour with an unfamiliar Cessna 210, looking for the battery after running it flat with some starting difficulty. We finally located it under the floorboards beneath the pilot's seat!

The demonstrator will show you the features of the landing gear, explaining the advantages of the system used in the airplane, whether it be spring steel, oleo shock struts, rubber bungees, or trailing-arm suspension. The special features of the airplane's construction should be explained—maybe fiberglass wingtips or honeycomb construction for a rivet-free wing. The type of paint will be pointed out, whether it be an enamel or a polyurethane. Is the aircraft

corrosion-proofed?

The baggage compartments will be shown and their capacities given. Can they be reached in flight? How much does carpeting in the baggage compartment cost? What sort of loading problems are there?

How easy is it to get in and out? Should the rear-seat passengers board first? Who gets in last? What are the door locks and latches like? Can the windows be opened on the ground or in flight? Are the seats easy to adjust? Does the aircraft have shoulder harness? Is the upholstery easy to keep clean? How do you clean it? Is there room on the panel for more radios than are there? (Note: new aircraft demonstrators tend to have very complete radio packages. Quite often a large amount of the demo flight is spent on demonstrating the radios and not the airplane! Good radio packages help to sell planes, even if the one *you* buy doesn't come similarly equipped.)

Who gets in the left seat? Assuming you are a pilot, you will almost certainly be invited to sit there. The salesperson is discouraged from having a lot of "hangers on" along for the ride, unless they have a definite interest in what you are doing. Anyone who may interfere with the prime purpose of the flight (which is to sell you the airplane) will be left on the ground unless you insist otherwise. Bear in mind that a lightly loaded airplane performs better than one at full gross, so there is another incentive to keep the passenger list down.

Who starts the engine? If it is easy, you will. If it is difficult to start, you may be relieved of the task. Ask about starting ease. Some airplanes can be real troublesome when the engine is hot or for some other reason known only unto themselves.

Off you go into the wild blue. You will probably get the takeoff. If not, why not? Is it that hard to fly? There may be another reason. I was having a demo flight in a brand-new Comanche 400—it was the second one built and was featured in the advertising brochure. We were at Rockford, Illinois at the Experimental

Aircraft Association fly-in, and the pilot asked if I didn't mind him doing the takeoff because he couldn't bear to miss the opportunity of showing all those thousands of people what this bird would do. So he did, and it felt like we were in a Lear Jet. But I got to do the landing!

If the aircraft has an autopilot, the salesperson will probably suggest that you go onto it rather quickly so that you won't be too distracted in flying the airplane to miss all those wonderful features, advantages, and benefits that will be shown to you.

Unless you ask for them, don't expect to have any violent maneuvers performed. The pilot shouldn't use the demo flight as an opportunity to show off.

What does it feel like? What is the visibility like in cruise, in a climb, in a turn? What about the noise level? Can you talk to each other without shouting? Is the airplane stable? Do the various controls come readily to hand or are you reaching all over the place? What sort of gear and flaps down speed do you have? Is it a problem to slow down? What sort of speed are you getting? If the aircraft does not have a true airspeed indicator, the TAS will be worked out and given to you when you are cruising along. (Note: new airplanes have their airspeed indicators in knots, so the numbers may look lower than you expect if you think in mph.)

Will you get the landing? Probably but perhaps not. You should ask for it anyway. First landings in a new aircraft are often less than the best, so don't be disappointed if you don't grease it on. If the *salesperson* insists on doing the landing and drops it in, you know the airplane is probably hard to land or else the other pilot lacks skill.

The last instruction from the dealer to the salesperson is "Close the throttle and the sale!" "Can we have one built for you, or will this fit your needs?"

Steady there!

Specifying options in a new aircraft

After you have looked through the glossy brochures, taken a demo ride, and made the basic decision that you want to buy the aircraft—a new one, not the demonstrator or one that is sitting on the line—you will need to go through the optional-equipment list and specify what extras you want.

Most manufacturers sell their aircraft at the standard price only with fairly basic instruments and equipment. Radios, landing lights, heated pitot tubes, reclining seats, and such often cost extra. Some manufacturers offer an excellent array of equipment as standard—even to the extent of complete avionics setups. And then there are the packages. These are combinations of desired items packaged together and offered as a group for one price. Cessna does this with their II option. A standard Skyhawk

comes with no radios or avionics wiring and lacks complete instrumentation and other niceties. The Skyhawk II comes with a full IFR package of Nav/Com and transponder plus other goodies. Piper does a similar thing with its Standard, Custom, and Executive models and offers separate avionics packages. Cessna will only install its own radios in its aircraft, which can be a problem if you want Narco, King, Collins, Bendix, or something other than the Cessna (ARC) line. Not only will they not install the competitive radios, but they won't put basic radio wiring and antennas in without their radio packages. The other manufacturers basically offer custom factory installation of most popular brands of radio. Your dealer may offer to sell you the radios himself and make the installation after the airplane arrives from the factory. This may or may not be a good idea, depending on the price, the amount of down time for the field installation, and the quality of the local radio shop (see page 182).

The main point in ordering accessories is to make sure that you get

the complicated stuff put on at the factory. Don't buy a new plane and then have de-ice boots installed after you get it home. The same applies to strobe lights, external power cables, air conditioning systems, and such. These are items best built in to the airplane on the production line.

Each optional extra you add not only costs but usually increases the weight. Bear this in mind as you say "yes" to each extra being proffered. Some options cost unbelievable amounts of money. Ask Cessna how much they charge for carpeting in the baggage compartment in a 310. You won't believe your ears! Air conditioning in a Baron 58 is around $6,000! Cars are proportionally just as bad. $500 for an FM radio?

Some options should be specified in terms of the type of flying you are going to be doing. I'm not talking about the obvious stuff, such as IFR instrumentation if you're going to fly IFR. I mean things such as external power receptacles if you do a lot of cold-weather flying (batteries get dead very fast in the cold, and there is *nothing* worse than trying to get a

Plane Profile 11: Beech B60 Duke

Seats	6
Cruise speed, 65% power,	
8,000 feet	185 knots
18,000 feet	201 knots
Range, 65% power, full optional fuel, 18,000 feet	1,005 nm
Maximum endurance	6.0 hours
Gross weight	6,819 pounds
Empty weight	4,425 pounds
Full optional fuel	1,392 pounds
	232 gallons
Useful load, full fuel	1,002 pounds
Fuel efficiency, 65% power	5.4 nmpg
Stall speed, gear and flaps down	73 knots
Rate of climb, sea level	1,601 fpm
	307 fpm s/e
Minimum field length	3,065 feet
Engine type Lycoming TIO-541-E1C4	380 hp
Engine TBO	1,600 hours
Remarks Pressurized and turbocharged	

jump start with cables when the temperature is below freezing and the wind is gusting to 30!), zinc-chromate finish if you operate near the sea (for anticorrosion), stainless-steel control cables (same reason), maybe a larger baggage door if you're going to be carrying bulky objects, quick-release individual seats instead of bench seats if you're going to carry varieties of freight or passengers, and so on.

Some aircraft have optional paint—the wet-look polyurethanes instead of the enamel standard finish. And don't forget to specify a custom N number if you want one (see page 96). It's easier to paint that on at the beginning than to repaint it after you get the airplane.

Should you buy a demonstrator?

A demonstrator with less than 50 hours on it is often a very good buy. It is usually well equipped. It should have been well maintained, and all the usual new airplane teething troubles should have been worked out. Obviously, the dealer wants the demonstrator to do a good job of selling airplanes, so it should be in tip-top shape—an aircraft with little things wrong with it does not present a very good image to a prospective buyer. Many demonstrators are offered with a new-airplane warranty. The only caution I would make is that in a twin some single-engine procedures may have been demonstrated, which means that the engines may have worked a little harder than you might have liked them to—being throttled back to zero thrust, maybe even shut down and feathered a few times, with the other engine running at a relatively high power setting for a few minutes. The engines have probably been worked quite hard in that time. Here are the instructions Piper gives its demonstrator pilots for single-engine demonstrations in the Navajo: "Single-engine perform-

ance can be demonstrated by either of two methods: actual engine shut-down or simulated engine out by use of zero thrust on one engine.

"Zero thrust—approximately 12 inches MP and 2200 RPM. Engine shutdown—prior to securing an engine in flight, *first cool engine to be shut down by reducing power to zero thrust for approximately 30 seconds...*" For restarting similar care is taken so as not to bring the cylinder-head temperatures up too fast right away.

The key is *how* the airplane is demonstrated to *you*. If you get an intelligent ride, with no hot-dogging, the airplane is probably going to be in good shape. If the demo pilot is a cowboy, forget it!

Warranties

Most new aircraft have a six-month warranty, while avionics warranties usually go up to a year. When you buy a new aircraft or piece of equipment, you will receive a warranty booklet. You may have to send in a card to record your ownership. Do this right away—you may be glad you did.

When the warranty period starts may be confusing. Some warranties start when the airplane is delivered to the *dealer*, others start when the *customer* takes delivery. This is an important question to ask.

Cessna warrants everything in the airplane, regardless of who made it. This includes engines, avionics, bat-

Beech 58 Barons, top to bottom 58TC, 58, 58P

teries, and so on. Obviously, Cessna has recourse to the individual manufacturers through *their* warranties, but their concept is that if something goes wrong with a Cessna during the warranty period, it's Cessna's problem, not yours. Beech has a similar approach. Piper only warrants its own aircraft and certain parts and equipment. Other components, such as engines, avionics, and certain autopilots, are warranted by the individual manufacturers of those components, although Piper *installations* of these components *are* warranted by Piper.

Warranty requirements have the usual stipulations about fair wear and tear, avoidance of abusive treatment, and operation in accordance with proper procedures and maintenance schedules.

Some warranties allow for troubleshooting time and removal and reinstallation of parts, but some do not—they just want you to ship the offending part, at your expense, back to the factory. The best advice I can

give in this area is to:

1. buy from factory-approved dealers
2. have any warranty work done by factory-approved service facilities

Some aircraft and radio dealers only want to sell you something. Once they have your money and you have the item, they want you to *go away*! Buying a radio through mail order and having it installed by a friendly A & P on his night off is not the best way to get good warranty service when something goes wrong.

The dealer network exists to provide you with continuing service, and they want you back as a continuing customer. If you find a dealer who does not give you the kind of service you think the manufacturer wants you to have, *complain to the factory*! Write to the president of the company and tell your story without histrionics. This works better than getting mad at a mechanic in the shop.

Used-aircraft price guides

As in the automobile industry, there are confidential price guides available to dealers, bankers, and insurance companies—but not to the public. These guides attempt to show the average wholesale price for each used aircraft, along with other information, such as appraisal points. The three most widely used guides are:

1. *Aircraft Price Digest*, published quarterly by Aircraft Appraisal Association of America, Inc., Box 59985, Oklahoma City, Ok. 73159
2. *ADSA Blue Book*, published quarterly by Aircraft Dealers Service Association, Box 621, Aurora, Colo. 80010
3. *Used Aircraft Price Guide*, published monthly by Interstate Aircredit Publications, Inc., 1700 Market, Suite 2600, Philadelphia, Pa. 19103

Plane Profile 12: Cessna Cutlass RG

Seats	4
Cruise speed, 65% power, 8,000 feet	129 knots
Range, 65% power, full optional fuel, 8,000 feet	748 nm
Maximum endurance	6.8 hours
Gross weight	2,658 pounds
Empty weight	1,591 pounds
Full optional fuel	372 pounds
	62 gallons
Useful load, full fuel	695 lbs
Fuel efficiency, 75% power	14.6 nmpg
Stall speed, gear and flaps down	50 knots
Rate of climb, sea level	800 fpm
Minimum field length	1,775 feet
Engine type Lycoming O-360-F1A6	180 hp
Engine TBO	2,000 hours
Remarks	Also available in a fixed-gear model as the Skyhawk.

The first one listed, *Aircraft Price Digest*, is the most useful guide in my opinion. It contains a wealth of information beyond raw price data. For instance, it shows all the ADs outstanding on each aircraft, and it even gives a one-line description of the essential requirements of each AD. It also has a detailed tabulation of specifications and performance for each aircraft. Ask your friendly dealer or banker to show you a copy. Shown here is a page from the *Aircraft Price Digest*.

The information used to assemble the prices in this guide comes from many sources. The parent company, for example, is in the title-search business, so every time they search a title, they can get all the lien and bill-of-sale information from each aircraft searched. (This is public information available to anyone.) In addition, they survey dealers constantly by WATS line, and they receive a large number of price-data cards mailed in by dealers showing the prices of the aircraft they have sold recently, along with the equip-

ment, condition, hours, etc. I would want my dealer to use this guide as a source when I was buying a used airplane.

Used-aircraft sources

There are many sources of used aircraft. The following list will give you an idea.

1. Aircraft dealers. As with cars, there are both new and used aircraft dealers. The new dealers are usually affiliated with one or more of the manufacturers, such as Piper of Cessna, and they almost always have an inventory of used airplanes. If you are shopping, ask to get on their mailing list. Then you will receive regular listings of available aircraft.

2. Aircraft brokers. They will try to find you what you want and charge you a fee when you buy. Aircraft

dealers will also act as brokers in many cases.

3. Publications specializing in used-plane listings. Trade-a-Plane, North Atlantic Aviation, Southern Aviation Times, Aviation Buyers' Guide, Air List-Ads, for example.

4. The ramp at the airport. Most airplanes for sale have a sign on them to that effect.

5. Airport bulletin boards. Often characterized by the fading Polaroid photograph attached to an often misspelled, ungrammatical, semilegible offering.

6. Want ads in national aviation magazines. Due to their long closing dates these are not usually the best source, since by the time the magazine comes out, the airplane may have been sold long ago.

7. Want ads in your local newspaper, Especially *The Wall Street Journal*, which tends to carry the bizjets, but you will often see light twins and singles advertised there. Surprisingly, *The New York Times*, which carries pages of boat advertising, has as yet failed to set up a special head-

CESSNA 177 RG Cardinal "NOTE" Value of aircraft with no yearly model change is determined by date put in service, not by mfg. date. These serial numbers are for information only, not to determine value.

Yr 19	MODEL	SERIAL NUMBER SERIES	FACTORY NEW LIST Standard / avg.equip'd	RETAIL avg.equip'd	AVERAGE EQUIPPED Inventory / Marketable	seats	ENGINE(s)	AIRWORTHINESS DIRECTIVES "AD NOTES"	avg.o'haul installed	TBO eng/hr	APPRAISAL POINTS
	CESSNA 177RG Cardinal (Retractable Gear) (S. eng.-piston)		Base Avg.=		Dual Nav-Comm † Vor/Loc † ADF † Xpnd † 200 Nav-O-Matic † G/S † Mkr B † 700 SMOH † Comp 85% of new † Orig logs † Good paint & Intr. † no MDH † 6 mo annual † AD's Complied						
71 72 73	177 RG Cardinal	177RG-0001 †-0212 177RG-0213†-0282 177RG-0283†-0432	$ 24,795 $ 32,200 $ 25,995 $ 34,385 $ 25,995 $ 34,385	20,000 21,750 23,500	A20P951D A20P271D A21P371D A21P781D A23P781D A23P202D	4 4 4	Lyc. 200 H.P. IO-360-A1B6	(72-3-3=71 only)73-10-2)73-23-1)74-8-1) (74-16-6)(74-24-13)(75-7-2)(75-8-9)(75-9-15) (76-4-3)	$ 3,950	*1400	Retractable tri-gear † fuel inj † C. spd 2 bld prop † Cantilever wing
	Add for-G/S $360 (0A72) † Enc. alt $530 (0A04) † DME $980 (0A47) † 300 A/P $530 (0A04) * IO-360 200 H.P. Eng. w/redesigned camshaft on s.n. 9762-51A up are 1600 Hrs.										
74	177 RG Card	177RG-0443 †-0592	$ 28,093 $ 37,298 $	27,000	A27P712D A27P232D	4	Lyc. 200 H.P. IO-360-A1B6	(74-8-1)(74-16-6)(74-24-13)(75-7-2) (75-8-9)(75-9-15)(76-4-3)	$ 3,950	1600	Retr. tri-gear
75 76	177 RG II Cardinal RG II	177RG-0593 †-0787 177RG-0788 †-1051	$ 30,950 $ 40,284 $ $ 35,550 $ 45,050 $	30,000 37,500	A30P242D A30P852D A37P303D A37P223D	4 4	Lyc. 200 H.P. IO-360-A1B6	(75-7-2 & 75-8-9 & 75-9-15=75 only) (76-14-8)(76-21-6=76 only)	$ 3,950	1600	Priced w/dual 300's, 200 A/P, Xpnd Priced w/Nav-Pac, 200 A/P, Xpnd
	Add-for-G/S $600 (0A54) † Enc Alt $860 (0A86) † DME $1,680 (06A21) † 300 A/P $900 (0A86) † Gyros $840 (0A36) †										
77	177 RG II	177RG-1052 † up	$ 39,950 $ 50,095 $	50,095	A50P083D A50P004D	4	Lyc. 200 H.P. None		$ 3,950	1600	Priced w/dual 300 Nav-Pac
	CESSNA CARDINAL 177 (Fixed gear) (s. eng.-piston)		Base Avg.=		360 ch Nav-Comm † VOR † ADF † Xpnd † 800 SMOH † Comp 85% of new † Orig Logs † Good Paint & Intr. † no MDH † 6 mo Annual † AD's Complied						
68	Cardinal 177	17700001 17701164	$ 14,500 $ 18,495 $	11,250	A11P88D A11P59D	4	Lyc. 150 H.P. O-320-E2D	(68-7-9)(68-17-4)(68-18-2)(70-1-2) (70-24-4)(71-1-3)(71-24-4)(72-3-3)(74-16-6) (75-7-2)(75-8-9)	$ 3,000	2000	Cardinal is Deluxe 177 † Cantilever High wing † Fixed Tri-gear
	Add-for-180 H.P. Dayn Conv. $1,250 (04P9) † 2nd Nav-Comm $500 (0A83) † G/S $260 (0A02) † Mkr B $120 (0A9) † Enc alt $380 (0A92) † DME $700 (0A35) † 200 A/P $330 (0A52)										
69	Cardinal 177 A	17701165 17701370	$ 16,995 $ 21,917 $	14,250	A14P211D A14P121D	4	Lyc. 180 H.P. O-360-A2F	(70-1-2)(70-24-4)(71-1-3)(72-3-3) (73-23-1)(74-16-6)(74-24-13)(75-7-2)(75-8-9)	$ 3,300	2000	Gross up † Fixed prop † Ded. $500 if 177
70	Cardinal 177 B	17701371 17701530	$ 17,500 $ 22,092 $	15,500	A15P321D A15P231D	4½	Lyc. 180 H.P. O-360-A1F6	(70-24-4)(72-3-3)(73-23-1)(74-16-6) (74-24-13)(75-7-2)(75-8-9)	$ 3,300	2000	McC. Const. spd. prop † New speed-form wing
	Add-for-2nd Nav-Comm $600 (0A54) † G/S $310 (0A32) † Mkr B $150 (0A11) † Enc alt $460 (0A53) † DME $840 (0A36) † 200 A/P $400 (0A03) † 300 A/P $840 (0A36) † Gyros $430 (0A23)										
71	177 B	177015311-01633	$ 17,995 $ 23,095 $	17,000	A17P531D A17P541D	4½	Lyc. 180 H.P. O-360-A1F6	(72-3-3)(73-23-1)(74-8-1)(74-16-6) (74-24-13)(75-7-2)(75-8-9)(76-4-3)	$ 3,300	2000	Fixed Tri Gear † C. Spd. Prop
72 73 74	177 B 177 B 177B Cardinal	177-0163†-01773 177-01774†-01973 177-01974†-02123	$ 19,300 $ 24,815 $ $ 19,300 $ 24,815 $ $ 20,651 $ 27,341 $	17,900 18,750 21,000	A17P141D A17P151D A18P941D A18P061D A21P761D A21P081D	4½ 4½ 4½	Lyc. 180 H.P. O-360-A1F6	(73-23-1 not on 74)(74-8-1)(74-16-6) (74-24-13)(75-7-2)(75-8-9)(76-4-3)	$ 3,300 $ 3,300	2000 2000	Fixed Tri Gear † C spd. Prop † More Range on 73 & 74 Deduct $750 if std 177
	Add-for-2nd Nav-Comm $810 (0A16) † G/S $410 (0A13) † Mkr B $200 (0A51) † Enc alt $610 (0A64) † DME $1,130 (0A58) † 200 A/P $530 (0A04) † 300 A/P $1,130 (0A58) † Gyros $570 (0A34)										

Page 54 "NOTE" When buying, selling or loaning - for hi-time engine(s) subtract ½ overhaul cost, for low-time add ½. On twins add or subtract full cost of one engine. Prices are avg. field cost with same accessories as installed by eng. mfr. - other accessories & props not inc. SPRING 1977

ing for aircraft. You will find a very limited, occasional listing in the Public and Commercial Notices want ads, which are usually located alongside the weather map. Sunday is the best day.

8. Auctions. Used-aircraft auctions are becoming more prevalent. You have an opportunity to inspect the aircraft on the ramp for maybe a couple of hours before the event, after which it's a good, old-fashioned auction. Terms usually call for cash or certified check for 10 or 20 percent of the purchase price after your bid has been accepted.

How to read a used-plane ad

Airplane ads, like real-estate ads, have their own lingo. The abbreviations used have come into effect by common use—there is no standard official code. Before we delve into the secret code, try your luck on this ad:

1965 CHEROKEE 180: 3200TTAF, 800 SCMOH, new int., Palmer paint, NDH, fresh ann., ELT, EGT, Mk 12 (90), VOA-4, KT-78 (TSO), ADF-31A, 3 LMB, all ADs c/w, clean $13,950.

What it means is the following. The aircraft is a 1965 Piper Cherokee 180, with 3,200 hours total time on the airframe and 800 hours since the engine had a major overhaul in which the cylinders were chromed. It has a new interior, and the paint job was done by Palmer (one of the best paint shops around). The aircraft has no damage history and a fresh annual inspection. It has an emergency locator transmitter, an exhaust-gas temperature gauge, a Narco Mark 12 Nav/Com with 90 communications channels and a Narco VOA-4 omni indicator, a King KT-78 transponder that meets TSO standards, a Narco ADF 31A, a 3-light 75 mHz marker-beacon indicator; all airworthiness directives have been complied with, the aircraft is "clean" and offered at $13,950.

Here is an idea of the abbreviations used. Like CB lingo, it is an evolving process, so you will undoubtedly find some new ones that aren't listed. Use your imagination!

AD	Airworthiness directive		NDH	No damage history
ADF	Automatic direction finder		O, OH	Overhaul
AH	Artificial horizon		OAT	Outside-air temperature gauge
AP	Autopilot		OBS	Omni-bearing selector
ASI	Airspeed indicator		PC	Positive control (wing leveler on Mooney aircraft)
BCN	Beacon			
CAT	Carburetor-air temperature gauge		PEP	Piper external power (ground-power plug)
CH	Channel		PET	Piper electric trim
CHT	Cylinder-head temperature gauge		PWI	Proximity warning indicator
			RB	Rotating beacon
CMOH	Chrome major overhaul		RC	Rate of climb
Cont	Continental engine		RDR	Radar
CTOH	Chrome top overhaul		RE	Right engine
C/W	Complied with		Reman	Remanufactured (rebuilt)
DG	Directional gyro		RG	Retractable gear
DME	Distance-measuring equipment		RH	Right-hand (copilot's side)
EGT	Exhaust-gas temperature gauge		RMF	Remanufactured (rebuilt)
ELT	Emergency-locator transmitter		RMI	Radio-magnetic indicator
FD	Flight director		RNAV	Area navigation
FGP	Full gyro panel		S	Since *or* single
FI	Fuel-injected		SCMOH	Since chrome major overhaul
Frank	Franklin engine		SCTOH	Since chrome top overhaul
Freman	Factory-remanufactured (rebuilt) engine		SFreman	Since factory remanufacture (rebuilt)
FRMF	Factory-remanufactured (rebuilt) engine		SFRMF	Since factory remanufacture (rebuilt)
FTO	Ferry time only		SMOH	Since major overhaul
FWFWD	Firewall forward (means complete engine and accessories)		SOH	Since overhaul
			SPOH	Since propeller overhaul
GPH	Gallons per hour		STOH	Since top overhaul
GS	Glideslope		STOL	Short takeoff and landing
GSI	Groundspeed indicator *or* glideslope indicator		TASI	True-airspeed indicator
			TB	Turn-and-bank indicator
GSP	Ground-service plug (external power source)		TBO	Time between overhauls
			TSO	Technical standard order
HF	High-frequency radio		TT	Total time
HP	Heated pitot *or* horsepower		TTAE	Total time, airframe and engine
IFR	Instrument-flight rules		TTAF	Total time, airframe
IRAN	Inspected and repaired as needed		TTSN	Total time since new
IVSI	Instantaneous vertical-speed indicator		TXP	Transponder
			UHF	Ultra high frequency
JATO	Jet-assisted takeoff		VFR	Visual flight rules
LE	Left engine		VHF	Very high frequency
LF	Low-frequency radio		VNAV	Area navigation with vertical guidance
LMB	(3) light-marker beacon			
LOC	Localizer		VOR	VHF omni range
LRT	Long-range tanks		VOR/LOC	VOR and localizer
Lyc	Lycoming engine		W/L	Wing leveler
MB	Marker beacon		XMTR	Transmitter
MKR	Marker		XPDR	Transponder
MO	Major overhaul		XTAL	Crystal

Choosing it

You will see many other abbreviations used in these ads. They are almost always radio-equipment designators. As a guide, most Cessna aircraft are equipped with Cessna avionics. These come in three series—300, 400, and 800. The 800 series is the top-of-the-line, fully TSO'd equipment. The 400 series is the middle-range line, and the 300 series is the least expensive line.

Narco used to employ the word "Mark" as a designator (e.g., Mark 5, Mark 12, Mark 16). Now they use abbreviations for the type of radio, followed by a model number (e.g. NAV 124, com 120). See the box for a summary of the Narco abbreviations.

King Radio also employs its own nomenclature, followed by a model number (e.g. KX175B, KMA20). See the box for a summary of the King abbreviations.

Narco abbreviations

ADF	Automatic direction finder
AR	Altitude reporting equipment
AT	Transponder
CLC	Area navigation equipment (CLC = course-line computer)
COM	Communications transceiver
CP	Audio-control panel
DGO	Horizontal situation indicator, unslaved (DGO = directional gyro/omni)
DME	Distance measuring equipment
ELT	Emergency locator transmitter
HSI	Horizontal situation indicator
ID	Indicator
M	Microphone
MKR	Marker beacon receiver
NAV	VHF navigation receiver
RMI	Radio magnetic indicator
RNAV	Area navigation equipment
UD	DME
UGR	Glideslope receiver

King abbreviations

KAE	Altitude encoder
KCI	Flight command indicator
KCS	Compass-slaved HSI
KCU	Keyboard control/display
KDF	ADF receiver
KDI	DME indicator
KDM	DME receiver
KE	Remote altitude encoder
KEA	Encoding altimeter
KFC	Autopilot/flight-control system or flight director system
KFS	Frequency selector
KGM	Glideslope/marker receiver
KGS	Glideslope receiver
KI	Navigation indicator
KMA	Audio-control system
KMR	Marker receiver
KN	Navigation receiver
KNC	Area navigation computer
KNI	Navigation indicator
KNR	VOR/LOC receiver and indicator
KPI	HSI (pictorial navigation indicator)
KR	Navigation receiver
KRA	Radar altimeter
KRT	Airborne telephone
KT	Transponder
KTR	Transceiver
KVN	Vertical/area navigation computer
KWA	RNAV waypoint annunciator
KWX	Weather radar
KX	Nav/com receiver
KXP	Transponder
KY	Transceiver

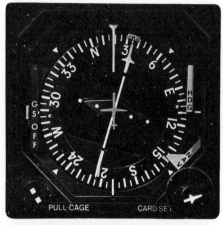

Above Narco HSI 100

Above King KI 204 VOR/ILS

Above Narco NAV 121 self-contained VOR

Left King KX 175B NAV/COMM

Used-aircraft checklist

Before you decide to go through with a used-aircraft deal, you should answer some key questions, preferably by interviewing the previous owner. Many of the answers can also be obtained by checking the log books. Then you should have the aircraft inspected by a certificated mechanic for mechanical soundness.

1. Review the following documents:

   All aircraft log books ☐ ⎫ Match log-
   All engine log books ☐ ⎪ book serial
   All propeller log books ⎪ numbers
      (may be in airplane ⎪ against air-
      or engine log) ☐ ⎬ frame, en-
   Avionics log book ☐ ⎪ gine, pro-
   Airplane flight manual ☐ ⎪ peller, and
   Equipment list ☐ ⎪ component
   Weight and balance ☐ ⎪ serial num-
   Any Form 337s ☐ ⎭ bers
   ADs ☐
   Factory-service pub-
      lications ☐
   Airworthiness certificate ☐
   Registration certificate ☐
   FCC radio-station license ☐
   Owner's handbook ☐
   Parts manual (rarely available
      from individual owners) ☐
   Service manual (rarely available
      from individual owners) ☐
   Bill of sale ☐

2. Year of manufacture _____

   Serial number _____

3. Exact model designation _____

4. Total hours on the airframe since

   new _____

5. Hours flown by seller _____

6. Date of last annual inspection _____

7. Date of last 100-hour inspection _____

8. Review of invoices and inspection
   reports ☐

9. Number of hours since last

   inspection _____

10. Hours since last oil change _____

11. Type of oil now in use _____
    Ashless dispersant ☐   Mineral ☐

12. Present oil consumption _____ hours
    per quart

13. Review of most recent series of oil-
    analysis reports ☐

14. Exact model designation of engine

    _____

15. Manufacturer's recommended TBO for

    engine _____

16. Engine hours since new _____

17. Engine hours since last major

    overhaul _____

18. Type of major: overhaul by:

    _____

    Exchange engine supplied by:

    _____

    Service limits ☐   New limits ☐
    Steel cylinders ☐ Chrome cylinders ☐
    Nitride cylinders ☐

19. Engine hours since top overhaul _____

    Nature of top: _____

    _____

    (see engine log book for description)

20. Top performed by _____

21. Date of last compression check _____

22. Findings of compression check _____

23. Estimated cost of replacement engine

    $_____ new ☐ exchange ☐ overhaul ☐

24. Estimated hours until overhaul _____
    (TBO hours minus hours in service)

25. Exact model designation of

    propeller _____

26. Manufacturer's recommended TBO for

    propeller _____

27. Propeller hours since new _____

28. Propeller hours since major

    overhaul _____

29. Overhaul carried out by _____

30. What ADs have been issued on this air-
    plane? (Make a list by AD number.
    Determine nature of AD and note
    any recurring items that you will
    have to carry out in the future.)

31. Have all outstanding ADs been complied
    with? Yes ☐ No ☐ Which ones
    are deficient?

32. Are there any outstanding mandatory
    factory-service publications to be
    complied with? Yes ☐ No ☐
    Which ones are deficient?

33. Is there any accident history? No ☐
    Yes ☐ What happened?

    Hours on airframe since accident _____

    Was the engine inspected after the
    accident? No ☐ Yes ☐
    Was any work required? No ☐ Yes ☐
    What was done?

34. If the engine is designed to run on 80-
    octane fuel, what steps have been
    taken to handle the lack of avail-
    ability of this fuel?
    Use regular 100 octane ☐
    Use 100 LL ☐   Use TCP ☐
    Use 80 octane when possible ☐
    Has the engine been modified to
       handle 100-octane fuel?
    No ☐ Yes ☐ What was done?
    Have there been any problems due to
       fuel octane? Since 80-octane
       became scarce, what percentage of
       flying hours since then has been
       flown with:
         80 octane _____ %
         100 octane _____ %
         100 LL _____ %

    Total hours flown since scarcity
    started _____

Now have your own mechanic carry out the following:

Aircraft Inspection Checklist:

1. Check ignition and master switches OFF
2. Open the cowling and check the engine:
   ☐ Is it clean?
   ☐ Free of rust and corrosion?
   ☐ Any sign of oil leaks?
   ☐ All hoses in good condition?
   ☐ Any sharp bends in lines?
   ☐ All clamps in good condition?
   ☐ No evidence of chafing?
   ☐ Metal particles in the oil screen?
   ☐ Turn propeller and check for compres-
      sion on each cylinder
   ☐ Check battery for condition
   ☐ Examine cowling for damage
   ☐ Close up engine

Choosing it

3. Examine propeller:
   - [ ] Blades in good condition?
   - [ ] Evidence of oil or grease leaks?
   - [ ] Check prop for looseness
   - [ ] Check condition of spinner
4. Examine the wings and tail surfaces:
   - [ ] Cuts or dents in leading edges?
   - [ ] All inspection plates present?
   - [ ] Any skin wrinkles?
   - [ ] Any sprung rivets?
   - [ ] Any fabric damage?
   - [ ] Fuel tank condition?
   - [ ] Fuel stains (look underneath for leaks)
   - [ ] All control surfaces in good condition?
   - [ ] Full and correct movement of all surfaces?
   - [ ] Lower the flaps and examine the runs, hinges, etc., for condition
   - [ ] All control cables properly safetied?
   - [ ] Any signs of rust or corrosion?
   - [ ] Everything secure and tight?
   - [ ] Check landing and taxi lights
   - [ ] Check navigation lights
   - [ ] Check stall-warning-horn actuator
   - [ ] Check pitot tube
   - [ ] Check static inlet
   - [ ] Check fuel vents
   - [ ] Drain sumps and gascolator for evidence of water, sediment, dirt, etc.
5. Examine the fuselage:
   - [ ] No evidence of damage or wrinkles?
   - [ ] All inspection plates present?
   - [ ] All radio antennas intact and secure?
   - [ ] Strobe lights and rotating beacons working?
   - [ ] Evidence of oil leaks?
   - [ ] Condition of overall paint job
6. Examine landing gear:
   - [ ] Condition of tires
   - [ ] Brake lines secure — no leaks?
   - [ ] Oleo struts properly inflated?
   - [ ] Shock absorbers, bungees, shock cords OK?
   - [ ] Do brakes hold properly?
   - [ ] Any nosewheel shimmy?
   - [ ] Nosewheel-steering linkage secure?
   - [ ] Gear doors in good condition and secure?
   - [ ] Wheel wells not blocked?
7. Examine the cabin:
   - [ ] Doors and windows — security and condition
   - [ ] Locks work?
   - [ ] Windows and vents open and close?
   - [ ] Glass condition?
   - [ ] Any loose or twisted hinges?
   - [ ] All latches working properly?
   - [ ] Seats adjust properly?
   - [ ] Upholstery condition
   - [ ] Carpet condition
   - [ ] Sidewall condition
   - [ ] Headliner condition
   - [ ] Heater and vents operate properly?
   - [ ] Cabin fire extinguisher installed?
8. Examine the radios and instruments:
   - [ ] All radios and instruments working?
   - [ ] Quality installations (look under panel for wiring and connectors)?
   - [ ] Are radios of legal type (some transponders and VHF transmitters are no longer acceptable)?
   - [ ] Do VORs and ADF work properly and check out?
   - [ ] Altimeter/static system check current (must be done within last 24 months if you want to fly IFR)?
   - [ ] All switches and circuit breakers working?
9. Do a test flight:
   - [ ] Wind noise around doors and windows?
   - [ ] Any smells from heating system?
   - [ ] All controls working properly?
   - [ ] All trims working properly?
   - [ ] Gear retracts and extends properly?
   - [ ] Aircraft properly rigged (flies hands-off when trimmed)?
   - [ ] All flight instruments working properly?
   - [ ] All navaids working properly?
   - [ ] Stall warner works?
   - [ ] Gear warning horn works?
   - [ ] General condition satisfactory?

Looking through the logs of a used airplane

Very careful inspection of the logs is essential when considering a used aircraft. Are all the required logs there? If the aircraft is old, there will probably be more than one book. Do the books maintain continuity, or are there any gaps in time between or within the books? (Check the engine logs against the airplane logs for complete information, year-by-year.) Have all the ADs been complied with? (Note: some ADs require a one-shot compliance; others require compliance at regular intervals, such as every 100 hours. Be careful to confirm that everything has been done that should have been done.) Look for damage reports. (Note: an accident will probably show up only in the form of the repairs made as a result. For example, the fact that the airplane had a gear-up landing may be indicated only by remarks such as: "Repaired underside of fuselage and lower engine cowl. Replaced nosewheel assembly, rerigged gear, and carried out retraction test." Look for these kinds of entries—in other words, *read all the entries*.) Look for recurring problem items. Why was the strobe light repaired seven times in nine months? If such an entry occurred a long time ago, you probably have no problem.

Another source of data on damage history is the FAA Form 337. Any substantial repairs to the airplane require that a Form 337 be filed with the FAA (see page 134) giving details of the work performed. Make sure the bottom of the form is signed out properly as "approved for return to service."

What about damage history?

Some people won't even look at an aircraft that has any damage history. Even though the airplane has been repaired, there seems to be a stigma attached to an airplane that has been dented at some point. An aircraft with such a history should sell for less than a similar aircraft with no damage history.

My Comanche has some damage in its past—the right wheel folded up once on landing, and another time someone ran it off the end of the runway. So I have some parts on the airplane that are newer than the whole! The airplane has been flying for many hours since the damage and has gone through several annual inspections. I'm not concerned about

Choosing it

its shady past. All is forgiven.

The main thing you need to watch for in an aircraft that has been damaged in the past is what happened to the engine. A sudden stoppage caused, for example, by the prop hitting the ground during a wheels-up landing is serious. Certainly the crankshaft should have been checked for misalignment. In fact, the whole engine should have been torn down and inspected. If the aircraft was submerged in water for any time, such as in a ditching, you want to look very carefully for signs of corrosion.

Buying an aircraft with a damage history really is a matter of the type of damage incurred and how long ago. If it was a bent wingtip 800 hours ago and the aircraft has had several annuals since then, it wouldn't worry me too much. An aircraft that has just come off repair from being flipped on its back might be something to think harder about. I'd want to make sure that the repairs had been made *very* properly, and I'd even go for a second opinion

on an inspection just to be sure. And the price should reflect the less-than-perfect condition.

Buying a wreck to fix yourself

Some people do this—it makes for a nice winter occupation. If you don't have an A & P certificate, you would have to perform the work under the direct supervision of an A & P mechanic, who would have to take responsibility for the work and would have to approve it for return to service.

Rebuilding is not an inexpensive operation, especially if you value your time highly. But people who have done it speak well of its therapeutic values, to say nothing of the opportunity to learn a lot about your own airplane!

Buying military-surplus aircraft

On my field right now we have three immaculate aircraft, a Stearman, a Beech T-34, and a North American T-28. All are painted in full navy training colors. They are individually owned, and it is a mere coincidence that they are all in the same hangar. You think you're at some navy museum when you walk in. Flying military-surplus aircraft can be a kick, especially for the more adventurous among us. Some military-surplus aircraft are very similar to civilian types—for example, the Beech 18, the Cessna 172, the Cessna Skymaster, the Beech Baron, and The Helio Courier have all flown in military uniforms. Others were never designed for civilian use but are to be found in civvies these days—aircraft such as the P-51, the T-33, the T-34, the T-28, the L-19, and so on.

The cheapest way to buy military-

Plane Profile 13: Piper Aerostar 602P

Seats	6
Cruise speed, 65% power,	
8,000 feet	203 knots
18,000 feet	220 knots
Range, 65% power, full	924 nm
optional fuel, 18,000 feet	
Maximum endurance	5.2 hours
Gross weight	6,029 pounds
Empty weight	4,075 pounds
Full optional fuel	993 pounds
	165.5 gallons
Useful load, full fuel	1,084 pounds
Fuel efficiency, 65% power	7.3 nmpg
Stall speed, gear and flaps down	77 knots
Rate of climb, sea level	1,460 fpm
	240 fpm s/e
Minimum field length	2,250 feet
Engine type 2 Lycoming IO-540-AA1A5	290 hp
Engine TBO	1,800 hours
Remarks Pressurized, turbocharged twin.	

surplus aircraft is to buy directly from the Department of Defense (DOD). The DOD occasionally disposes of aircraft it no longer wants. To find out about this, write to the following address and ask to be put on the mailing list for sale information:

Defense Surplus Sales Office
Dept RK-24, Box 1370
Battle Creek, Mich. 49016

Buying direct may be the cheapest way in, but it may not be the cheapest way out. If you intend to fly your purchase, the FAA requires that you bring the aircraft into airworthy condition (complying with FAA certification standards or otherwise satisfying them of the aircraft's suitability). This can be a very expensive process. If you want a warbird to fly right away, you should buy one that is already civilianized and legal.

When the DOD announces a sale, the FAA prescreens the aircraft in most cases to alert prospective buyers of the certification potential of the aircraft. This is no guarantee that you will be able to get the aircraft certificated, however. The buyer is the person responsible for obtaining FAA type certification of the aircraft or for showing that the aircraft conforms to an existing model that has an FAA type certificate and is in airworthy condition. Aircraft that the FAA does not consider to be suitable for certification are usually sold for scrap or parts recovery rather than for the purpose of flight.

Assuming that you attend a sale and walk away with the title to a slightly worn surplus aircraft, how do you get it to your base so you can bring it up to FAA standards? First, it *must* be registered before flight and you must obtain a special flight permit.

Send an application for registration to the FAA along with proof of ownership (see page 94 and 96). You will receive an N number and a registration certificate in the mail.

Once your aircraft has been registered and you have affixed the N number to the aircraft, you must then apply to the nearest FAA dis-

The Cessna L 19 is a popular surplus aircraft

trict office for a flight permit. This will only be issued when the FAA has determined that the aircraft is safe for flight. You should have all documents available for inspection so that its identity and safe condition can be determined. An FAA inspector will want to inspect the aircraft before you can fly it. When you get your permit, it will only authorize you to fly to your base or designated destination. Subsequent flights under this permit are not allowed.

Once you get the aircraft to your base, the process of obtaining civil certification begins in earnest. Prior to beginning work you should contact your nearest FAA engineering and manufacturing district office. The FAA will help you to determine what is needed to certificate the aircraft. A mutually agreeable inspection program can be established at this time.

Establishing conformity with the type design officially identifies the aircraft for civilian use. It confirms that the basic design is one that has been tested and approved by the FAA. You must show the FAA that the aircraft conforms to the FAA type certificate and that the aircraft is in a safe condition for operation. You have to obtain any technical data needed to show this. The FAA is responsible for determining that the aircraft is safe and conforms to the FAA-approved design. You must be prepared to compare parts of your aircraft against the FAA-approved

drawings to show conformance. The FAA inspector may want to check some details to verify this. This can take a lot of time. The big question is whether all parts replaced by the military are approved for use in civil aircraft. Some parts may not be FAA-approved. If you find this to be so, you must either prove conformity to the approved type design or replace the parts with FAA-approved parts.

When an aircraft has been modified by the military, you must either return the aircraft to the originally approved civilian configuration or obtain FAA design approval for the military modification. This is done through a Supplemental Type Certificate (STC). See page 164 for details.

When the aircraft's identity has been clearly established, it has been inspected and shown to conform to an FAA-approved type design and is in a condition for safe operation, and you have conducted a weight-and-balance procedure, an experimental certificate can be issued for the purpose of showing compliance to the rule. You are then allowed to fly the aircraft—for flight test only. The test program must be coordinated with the FAA for approval prior to carrying it out. You will have to report on progress to the FAA inspector, who may ask for additional flights and will want to flight-test the aircraft. Following satisfactory completion of these tests an application for a certificate of airworthiness may be made to the FAA. Once you have that, you can fly the aircraft as you wish.

18. Select the right aircraft for you

If you have been following through on the suggestions made so far, you should by now have a very good idea of what you want and you should have selected several aircraft from which to choose. There may be a Bonanza at Mercer County Airport—a '68, with 1,600 TTAF and the engine about to run out, with an asking price of $41,000. Then there's a '70 Cessna 210 at Westchester, only 800 TTAF and a brand-new chrome-top overhaul, asking $37,000. And there's a Piper Arrow—a '72, at Republic, 1,200 hours TTAF&E, asking $24,500. Which is the best one for you? That's where the specific-aircraft-comparison chart comes in.

Specific-aircraft-comparison chart

When you have selected four or five aircraft candidates, fill out the details about them on the chart on the next page. (Some or all of these could be the same type.) You'll notice that under each candidate there is space for detail and a ranking for each item being considered. This is to help you make a logical decision about which aircraft to select.

For each item enter the information under the appropriate aircraft, but do not enter anything in the "Rank" column yet. When you have put down all the pertinent information for all the aircraft you are thinking about, go across each item and rank the aircraft from 1 to 5 for that item. For example, considering "Year," if you had aircraft with the following years of manufacture:

1972, 1968, 1956, 1971, 1970

you would rank them
1 4 5 2 3

assuming that newer ranked higher with you than older. Likewise, under price, you might have the following (in thousands of dollars):

$27.0 $22.0 $16.0 $28.0 $26.0

which you might rank

4 2 1 5 3

Rank each item going across, comparing each airplane with the others in order of importance to you for your requirements or situation. Then add up vertically the rankings for each aircraft. The lowest figure should be your best choice, the next lowest, your second best, and so on.

The "location" item specifies where the airplane now is. It is there so that you can consider how far away you have to go to view the airplane or have it ferried from if you buy it.

"TTAF" means "total time airframe."

"TSMOH" means "time since major overhaul." There is room for you to enter data on two engines.

The cruise speeds and ranges are shown at 75-percent power. If you would rather use a lower power setting, show that data and change the 75-percent figure on the chart.

To calculate the fuel efficiency, divide the cruise speed by the gallons-per-hour figure. For example, a cruise speed of 150 knots and a fuel use of 15 gph gives an efficiency of 10 mpg.

The "useful load" figure should be the difference between the gross weight and the empty weight.

The maintenance, AD, and avionics ranks are subjective. Assuming that you have reviewed the maintenance and AD situation on each candidate, rank the aircraft according to how you feel. Do the same with the avionics installed in the aircraft.

Three Bonanzas, the A 36, the V 35B and the F 33A

Specific-Aircraft-Comparison Chart

Item	Aircraft #1		Aircraft #2		Aircraft #3		Aircraft #4		Aircraft #5	
	Detail	Rank	Detail	Rank	Detail	Rank	Detail	Rank	Detail	Rank
Type										
Year										
Location										
Price $										
TTAF										
TSMOH Left										
TSMOH Right										
Engine type — TBO TBO hours										
Cruise speed, 75% — knots										
Range, 75% — nm										
Fuel used, 75% — gph										
Fuel efficiency — nmpg										
Useful load — lbs										
# seats										
Maintenance Rank										
AD Rank										
Avionics Rank										
Rank totals										

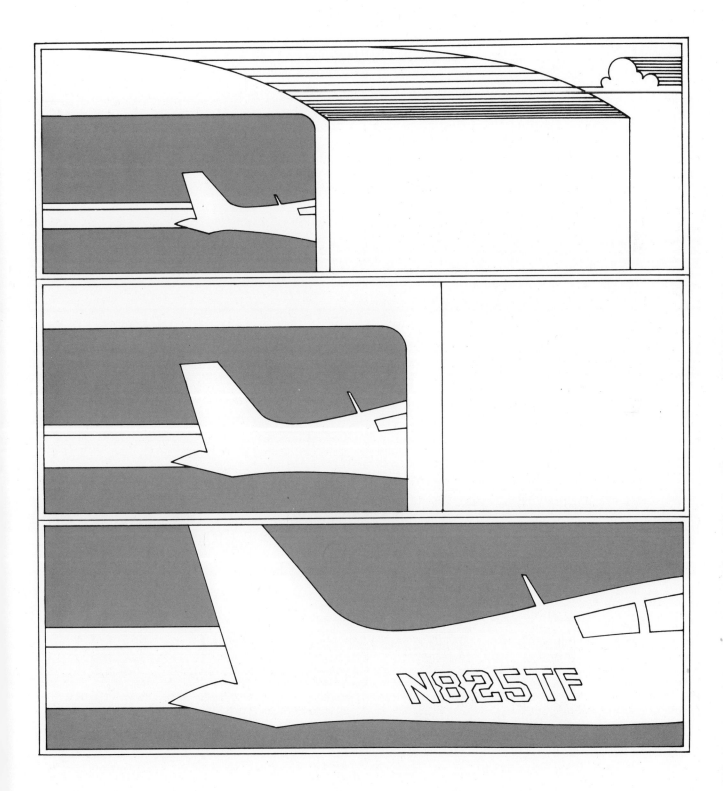

Owning it

Government agencies and the aircraft operator

When you own or operate an aircraft, you will find yourself dealing with many different manifestations of the government.

The most significant is the Department of Transportation (DOT), a cabinet-level department created in 1967 to unite 34 transportation agencies that had been scattered throughout the U.S. Government.

The most important part of the DOT for aircraft owners is the *Federal Aviation Administration (FAA)*. The agency is responsible for the administration of all civil aviation certification (airplanes, pilots, air traffic controllers, mechanics, repair stations, etc.); operation of the air traffic control system, including the associated navigational aids, control towers, ATC Centers, etc.; aviation safety through the issuance of aircraft type certificates, maintenance requirements, airworthiness directives, flight testing of pilot applicants, and so on. Its rules are called Federal Aviation Regulations (FARs), which are divided into several Parts. The pertinent FARs are:

FAR 1—Definitions and abbreviations
FAR 23—Airworthiness Standards
FAR 43—Maintenance, preventive maintenance, rebuilding, and alteration
FAR 47—Aircraft registration
FAR 49—Recording of aircraft titles and security documents
FAR 61—Certification: pilots and flight instructors
FAR 91—General operating and flight rules
FAR 135—Air-taxi operators and commercial operators of small aircraft
FAR 141—Pilot schools

Throughout this book bracketed FAR figures (e.g., FAR 91.173) indicate the pertinent FAR governing the stated requirement. Copies of the FARs may be bought on subscription from the government printing office. They are issued in volumes as follows:

Volume	FAR Part
I	1
II	11, 13, 15, 21, 37, 39, 45, 47, 49, 183, 185, 187, 189
III	23, 25, 36
IV	27, 29, 31, 33, 35
V	43, 145, 149
VI	91, 93, 99, 101, 103, 105
VII	121, 123, 127, 129
VIII	133, 135, 137
IX	61, 63, 65, 67, 141 143, 147
X	151, 153, 155, 159, 165, 167
XI	71, 73, 75, 77, 95, 97, 157, 169, 171

The price varies by volume. They may be ordered from:

Superintendent of Documents,
U.S. Government Printing Office,
Washington, D.C. 20402

A good way to receive constantly updated, pertinent FARs is to subscribe to the Jeppesen J-Aid, which covers you on FARs 1, 61, 91, 121, 135, and 141 as well as the *Airman's Information Manual*. This service is available by subscription and may be ordered from:

Jeppesen Sanderson,
Box 3279
Englewood, CO 80112
Telephone: (303) 779-5757

Various other publishers make available reprints of the FARs, but these are not often sold on a subscription basis, so they will go out of date. I recommend the J-Aid service. It also includes a regional airport directory, with diagrams covering most VFR and all IFR airports. (J-Aid is not the Jeppesen Airway Manual Service, which provides IFR enroute and approach charts in various regional editions, see page 116.)

The FAA also publishes advisory circulars. Some are sold; others are free. The advisory circular system is used to aid in the interpretation of FARs and to pass on important and useful information. Three times a year a free checklist is published in the *Federal Register* that shows the currently available circulars and how they may be ordered.

Many advisory circulars are well-known books, which can be found at most FBO counters—books such as *Aviation Weather*, *Pilot's Handbook of Aeronautical Knowledge*, the various written exam and flight-test guides, *Terrain Flying*, and such. You can also buy these through the government printing office. Free circulars may be ordered through:

Department of Transportation,
Publications Section, TAD 443.1,
Washington, D.C. 20590

Advisory circulars are numbered in relation to the FARs they correspond to. For example, AC 43.13-1A, *Acceptable Methods, Techniques, and Practices–Aircraft Inspection and Repair* relates to FAR Part 43, which is the maintenance part. The AC that lists the available ACs is 00-2KK, *Advisory Circular Checklist*, and it's free.

The FAA publishes a free catalog "Guide to Federal Aviation Administration Publications" which outlines all their publications and how to get them. You can order this from:

Public Inquiry Center APA-430,
800 Independence Ave. SW,
Washington, D.C. 20591

Department of Commerce.

This is the former home of the old Civil Aeronautics Authority (CAA), which was replaced by the FAA in 1958. This department maintains a relationship with aviation through the weather and mapping services, both of which are provided through the *National Oceanic and Atmospheric Administration*. Weather services are provided through the *National Weather Service*. NWS provides weather observation and forecasting services. In some cities you can get aviation briefings from NWS forecasters, which will generally be better than the ones you get from a flight service station because you will get more interpretive information in-

Owning it

stead of a reading off a teletype. NWS aviation-briefing numbers are usually unlisted, but you can find them in *Airman's Information Manual* or Jeppesen's *J-Aid* and other airport directories. NWS also supplies the recordings for PATWAS—Pilot's Automatic Telephone Weather Answering Service—found in many cities throughout the U.S.A. NWS maintains about 50 weather-service forecast offices (WSFOs) around the country where you can get direct briefings. Flight service specialists, who are to be found at FAA flight service stations (FSS), have been trained by the NWS to give aviation weather briefings.

National Ocean Survey (NOS).

This service provides mapping and charting services for aviation. It is a part of the National Oceanic and Atmospheric Administration and thus the Department of Commerce. VFR charts in scales of 1:250,000 (about 4 miles to the inch) for VFR terminal-area charts, 1:500,000 (about 8 miles to the inch) for sectional charts, 1:1,000,000 (about 16 miles to the inch) for world charts, and smaller-scale planning charts are issued on a scheduled basis roughly every six months or more. IFR charts, including enroute, terminal, and instrument approach charts, are issued on a scheduled or demand basis at frequent intervals and are sold by subscription. Nevertheless, the best IFR chart service is that provided by Jeppesen. See page 116 for information on how to buy charts.

Federal Communication Commission (FCC).

This independent agency regulates interstate and foreign communications by wire and radio, which for aviation means FCC restricted radiotelephone-operator permits for pilots and aircraft radio station licenses for aircraft. I recommend that, if you need any FCC application forms, you order them through the Aircraft Owner's and Pilot's Association (AOPA). AOPA will also be able to answer your questions about FCC requirements better and faster. The FCC is notoriously slow. Their address is:

AOPA,
421 Aviation Way
Frederick, MD 21701

FCC Licenses.

To operate a radio transmitter in an aircraft, you must have both a radio station license and a radio operator's license, both of which are issued by the FCC. The radio station license must be displayed in the aircraft.

To apply for a new FCC aircraft radio station license or to modify such a license, use FCC Form 404. To apply for renewal of an aircraft radio station license, use FCC Form 405-B. Renewal applications must be filed within 90 days of and not less than 30 days prior to the expiration of the license. Applications should be sent to:

FCC, Box 1030,
Gettysburg, Pa. 17325

When you buy a used aircraft, the previously issued license (the one issued to the previous owner) is valid for your own use for 30 days. When you buy a new aircraft, you also have 30 days in which you may operate aircraft radio equipment installed at the factory before a license is issued. But apply right away! The FCC takes more than 30 days to respond!

Aircraft Radio Operator Licenses.

The radio transmitter must be operated by or under the supervision of a licensed radio operator. The appropriate license is the restricted radiotelephone operator's permit. To obtain one, complete FCC Form 753 and send it to:

FCC, Box 1050,
Gettysburg, Pa. 17325

No oral or written examination is required.

If you are an alien, you have to get an alien's permit by completing FCC Form 755. Alien permits are valid for five years.

The FCC used to charge fees for these permits but then rescinded them. Check with AOPA or the FCC before completing the forms to find out the current fee requirements.

National Aeronautics and Space Administration (NASA).

Unless you are planning to go into orbit, you will probably have little to do with NASA as an aircraft owner. However, NASA conducts research on some general aviation aircraft in such areas as stability and control, airfoil sections and such, so they appear here as a matter of record. NASA is an independent agency.

Civil Aeronautics Board (CAB).

Unless you run an airline, you will have little to do with the agency that regulates the nation's interstate airlines.

The Department of Defense.

This unit runs the military services—air force, navy, and army—but not the coast guard, which is part of the Department of Transportation. Your involvement with DOD should be limited to not bumping into their high-performance aircraft (or any) and keeping out of their airports, except in emergencies.

Owning it

Aircraft owner responsibilities

The registered owner of an aircraft is responsible for the following.

1. Having a current airworthiness certificate appropriately displayed in the aircraft. For *standard* aircraft this is FAA Form 8100-2. For aircraft other than standard, namely *experimental*, *restricted*, *limited*, or *provisional*, FAA Form 8130-7 is used.

2. Maintaining the aircraft in an airworthy condition.

3. Assuring that maintenance is properly recorded.

4. Keeping on top of current regulations concerning the operation and maintenance of the aircraft.

5. Notifying the FAA Aircraft Registry immediately of any change in permanent mailing address or of the sale or export of the aircraft. Their address is:

Department of Transportation
FAA Aeronautical Center
Aircraft Registration Branch
Box 25082
Oklahoma City, Okla. 73125

Registration of U.S. Civil Aircraft

FAR 47 is the regulation pertaining to aircraft registration. Here are some of the key points.

1. Eligibility.

An aircraft is eligible for U.S. registration only if it is owned by a U.S. citizen (other than a corporation) or by an individual citizen of a foreign country who has lawfully been admitted for permanent residence in the United States, or owned by a corporation lawfully organized and doing business under the laws of the

United States or any State thereof; or by a government unit; and is not registered under the laws of any foreign country. Operation of an unregistered aircraft may subject the operator to a civil penalty.

2. How to register.

The owner of the aircraft must apply to the FAA Aircraft Registry for a certificate of registration by submitting an application for aircraft registration (FAA Form 8050-1) accompanied by evidence of ownership and a $5 registration fee. The application form consists of an original and two copies. Two parts are sent to the FAA, and the pink copy is retained by the owner and must be kept in the aircraft until the permanent certificate of registration (FAA Form 8050-3) is received. An application by an alien must be accompanied by the declaration shown in the box.

CERTIFICATE OF AIRWORTHINESS

UNITED STATES OF AMERICA
FEDERAL AVIATION AGENCY

1. NATIONALITY AND REGISTRATION MARKS: N8251P

2. AIRCRAFT AIRWORTHINESS CLASSIFICATION: STANDARD

3. This Certificate of Airworthiness is issued pursuant to the Federal Aviation Act of 1958. The aircraft identified hereon is considered airworthy when maintained and operated in accordance with the Civil Air Regulations and applicable aircraft Operation Limitations. Issued under the provision of Part 410

4. This Certificate will remain in effect as long as the aircraft is maintained in accordance with Part 43 of the Civil Air Regulations unless surrendered, suspended, revoked, or a termination date is otherwise established by the Administrator of the Federal Aviation Agency.

5. DATE OF ISSUANCE: 7-22-63

6. FAA REPRESENTATIVE: J.W.McNary, Asst.Chief Engr. Piper Aircraft Corporation

7. DESIGNATION NO.: DMCR 1-1

8. Any alteration or misuse of this Certificate is punishable by a fine of not exceeding $1,000 or imprisonment not exceeding 3 years, or both.

GPO . 1959 OF—508938   Form FAA 1362B (5-59)

CERTIFICATE OF AIRCRAFT REGISTRATION

UNITED STATES OF AMERICA
DEPARTMENT OF TRANSPORTATION – FEDERAL AVIATION ADMINISTRATION

This certificate must be in the aircraft when operated.

NATIONALITY AND REGISTRATION MARKS: N12345X

AIRCRAFT SERIAL NO: 29-270

MANUFACTURER AND MANUFACTURER'S DESIGNATION OF AIRCRAFT: FLITMORE FLIVVER MK 1   FF-29-1

ISSUED TO:
DOE   JOHN ALBERT
123 MAIN STREET
CITY   STATE   00000

INDIVIDUAL

This certificate is issued for registration purposes only and is not a certificate of title. The Federal Aviation Administration does not determine rights of ownership as between private persons.

It is certified that the above described aircraft has been entered on the register of the Federal Aviation Administration, United States of America, in accordance with the Convention on International Civil Aviation dated December 7, 1944, and with the Federal Aviation Act of 1958, and regulations issued thereunder.

DATE OF ISSUE: APRIL 05, 1976

DURATION - See reverse side.

Alexander P. Butterfield
Administrator

AC Form 8050-3 (8/74)

Owning it

The pink temporary certificate is valid only for 90 days.

3. Name requirements.

An aircraft may be registered only by and in the legal name of its owner. It is important that the name be the same on all conveyances submitted (e.g., on the application and on the bill of sale). A corporation has only one name under which it is incorporated. Abbreviations or shortened names should not be used. An individual should not use nicknames and should show "Junior" or "Senior" if applicable. A woman's full name should be used (Jane A. Doe) rather than her married name (Mrs. John Doe). When a trade name is used by an individual, by co-owners, or by a corporation, the trade name alone is not sufficient since it is not the legal entity owning the aircraft. The trade name may appear on conveyances in addition to the legal name of the owner (e.g., Joseph Doe, dba [doing business as] Crazy Joe's Appliances).

4. Aircraft Registration Application.

This must be signed by the owner-applicant. The owner's name on the application must be identical to that shown on the evidence of ownership. The type of registration block checked and the title of the signer must agree. These are the types of registration permitted:

a. Individual. When an aircraft is owned by one person, he or she is the individual owner. The individual's title in connection with aircraft documentary instruments is "owner." If more than one person is shown as the applicant of the instrument, registration must be made to them as co-owners or partners.

b. Co-owners. When an aircraft is owned by two or more persons as co-owners, each person who shares title to the aircraft must sign all instruments and show title as "co-owner." Each co-owner's name must appear,

---

Representation in support of application for registration of an aircraft owned by a resident alien.

The undersigned is not a citizen of the United States but was lawfully admitted for permanent residence in the United States as of _____ (date) _____, and is the holder of alien registration (Form I-151) number _____ . This representation is furnished in support of that AC Form 8050-1, Aircraft Registration Application, for civil aircraft identified as N _____ , executed on _____ (date) _____ and furnished to the FAA Aircraft Registry.

Name _____

Signature _____

Date _____

FORM APPROVED. OMB No. 04-R0076

UNITED STATES OF AMERICA
DEPARTMENT OF TRANSPORTATION — FEDERAL AVIATION ADMINISTRATION

AIRCRAFT REGISTRATION APPLICATION

TYPE OF REGISTRATION   (Check one box) [X] 1. Individual
[ ] 2. Partnership [ ] 3. Corporation [ ] 4. Co-Owner [ ] 5. Gov't.

CERT. ISSUE DATE

NATIONALITY AND REGISTRATION MARKS   N12345

AIRCRAFT MAKE AND MODEL Flitmore FT-3

AIRCRAFT SERIAL No.   F-123

FOR FAA USE ONLY

NAME OF APPLICANT (Person(s) shown on evidence of ownership. If individual, give last name, first name, and middle initial.)

Doe, John A.

ADDRESS (Permanent mailing address for first applicant listed.)
Number and street: 100 Main Street

Rural Route: P. O. Box:

[ ] CHECK HERE IF ADDRESS CHANGE

CITY City   STATE State   ZIP CODE 00000

(No fee required for revised Certificate of Registration)

ATTENTION! Read the following statement before signing this application. A false or dishonest answer to any question in this application may be grounds for punishment by fine and/or imprisonment (U.S. Code, Title 18, Sec. 1001).

CERTIFICATION

I/WE CERTIFY that the above described aircraft (1) is owned by the undersigned applicant(s), who is/are citizen(s) of the United States as defined in Sec. 101(13) of the Federal Aviation Act of 1958; (2) is not registered under the laws of any foreign country; and (3) legal evidence of ownership is attached or has been filed with the Federal Aviation Administration.

NOTE: If executed for co-ownership all applicants must sign. Use reverse side if necessary.

EACH PART OF THIS APPLICATION MUST BE SIGNED IN INK.

SIGNATURE *John Doe*	TITLE	DATE 1-20-78
SIGNATURE	TITLE	DATE
SIGNATURE	TITLE	DATE

NOTE: Pending receipt of the Certificate of Aircraft Registration, the aircraft may be operated for a period not in excess of 90 days, during which time the PINK copy of this application must be carried in the aircraft.

AC Form 8050-1 (4-71) (0052-628-9002)

in addition to the trade name if one is used.

c. Partnership. The names of all general partners must be stated with the partnership name on the application for registration. If there is only one general partner, this must be stated. One partner may sign instruments for the partnership if the full partnership name is shown and the title "partner" follows the signature. The partnership name is either the name under which the partners do business or, if none, the names of all general partners.

d. Corporation. The name of the corporation must be shown, and a corporate officer or a person in a managerial position should sign the instrument and show his or her organizational title.

e. Government. Persons signing conveyances for government-owned aircraft must show their title as evidence of the capacity in which they act.

5. Authority to sign for another.

If another person is signing certificates, applications, and so on for and on behalf of the applicant, the FAA requires a certified true copy of the document authorizing the signer to act. Examples of such others are agent, guardian, estate executor or administrator, heir-at-law, trustee, or trustee in bankruptcy.

6. Change of name.

When a change of name occurs, the original or certified true copy of the instrument approving the change is required (e.g., marriage certificate, certificate from the Secretary of State, approved merger agreement, etc.). When the registered owner's name is changed, an application for registration in the new name must be submitted for each aircraft affected in addition to the name-change document. If a merger is involved, a fee of $5 is charged.

7. Evidence of ownership.

The applicant for registration of an aircraft last registered in the U.S. must submit conveyances completing the chain of ownership from the last registered owner through any intervening owners to the applicant. The following are examples of evidence of ownership.

a. Bill of sale. FAA Form AC 8050-2 or its equivalent, which transfers all

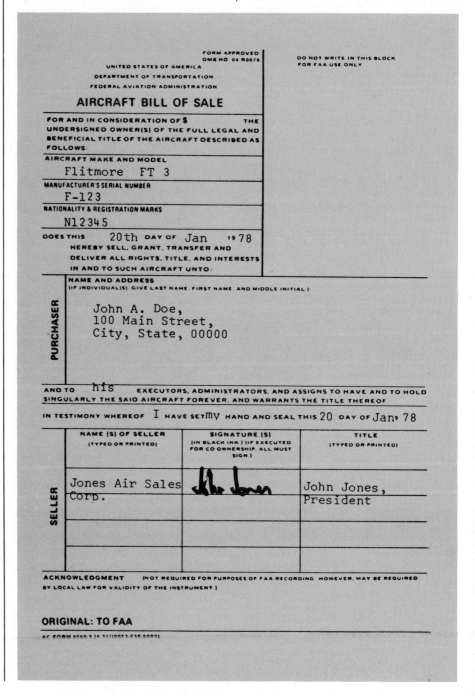

right, title, and interest in a specifically described aircraft.

b. Conditional sale contract. This may be recorded as evidence of ownership.

c. Transfer of interest. An agreement that provides that the buyer shall assume the debt under a recorded security instrument and that transfers all right, title, and interest in the aircraft,which is signed by the buyer, the seller, and the lienholder as evidence of the lienholder's assent to the transfer, may be used. The agreement must describe the original security instrument by date, parties, description of aircraft, and FAA recording date and conveyance number.

d. Repossession. The repossessor of an aircraft must submit a certificate of repossession on FAA Form AC 8050-4 or its equivalent, accompanied by an original or a certified true copy of the security instrument upon which repossession is based, unless such instrument is already recorded with the FAA.

e. Foreclosure. When repossession is through foreclosure proceedings resulting in a sale, a bill of sale is required in addition to the certificate of repossession mentioned in (d) above. The bill of sale must be signed by the sheriff or other authorized person who conducted the sale and must include a statement that the sale was made under applicable local law.

f. Judicial Sale. The buyer of an aircraft at a judicial sale or at a sale to satisfy a lien or charge must submit a bill of sale signed by the sheriff, auctioneer, or other authorized person who conducted the sale, stating that the sale was made under applicable local law.

g. Court Order. If title to an aircraft has been in controversy and ownership has been determined by a court of law, a certified copy of the court order may be used as evidence of ownership. The aircraft must be specifically described in the order, and the owner of record must be a party to the action.

h. Affidavit. If, for good reason, the applicant can't produce the required evidence of ownership, an affidavit may be submitted for consideration, along with a statement explaining why the required evidence cannot be produced accompanied by whatever further evidence is available to prove the transaction.

i. Aircraft assembled from parts. The applicant for registration of an aircraft that is assembled from parts to conform to an approved type design must describe the aircraft by class (airplane, rotorcraft, glider, etc.), by serial number, number of seats, type of engine (reciprocating, turboprop, turbojet), number of engines, and manufacturer, model, and serial number of each engine. The applicant must also state whether the aircraft is built for land or water operation. Bills of sale of all major component parts are required as evidence of the applicant's ownership.

8. Information re conveyances.

The term "conveyance" refers to any document used to convey information pertaining to the title or encumbrance on the aircraft. All conveyances filed become a part of the permanent record and may not be returned. Copies may be obtained on request and on payment of search and copy fees. If an original is submitted and it needs to be returned, a certified true copy of the original must accompany it. The FAA will keep the copy and return the original stamped with the date and time of recording. Certain specific conveyances have specific requirements. These include the following (FAR 49).

a. Transfer of equitable interest. A transfer of equitable interest under a contract of conditional sale may be recorded if it is signed by the transferer (last owner) and by the lienholder of the security interest to show assent. The orginal contract must be described by date, parties, collateral, and FAA recording date and conveyance number. A $5 recording fee must accompany each transfer of equitable interest.

b. Assumption agreement. An agreement to assume an obligation on a recorded security conveyance must be signed by the new obligor (debtor) and assented to by the lienholder. The security instrument must be described by date, parties, collateral, and FAA recording date and conveyance number. There is a $5 recording fee.

c. Mortgage by one co-owner. A security instrument executed by one co-owner may be recorded if the conveyance specifically sets forth that only the said co-owner is mortgaging an interest. The title "co-owner" must appear after the signature.

d. Assignment. An assignment of a security interest by a secured party that is not attached to or a part of the original instrument may be recorded separately. The assignment must describe the original security instrument by date, parties, collateral, and FAA recording date and conveyance number. The assignment must be signed by the assignor and accompanied by the $5 recording fee for each piece of collateral affected.

e. Amendment or supplement. An amendment or supplement to a recorded conveyance may be recorded if it describes the original conveyance by date, parties, and FAA recording date and conveyance number. It must meet the signature requirements of the original instrument. The usual $5 fee applies.

g. Incompleted sale or conveyance filed in error. When a conveyance is filed in error or a transaction is not completed after documentation is submitted to the FAA, the record may be set straight by the submission of an affidavit signed by the parties to the conveyance explaining the circumstances. The erroneous conveyance should be described by date, parties, collateral, and, if recorded, FAA recording date and conveyance number. There is a $5 fee.

h. Disclaimer of interest. A statement disclaiming any interest in a specifically described aircraft may be recorded upon payment of a $5 recording fee. Such a statement is appropriate to clear the record when a conveyance on file indicates the possibility of an interest of someone outside the chain of ownership.

9. Eligibility for recording conveyances.

To be eligible for recording, an instrument granting a security interest in an aircraft must be signed in ink and describe the aircraft by manufacturer, model, serial number, and registration number. The debtor must be the registered owner of the aircraft or the owner of record on the date the instrument is executed, as evidenced by documents on file with the FAA aircraft registry.

(Note: certain engines and propellers may be registered with the FAA. Engines of more than 750 rated takeoff hp [1,700 lbs or more thrust in a jet engine] and associated propellers may be so registered. The manufacturer, model, serial number, and horsepower [or thrust] of each engine and propeller must be shown. There is a $5 registration fee for each item. Certain spare parts may also be recorded [air carriers only].)

Registration of aircraft obtained from military surplus

To register an aircraft obtained from military surplus, you must submit a bill of sale from the government disposal officer or an invitation to bid and acceptance document describing the aircraft by make, model, and serial number, signed in ink by the disposal officer. If this is accepted by the FAA, it will not be recorded but will be stamped "accepted in lieu of a recordable document."

Registration of amateur-built aircraft

In addition to the application for registration you must submit evidence of ownership in the form of a verified instrument—i.e., an affidavit showing the FAA identification number signed in ink, setting forth that the aircraft was built from parts and that you are the owner of all right, title, and interest. If the aircraft was built from a kit, submit a bill of sale from the manufacturer of the kit. Follow the instructions on applications for an aircraft built from parts (page 95).

Registration of an aircraft previously registered in a foreign country

In addition to the application for registration and the bill of sale from the foreign seller you must submit acceptable evidence of cancellation of foreign registry, which must be in the form of a letter signed in ink by the appropriate official of that country, describing the aircraft by make, model, and serial number, stating that the foreign registration has been terminated or is invalid or that the aircraft was never entered on the foreign registry. Telegrams may be accepted if the name and title of the proper official are shown.

It is not necessary for the bill of sale to be in recordable form. If the document describes the aircraft in sufficient detail and is in a bill-of-sale form, bearing foreign acknowledgment, it may be accepted in lieu of a recordable document.

If you are applying for registration of an aircraft assembled from a kit made in a foreign country and assembled in the U.S., you need not furnish evidence of cancellation of registration.

How to get a custom N number

Many of us like to have our aircraft identified with some personal type of N number. This is an easy thing to do and costs only $10 (plus paint!).

Start by writing a letter to the FAA Aircraft Registration Section, Box 25082, Oklahoma City, Ok. 73125, requesting reservation of the desired N number for assignment to the existing N number (which you show). Include a $10 check, made out to the Treasury of the U.S. In a few weeks, if the number is available, you should receive notice that it has been reserved for you, and you will receive FAA Form 8050-64. This is a form for you to declare that you have painted the new number on the aircraft. You have up to a year to paint it on, and you have five days after you paint it to get the Form 8050-64 in to the FAA. You *must* return the form, or the FAA will have your airplane recorded under the old number. If you don't paint it on, you simply lose the reservation, and the number would become available for someone else to use. Easy, isn't it?

It may be preferable to do the whole thing through a title-search company. They can breathe down the FAA's neck for you.

Expiration date

The certificate of registration expires when:

1. the aircraft is registered under the laws of a foreign country
2. the registration is cancelled at the written request of the owner
3. the aircraft is totally destroyed or scrapped
4. the ownership of the aircraft is transferred.

When you sell an aircraft, you must notify the FAA by filling in the back of the certificate of registration and mailing it to the FAA aircraft registry.

Another form of registration certificate, FAA Form 8050-6, the dealer's aircraft registration certificate, which is used by aircraft manufacturers and dealers, may not be used for purposes other than those necessary for or incidental to the sale of the aircraft or for flight checks.

The FAA does not issue any certificate of ownership or endorse any information with respect to the ownership on a certificate of aircraft registration.

The title search

The FAA aircraft registry is in the FAA Aeronautical Center at Will Rogers Field in Oklahoma City. There are 14 title-search firms in the area. Two of them are on the FAA grounds, literally across the street from the registry office. These are the AOPA Title Search Service (telephone: 800-654-4700) and Insured Aircraft Title Service, Inc. (telephone: 800-654-3282). The FAA supplies a list of title-search firms. If you phone the FAA for information and ask for the name of a title-search firm, they will ask you to pick a number from 1 to 14. Then they give

you the corresponding firm name from their list.

When a firm receives a request for a search, they order the file out of the archives from the FAA. Most of the firms have staff on hand all the time at the registry office (which is a public place), and they have their own direct phone lines into the office. A file can be pulled very quickly if necessary, but usually it takes a few hours. I went there and searched my own file for my Comanche. It was interesting to see the path of ownership over 14 years!

The file has two sections—the registry section, which has all the conveyances attached in sequence, and the air-data section, which has all the copies of FAA Form 337 that have been filed (see page 134 for a description of the FAA 337 form). The file may not be removed from the FAA premises, but photocopies may be made. When you order a title search, a clerk goes through the file and writes down all the details of the encumbrances and registered owner-

Plane Profile 14: Wing Derringer

Seats	2
Cruise speed, 65% power, 8,000 feet	182 knots
Range, 65% power, full optional fuel, 8,000 feet	764 nm
Maximum endurance	5.2 hours
Gross weight	3,050 pounds
Empty weight	2,100 pounds
Full optional fuel	522 pounds 87 gallons
Useful load, full fuel	428 pounds
Fuel efficiency, 65% power	11.5 nmpg
Stall speed, gear and flaps down	63 knots
Rate of climb, sea level	1,700 fpm 420 fpm s/e
Minimum field length	2,100 feet
Engine type 2 Lycoming IO-320-B1C	160 hp
Engine TBO	2,000 hours
Remarks Two-seater twin.	

ship current. It is possible to obtain a certified copy of the title documents or the search report, if desired. The details are sent to you or your bank. (Your bank won't lend you any money on an airplane until this search has been done and reported to them.) Fees for searches run around $10 and up.

Title insurance

Many title-search firms also offer title insurance. This protects you against liens or encumbrances that have not been filed with the FAA. For example, federal tax liens do not have to be filed with the FAA! Or a document may have been forged or falsely filed with the FAA, showing the aircraft to be clear when in fact it is not. AOPA title insurance costs $4 per $1,000, with a $40 minimum fee and a maximum insurance available of $100,000.

Recent flight experience: pilot in command

FAR 61.57 gives the recent-flight-experience requirements for FAA-certificated pilots. Here are some key points.

1. Flight review. Biennial flight review [BFR]). You may not act as pilot in command of an aircraft unless, within the preceding 24 months, you have:

a. Accomplished a flight review in an aircraft for which you are rated, given by an appropriately rated flight instructor or other person designated by the FAA

b. Had your log book endorsed by the person who gave you the review, certifying that you have satisfactorily accomplished the review

The requirement for a BFR may be satisfied alternatively by, within the preceding 24 months, satisfactorily completing a pilot proficiency check conducted by the FAA or an approved check pilot (such as an instrument check ride, a multi-engine ride, or the like). The BFR consists of a review of FAR 91 rules and an in-flight review of those maneuvers and procedures the check pilot considers to be necessary to demonstrate your ability to safely exercise the privileges of your certificate.

2. General experience. You may not act as pilot in command of an aircraft carrying passengers nor of an aircraft certificated for more than one pilot crewmember unless within the preceding 90 days you have made three takeoffs and three landings as the sole manipulator of the controls in an aircraft of the same category (e.g., airplane, helicopter, balloon), class (e.g., single-engine land, multi-engine land), and, if a type rating is required, type (e.g., Lear Jet 24). If the aircraft has a tailwheel, the landings must have been to a full stop.

3. Night experience. You may not act as pilot in command of an aircraft carrying passengers during the period beginning one hour after sunset and ending one hour before sunrise unless, within the preceding 90 days, you have made at least three takeoffs and landings to a full stop during that period in the category and class of aircraft to be used.

4. Instrument experience. a. Recent IFR experience. You may not act as pilot in command under IFR nor in weather conditions less than VFR minima unless you have, within the past six months:

(1) In the case of an aircraft other than a glider, logged at least six hours of instrument time under actual or simulated IFR conditions, at least three of which were in flight in the category of aircraft involved, including at least six instrument approaches, or passed an instrument-competency check in the category of aircraft involved.

(2) In the case of a glider, logged at

least three hours of instrument time, at least half of which were in a glider or an airplane. If a passenger is carried in a glider, at least three hours of instrument-flight time must have been in gliders.

b. Instrument competency check. If you *don't* meet the above recent-instrument-experience requirements during the *prescribed time* or *within six months thereafter*, you *must* pass an instrument-competency check flight in the category of aircraft involved, given by an FAA inspector, an FAA-approved check pilot, a certificated instrument-flight instructor, or an authorized member of the armed forces before you may fly as pilot in command under IFR or in weather conditions below VFR minima. The FAA may approve all or part of this check to be done in a flight simulator.

FAR 61.53 says you may not act as pilot in command or in any other capacity as a required flight crewmember while you have a known medical deficiency or increase of a known medical deficiency that would make you unable to meet the requirements for your current medical certificate. FAR 61.23 gives the following:

1. A first-class medical certificate expires at the end of the last day of:

a. The sixth month after the month of the date of examination shown on the certificate for operations requiring an airline transport certificate

b. The 12th month after the month of the date of examination shown on the certificate for operations requiring only a commercial pilot certificate

c. The 24th month after the month of the date of examination shown on the certificate for operations requiring only a private or student pilot certificate

2. A second-class certificate covers items b and c above.

3. A third-class certificate covers item c above.

What to do if your pilot certificate is lost

Lost or destroyed *airman* certificates may be replaced on application to the FAA. You have to write a letter to:

Department of Transportation,
Federal Aviation Administration,
Airman Certification Branch,
Box 25082,
Oklahoma City, Okla. 73125

The letter must state your name, permanent mailing address, social-security number (if any), date and place of birth, and any available information regarding the grade, number, date of certificate, and ratings on it. Send this with a $2 check made out to the Federal Aviation Administration.

A lost *medical* certificate may be replaced by following the same procedure (and sending another $2) to the same address. If it's only a medical certificate you need, amend the address to show Aeromedical Certification Branch instead of Airman Certification Branch. If you need both, use the Airman address.

You can request a telegram confirming that the certificate was issued, which may be carried as a certificate for up to 60 days pending receipt of the duplicate certificate. You can request such a telegram by letter or prepaid telegram to the previously given addresses (FAR 61.29).

Aviation insurance

The purpose of aviation insurance is to protect you, the aircraft owner. You need to protect your investment in the airplane, which you do by buying "hull" insurance. This will probably have a set deductible, such as $500, after which payments are made by the insurance company to satisfy proper claims for damage or loss. And you need to protect yourself against liability in the event that you cause damage or harm to other people's property or person. You could think of the liability insurance as a fund designed to defend you against a suit—up to the limit that you buy. You can also think of liability coverage as a fund to pay damages to innocent third parties who suffer due to some accident your airplane has. If you don't have the coverage, you might become personally liable for such damages, which theoretically could run into the millions.

Most aviation insurance will not protect *you*. You should carry life insurance or disability insurance to cover yourself. Some life and casualty companies will "rate" you for being a pilot—i.e., charge you a higher premium—or else they simply won't cover you when you're flying. This is especially noticeable in corporate group policies. With reasonable flying experience, you should be able to buy these types of policies without paying a rating for being a pilot.

How aviation insurance is offered

You can buy aviation insurance directly from an underwriter, such as Avemco or National Aviation Underwriters, through an aviation broker, such as Don Flower Associates or Bayly, Martin & Fay, Inc., or through your own fire, casualty, and property insurance agent.

The underwriter is the firm that actually carries the insurance and that pays you in the event of a claim. Some underwriters deal directly with the public; others deal through brokers or agents. A broker is an agent who shops around for you and finds you the best deal, according to your own special needs. An agent represents one or more specific insurance companies. I recommend that you deal either with a direct underwriter or an aviation broker. Your regular (nonaviation) local agent or broker is not likely to be qualified to seek out the kind of coverage you should have and probably won't know where to go for it beyond one or two companies.

The advantage of dealing with a direct underwriter is that it is relatively straightforward. They have toll-free telephone numbers and they specialize in aviation insurance. The person who handles your policy request is a pilot. If your insurance requirements are simple, you may save money by dealing direct. The person you speak to does nothing all day but talk to people about aviation insurance issued by the one company, so the area is a familiar one. However, you don't get to shop around at the direct underwriter. They have one deal, take it or leave it. Sure, you can modify the policy to save money, but their rates are their rates. The direct underwriters seem to be less flexible than those you find through a broker. They have set guidelines as to what each piece of coverage costs. Of course, the direct underwriter is also the outfit that pays your claim, so they are on the other side, so to speak, if you have to ask for money. They are less likely to go to bat for you if there are some gray areas about your claim.

A broker, on the other hand, is your agent. An *aviation* broker is the only kind to consider. Forget your Uncle Freddie. There are about 50 specialist aviation-insurance brokers in the U.S. The best way to pick one is to ask around. Note some of the advertising, find one that looks good, and ask the people at the airport whom *they* deal with. Ask your FBO. Best of all, ask people who have had claims in the last year or so. Ask about experience. Some brokers have been around for a long time, which speaks well for them. Talk to one or two brokers that you feel might be suitable. Find out if they speak your language or if they snow you with jargon.

There is absolutely nothing wrong with shopping around between direct underwriters and one or two brokers. You need to tell the important facts about the risk (that's you and your airplane) and then get some quotes. Aviation-insurance rates are totally unregulated, so they can vary widely for similar coverage. Shopping around between brokers is less effective, since they could well be quoting from the same underwriter.

Coverages available

You can insure almost anything you want to if you're prepared to pay the premium. If you're fairly standard in your requirements, you'll get a fairly standard quote. Here are the types of risks you can cover:

Liability. This can be specified as follows:

1. Each person—the limit to which liability claims will be met for each individual person in any one incident.

2. Property damage—the limit to which liability claims will be met for damage to property for each incident.

3. Each occurrence—this is the total limit of liability claims for both personal injury and property damage.

In other words, the total of (1) and (2) cannot exceed (3). Typical coverages might be: $50,000 each person, $300,000 property damage, $300,000 each occurrence. If you've got three passengers, you do property damage in an accident, and the passengers sue you and win $50,000 each, your insurance policy would only pay $150,000 for the property damage, since the single-occurrence limit is $300,000.

When buying this type of coverage, consider how many passenger seats

you have (obviously, your liability coverage does not extend to *you*, the pilot, since you can't sue yourself!) and your personal net worth. If you're worth $600,000, you should carry at least that in insurance. If you carried less than that, a suit could be won to collect $600,000 or more, and only part of that would be met by insurance. The difference would have to come from your own assets.

You can also buy single-limit liability coverage. This does not impose any maximum payment for each passenger. It merely sets a total limit for the whole occurrence. The more seats you have in the airplane, the greater the coverage you should have in this area. Low-time pilots may have difficulty getting single-limit liability. You can also get liability coverage that excludes your occupants. If you only carry your spouse in your two-seater, it would be silly to carry coverage on the occupants. So when you are talking to your insurance quoter, discuss who will ride with you. It could affect your needs and thus your rate.

If you are carrying passenger-liability insurance, it might be a good idea to have medical-payments coverage. This can provide you with extra protection.

All-risks. This can cover the airplane in flight or just on-the-ground not-in-motion. The term "all risks" means that the coverage extends to such things as wind damage, theft (including avionics and other components), taxiing damage, write-offs, fire, and so on. Some policies cover you for a stated value (which *you* state), upon which the premium is based, and others cover for current market value. The type to buy is "stated value." One that pays you the actual cash value of the plane is no good. You may end up with a replacement not to your taste foisted upon you. Another thing to avoid is a depreciation exclusion. This will also serve to reduce the payout in the event of a claim.

Some policies will return the unused premium to you if you have a total write-off. Others keep you paying until the policy expires. Some automatically cover a new airplane

1956 Cessna 172, the first year of production

that you buy for a few days—but you may only have a week or so to tell the insurance company about it. See page 127 for procedures to follow if you have an accident or your plane is stolen. And hope it doesn't happen!

Factors affecting premiums

There are three main factors affecting the premium you'll have to pay—pilot experience and qualifications, value of the aircraft and ease of repair, and type of flying.

1. Pilot experience. Obviously, the more experience you have, the better. Time in type is very important, as is "exotic" time—for example, retractable or multi-engine time if you are insuring a high-performance single or twin. Probably the biggest moneysaver of all insurance-wise is an instrument rating. It's not just that you can handle the airplane in a cloud. Being instrument-rated means that you are a better-disciplined pilot, and that counts.

2. Value of aircraft and ease of repair. An antique will cost more to insure than a Cessna 172. The way to save money on insurance in this area is to buy standard airplanes—Cherokees, 172s, Tigers. A Navion will probably cost you more to insure than a similar-year Bonanza since it isn't made any more, while the Bonanza is still being lovingly produced in Wichita.

3. Type of flying. Crop dusting? Fire fighting? Expect high premiums. Training also. But straight business and pleasure flying won't cost you nearly so much.

Coverage restrictions

1. Broken FARs. Good policies will cover you even if FARs are broken. This is a good question to ask your vendor. Even if you don't intentionally go around infringing regulations, FARs can be broken inadvertently, and the last thing you want is an insurance policy that penalizes you for that—you're probably in enough trouble already!

2. Other pilots. Coverage depends on the policy. Some policies allow certain types of pilots to fly your plane; others require you to specify who and give the relevant experience. You may be charged extra. You'll certainly be charged more if you're going to rent your plane to another pilot. Tell all to your insurance person.

3. Outside the U.S. Some policies provide coverage outside the U.S. You may have to activate this coverage by letting the underwriter know. You may also be covered in some areas but not others nearby, e.g., in the Bahamas but not in Cuba. You can, of course, arrange coverage almost anywhere for a price. Check with the company.

4. People not covered. Many liability policies specifically exclude the employees of the insured (workmen's compensation is supposed to handle

Plane Profile 15: Cessna Skyhawk

Seats	4
Cruise speed, 65% power, 8,000 feet	112 knots
Range, 65% power, full optional fuel, 8,000 feet	761 nm
Maximum endurance	7.8 hours
Gross weight	2,407 pounds
Empty weight	1,427 pounds
Full optional fuel	372 pounds 62 gallons
Useful load, full fuel	608 lbs
Fuel efficiency, 75% power	14.6 nmpg
Stall speed, flaps down	46 knots
Rate of climb, sea level	700 fpm
Minimum field length	1,390 feet
Engine type Lycoming O-320-D2J	160 hp
Engine TBO	2,000 hours
Remarks	Also available in a retractable-gear model as the Cutlass RG.

that)—some also exclude the close relatives of employees. A good question to ask if you fly for business. Many policies also won't cover crew members.

Renter-pilot insurance

Most aircraft insurance is written to protect the owner of the aircraft against liability and physical damage to the aircraft. The owner is protected even if not flying the aircraft. If the owner has not arranged specific coverage for a nonowner pilot, such a pilot may be liable for damage to the aircraft and even liability and property damage. Even if the owner has arranged coverage that respects you, you need to consider these points.

1. Is the owner's insurance in force? It might have been cancelled without your knowing.

2. Are the coverage limits enough? You may not think so.

3. Could your operation of the aircraft go beyond the scope of the existing coverage?

To be sure of adequate insurance coverage, your name should be on the policy. You can buy nonowner coverage through several underwriters. If you fly airplanes you don't own, it's a good idea to protect yourself. You can buy either liability coverage or aircraft-damage coverage or both.

Insurance and your leaseback

If you are leasing your aircraft back to an FBO, you should be covered under the FBO's insurance. However, you should also carry your own insurance that takes the leaseback into

consideration. No matter what the FBO's policy says, your own policy will probably protect you better. Talk this over with your FBO and his insurance outlet. Don't let the FBO get *you* to buy the coverage for the

Above The prototype Cessna 210, 1956
Below 22 years later, the Cessna Centurion.

leaseback. But you should have additional protection for yourself. Suppose something went wrong with the airplane and you forgot to tell the FBO. He goes out on a trip the next day, writes off the airplane, and kills three people. The accident investigation finds that something was wrong that you would have known about. The FBO's insurance company will cover him and promptly turn around and come after *you*. You definitely need your own protection.

Reading the insurance policy

Of course you should read your policy. It is a legal document and spells out just what the insurance company will and won't do for you. What they *will* do for you is given in the section entitled "insuring agreements." What they won't do is covered in the section called "exclusions." In addition, you will find "definitions," which is self-explanatory, "declarations," which is the part printed out by the computer listing the named insured,

the policy period, the coverages (limits of liability of the company), the description of the aircraft covered, the purposes of the flying involved, the pilots who are specified and the encumbrance, if any, and the endorsements. "Endorsements" include such things as a renewal guarantee, the fact that the airplane will be kept in an enclosed, locked, or guarded hangar while at home base, extended geographic limits, or a "breach of warranty" endorsement, which is a protection to the lender in the event that your claim is denied by the insurance company.

Payment of premiums

Most policies run for a year. You can pay the premium in one shot or in multiple payments, such as monthly

or quarterly. You may pay a slight extra charge for spreading the payments out. If you are late in making a payment, the insurance company can start to cancel the policy. You get a certain number of days of grace after the payment is due, after which you get a notice of cancellation with a due date. If payment is not made by this date, the policy is cancelled. Avoid this!

Inflation notwithstanding, you should expect a reduction of premium each year if you have made no claims—a "safe flying" discount. Furthermore, if you have low experience when you start buying your insurance and keep plugging away at the ratings, you should expect a reduction of premium each year in recognition of your increased experience and qualifications. You will pay a much higher pemium if your experience is low or your ratings are barren. The best risk is an instrument-rated pilot with a commercial certificate and at least 1,000 hours, with at least 200 hours in the type of air-

Plane Profile 16: Piper Tomahawk II

Seats	2
Cruise speed, 65% power, 8,000 feet	92 knots
Range, 65% power, full optional fuel, 8,000 feet	442 nm
Maximum endurance	5.8 hours
Gross weight	1,670 pounds
Empty weight	1,108 pounds
Full optional fuel	180 pounds
	30 gallons
Useful load, full fuel	382 pounds
Fuel efficiency, 65% power	19 nmpg
Stall speed, flaps down	47 knots
Rate of climb, sea level	718 fpm
Minimum field length	1,544 feet
Engine type Lycoming O-235-L2C	112 hp
Engine TBO	2,000 hours
Remarks Trainer	

plane involved. If you are a private pilot with 75 hours and you are buying a Beech Baron, expect to pay very high insurance premiums at first. Two years later, with 1,000 hours, an instrument rating, and no accidents, your premium should drop to an affordable amount.

Buying insurance for a short period of time

Sometimes you need insurance only for a short time—say, you are leasing an airplane for two months to take a trip. It is probably smarter to buy your insurance for the normal one-year period and cancel it when you no longer need it. You will then get a refund of unused premium. If you buy for just the two-month period, you could get into an awkward situation if you had to keep the plane a few extra days. You would have to arrange to extend the insurance or buy some new coverage— you might even forget and fly uncovered for a few days! Better to cancel it *after* you no longer need it.

Aircraft Storage

Storing your aircraft can represent one of the larger parts of your fixed costs, especially if you are near a large city. The cheapest form of storage is the *tiedown*. You are pretty much on your own here. *You* park it. *You* tie it down and untie it. And the aircraft is out, exposed to the elements, all the time. This can make for problems in cold weather, with the need for snow removal, preheating of engines, and general inconve-

nience. If you have to tie down, I recommend that you use a set of interior window covers. These are special heat-resistant covers that attach by Velcro inside the cabin and keep it relatively cool. They cost about $50. Without this kind of protection interior-cabin temperatures can get up to 150°F in the summer, which will ruin your radios very quickly, to say nothing of being very uncomfortable to get into at the start of a flight.

You can also obtain exterior window covers and wing and prop covers. There are engine air-intake covers, made out of plastic or even large chunks of foam. These are also a good idea, because they keep birds from building nests in the nice, warm engine compartment. You can even buy a fierce-looking plastic owl to stick on the tip of the prop, which is supposed to scare the birds away. Pitot-tube covers and external control locks are also desirable items to have if you are keeping the airplane outdoors. Naturally, the aircraft should in fact be *tied down* in the tiedown. You might invalidate your insurance if you didn't tie it down. Your insurance rate will probably be a little higher if you tie down rather than hangar your bird.

The ideal storage method is probably the T-hangar. Again, you are on your own as far as getting it in and out are concerned. I suggest you invest in an electric winch if your aircraft is heavy to move on your own. Then you can haul it in easily. T-hangars are not available at all airports, and there is usually a long waiting list for existing ones. What you can do at some airports is work a deal in conjunction with a few other aircraft owners to have a set of T-hangars built. You do it like a condominium apartment or in some similar joint manner. This might be worth looking into if the idea is feasible and appealing.

If you are lucky enough to base at a former military field, there are probably more hangars than airplanes on the field. One or two of the best ones will be used for aircraft storage en masse. The only problem here is that

you need people to help move the airplanes around if you want the one at the back out. If you are lucky, the hangar will be heated, which is desirable in the north in winter. Many small airports have only one hangar, which is used mostly for maintenance and storing the local Aerostar and Navajo. Your 172 will probably see the inside of it only when work has to be done or you want to melt the snow off the wings.

Another innovative storage idea is the Mini-Hangar. This is made out of fiberglass and is a housing that covers the nose of the aircraft back to the trailing edge of the wing.

In hot climates you will often find wall-less hangars or plane ports. These act purely as sun shields and help to cool things down a bit.

Choosing a fixed base operator

The FBO can make owning your own plane a very rewarding experience or an agony. If you have an opportunity to select one of several, what should you look for?

1. Maintenance facilities. Your ideal FBO should be a dealer for the type of aircraft you fly. If you have a Cherokee, the FBO should be a Piper dealer. If you fly a Baron, you want a Beech dealer, and so on. The maintenance staff should be experienced and skilled. When you go into the shop, look for certificates indicating that the personnel have gone through factory training programs. Is there more than one person with an IA (inspection authorization)? This would be preferable. One IA on vacation can ruin your plans. Talk to the chief mechanic and find out if he sincerely wants your business. Some FBOs are so tied up with corporate flight departments that they may not give you the kind of service you want. The corporation will probably come first if both of you need something *now*. Ask to see the inspection checklist they use for a 100-hour check or annual on your type of aircraft. Ask about rates. Do they have a flat rate for regular inspections? See if one of the A & Ps has special expertise in your type of plane. An A&P who is rebuilding his own TriPacer from a wreck would be the ideal person to work on *your* Tri-Pacer. If you find a mechanic whose work you like and whom you trust, request that mechanic! Don't be afraid to ask. Look around at the types of aircraft being worked on. Would your airplane fit in that environment? I would be reluctant to leave my shiny new Bonanza with people who are spending all their time on bunch of tatty old Navions and 170s. If you are in doubt about finding a mechanic, ask the local distributor or factory-service rep to recommend one who knows about your airplane and does good work.

2. Hangar facilities. Check the physical amenities in the hangar. Is it clean? Heated? What kind of fire protection is provided? Is it sprinklered?

Are the doors easy to operate? If you are going to store your aircraft in the hangar, what do you have to do to get it out? When can you *not* get it out? (I had to cancel a trip and go by car because I didn't realize that my FBO was closing on a certain holiday, and I couldn't get the Comanche out of the locked hangar!) What do they do in the winter? (My hangar opens on a scheduled basis only in cold weather. About every three hours you can move an airplane, otherwise forget it.) Does the hangar have suitable lounge, toilet, and flight-planning facilities? Some hangar toilets look like they belong in a Latin American jail. Are there telephones, direct lines to Flight Service, weather teletypes? What about food? Are there vending machines and do they work? Where can you park when you're on a trip? Can you drive out to the airplane if you have a lot of baggage? Is the hangar secure, or can anyone walk in anytime? Is it guarded or locked when closed? Is it patrolled by local or air-

port police?

3. Tiedown facilities. If you are going to tie your airplane down, what are the tiedowns like? Are they paved? What do you tie with—ropes, chains, straps? What is the tiedown point—a hook in the ground, a concrete block, or a wooden stake? Will the aircraft face into the prevailing wind when it is tied down? What assurance do you have that a strange, unkown Skylane won't be tied into your spot with the brakes on and the doors locked when you come back from a trip? Can you start the airplane at the tiedown, or will you have to move it first? Some tiedowns have a lot of gravel lying around just beneath your prop, and you know what *that* does to the propeller. Or the gravel might be on the tiedown *ahead* of you, so every time *he* moves out, you get sprayed with gravel!

4. FBO financial condition. It's sad but true that many FBOs are in desperate financial shape. It is a characteristic of the aviation business to attract dreamers rather than hard-

Profile 17: Beech Duchess 76

Seats	4
Cruise speed, 65% power, 8,000 feet	156 knots
Range, 65% power, full optional fuel, 8,000 feet	640 nm
Maximum endurance	5.1 hours
Gross weight	3,916 pounds
Empty weight	2,466 pounds
Full optional fuel	600 pounds
	100 gallons
Useful load, full fuel	850 pounds
Fuel efficiency, 65% power	8.4 nmpg
Stall speed, gear and flaps down	60 knots
Rate of climb, sea level	1,248 fpm
	235 fpm s/e
Minimum field length	2,119 feet
Engine type Lycoming O-360-A1G46D	180 hp
Engine TBO	2,000 hours
Remarks Contra-rotating propellers.	

Owning it

nosed businessmen. You should try to check out the proposed FBO's financial condition before getting heavily involved. A glance around the facilities should give you a basic idea, but a few discreet questions wouldn't hurt. You don't want to arrive at the airport to find that you can't get into the hangar because there is a big padlock and a bailiff's order on the door.

5. Convenience. One FBO may be on one side of the airport and another on the other side, a five-mile drive through the country beyond the main airport entrance. Consider your own ground-transportation time.

6. Airport facilities. If you have a choice of airports, consider these factors.

a. Runway lengths, widths, directions.
b. Tower or no tower?
c. FSS on the field?
d. Instrument approaches available?
e. Are the IFR approaches appropriate to the prevailing weather conditions? A high-limit VOR approach is not much good at an airport that gets a lot of fog—you want an ILS.
f. Customs on the field or available?
g. Convenience to your normal ground location.
h. Traffic situation. Do you have to wait 10 minutes for a takeoff clearance on a Saturday morning?
i. Are landing fees charged to aircraft based on the field?
j. What are the surrounding obstructions like? Is the airport surrounded by TV towers, with a factory at the end of the main runway?
k. Night-lighting availability and type. How do you turn it on if everybody's gone home? (Many airports have lighting that can be activated by keying the mike on a certain frequency.) Is there a **VASI** (visual approach-slope indicator)?
l. What about snow removal?
m. Do they have the type of fuel

you need? Do they truck it to you or must you taxi up to the pumps?
n. Is the airport very close to another one, enough to cause traffic problems? Is it in a TCA (terminal control area) or control zone? These may affect the type of equipment you need in the airplane or whether you can fly VFR in certain conditions.

Creating your own airplane reference manual

I have a large three-ring binder that I use as a complete reference manual for my Comanche. It is invaluable to me to have everything laid out in an easy-to-find format, so that when I'm talking to the FBO, the parts distributor, the avionics shop, or just reviewing my budget, I've got everything in one place. I recommend that you take this approach. Here's how to start. You will need the following ingredients.

1. A large, sturdy three-ring binder. Mine has 2¼" rings. It takes standard 8½"-x-11" sheets. The spine is 3" thick on the outside.
2. Two sets of five tabbed-divider index sheets.
3. A supply of 3-column ledger sheets, 3-hole punched.
4. A supply of blank paper.
5. A three-hole puncher.

Here are the headings I use for the divider sheets:

1. Suppliers
2. ADs and service bulletins
3. Flight manual
4. Maintenance
5. Expenses
6. Installed equipment
7. Potential equipment
8. Correspondence
9. Miscellaneous

Let's look at the contents of each section in greater detail.

1. Suppliers. This is simply a sheet I typed up with the details of all the suppiers I deal with. I show the name, address, phone number, and person to contact for the following:

a. Airframe manufacturer
b. Local distributor
c. Local dealer
d. Engine manufacturer
e. Engine overhauler
f. Propeller manufacturer
g. Propel overhauler
h. Radio manufacturers
i. Radio shop
j. FBO (list names of all the people you know who work on the airplane—when you are calling in to get an answer on "when it will be ready." It helps to know more than one person in case your main contact is not available)
k. The airport manager and fuel dealer, if different from the FBO
l. Autopilot manufacturer
m. Autopilot service
n. The paint shop that painted the airplane last
o. The people involved in refurbishing the interior, if applicable
p. The oxygen supplier and where to get it serviced
q. Your chart-subscription agency and the expiration dates—show what coverage you subscribe to
r. Your insurance outlet—show policy number and expiration date
s. The local FAA General Aviation District Office
t. The local FAA Flight Service Station
u. Record the airplane serial number, N number, and year of manufacture and your own pilot certificate number

2. ADs and bulletins. Place these here in numerical order as you receive them.

3. Flight manual. My flight manual was very tatty since the airplane was

13 years old when I got it. I simply made Xerox copies and inserted one set in this binder. The other set I kept in the airplane file. The original tatty set I put in an envelope for safekeeping.

4. Maintenance. In this section I keep a copy of the Piper inspection which lists the items to be performed during an inspection. I also file the detailed reports supplied by the FBO of work done.

5. Expenses. This is where the ledger sheets come in (see examples). Here I record *all* expenses relating to the airplane under the following separate headings (a different sheet for each heading):

  a. Fuel and oil—every separate purchase is recorded in chronological order

  b. Cost of new items bought to upgrade aircraft, including labor

  c. Cost of items bought to re-place or repair worn parts, including labor

  d. General maintenance expense

  e. Cost of complying with ADs

  f. Hangarage or storage fees

  g. Parking and landing fees

  h. Charts, etc.

  i. Insurance and licensing fees

  j. I keep a separate record of sales taxes paid for tax-deduction purposes

  k. Record of fuel-tax rebates obtained from the various states

6. Installed equipment. In this section I simply keep the brochures for all equipment I have in the airplane—avionics, unusual instruments, oxygen system, and so on.

7. Potential equipment. This is my dream file. In here I put the brochures for the items I would like to add in the future or ones I am thinking about.

8. Correspondence. Any letters about the airplane go in here—quotes from suppliers, questions answered and so on.

9. Miscellaneous. This is where you put anything else that you can't find a home for that relates to the airplane.

One more thing. I keep a sharp color photo of the instrument panel in the book (in the flight-manual section) for reference when I'm talking to the shop on the phone. It's handy to have, and you can look at it when you feel lonesome for your bird!

This is my instrument panel

Plane Profile 18: Cessna Stationair 8

Seats	8
Cruise speed, 65% power, 8,000 feet	136 knots
Range, 65% power, full optional fuel, 8,000 feet	530 nm
Maximum endurance	4.9 hours
Gross weight	3,812 pounds
Empty weight	2,123 pounds
Full optional fuel	438 pounds
	73 gallons
Useful load, full fuel	1,251 pounds
Fuel efficiency, 65% power	10 nmpg
Stall speed, flaps down	58 knots
Rate of climb, sea level	810 fpm
Minimum field length	1,970 feet
Engine type Continental IO-520-F	300 hp
Engine TBO	1,400 hours
Remarks Also available in turbocharged version.	

Owning it

Factory publications

When you buy an aircraft, you should receive at least the following materials, whether the airplane is new or used:

1. Pilot's operating handbook
2. Airplane flight manual
3. Equipment list
4. Weight and balance report
5. Aircraft log book
6. Engine log book(s)
7. Warranties, if applicable

In addition you can obtain from the manufacturer copies of the parts manual and service manual, if you desire.

Factories issue various service publications as needed. Piper has *Service Bulletins* and *Service Letters*. Piper considers bulletins to be mandatory service items, while letters are optional. Beech publishes *Service Instructions* in three classes. Class Is cover changes, inspections, and modifications that could affect safety.

Beech considers these to be mandatory compliance items. Class IIs cover changes and modifications considered beneficial to the owner and highly recommended. Class IIIs cover optional suggestions. Cessna also publishes *Service Letters*.

These may be free or available on a subscription basis, depending on the factory and how long you have owned the airplane. In any event, here is a piece of good advice: if you buy a used airplane, write immediately to the factory telling them what you have done, giving the model and serial number of the aircraft and asking for a complete set of service bulletins or letters to date. And ask to be put on the mailing list for future copies (which may cost you a nominal amount). Piper automatically sends their bulletins free to all registered owners per the FAA lists, but they don't send you back issues unless you ask for them.

GAMA format handbooks

The General Aviation Manufacturers' Association has established standard formats for pilot's operating handbooks and service manuals. All handbooks and manuals for new aircraft are produced on these formats. This is a major breakthrough from what went before in many cases. Much more information is given. The following headings in any pilot's operating handbook are standard, for example:

Section 1. General
Section 2. Limitations
Section 3. Emergency procedures
Section 4. Normal procedures
Section 5. Performance
Section 6. Weight and balance
Section 7. Systems description
Section 8. Handling, servicing, and maintenance
Section 9. Supplements
Section 10. Safety information

A covey of Centurions. Back up a bit, three!

Beechcraft has reformatted all its pilot's handbooks to the GAMA format—even for the early Bonanzas—but the other manufacturers have not indicated that they would do this. They should, I think.

The new format makes it much easier for a pilot to switch from one aircraft to another. Everything is in the same place. Now if we can just get the cockpits standardized!

Weight and balance

As airplanes acquire more seats and remote baggage compartments, proper weight and balance control becomes increasingly necessary. It's pretty hard to load a Cessna 182 outside its approved limits. A hypothetical load of a lady driver at 120 lbs, two 200-lb football payers in the rear seat, 120 lbs of baggage in the rear compartment, and 40 gallons of fuel still keeps the aircraft within its aft center-of-gravity (CG) limit. But start messing around with an Aztec or a Cherokee Six, with all those seats and baggage spaces, and you could be in trouble.

It is important that the aircraft be operated within its CG range at all times. Some aircraft may be within the range on takeoff with full tanks and go out of the range as the fuel is used up. The pilot's operating handbook for the aircraft will have a complete description of the weight and balance calculations required, and these should be studied before each flight if you think there might be a loading problem. If you misload the aircraft, you will have undesirable characteristics in flight. An overloaded aircraft will not take off so fast or climb so well as a properly loaded bird. If the CG is too far forward, it may be difficult to rotate the aircraft for takeoff or landing. If the CG is too far aft, the airplane may rotate prematurely on takeoff or tend to pitch up during climb. Longitudinal stability will be reduced. This can lead to inadvertent stalls or spins, and spin recovery will be more difficult than when the CG is within approved limits.

Each airplane has its own individual weight and balance data. This will be found in the airplane flight manual. It is the owner's responsibility to ensure that changes in equipment are reflected in a new weight and balance and in an addendum to the equipment list. A good way to do this is to keep a running tally of changes in equipment and the effect of these on the basic empty weight and CG. The current equipment list and basic empty weight and CG information must stay with the aircraft when it is sold. If the data is lost, the FAA requires that the airplane be reweighed and that an inventory of installed equipment be conducted to create a new equipment list.

1982 Piper Turbo Saratoga

State sales and use taxes

Most states and some cities impose sales and use taxes on aircraft. At the end of 1977 only Alaska, Delaware, Montana, New Hampshire, and Oregon did not have such taxes.

The *sales tax* is usually imposed on the price of tangible personal property sold within the taxing state. If you live in a state that charges a sales tax and you buy an aircraft in a state that has no tax, you will most likely have to pay a *use tax* at the same rate as the sales tax. If you paid a state sales tax where you bought the aircraft, your home state will probably give you a credit for what you paid.

Some states exempt casual sales, e.g., between two private individuals, from these taxes, while others do not. Other states do not tax the sale of an aircraft that is to be used outside the state. Some states may charge a use tax on an out-of-state purchase if the aircraft is based within the state and the owner lives outside the state. Some states, such as Illinois, South Dakota, Virginia, and Wisconsin, will impose a use tax when the aircraft is registered in the state. Some states allow exemptions from these taxes if the aircraft is used for certain purposes only, such as training or agricultural purposes.

The various laws are so complex that it is impossible to give any specific advice for each state. The best thing to do is to save any evidence of taxes paid or that the transaction was a casual one. Then sit back and wait for someone to contact you and suggest that your airplane is subject to a sales or use tax. If you haven't paid the tax and are found liable, you may have to pay the tax, which could be as much as 7% of the cost of the aircraft, depending on the state, even many months after your purchase.

State aviation-gas-tax refunds

In 1982, 38 states charged a tax on aviation gasoline. This charge is often a motor-vehicle road tax, and in 21 of the states a full or partial refund of the tax may be obtained. Twelve states charged no tax on aviation gasoline. The box shows the states' action and what they did in 1982.

States charging tax	Some exemption or refund available
Alabama	
Alaska	
Arizona	X
California	X
Delaware	X
Georgia	
Hawaii	
Idaho	
Iowa	X
Kansas	X
Kentucky	X
Louisiana	X
Maine	X
Maryland	X
Michigan	
Minnesota	X
Mississippi	X
Missouri	X
Montana	
Nebraska	X
Nevada	X
New Hampshire	
New Jersey	X
New Mexico	X
New York	X
North Dakota	X
Oklahoma	
Oregon	
Pennsylvania	
Rhode Island	X
South Dakota	X
Tennessee	
Utah	
Vermont	
Virginia	
Washington	
Wisconsin	X
Wyoming	

Two old favorites, the Piper Comanche B and Twin Comanche B over Toronto harbor.

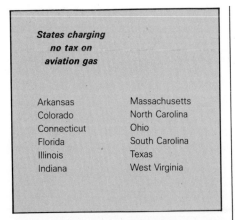

**States charging
no tax on
aviation gas**

Arkansas	Massachusetts
Colorado	North Carolina
Connecticut	Ohio
Florida	South Carolina
Illinois	Texas
Indiana	West Virginia

Procedures for obtaining refunds vary by state. In some states you sign an exemption form when you buy the gas and so are not charged. In others you have to file a request for a refund. Some states will not accept credit-card invoices unless they are marked "Paid," which means that you have to go back to the credit-card company and ask them to mark your invoices as paid—bureaucracy works in wondrous ways! Some states give a deadline within which the refund claim must be made. Ask where you buy gas how to do it. Refunds run up to about 10¢ per gallon, so it is worth it if you go through a lot of aviation gas.

Keeping track of your expenses

If you are making any claims for tax deductions due to business use of your aircraft, you *must* keep good expense records. Even if you are flying strictly for pleasure, it is a good idea to keep a record of your expenses so that you can make the most efficient use of your resources.

The best way to record expenses is to invest in a copy of the *Pilot's Taxlog Flight Record*. This costs about $15 and provides you with both a record of expenses and a log book so that you can quickly substantiate and relate the expense to the trip. The book is well worth the money, and it's even tax-deductible! You can order it through:

Taxlogs Unlimited,
20 Galli Drive,
Ignacio, CA 94947.
Telephone: 800-453-2444

If you prefer to keep your own records, here are some suggested formats. You will need a pad of multi-columned analysis paper—the kind accountants use. You should have at least three columns per page. If you get it in the 8½-×11-inch size, you can keep the sheets in your own airplane reference manual (see page 106). I suggest that you use separate sheets for each of the following.

1. Fuel and oil. Record every separate purchase in chronological order. Show the state where purchased so that you can determine whether it is worthwhile to claim an aviation-gas-tax refund if there is one available (see opposite page).
2. Cost of new items bought to upgrade aircraft, including labor.
3. Cost of items bought to replace or repair worn parts, including labor.
4. General maintenance expense.
5. Cost of complying with ADs.
6. Hangarage or storage fees.
7. Parking and landing fees, etc.
8. Charts, etc.
9. Insurance and licensing fees.
10. A separate record of sales taxes paid (taken from the previous pages) for tax-deduction purposes.
11. A separate record of fuel-tax rebates obtained.

See the illustration on page 114 for suggested formats. Your accountant will help you set up recordkeeping if you are running your plane on a leaseback.

Staying with it

Staying with the ownership of an airplane demands that you keep in touch with what's going on. I recommend at least that you become a member of the Aircraft Owners and Pilots Association. Their address is:

AOPA,
Box 5800,
Washington, DC 20014.

In addition, I recommend that you read "The Aviation Consumer", which carries no advertising and has been known to refer to a spade as a spade. Their address is:

The Aviation Consumer,
1111 East Putnam Ave.
Riverside, CT 06878.

This Ercoupe offers cheap flying, but the owner has spent a lot of money upgrading it

Owning it

Calculating your direct operating costs

Let us now develop direct operating costs for your own situation. We will work these figures out on the basis of 100 hours of utilization, and then you can factor them for your actual or expected utilization.

1. Fuel

What power setting will you use? Indicate the fuel consumption in gallons per hour for the proposed setting:

Power setting		Fuel consumption	
55%	☐	_____	GPH
65%	☐	_____	GPH
75%	☐	_____	GPH

Multiply answer by 110 to give gallons used per 100 hours (with an additional 10 percent for takeoff, taxi, climb, and landing fuel). For example, if you intend to use 65% power and your fuel consumption at this setting is 12 GPH, multiply 12 × 110 = 1,320 gallons per 100 hours. What do you pay for fuel? Exclude recoverable fuel taxes (see page 110).

Price of fuel = $ _____ per gallon.

Work this out for your 100 hours. For example, if your pay $1.80 per gallon, 1.80 × 1320 = $2,376 per 100 hours.

Cost for 100 hours is:

$ _____ per gallon X _____ gallons

= $ _____ per 100 hours.

2. Oil

What is your oil consumption? What is your oil capacity? How often will you carry out an oil change? Assuming, for example, that you consume 1 quart of oil over three hours and that you have a 12-quart oil tank and that you change the oil every 50 hours, your calculation would look like this:

Oil used per 100 hours = $\frac{100}{3}$ = 33.3 quarts

Plus 2 12-quart oil changes = 24 quarts

Total oil used = 57.3 quarts.

How much do you pay for oil? Work that out as a cost. At $2 a quart, our cost in the example is $114.67 per 100 hours. Yours?

Oil used per 100 hours divided by number of hours per quart (HPQ) =

$\frac{100}{HPQ}$ = _____ quarts per 100 hours.

Plus oil used for oil changes:

changes _____ X _____ quarts

per change = _____ quarts per 100 hours.

Total oil used per 100 hours = _____ quarts.

Cost per quart $ _____ = $ _____ per 100 hours.

3. Oxygen

(If you have no oxygen, skip to item 4.) What does it cost you for a refill?

Average cost per refill $ _____

How long does one refill last?

One refill lasts _____ hours for one person.

How many people on average will use the oxygen? _____ people.

How many flying hours will one refill last?

One refill _____ hours

divided by _____ people using

equals _____ flying hours capacity.

Of 100 hours, how many will be spent above 10,000 feet? _____ hours.

How many refills will you need per 100 hours? Number of hours above 10,000 feet divided

by capacity equals _____ refills X

cost per refill $ _____ equals cost of

oxygen per 100 hours $ _____.

For example, my oxygen feeds two people for 1.5 hours each. I fly about 5 hours per 100 above 10,000 feet: 5 divided by 1.5 = 3.3, so I need 3.3 refills per 100 hours. At $12 per refill, my cost per 100 hours for oxygen is 12 × 3.3 = $39.60.

4. Maintenance

This does not include regular maintenance checks, which are covered in (6). How can you figure how much maintenance you're going to need? You can't. You should ask other owners what their story is and talk to your FBO. The factors affecting the need for maintenance outside regularly scheduled maintenance are listed below.

a. Airplane age. A new aircraft should need little unexpected maintenance, and anything needed should be covered by warranty. An older airplane, especially one that is out of shape, will probably need a fair amount. Based on your own judgment, you could figure maybe one hour of maintenance for every five hours of flying on an older aircraft.

b. Airplane complexity. The more complex an aircraft, the more things there are to go wrong. Retractable gear, adjustable propellers, more than one engine, hydraulic

systems, complicated avionics installations, pressurization — these are the sorts of things that will drive your maintenance bills up. Depending on complexity, you may like to make an allowance of an hour or so every ten flying hours.

c. Type of operation. An aircraft subjected to basic training flights all the time is going to need much more maintenance than one that is owner-flown on long cross-country trips by an experienced pilot. If you own an airplane and lease it back to a flight school or rental operation, figure on quite a bit more maintenance, especially if it is also old or complex.

Based on the above, what do you estimate your need for maintenance (labor costs only) to be outside regularly scheduled maintenance?

Per 100 hours, _____ extra maintenance

hours will be needed at $ _____ per hour =

$ _____ maintenance cost per 100 hours.

For example, I figure I need 1 hour of maintenance per 10 hours. This is 10 hours per 100 at $25 per hour for labor = $250 per 100 hours.

5. Spare parts

These are also very hard to predict as an expense item. The same factors affecting maintenance will affect your parts expense. You're talking here about things that go wrong and need to be replaced. Here's what I had to replace in the first 150 hours of flying my 13-year-old Comanche (it had 3,450 hours on it when I bought it):

Item	Parts cost	Labor cost
Left aux fuel cell	$157	$ 58
Turn & bank gauge	75	25
Battery	47	—
Landing light (2)	18	30
Rebuild starter & generator	133	72
Door restraint	22	—
Vacuum pump	129	45
Right tire	42	30
Right brake lining	11	15
Repair stall warner	5	60
Fix leak in manifold pressure gauge line	1	15
Total cost	$640	$350

This worked out to a cost per hour of $4.27 for parts and $2.33 for labor. However, many of the things that needed to be fixed related to the condition of the airplane when I bought it. It is now in much better shape, and my costs have dropped accordingly. The labor worked out to about 1.5 hours per 10 hours flying.

6. Reserve for inspections

Unless you are operating under FAR 135, there is no requirement for a private aircraft operator to have any regular inspections other than the annual. We include the cost of the annual inspection as one of our fixed costs of operation. If you run regular inspections beyond the annual, which I recommend, find out what the FBO rate is for the inspection and amortize this over your use. Since we are figuring here on a per-100-hour utilization, show the 100-hour rate if you are going to have these performed:

Cost of 100-hour inspection $ _____.

If you also schedule 50-hour inspections, then show the cost of two of these, instead:

Cost of two 50-hour inspections $ _____.

7. Reserve for engine overhaul

(If you have a twin, work this out for each engine.*)

What is the TBO for your engine?

TBO is _____ hours.

What is the time since major overhaul (SMOH) or since new? _____ hours ☐SMOH ☐new

How many hours do you have left to TBO?

Hours to recommended overhaul:

_____ hours.

What is the cost of replacing the engine?

Cost of replacement $ _____

This is for:
New exchange ☐
Factory-remanufactured engine ☐
Overhaul existing engine ☐

What is the cost per engine hour to amortize replacement? Figure it out:

TBO hours _____

minus hours
SMOH or new _____

equals hours
remaining _____

Cost of overhaul $ _____

divided by hours
left on engine _____

equals cost per
hour $ _____

X 100 equals cost
per 100 hours $ _____

*Twin cost $ _____

8. Reserve for repetitive ADs

What ADs are outstanding that need to be complied with at regular intervals (for details see page 71)? List them here:

AD number	Frequency (hours)	Cost $	Cost per 100 hours
_____	_____	_____	_____
_____	_____	_____	_____
_____	_____	_____	_____
_____	_____	_____	_____
_____	_____	_____	_____
_____	_____	_____	_____

Total cost per 100 hours of repetitive ADs:

$ _____ per 100 hours.

9. Reserve for life-limited components

What components have life limitations?

Propeller _____ hours. Cost $ _____

Cost per 100 hours $ _____. X 2 (for twin) $ _____

Others:

Item	Life	Cost to replace	Cost per 100 hours
_____	_____	_____	_____
_____	_____	_____	_____
_____	_____	_____	_____
_____	_____	_____	_____

Total cost per 100 hours of life-limited items $ _____ per 100 hours.

10. Landing and parking fees

Do you fly regularly into any airports that charge landing or parking fees? Figure your approximate outlay per 100 hours for these items:

Airport	Landing fee	Parking fee	Frequency per 100 hours	Total cost per 100 hours
_____	$ ___	$ ___	_____	$ _____
_____	$ ___	$ ___	_____	$ _____
_____	$ ___	$ ___	_____	$ _____
_____	$ ___	$ ___	_____	$ _____
_____	$ ___	$ ___	_____	$ _____
_____	$ ___	$ ___	_____	$ _____
_____	$ ___	$ ___	_____	$ _____
_____	$ ___	$ ___	_____	$ _____
_____	$ ___	$ ___	_____	$ _____
_____	$ ___	$ ___	_____	$ _____

Total cost per 100 hours for landing and parking fees: $ _____ per 100 hours.

11. Putting it all together

Now assemble all these costs to determine the direct operating cost for the aircraft:

Item	Cost per 100 hours
1. Fuel	$ _____
2. Oil	$ _____
3. Oxygen	$ _____
4. Maintenance	$ _____
5. Spare parts	$ _____
6. Reserve for regular inspections	$ _____
7. Reserve for engine overhaul	$ _____
8. Reserve for repetitive AD compliance	$ _____
9. Reserve for life-limited components	$ _____
10. Landing and parking fees	$ _____
Total cost per 100 hours	$ _____

Divide this by 100 to achieve the direct operating cost per hour:

Direct operating cost per hour $ _____

FUEL & OIL 1981

DATE		LOCATION	FUEL				OIL	
			1 GALLS	2 $/GAL	3 COST	4 STATE TAX	5 QTS	6 $
2	19	LDJ	57.0	1.80	91.80	NJ	3.	6 —
2	21	DCA	41.0	1.96	80.36	VA		
2	26	HYA	21.0	1.93	40.53	MA	—	
2	5	LDJ						

MAINTENANCE 1987

DATE		ITEM	1 W/O #	2 TACH	3 PARTS $	4 LABOR HRS	5 LABOR $	6 TAXES
4	23	Pk brake, A/P Fuel gauge	7736	691.2	4.69	3.25	52.00	.33
6	22	Prop Grease leak	S 3022	771.0	108.70	8.25	132.00	21.95
9	17	Compass swing	8022	842.2	—	3.0	45.00	—
9	27	Inter Checks	8022	845.1		3.0	45.00	

A-D COMPLIANCE 1987

DATE		AD #	1 TACH	2 PARTS $	3 LABOR HRS	4 LABOR $	5 TAXES	6
4	23	68-13-3	609.6	1.52	7.0	101.50	19.91	
9	14	75-12-6	840.0	—	3.0	45.—	—	
11	20	77-13-21	900.2	7.591	8.0	120.50	22.57	

LANDING & PARKING FEES ETC 1987

DATE		LOCATION	1 LANDING	2 PARKING	3 HANGAR	4 CHARTS	5 MISC	6
6	25	HFD	—	3 —		2.08		
7	17	ACK	1 —	2 —			2 —	
8	15	BOS	5 —	2 —				
8	20	BUF	—	2.50				

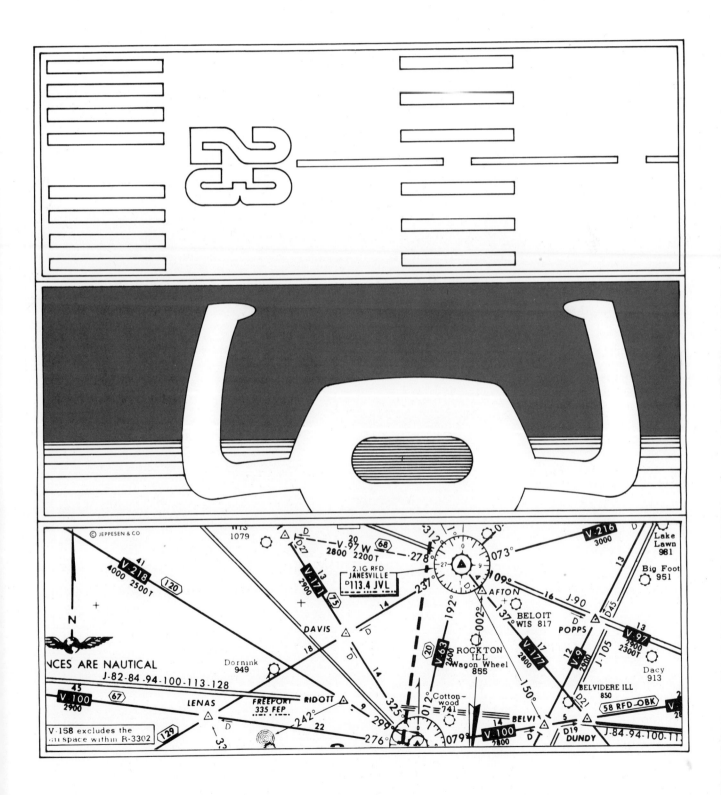

Operating it

Charts

Your need for charts is related to the type of flying you do. You can get supersophisticated coverages, moderately so, or bare-minimum materials.

You can divide your needs into three basic categories—enroute charts, approach charts, and basic airport guides. The best service you can get, and I recommend it strongly, is the Jeppesen Airway Manual service. This is issued on a subscription basis (minimum one year). You can buy just the coverage you need to suit both IFR and VFR requirements. The service consists of enroute radio-navigation charts, area charts of congested regions, SID and STAR (standard instrument departure and standard terminal arrival route) charts, and instrument approach procedure charts. The latter include airport diagrams with runway and taxiway layouts. Revisions are issued every week.

You can also buy VFR and RNAV charts and a service called J-Aid, which gives you airport diagrams and data for VFR fields as well as most of the stuff found in the Airman's Guide and appropriate FARs. This is also amended regularly. One of the best features of the Jeppesen service is the "trip-kit." Subscribers can order coverage for an area outside their normal subscription area for one-shot trips. This service will supply anything you need, from one approach plate right up to complete coverage. However, this service is not amended.

Jeppesen is very good at filling your needs. They ask for a couple of weeks notice, but you can phone in your order and they'll get it out to you right away. I once phoned them at 1 P.M. New York time on a Friday and I had the charts in the next morning's mail (from Denver to New York!). Obviously, they don't guarantee it'll get there, and they won't take them back if they're too late. I can't recommend Jeppesen too highly. It's simply the best. All the airlines use it (they get custom coverages for their routes, so every-

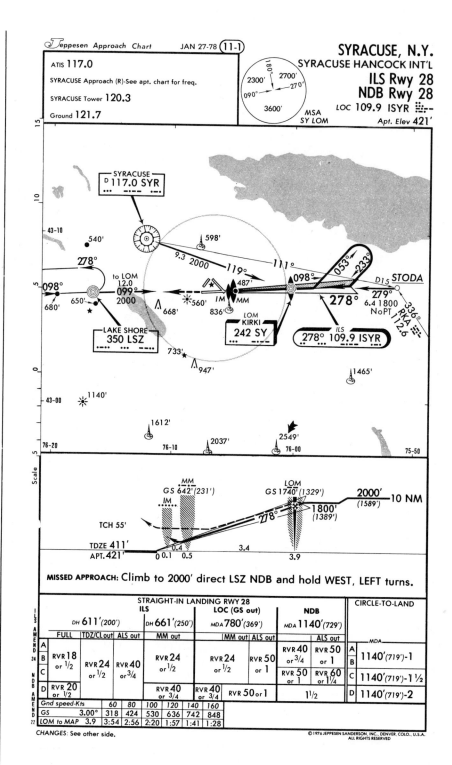

Copyright Jeppesen Sanderson. Chart slightly reduced for illustration. Not to be used for navigation.

116

Operating it

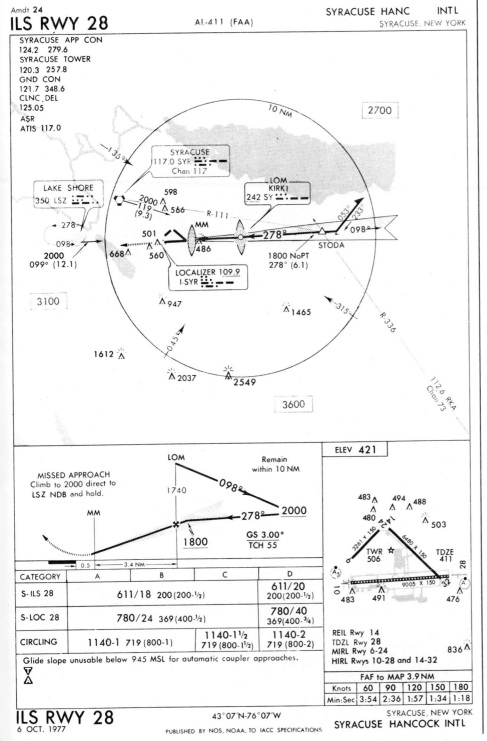

ILS RWY 28 AL-411 (FAA) SYRACUSE HANC INTL
SYRACUSE, NEW YORK

SYRACUSE APP CON
124.2 279.6
SYRACUSE TOWER
120.3 257.8
GND CON
121.7 348.6
CLNC DEL
125.05
ASR
ATIS 117.0

10 NM
2700

LAKE SHORE
350 LSZ

SYRACUSE
117.0 SYR
Chan 117

LOM
KIRKI
242 SY

R-111

598
2000
119
(9.3) 566

278

233

098

STODA

501
668 560

2000
099° (12.1)

486

MM

278

1800 NoPT
278° (6.1)

LOCALIZER 109.9
I-SYR

3100

947

1465

315

R-336

1612

2037 2549

3600

112.6 RKA
Chan 73

MISSED APPROACH
Climb to 2000 direct to
LSZ NDB and hold.

LOM

Remain
within 10 NM

098°

1740

MM

278° 2000

1800

GS 3.00°
TCH 55

0.5 3.4 NM

ELEV 421

483 494 488
480 503
142

TWR
506

TDZE
411

3761 x 150 6480 x 150

28

10

9005 X 150

32

483 491 476

REIL Rwy 14
TDZL Rwy 28
MIRL Rwy 6-24
HIRL Rwys 10-28 and 14-32

836

CATEGORY	A	B	C	D
S-ILS 28	611/18 200 (200-½)			611/20 200 (200-½)
S-LOC 28	780/24 369 (400-½)			780/40 369 (400-¾)
CIRCLING	1140-1 719 (800-1)		1140-1½ 719 (800-1½)	1140-2 719 (800-2)

Glide slope unusable below 945 MSL for automatic coupler approaches.

FAF to MAP 3.9 NM					
Knots	60	90	120	150	180
Min:Sec	3:54	2:36	1:57	1:34	1:18

ILS RWY 28 43°07'N-76°07'W SYRACUSE, NEW YORK

thing fits in one binder). Their address is:

Jeppesen Sanderson,
Box 3279,
Englewood, CO 80112
Telephone: 303-779-5757

Jeppesen Trip Kits are also available to AOPA members through AOPA.

The alternative to Jeppesen is the NOS (National Oceanic Survey) service. Their charts look a little different from Jeppesen's. You can buy similar area coverages on an annual subscription basis. I used to use NOS a few years ago. One advantage is that the NOS charts come in bound booklets rather than in loose-leaf form, as do Jeppesen's. Another is that the airport diagram is included on the front of the instrument-approach chart, whereas Jepp puts it all by itself on the back, necessitating a bit more shuffling. If you use NOS, you'll also need some kind of VFR airport charts and a subscription to the Airman's Information Manual (AIM) to approach the coverage of the Jepp service.

Something you should know is that all FAA facilities have the NOS charts in front of them, not the Jepps. The two sets of charts are different in format. If you are having a problem interpreting a chart and you are trying to get guidance from the tower or approach control over the radio while using Jepps, bear in mind that the FAA person will be looking at a different-format document than yours. Their address is:

NOS,
Riverdale, Md. 20840
Telephone: 301-436-6993

There are two other alternatives to Jepp and NOS, which are strictly low-budget deals and quite satisfactory for the simple approach (i.e, no heavy IFR all over the place). One service is Sky Prints. This is a large atlas that is issued every year and contains its own format enroute charts. It is amended by a monthly sticker that you place on the appropriate chart to show, in text form only, the changes. Another service is Pro-Plates. This reproduces, from NOS charts, the main IFR approach at all civilian airports (excluding

Operating it

ADF approaches for some reason). Monthly update sheets are issued. The disadvantage is that if you are going into an airport where a secondary approach is being used, you won't have the chart. This could prove awkward in a solid IFR environment. But the service is not very expensive and easy to keep up. It is particularly useful if you don't have an ADF in your airplane, because then you're twice damned if that's the only type of approach available. No ADF and no ADF chart!

For VFR navigation you have a choice between the NOS VFR sectional charts and the world aeronautical charts. The sectionals are best for VFR navigation, being on a scale of 1:500,000 (about 8 miles to the inch), whereas the WACs are on a 1:1,000,000 scale (about 16 miles to the inch). Terminal area charts on a

1:250,000 scale (about 4 miles to the inch) are available for many metropolitan areas. An excellent Flight Case Planning chart is also issued by NOS, along with IFR and VFR wall planning charts.

A cheap alternative to the NOS charts for VFR navigation are the charts put out by the various state aeronautical commissions. Not all states do them, but many are available and are perfectly satisfactory and usually free of charge. Check with your state aeronautics commission to see if one is available (see page 222).

There are several airport guides available. These feature airport diagrams and data such as service facilities, local navaids, phone numbers, and so on.

AOPA's *Airports USA* is a very comprehensive listing-type guide. (It includes airport diagrams of IFR

airports picked up from the NOS IFR approach charts, but these are grouped together in a section at the front of the book. The diagrams do not accompany the airport listings.) The big advantage is that they have very good telephone-number information. They list local hotels and motels for each airport, with the phone number. This is a very useful feature. The book is available as a membership item but may also be purchased by nonmembers of AOPA. The guide also includes weather and FSS phone numbers and customs information.

Flight Guide, published by Airguide Publications, Inc., provides an airport directory in two looseleaf volumes for the east and west. It is very compact and contains good airport diagrams. It has a revision service.

If you are going to Canada, you

A part of the Sky Prints enroute chart, actual size

Copyright Sky Prints Corporation. Used with permission.

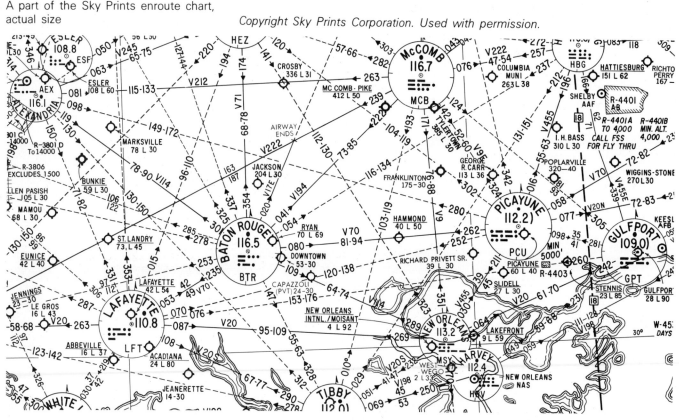

can get good IFR coverage through Jeppesen. If you are a Jepp subscriber, you can order a trip kit for the regions you visit (with no revision service).

The Canadian government publishes charts on the same scales as the U.S. charts—world charts at 1:1,000,000; Canadian pilotage charts (similar to sectionals) at 1:500,000; and a useful series of route charts on the world-chart scale (1:1,000,000) covering most commonly traveled routes.

IFR charts produced by the Canadian government have almost the same format as the NOS IFR charts. Approach charts (and VFR airport diagrams) come in two binders for east and west. The dividing line is about Winnipeg. Enroute charts come in low- and high-altitude sets, with the low-altitude service including area charts and SIDs.

For charts and procedures for the rest of the world I recommend that you contact the AOPA's flight department in Washington, D.C. They can not only get you the information and charts you need but they also publish an excellent series of booklets giving you virtually everything you need to know about flying to various areas. Booklets are available for the following areas:

U.S.A.
Alaska
Chicago
Florida
New York City
Washington, D.C.

Foreign:
Bahamas
Bermuda
Canada
Central America
Latin America
Mexico
Transatlantic & Europe
West Indies

Their address is:
AOPA,
421 Aviation Way
Frederick, MD 21701

Landing and parking fees

There is no logic to the way landing and parking fees are charged. You can go into the most exotic airport, replete with navaids, lights, good paved parking areas, and everything and pay nothing. And you can go into the grungiest strip, with potholes in the runway and loose gravel all over the place to chew up your prop, and you'll be charged $5.

The main thing to remember is that most places that charge a landing fee do so on the basis of the type of operation you are carrying out. If you are flying passengers for hire, you may be charged $10. If you are on a pleasure flight, you may be charged only $2. Some airports charge a flat fee; others vary the fee by aircraft weight. Some charge no landing or parking fee if you buy gas. Others charge a parking fee and no landing fee or vice versa. Some places appear not to charge a fee, and then you get a bill 11 months later. Some airports charge a punitive fee in rush hours to discourage operations at those times. JFK and La Guardia charge over $50 a crack in rush hours, for example.

Parking fees are surprisingly reasonable when you compare what it would cost you to park your car downtown in the same city. Last year the highest parking fee I paid was $6 a night at Washington National. The highest landing fee I paid was $5 at Boston Logan.

Getting maintenance when you're on a trip

Before you go on any lengthy trip where you're going to be away from base for a few days, schedule a minor inspection of the aircraft. The sorts of things to do include maybe an oil change, a new oil filter, maybe a look at the sparkplugs, depending on when they were last examined. Do the sorts of things that are done on a 50-hour inspection. Be sure to check the battery, tires, brake linings, and so on. In this way you should be reasonably assured that you won't encounter any surprises when you are 1,000 miles from home, with a need to be 400 miles away the next day.

La Guardia. Stay away in rush hours! Note STOL runway to left of tower

Operating it

If there is any little item that has been acting up intermittently, the time to get it fixed is before you leave. If you don't, more than likely it will become a nonintermittent unserviceability at the most awkward place on your trip. I made a 3,000-mile trip one summer, and my DME was acting up and my number-one nav was weak—I'd lose the signal much sooner than I'd lose it on number two. I had the DME fixed before I left and it worked perfectly all the way. I didn't have the nav fixed before I left and it went out halfway through the trip. The result was a one-day delay and a lot of unnecessary expense, since the fixing had to be done by people not familiar with the equipment. In this regard, my advice is to stay away from the big-deal avionics shops if you don't have big-deal avionics. Their rates are higher and they often don't know your radios well enough, so you spend a lot of labor dollars while the technician learns about your system.

The advantage of owning your own airplane is that you have a pretty good idea of how well it is being looked after, so you should get fewer unexpected unserviceabilities. The problem becomes more significant if you are using a rented airplane. This is where you can really get into maintenance headaches on a trip. First of all, the airplane is an unknown quantity to you as far as its history is concerned. You don't know what has been done with it. Did some idiot start the engines with all the radios on several times? How about changing the gear selector in mid-cycle? This is a good way to mess up the gear transmission and give some future pilot a problem out of the blue. All of the major problems I've had on trips have been with rented aircraft. You get it fixed, and who pays for it? Who can authorize the repairs? What if it ends up costing $500? I recommend that, before you take a rented aircraft on a long trip, you have a clear understanding with the rental outfit about what to do if something goes wrong.

Fortunately, most FBOs understand why you are flying and will go out of their way to help you if you have a service problem while away from base. There are two key areas where you may have difficulty, however. One is scheduling. Few FBOs are sitting around with an empty hangar and an unoccupied mechanic waiting for you to walk in with your burned-out starter motor that needs to be fixed right away because you need to be in Abilene by tomorrow morning. When you do walk in, the FBO has to take a mechanic off a job that's already underway, and *that* airplane may have to be in Abilene tomorrow too, and the owner is based there and gives the FBO $2,000 a year in business. So when you have a problem and you want if fixed *now*, don't come on like a big shot. It's not the FBO's problem, it's yours. The FBO is probably doing you a favor to drop everything else and fix your bird. Amazingly, you can usually get it done—but be considerate of the FBO's priorities.

Plane Profile 19: Piper PA 32-301 Saratoga

Seats	6/7
Cruise speed, 65% power, 8,000 feet	140 knots
Range, 65% power, full optional fuel, 8,000 feet	728 nm
Maximum endurance	6.2 hours
Gross weight	3,615 pounds
Empty weight	1,940 pounds
Full optional fuel	612 pounds
	102 gallons
Useful load, full fuel	1,063 pounds
Fuel efficiency, 65% power	8.8 nmpg
Stall speed, flaps down	60 knots
Rate of climb, sea level	990 fpm
Minimum field length	1,800 feet
Engine type Lycoming IO-540-K1G5D	300 hp
Engine TBO	2,000 hours

Remarks Also offered with turbocharging as the Turbo Saratoga, and with retractable gear, both turboed and non-turboed as the Saratoga SP.

Operating it

The other area of difficulty is in parts availability and FBO familiarity with your aircraft. The best solution is for you to schedule your trips, wherever possible, so that you stop over at FBOs that handle your model of aircraft. If you fly a 172, stop over at Cessna dealers. If you have a Bonanza, aim at Beech dealers on your itinerary. A good source of this information is AOPA's *Airports USA* guide. In the listings for each airport they show the names of the operators and their dealership affiliations. This may mean using a different airport than you thought of using so that you can be near knowledgeable help.

But the most important thing is to eliminate the likelihood of problems in the first place by making sure that the aircraft is in good shape before you leave.

Traveling abroad with your plane

First, check that your insurance covers you for the intended trip. Most policies cover trips to Canada, but you often have to get a rider to cover you for other parts of the world. Second, know about U.S. customs. Clearance services are provided by U.S. customs at two types of airports—*international airports* and *landing-rights airports*. You could interpret the difference between these in terms of whether the customs officers are on hand as a rule or whether they have to make a special trip to make a clearance. In either case, advance notice to customs is required if clearance is wanted, and at landing-rights airports specific permission to land must be obtained in advance of contemplated use. However, at many landing-rights airports this permission may be automatically obtained

by simply requesting customs service in the flight plan. If it is not possible to use a flight plan for this purpose, U.S. customs must be notified directly and in advance that service will be required.

Outward clearance

For private flights (i.e., those not carrying passengers or freight for hire) no outward customs clearance is required. However, if you are carrying articles of value on which you might be challenged on return to the U.S. (e.g., an expensive Japanese camera), it would be wise to go to U.S. customs before leaving to file a Customs Form 4457, *Certificate of Registration For Personal Effects Taken Abroad*. A copy will be given to you to show to customs when returning to prove that you're not trying to smuggle the camera in. These forms are valid for three years, after which they must be renewed. It is not mandatory to file this form, but it makes life a lot easier and will eliminate any delays caused by this kind of thing.

Private aircraft leaving the U.S. with passengers or freight carried for hire must file an outward declaration form with U.S. customs prior to departure.

If you are carrying aliens, have them check with U.S. immigration to make sure they won't be hassled on return. Resident aliens carrying their green card or its new replacement will have no problem. Nonresident aliens may require special forms, depending on their status in the U.S.

The Cherokee Six has an extra-large rear door

Inward clearance

All aircraft entering the U.S. from another country must clear customs inbound. Advance notice to U.S. customs is required, and at many airports this information may be transmitted by a notification on the flight plan. The term "ADCUS" (advise customs) in the remarks box does the trick. Some airports do not have this flight-plan-notification ability, and direct notification to customs is required, giving expected time of arrival. You must also indicate how many U.S. and non-U.S. citizens are on board. FAA flight service stations and the better airport directories can tell you which airports can handle the flight-plan message.

Southern border crossing

When crossing the southern border of the U.S. inbound, a *special reporting requirement* exists. The limits within which this report must be made are from anywhere south of 33° N latitude between 95° and 120° W longitude. Not only do you have to notify Customs that you're going to be needing them, but you also have to tell them at what time and at what point you intend to cross the border. The report must include the following:

1. Type of aircraft and registration number
2. Captain's name
3. Number of U.S.-citizen passengers
4. Number of alien passengers

Plane Profile 20: Taylorcraft F21

Seats	2
Cruise speed, 65% power, 8,000 feet	96 knots
Range, 65% power, full optional fuel, 8,000 feet	298 nm
Maximum endurance	4.1 hours
Gross weight	1,500 pounds
Empty weight	990 pounds
Full optional fuel	174 pounds
	29 gallons
Useful load, full fuel	336 pounds
Fuel efficiency, 65% power	13.7 nmpg
Stall speed, flaps down	47 knots
Rate of climb, sea level	875 fpm
Minimum field length	400 feet
Engine type Lycoming O-235-L2C	118 hp
Engine TBO	2,000 hours

Plane Profile 21: Beech Bonanza A 36

Seats	6
Cruise speed, 65% power, 8,000 feet	158 knots
Range, 65% power, full optional fuel, 8,000 feet	695 nm
Maximum endurance	5.4 hours
Gross weight	3,612 pounds
Empty weight	2,195 pounds
Full optional fuel	444 pounds
	74 gallons
Useful load, full fuel	973 pounds
Fuel efficiency, 65% power	12 nmpg
Stall speed, gear and flaps down	52 knots
Rate of climb, sea level	1,030 fpm
Minimum field length	2,040 feet
Engine type Continental I0-520-BB	285 hp
Engine TBO	1,700 hours

Remarks   Also offered with turbocharging as the Bonanza A 36TC.

5. Place of last foreign departure
6. Estimated time and location of crossing the U.S. border
7. Name of U.S. airport of first intended landing
8. Estimated time of arrival

Unless an exemption has been obtained in advance (by at least 15 days), all such southern border crossings must terminate at certain specially designated airports, all of which are located in Texas, Arizona, or California. Check with an FAA flight Service Station for which airports apply.

Emergency landing

If an emergency landing is made in the U.S. at an airport other than an airport of entry, the pilot must report as soon as possible to the nearest customs, immigration, and public-health officers. Except for the preservation of life, health, or property, baggage should not be removed from the aircraft, and crew and passengers should remain with the aircraft and not mix with the public without official permission.

An aircraft that has left the U.S. and returns without landing does not have to advise or clear U.S. customs.

Overtime charges apply for service outside normal working hours (generally 8 A.M. to 5 P.M.). The rates for overtime services are based on a formula, but are limited to a maximum of $25 per aircraft.

Payments for overtime must be made in cash or by check drawn on a U.S. bank.

If overtime services are requested but not used (e.g., if the customs officer sits there waiting while you shoot two missed approaches and then go to an alternate), you are liable for the overtime charges just as if you had used them. Obviously, if you know you're going to change destinations, you should cancel the customs you don't want to avoid paying extra charges for services you don't use.

Clearing customs into the Bahamas

Island hopping is one of the most enjoyable ways to use your airplane.

The Bahamas are only a few minutes away from Florida, and the entry procedures are very simple.

Flights arriving in and departing from the Bahamas must go through Bahamian airports designated as ports of entry. Flights to the Bahamas may originate at any airport in the U.S., provided neither passengers nor cargo are carried for hire. Aircraft cruising at over 180 kts must file a DVFR (Defense Visual Flight Rules) or an IFR flight plan for penetration through the Air Defense Identification Zone (ADIZ), which is located about 20 miles off the Florida coast.

If you feel lacking in confidence about making the flight to the Bahamas for the first time, I suggest that you visit one of the FBOs at Miami, Fort Lauderdale, or West Palm Beach. These people are totally familiar with entry requirements and

Actually you don't need a seaplane to tour the Bahamas—there are over 50 airports and airstrips there

The author's Comanche at Loch Haven

can rent or sell you survival equipment, such as dinghies and life jackets for the overwater flight. They will help you fill out the documents you'll be needing.

On arrival at the port of entry in the Bahamas, you must immediately clear customs and immigration. Bahamian special declarations must be filled out in triplicate and surrendered to customs and immigration officials. These forms can be obtained from the U.S. FBOs in Florida or from the officials in the Bahamian port of entry. U.S. and Canadian citizens don't need passports or visas, but they must have identification. Your pilot certificate will do.

You may need to have your airplane insurance extended to cover a trip to the Bahamas. Not all policies are good for this. Some are good but require you to file a notification with the insurance company before you leave. Check yours.

On flights from one Bahamian island to another, carry an extra copy of the special declaration. This is your cruising permit. On arrival at an out-island airport, you may be required to produce this for an official. Surrender it only when you leave the Bahamas. Flight plans are required for inter-island flights departing from Nassau, but they are not required at other island airports. IFR flight plans are required for all night flights.

There are over 50 airports and landing strips in the Bahamas. Fuel (100-octane) is available at most locations, but it becomes more expensive the further out you go. Repair service is only available in Nassau.

The Bahama Island tourist offices will give you a lot of helpful information, including a special brochure on flying there in your own plane. These offices are located in most major U.S. cities, or you can write to:

Bahamas Ministry of Tourism
Nassau Court,
Box N3701,
Nassau, Bahamas

The AOPA offers a special Jeppesen Bahamas trip kit, a Bahamas flight report booklet, and their usual excellent planning services.

Clearing customs into Canada

Prior to departure for Canada advance notice must be forwarded to the appropriate Canada customs office. This can be done on the flight plan (which should be filed) by writing the word "ADCUS" in the remarks column for many airports. If the ADCUS facility is not available at your destination, then you must notify customs yourself by telephone or telegraph. Your FSS in the U.S. should be able to tell you if your destination can accept an ADCUS message. Customs service is free to pleasure flights, although mileage charges may be levied.

On arrival in Canada, the owner or pilot of the aircraft must report to the customs office and complete all necessary documentation. This report constitutes both an inward and outward report, unless you are carrying goods that require outward documentary control when you leave. The customs officer will issue a cruising permit valid for a period not exceeding 12 months. And that's it. No further contact with customs is required. When you return to the U.S., the U.S. customs officer will ask you for this cruising permit, so don't lose it. You do not have to clear Canadian customs when you leave Canada unless you have those goods mentioned above.

There are no operational fees for communications and navigational aids in Canada for private aircraft. Landing and parking fees are charged at many airports, including all government-operated fields.

There are a few differences in air regulations between the two countries.

1. No "VFR on top" permitted (over solid or broken clouds)

2. VFR flight in controlled airspace above 9,500 feet ASL east of 114°W (Calgary, Alberta) and above 12,500 feet west of 114°W is subject to an ATC clearance. This is called block airspace.

3. *All* cruising altitudes are even or odd thousands of feet, as IFR altitudes in the U.S. The "plus 500 feet" VFR altitudes are not used.

4. Flight plans are mandatory for night flights, except for those confined to an airport area.

5. Flight plans or flight notifications are mandatory for flights in certain areas (block airspace and "sparsely settled areas").

The Canadian government publishes an excellent guide for people traveling within Canada in their own airplane. It is called *Air Tourist Information Canada*. It contains important data, such as NOTAMs, procedures, and other information. It is basically a Canadian tourist's "Airman's Guide." It is catalog number T53-6 and may be ordered through:

Aeronautical Information Services,
Canadian Air Transportation Administration,
Ministry of Transport,
Ottawa, Canada K1A 0N8

Canadian charts, may be ordered through AOPA at:
AOPA,
421 Aviation Way
Frederick, MD 21701

AOPA also publishes its own guide to Canada, which you can order from them.

The Canadian equivalent to AOPA is COPA—the Canadian Owner's and Pilot's Association. Their address is:
COPA,
Box 734,
Ottawa, Canada K1P 5S4

Clearing customs into Mexico

This information pertains only to private-aircraft operations, with no more than 14 passenger seats on a nonpaying basis. Such aircraft may only carry passengers and may not carry goods or articles of any kind that are not for the personal use of the passengers or crew. In other cases prior permission is required from the Mexican Director General of Civil Aviation (DGAC). Entry is only permitted at certain airports.

All the requirements stipulated by the customs, immigration, and health authorities must be complied with both upon arrival at the airport of entry and upon departure from Mexican territory.

A flight plan must be filed, and if you are overflying an airport of entry near the border, you must communicate with that airport's control tower and give your ETA at your intended-destination airport of entry.

At the airport of entry the owner of the aircraft (or pilot, in the case of a rented aircraft) must fill out and sign the general declaration (Form DGAC-40) and obtain the necessary authorization from customs, immigration, and health authorities. The general declaration must be given to the airport official for approval, who will then return the original. This must be kept on board the airplane to be shown to any Mexican authority who requests it. The copies of the general declaration go to DGAC, immigration, and health (one each), and two copies go to Customs.

When all these requirements have been complied with, foreign (non-Mexican) aircraft may be flown anywhere in Mexican territory, subject to the conditions stated in the General Communications Law and regulations. Rented aircraft may be admitted, providing they have no more than six seats. Otherwise, prior permission is required.

At the port of departure from Mexico the original of the general declaration must be surrendered. (NOTE: all aircraft when departing Mexican soil must carry on board *the same crew and passengers who were listed on the DGAC-40 form*. In the case of any change the airport official may authorize departure of other than the original passengers for plau-

sible reasons as long as there are no violations to the General Communications Law. *This is very important.*)

Any infraction of regulations will entail penalties in the form of fines and/or confiscation of the aircraft. You have been warned!

The address of the DGAC is:

Direccion General De Aeronautica Civil,
Departmento De Transporte Aero Internacional,
Mexico City, D.F., Mexico
Telephone: 905-519-6996
Telex:177-1097

When you enter Mexico, you will be given a tourist card, which is valid for a week, a month, or up to 180 days (six months). The card is free and may also be obtained from any Mexican consulate or Mexican government tourist bureau in advance. You do not need a passport to enter Mexico if you are a U.S. citizen. If you are naturalized, you must have proof of citizenship. You don't need a visa for pleasure travel. For business travel you must have a busi-

Plane Profile 22: Piper PA 28RT-201 Arrow IV

Seats	4
Cruise speed, 65% power, 8,000 feet	131 knots
Range, 65% power, full optional fuel, 8,000 feet	812 nm
Maximum endurance	7.2 hours
Gross weight	2,750 pounds
Empty weight	1,637 pounds
Full optional fuel	432 pounds 72 gallons
Useful load, full fuel	681 pounds
Fuel efficiency, 65% power	13.6 nmpg
Stall speed, gear and flaps down	53 knots
Rate of climb, sea level	831 fpm
Minimum field length	1,600 feet
Engine type Lycoming IO-360-C1C6	200 hp
Engine TBO	1,600 hours
Remarks Also available in turbocharged version.	

ness visa, which you can apply for at any Mexican consulate or the Mexican embassy.

Air-navigation services in Mexico used to be charged for through a RAMSA card (Radio Aeronautica Mexican, S.A.), but this is no longer needed. Facilities charges, landing, fees and parking costs are now covered through fuel taxes. Once again, remember to make sure that your insurance is valid in Mexico before you leave.

In Mexico, all flight plans must be filed *in person*. You cannot file by radio. All night flying must be carried out IFR, which requires the relevant airports to be staffed during the flight. If your flight is conducted at other than normal airport hours, you may have to pay overtime to the personnel being kept on duty. *All flights require a flight plan, whether VFR or IFR*. Some airports have no facilities for filing a flight plan or closing one. In any event, you must file one when *going* to such an airport, and you

must file an arrival report ("closing your flight plan") when arriving from such a field.

The Commandante at any airport has the legal authority to refuse to allow a pilot to take off if he deems it unsafe. Arguing is pointless.

AOPA publishes their own guide to Mexico, which you can order, along with charts and Jeppesen trip kits, directly from AOPA. See page 119.

The best guide to flying in Mexico is published by the Texas Aeronautics Commission. It is called the "Mexico Flight Manual" and is free on request from

Texas Aeronautics Commission
Box 12607,
Capitol Station,
Austin, Texas 78711.

The Mexican government also publishes a booklet called "Fly to Mexico" which is free from any Mexican Tourist Office or Consulate or from the DGAC address given earlier.

Security

Aircraft theft is becoming an increasing problem. Some ways to help beat it include special wheel-locking devices and throttle or mixture control locks. The wheel device fits like a chock around the wheel and then locks onto the brake disc. Once in place, the aircraft wheels cannot be rolled. The other device fits over the shaft of a push-pull throttle or mixture control and, when locked in place, makes it impossible to move.

The International Aviation Theft Bureau (IATB) has an equipment-registration form on which you can list the serial numbers and descriptions of the equipment in your airplane. You can get one through you insurance company or from:

International Aviation Theft Bureau,
7315 Wisconsin Avenue,
Washington, D.C. 20014

AOPA supplies members with an antitheft warning sticker. You can place this on the door of your plane. It warns that interference with or theft of an airplane is a federal offense and offers a reward for information leading to the arrest and conviction of the perpetrators.

You should mark all your radios with the aircraft registration number or your name. Put some innocuous sort of identification that won't be so obvious on the radios as well, such as a spot of red paint in a certain place. Take a photograph of your instrument panel to show the equipment installed. Don't forget that some radios have remote boxes in other parts than the instument panel. Mark these, too.

Always leave your airplane locked, with the windows closed. The best way to keep it cool is with a sun shield on the inside, not by leaving the small pilot's window open. Insects can get in through here, and so can hands stealing microphones and headsets. Mikes are always being stolen. Check that you have yours before you leave on every flight. You

AOPA's anti-theft deterrent

should also carry a spare mike just in case the standard one conks out.

According to the IATB, 83 airplanes were reported stolen in 1976, with a total value of almost $3 million. There were reports of avionics and miscellaneous equipment thefts amounting to 312 units, valued at over $400,000. Nineteen airplanes were recovered—mostly in Mexico. For some reason the most popular plane among thieves is the Cessna 210—27 were stolen in 1976.

The IATB seems to be effective, since thefts of airplanes and radios were down considerably over the previous year.

27 Cessna Centurions were stolen in 1976—one out of three of all stolen aircraft was a Centurion!

What to do if your aircraft is stolen

The first thing to do when you find that your aircraft or parts from it have been stolen is to report the loss to the police. Then contact your insurance company. They will take it from there.

Most policies allow the insurance company 60 days to try to recover the airplane. If they are unsuccessful, you should shortly thereafter receive payment.

If the company locates the airplane, congratulations! But the cost of retrieving it is not covered in most cases. So if you live in Maryland and your plane is found in Saskatchewan, it's your problem to get it back home! If the aircraft is damaged when it is found, your policy should cover you for repairs.

Most policies will *not* cover you for seizure by a government agency. So if your airplane is stolen and flown to Mexico to bring back a load of marijuana and captured on the way back, it will probably be impounded by the Mexican authorities. Your recourse is through the courts, not through your insurance company. Apparently, if you are not involved,

it is not too hard to get it back. They might be harder to deal with if they suspect you, however. If the airplane was seized and is now damaged, either as a result of the seizure or for other reasons, you policy will probably cover you for the damage and the insurance company will probably pay for repairing the aircraft or at least making it able to fly to a base where it can be repaired.

Speaking of marijuana offenses, did you know that the FAA will lift your pilot certificate for one year if you are convicted of any offense relating to the growing, processing, manufacture, sale, disposition, possession, transportation, or importation of narcotic drugs, marijuana, depressant or stimulant drugs, or substances? Look at FAR 61.15!

What to do if you have an accident

What is an accident? National Transportation Safety Board (NTSB) Part 830.2 defines an accident as: "an occurrence associated with the operation of an aircraft which takes place

between the time any person boards the aircraft with the intention of flight until such time as all such persons have disembarked, and in which any person suffers death or serious injury as a result of being in or upon the aircraft or by direct contact with the aircraft or anything attached thereto, or in which the aircraft receives substantial damage."

Substantial damage is defined as: "Damage or structural failure which adversely affects the structural strength, performance, or flight characteristics of the aircraft, and which would normally require major repair or replacement of the affected component. However, engine failure, damage limited to an engine, bent fairings or cowling, dented skin, small punctured holes in skin or fabric, ground damage to propeller or rotor blades, damage to landing gear, wheels, tires, flaps, engine accessories, brakes, or wingtips are not considered "substantial damage" for the purpose of Part 830.2."

A *fatal injury* is defined as: "any injury resulting in death within seven days of the accident."

A *serious injury* is defined as: "any injury which (1) requires hospitalization for more than 48 hours, commencing within seven days from the date the injury was received; (2) results in a fracture of any bone (except simple fractures of fingers, toes, or nose); (3) involves lacerations which cause severe hemorrhages, nerve, muscle, or tendon damage; (4) involves injury to any internal organ; or (5) involves second- or third-degree burns, or any burns affecting more than five percent of the body surface."

The *operator* of the aircraft is defined as: "any person who causes or authorizes the operation of an aircraft, such as the owner, lessee, or bailee of an aircraft."

NTSB Part 830.5 calls for immediate notification of aircraft accidents or incidents or overdue aircraft. The aircraft operator must immediately, by the fastest means available, notify the nearest NTSB Field Office if any of the following events occur:

1. An aircraft accident
2. An overdue aircraft believed to have been involved in an accident
3. Any of the following incidents:
   a. flight-control-system malfunction or failure
   b. inability of any flight crewmember to perform any of his or her normal flight duties as a result of injury or illness
   c. turbine-engine rotor failures excluding compressor blades and turbine buckets
   d. in-flight fire
   e. in-flight collision between aircraft.

The following information must be given in the notification, if available:

1. Type, nationality, and registration marks of the aircraft
2. Name of owner and operator of the aircraft
3. Name of the pilot-in-command
4. Date and time of the accident
5. Last point of departure and point of intended landing of the aircraft
6. Position of the aircraft with reference to some easily definable geographical point
7. Number of persons on board, number killed, and number seriously injured
8. Nature of the accident, the

weather, and the extent of the damage to the aircraft, so far as is known
9. A description of any explosives, radioactive materials, or other dangerous articles carried.

NTSB Part 830.10 then goes on to call for the preservation of the wreckage, cargo, and mail on board and all records pertaining to the operation and maintenance of the aircraft. It may only be disturbed to remove injured or trapped people, to protect the wreckage from further damage, or to protect the public from injury. Part 830.15 requires the operator to file any report required by the NTSB within ten days after an accident and within seven days after an overdue aircraft is still missing. All crewmembers are required to submit a statement about the facts of the occurrence with the operator's report or as soon after as possible if

they are incapacitated at the time that the report is filed.

The accident or incident notification must be filed with the nearest NTSB field office to the operator. The post-accident report must be filed with the nearest NTSB field office to the accident or incident.

The NTSB maintains Bureau of Accident Investigation Field Offices at the following locations:

Alaska	Anchorage
California	Los Angeles
	Oakland
Colorado	Denver
D.C.	Washington
Florida	Miami
Georgia	Atlanta
Illinois	Chicago
Missouri	Kansas City
New York	New York City
Texas	Fort Worth
Washington	Seattle

What to do if your plane is damaged

After you have secured the property and notified the NTSB, contact your insurance company as soon as possible and tell them what happened. Securing the property is your responsibility. You may even have to hire a security guard. Do it. Your insurance company will probably reimburse you for this type of expense. If the airplane is vandalized after the accident, your insurance may not cover this aspect of the loss if you haven't tried to protect it.

Depending on who is insuring you and what happened, your insurance company may send an adjuster to view the damage and report to the company on the best way to handle

Left What can you say?

Operating it

it. For example, if you go off the end of the runway at home base and shear off the nosewheel, they'll probably get your own FBO to fix it. The adjuster should suggest what course of action to take—whether you need more than one bid to repair, whether in fact it is worth repairing, and so on.

The NTSB is solely responsible for the investigation of all accidents involving civil aircraft within the U.S. It is also responsible for investigating accidents involving civil U.S. aircraft that take place outside the U.S. to the extent allowed by the foreign government. Certain field investigations are carried out by FAA people, but the determination of the probable cause is made by the NTSB. NTSB Part 831 gives all the details of the legal aspects of accident investigation.

Safety considerations

Few aircraft accidents are caused by mechanical or structural failure. According to the NTSB, the "typical" accident features a private pilot with between 100 and 300 hours who crashes in rain and fog. An instrument rating is a very good step in the right direction—only 20 percent of weather-related accidents happen with instrument-rated pilots on IFR flight plans. Time-in-type is an important factor. Low time-in-type comes up often in the accident statistics, especially in the more complex aircraft. Non-instrument-rated pilots

flying at night are running a risky operation—one study showed that 20 percent of all weather-related accidents occurring to VFR pilots took place at night.

The most common cause of engine failure is that the engine stopped receiving fuel. Sometimes this is because the pilot literally ran out of fuel. But often the fuel exhaustion was in one tank and there was fuel available in another tank. There is no excuse for running out of fuel. It is available at almost every airport, and you should be landing with at least 45 minutes of fuel in the tanks. So those types of engine failures are really management problems.

What steps can you take to reduce the chances of being involved in an accident or at least surviving one if you are? See the box for some ideas.

1. Obtain and maintain competence in the types of airplane you fly. Practice every few months, even if you fly two or three times a week.
2. Get an instrument rating if you don't have one. Make it a general rule to file IFR where it makes sense. Maintain instrument proficiency.
3. Make sure that the aircraft receives first-class maintenance. Don't let squawks accumulate — fix them fast.
4. Use current charts, especially for IFR operations.
5. Check the weather intelligently and stay on top of it.
6. File a flight plan on cross-country trips of more than one hour if you're going VFR. Make position reports to flight service stations every 100 miles or so, especially over underpopulated areas.
7. Make use of the flight-following services available over the Great Lakes, Long Island Sound, the Florida swamps, and other areas.
8. Don't fly night VFR unless you are *competent* at instrument flying. Preferably, do all night cross-countries on an IFR flight plan.
9. Check your ELT regularly.
10. Always preflight the airplane carefully, checking the fuel and oil before

each flight.
11. Don't be afraid to land at an airport other than your destination if you are concerned about the weather or your fuel supply or if you feel tired.
12. Stay off the booze before flying. Avoid flying when you are taking medication, especially antihistamines.
13. Keep your eyes open and look around all the time when you're flying. Get your passengers to do this, too.
14. Use oxygen above 10,000 feet.
15. Always check to make sure the wheels are down just before you flare.
16. Stay above the flight path of large aircraft to avoid wake turbulence.
17. Wear a shoulder harness. Crop dusters, who are very experienced at crashing, always do.
18. Don't let anyone in or out of the aircraft when the engine is running.
19. Don't show off. Buzzing is for bees.
20. Carry a fire extinguisher in the aircraft.
21. Carry a first-aid kit in the aircraft.
22. Carry a survival kit if you're flying on trips over two hours, or over unpopulated areas.
23. Check the important little instruments such as oil pressure, suction, ammeter, fuel pressure, oil temperature, fuel

quantity, and such every five or ten minutes. It gives you something to do on those long, boring legs between VORs.
24. Always stay ahead of the airplane. Plan ahead so that the action you are doing *now* is the one you thought about *earlier*. While you are doing the *now* thing, think about the *next* thing.
25. Never overload the airplane or exceed the CG limits.
26. Carry life jackets for flights beyond gliding distance from land. Take a dinghy, too, for long trips.
27. Carry a parachute if you're doing aerobatics, but don't do aerobatics unless you are competent at them and the airplane can handle them.
28. Don't let considerations other than those involved in flying the airplane govern you. Large numbers of accidents occur because the pilot *had* to get there. Flying is not a "get there or die!" activity unless you make it so.
29. Always use a checklist.
30. Only use runways that are long enough for the planned operation, considering aircraft weight, wind, runway surface, braking action, temperature, and field elevation.

These items were deliberately given in a random sequence to eliminate the tendency to skip over the parts you know. I *hope* you know them all, but why not go back and read them all, only this time starting at the end and working forwards? Then write down three more rules of your own:

1. _____

2. _____

3. _____

Making a survival kit

You can buy prepackaged survival kits. However, it's more fun and sobering to make your own. A visit to a camping-supplies store will yield all kinds of goodies. Here are some of the things you should have on board the airplane in case you go down in the wilderness (the quantities are for two people):

1. 2 "space blankets"
2. 2 hunter's emergency food packs
3. 8 cans of food, such as baked beans
4. 1 can opener
5. 1 folding sterno stove
6. 3 cans of sterno

7. A supply of matches wrapped in foil and kept in a plastic bag
8. 1 large hunting knife
9. Some large nails
10. Some heavy string or light rope
11. Some water-purification tablets
12. Insect repellent
13. A portable compass
14. A signaling mirror
15. Cooking and eating utensils
16. A plastic jug of drinking water
17. A small survival handbook
18. Additional concentrated food in waterproof packages (suggest 5 lbs per per person)

If you're really going over the wilds, you should also carry:

1. An axe
2. 30 feet of snare wire
3. Fishing trawls, lines, hooks, nets
4. Mosquito nets

And in the winter I suggest:

1. A tent
2. Sleeping bags
3. 2 pairs of snow shoes
4. Ice chisel
5. Snow knife
6. Snow shovel

All in one neat package. My kit contains the items in the first list, weighs about ten pounds, and fits in a small bag about one cubic foot in size.

Don't forget you have other things on the airplane that could help if you go down in the woods. Your luggage probably has extra clothes, toothbrushes, etc. You should carry a few essential tools. Engine oil can help to make a smoky fire. Avgas can help you start one. The seats can give you something comfortable to sit or sleep on. You should have a first-aid kit. Be resourceful!

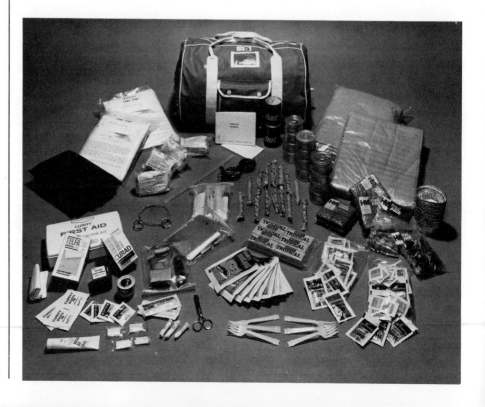

The contents of a typical pre-packaged kit, this one by Nicolet survival Products

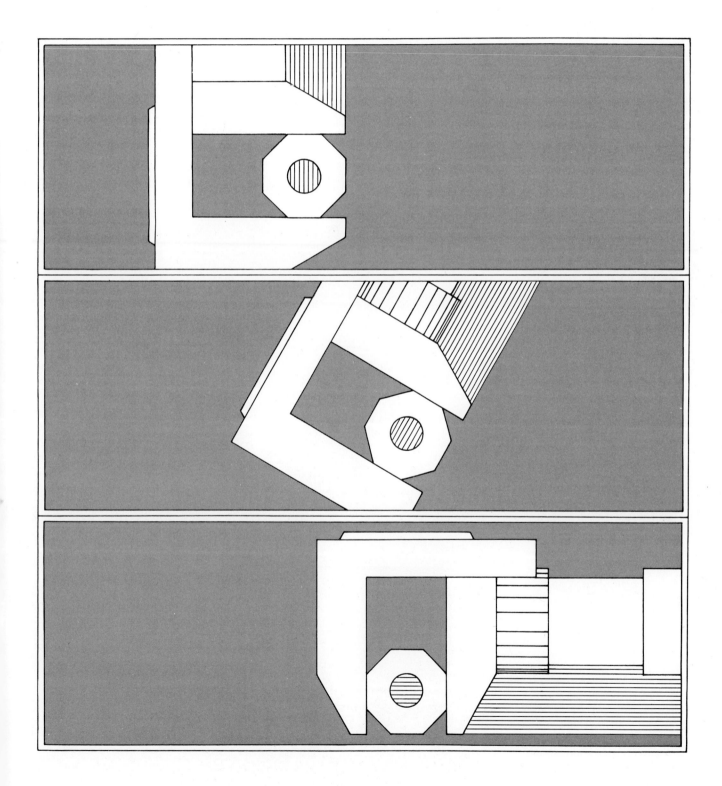

Aircraft maintenance and inspections

Maintenance means the inspection, overhaul, and repair of aircraft, including the replacement of parts. Its purpose is to ensure that the aircraft meets acceptable standards of airworthiness throughout its operational life.

Although maintenance requirements vary for different types of aircraft, most aircraft need some kind of preventive maintenance about every 25 hours of flying and minor maintenance every 100 hours. This is influenced by the kind of operation, climatic conditions, storage facilities, age, and construction of the aircraft. Most manufacturers supply service information that should be used in maintaining your aircraft.

The owner or operator has primary responsibility for maintaining an aircraft in an airworthy condition (FAR 91.165). Certain inspections must be performed on your aircraft, and you must maintain the airworthiness of the aircraft between required inspections by having any defects corrected.

FARs require the inspection of all civil aircraft at specific intervals to determine the overall condition. The interval depends generally upon the type of operations engaged in. An aircraft that is not operated for hire requires at least an annual inspection in accordance with the requirements of FAR Part 43. It may only be returned to service after it has been so approved by the holder of an inspection authorization (IA). The exceptions to this rule are:

1. Aircraft being maintained on a progressive maintenance schedule under FAR 91.171

2. An aircraft operating under a special flight permit or one with a current experimental or provisional certificate of airworthiness

3. An aircraft operated by an air-travel club that is being inspected under FAR 123

4. An aircraft operated under FAR 135 and being inspected under an approved aircraft-inspection program in accordance with Part 135

5. A large airplane (i.e., over 12,500 lbs gross weight), jet, or turboprop being inspected in accordance with an inspection program authorized under Sub-part D of FAR 91

The inspection for the original issuance of an airworthiness certificate counts as the first annual, and thereafter each 12 calendar months an annual inspection must be carried out as defined above.

Aircraft that are operated for hire must also have the same type of inspection carried out every 100 hours of flight time. The only difference between an annual and a 100-hour is that the annual must be signed out by the holder of an IA, whereas the 100-hour need only be approved by a certificated A&P mechanic. The 100 hours may be exceeded by up to 10 hours in order to reach a place where an inspection may be done, but such a carryover must be deducted from the next 100 hours.

Annual inspections may also be carried out by an appropriately rated certificated repair station or by the aircraft manufacturer. The due date for the annual is the last day of the same month in which the previous annual (or airworthiness inspection) was done. Hint: schedule your annual inspection close to the end of the month, so that the IA can date the annual on the first of the next month—this will gradually move your annuals up one month each year, and gives you almost 13 months of flying per annual.

An aircraft with an overdue annual may be flown under a special flight permit to a place where the inspection can be carried out. This permit is obtained from the local FAA Flight Standards or General Aviation District Office.

Note that an annual inspection will count as a 100-hour inspection, but a 100 hour inspection will *not* count as an annual inspection.

After the requirement for an annual inspection has been met, the IA may either approve or disapprove the aircraft for return to service. If the IA disapproves it, the owner is given a list of discrepancies that must be corrected before the aircraft may be certified airworthy. If you get such a list, it doesn't mean that you have to go through the whole inspection routine again. For example, you might have an annual, and the IA says: "Annual inspection carried out. Left main gear strut cracked and must be replaced." At this point you have satisfied the legal requirement to have an annual inspection. Now, to make the plane airworthy, you must get the landing gear fixed. When you've done that, the aircraft may be certified as airworthy.

A Twin Comanche undergoing minor surgery.

Types of FAA-approved repair stations

FAR 145.31 classifies the types of repair stations that the FAA approves. Here are the types of ratings issued:

a. Airframe ratings:
Class 1: Composite construction of small aircraft
Class 2: Composite construction of large aircraft
Class 3: All-metal construction of small aircraft
Class 4: All-metal construction of large aircraft

b. Powerplant ratings:
Class 1: Reciprocating (piston) engines of 400 horsepower or less
Class 2: Reciprocating engines of more than 400 horsepower
Class 3: Turbine engines

c. Propeller ratings:
Class 1: All fixed-pitch and ground-adjustable propellers of wood, metal, or composite construction
Class 2: All other propellers, by make

d. Radio ratings:
Class 1: Communication equipment
Class 2: Navigation equipment
Class 3: Pulse and radar equipment

e. Instrument ratings:
Class 1: Mechanical (e.g., tachometers, ASIs, altimeters, compasses, etc.)
Class 2: Electrical
Class 3: Gyroscopic
Class 4: Electronic

f. Accessory ratings:
Class 1: Mechanical accessories (e.g., brakes, carburetors, pumps, shock struts, etc.)
Class 2: Electrical accessories (e.g., starters, generators, electric pumps, etc.)
Class 3: Electronic accessories
Under FAR 145.33 the FAA may issue limited ratings for particular makes and models of airframes, engines, propellers, instruments, radios, accessories, and other parts and purposes.

Mechanics are certificated under FAR 65. There are two basic mechanic certificates—*airframe* and *powerplant* (A&P). In addition, there is the *inspection authorization* (IA), which allows the holder of both an A and a P certificate to carry out such things as annual inspections. Finally, there is the *repairman* certificate. This is issued to people who have at least 18 months experience and is related to the specific repair station where the repairman is employed.

Aircraft-maintenance records

You must have a good system of maintenance records to properly manage your operation of your aircraft. These will give the maintenance people the information they need about what has been done in the past, and they will give you the cues as to when scheduled maintenance must be done. It is the owner's or operator's responsibility to make sure that maintenance is carried out on schedule and that entries are made in the records (FAR 91.173).

I recommend a service supplied by Aerotech Publications, Inc. It's called the Adlog System and consists of an 8½-X-11-inch binder containing separate log book sections for the airframe, engines, propellers, and avionics. In addition it has an AD section and you are sent all ADs on a subscription basis. It has other features too, such as an inspection check-list and space for weight and balance, FAA Form 337s and factory bulletins. This is an ideal system to use if you are starting with a new airplane. It is available from:

Aerotech Publications, Inc.,
Box 528B, Old Bridge, NJ 08857
Telephone: 201-679-5151

If you buy a used airplane, you will also get the log books. They must be transferred to the new owner with the airplane (FAR 91.174). FAR 91.173 requires that records be kept on the aircraft, the engine or engines, propeller or propellers, the rotor if a rotorcraft, and the aircraft appliances (meaning pumps, generators, and such). What you will probably get will be an aircraft log book and an engine log book. Any propeller entries will probably have been made in the engine log. I have a very nice propeller log book supplied by Hartzell, which gives much useful information about the prop and its systems. I got this when I had some work done on the prop at Sensenich. I also have a useful avionics log, which I got when I had a radio installed. This has room for separate records on each piece of avionics equipment. This log is supplied by:

Aviation Maintenance Foundation, Inc.
Box 739,
Basin, Wyo. 82410

FAR 91.173 calls for records to be made of the following items for each aircraft, engine, propeller, and appliance:

1. Maintenance and alteration
2. 100-hour inspections
3. Annual inspections
4. Progressive inspections
5. Other required and approved inspections

These records must include:

1. A description of the work performed (or reference to FAA-approved data)
2. The date of completion of the work carried out
3. The signature and certificate number of the person approving the aircraft for return to service.

The above records must be kept until the work is repeated or superseded by other work or for one year after the work is performed. Records containing the following information must be kept for the life of the aircraft and transferred to the new owner when the aircraft is sold:

1. The total time in service of the airframe
2. The current status of life-limited parts of the airframe, engine, propeller, rotor, and appliance
3. The time since last overhaul of

all the items installed on the aircraft that are required to be overhauled on a specified time basis

4. The identification of the current inspection status of the aircraft, including the times since the last inspections required by the inspection program under which the aircraft and its appliances are maintained

5. The current status of applicable ADs, including the method of compliance

6. A list of current alterations to each airframe, engine, propeller, rotor, and appliance.

If the records for an aircraft and its bits are lost or destroyed, it is necessary to recreate them by such means as:

1. Getting information from other records kept by the owner, such as pilot log books, FBO bills, other log books (e.g., an engine log book might be quite helpful in reconstructing a lost aircraft log)

2. Checking with records kept by the maintenance facility or individual mechanics.

A method acceptable to the FAA is for the owner or operator to make a statement describing the loss and then to establish the time in service, followed by the owner's notarized signature.

The current status of ADs may present a more formidable problem. It may require a detailed inspection by maintenance personnel to re-establish that applicable ADs have been complied with.

There is no FAA requirement that preventive maintenance be entered in the maintenance records. But why not do it anyway?

FAA Form 337

FAA Form 337 must be filed with the FAA when major repairs or alterations are made to the airframe, engine, propeller, or appliance. It contains details of the aircraft (make, model, serial number, and so on), the owner's name, the mechanic's or repair station's name and certificate number, a statement of compliance with FARs, an approval for return to service (or a rejection thereof), and a description of the work accomplished. The requirements for the filing of an FAA Form 337 are in FAR 43.9 (a). A copy of all Form 337s should be kept in the aircraft file for reference by maintenance personnel.

The description of work done on an FAA Form 337

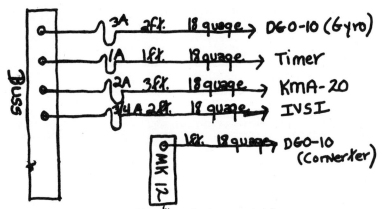

NOTICE

Weight and balance or operating limitation changes shall be entered in the appropriate aircraft record. An alteration must be compatible with all previous alterations to assure continued conformity with the applicable airworthiness requirements.

8. DESCRIPTION OF WORK ACCOMPLISHED *(If more space is required, attach additional sheets. Identify with aircraft nationality and registration mark and date work completed.)*

    Installed following equipment in accordance with manufacturer's instructions: Narco DGO-10, Davtron 822 Count-down timer, Davtron 701A-1 ADF freq. indicator, King KMA-20 Audio panel, Teledyne SLZ 9541 IVSI

Units were wired for power as illustrated below:

All connectors were supplied manufacturers and harnesses were made to their specs.

W & B and equipment list revised.

Electrical load analysis performed in accordance with A.C. 43-13-1. Maximum continous running load <u>does not</u> exceed 80% of maximum generator output of 50 Amps.

Static system tested per FAR 91.170 and found operational.

Anatomy of an annual inspection

These are the typical steps taken by the inspector when carrying out an annual inspection.

1. Paperwork check.

The inspector examines the log books for the aircraft, engine, and propeller to determine past history, time in service, and compliance with AD notes. Any outstanding ADs are to be complied with before the inspection is completed. He checks the equipment against the equipment list and makes sure that the weight and balance data are up to date. If repairs or alterations have been made, FAA Form 337s to cover these should be in the aircraft file. He checks that the aircraft has an Aircraft Airworthiness Certificate (FAA Form 8100-2), an Aircraft Registration Certificate (FAA Form 8050-3), and an Aircraft Radio Station License (FCC Form 404-2). These forms should be on display in the aircraft.

2. Run-up check.

Before the aircraft is taken apart, a complete run-up of the engine is made. The following items are covered:
- ☐ Oil pressure and temperature, fuel pressure and temperature, cylinder-head and carburetor temperatures
- ☐ Static RPM at full throttle
- ☐ Magneto drop
- ☐ Engine response to throttle movement
- ☐ Propeller cycling and response
- ☐ Unusual engine noises
- ☐ Idle RPM and idle mixture
- ☐ Proper fuel feed from each tank
- ☐ Electric fuel pump and fuel flow at idle and full power
- ☐ Alternator or generator output
- ☐ Suction (for vacuum instruments)
- ☐ Ignition-switch dead cut
- ☐ Proper shutdown behavior

3. Systems check.

Each system of the aircraft is inspected in turn. The following sequence is that recommended by Piper for the Comanche:

A. Propeller group
- ☐ Inspect spinner and back plate for cracks
- ☐ Inspect blades for nicks and cracks
- ☐ Check for grease and oil leaks
- ☐ Lubricate per lubrication chart
- ☐ Check spinner mounting bracket for cracks
- ☐ Check propeller mounting bolts and safety wire (check torque if safety wire is broken)
- ☐ Check pitch-actuating arms and bolts
- ☐ Inspect hub parts for cracks and corrosion
- ☐ Rotate blades and check for tightness in hub pilot tube

B. Engine group
[CAUTION—ground magneto primary circuit before working on engine]
- ☐ Remove engine cowling
- ☐ Clean and check cowling for cracks, distortion, and loose or missing fasteners
- ☐ Drain oil sump
- ☐ Clean suction-oil strainer
- ☐ Clean pressure-oil strainer or change full-flow (cartridge-type) oil-filter element (check strainer or element for foreign particles)
- ☐ Check oil-temperature sender unit for leaks and security
- ☐ Check oil lines and fittings for leaks, security, chafing, dents, and cracks
- ☐ Clean and check oil-radiator cooling fins
- ☐ Remove and flush oil radiator
- ☐ Fill engine with oil of suitable type
- ☐ Clean engine
- ☐ Check condition of spark plugs (clean and gap as required)
- ☐ Check ignition harnesses and insulators (high-tension leakage and continuity)
- ☐ Check magneto main points for clearance
- ☐ Check magneto for oil-seal leakage
- ☐ Check breaker felts for proper lubrication
- ☐ Check distributor block for cracks, burned areas, or corrosion and height of contact springs
- ☐ Check magnetos to engine timing
- ☐ Remove and clean air-cleaner screen
- ☐ Drain carburetor and remove and clean carburetor inlet screen or fuel-injector inlet screen (clean injector nozzles as required—with acetone only)
- ☐ Check condition of carburetor heat or alternate air door and box
- ☐ Check intake seals for leaks and clamps for tightness
- ☐ Inspect condition of flexible fuel lines
- ☐ Check fuel system for leaks
- ☐ Inspect and lubricate fuel-selector valve
- ☐ Clean screens in electric fuel pumps
- ☐ Check fuel pumps for operation (engine-driven and electric)
- ☐ Check vacuum pump and lines
- ☐ Check throttle, carburetor heat or alternate air, mixture, and propeller governor controls for travel and operating condition
- ☐ Inspect exhaust stacks, connections, and gaskets—replace gaskets as required
- ☐ Inspect muffler, heat exchanger, and baffles
- ☐ Check breather tube for obstructions and security
- ☐ Check crankcase for cracks, leaks, and security of seam bolts
- ☐ Check engine mounts for cracks and loose mounting
- ☐ Check rubber engine-mount bush-

Fixing it

ings for deterioration (replace every 500 hours)
- [ ] Check all engine baffles for cracks
- [ ] Check firewall for cracks
- [ ] Check condition of firewall seals
- [ ] Check condition and tension of generator or alternator drive belt
- [ ] Check condition of generator or alternator and starter
- [ ] Lubricate all controls
- [ ] Reinstall engine cowling

C. Cabin group
- [ ] Inspect cabin entrance, door, and windows for damage and operation
- [ ] Check upholstery for tears
- [ ] Check seats, seat belts, securing brackets, and bolts
- [ ] Check trim operation
- [ ] Check rudder pedals, brake pedals, and cylinders for operation and leaks
- [ ] Check parking brake
- [ ] Check control wheels, column, pulleys, and cables
- [ ] Check landing, navigation, cabin, and instrument lights
- [ ] Check instruments, lines, and attachments
- [ ] Check instruments and central air-filter lines and replace filter
- [ ] Check condition of vacuum-operated instruments and electric turn and bank (overhaul or replace as required)
- [ ] Replace vacuum regulator filter
- [ ] Check altimeter (calibrate altimeter system in accordance with FAR 91.170, if appropriate [required for IFR flight every 24 months])
- [ ] Check oxygen outlets for defects and corrosion
- [ ] Check oxygen-system operation and components

D. Fuselage and empennage group
- [ ] Remove inspection panels and plates
- [ ] Check fluid in brake reservoir (fill as required)
- [ ] Check battery, box and, cables—flush box as required and fill battery per instructions in service manual
- [ ] Check electronic installations

- [ ] Check bulkheads and stringers for damage
- [ ] Check loop and loop mount, antenna mount, and electrical wiring
- [ ] Remove, drain, and clean fuel-filter bowl and screen
- [ ] Check fuel lines, valves, and gauges for damage and operation
- [ ] Check security of all lines
- [ ] Check stabilator and stabilator trim tabs for security of mounting, free play of components, and ease of operation
- [ ] Check stabilator bearings, bungee, and stabilator trim horns, control rod, and trim mechanism for security of installation, damage, and operation
- [ ] Check fin, rudder, and stabilator surface for damage
- [ ] Check rudder and rudder tab hinges, horns, and attachments for security, damage, and operation
- [ ] Check rudder-trim mechanism operation
- [ ] Check all control cables and trim cables for correct cable tension and turnbuckles, guides, and pulleys for damage, operation, and safeties
- [ ] Check rotating beacon or strobe lights for wear
- [ ] Lubricate per lubrication chart
- [ ] Check security and condition of autopilot bridles and clamps
- [ ] Reinstall inspection panels and plates

E. Wing group
- [ ] Remove inspection plates and fairings
- [ ] Check wing, aileron, and flap surfaces for damage and loose rivets—check condition of wing tips
- [ ] Check condition of walkway
- [ ] Check aileron attachments and hinges for damage, looseness, and operation
- [ ] Check aileron cables for correct tension; check pulleys, bellcranks, and control rods for corrosion, damage, and operation
- [ ] Check flap attachments and hinges or tracks and rollers for damage, looseness, and operation—clean tracks and rollers
- [ ] Check flap cables, pulleys, step

lock, bellcranks, and rods for corrosion, damage, and operation
- [ ] Lubricate per lubrication chart
- [ ] Check wing-attachment bolts and brackets
- [ ] Check fuel tanks and lines for leaks and water
- [ ] Fuel tanks marked for capacity
- [ ] Fuel tanks marked for minimum octane rating
- [ ] Check switches to indicators registering fuel-tank quantity
- [ ] Check fuel cell vents
- [ ] Check thermos-type fuel-cap rubber seals for brittleness and distortion
- [ ] Reinstall inspection plates and fairings

F. Landing-gear group
- [ ] Check oleo struts for proper extension—check for proper fluid level as required
- [ ] Check nose-gear steering control
- [ ] Check wheels for alignment
- [ ] Put airplane on jacks
- [ ] Check tires for cuts, uneven or excessive wear, and slippage
- [ ] Remove wheels, clean check, and repack bearings
- [ ] Check wheels for cracks, corrosion, and broken bolts
- [ ] Check tire pressures
- [ ] Check brake linings and discs for wear and cracks
- [ ] Check brake backing plates for cracks
- [ ] Check condition of brake hydraulic lines
- [ ] Check condition of shimmy dampener
- [ ] Check gear forks for damage
- [ ] Check oleo struts for fluid leaks and scoring
- [ ] Check gear struts, attachments, torque links, retraction links, and bolts for operation
- [ ] Check torque-link bolts and bushings—rebush as required
- [ ] Check drag-link bolts—replace as required
- [ ] Check gear doors and attachments
- [ ] Check warning horn and lights for operation
- [ ] Retract gear—check operation
- [ ] Retract gear—check doors for clearance and operation

Fixing it

☐ Check emergency operation of gear
☐ Check landing-gear motor, transmission, and attachments
☐ Check anti-retraction system
☐ Check position indicating switches and electrical leads for security
☐ Lubricate per lubrication chart
☐ Remove airplane from jacks

G. Operational inspection
☐ Check fuel-pump and fuel-tank selector operation
☐ Check indication of fuel quantity and pressure or flow gauges
☐ Check oil pressure and temperature indications
☐ Check generator or alternator output
☐ Check manifold-pressure indications
☐ Check operation of carburetor heat or alternate air

☐ Check operation of brakes and parking brake
☐ Check operation of vacuum gauge
☐ Check gyros for noise and roughness
☐ Check cabin-heat operation
☐ Check magneto-switch operation
☐ Check magneto-RPM variation
☐ Check throttle and mixture operation
☐ Check engine idle
☐ Check propeller smoothness
☐ Check propeller-governor action
☐ Check electronic equipment operation
☐ Check operation of controls
☐ Check operation of flaps
☐ Check override function of autopilot
☐ Check operation of pitch-trim installation if installed

H. General
☐ Aircraft conforms to FAA specifications
☐ All FAA ADs complied with (any that were due would have been detected in the initial paperwork review and complied with during the check of the appropriate aircraft system)
☐ All manufacturer's service letters and bulletins complied with
☐ Check for proper airplane flight manual and weight and balance
☐ All aircraft papers in proper order and log-book entries made.

There is one thing that is not in the above checklist and that is "prepare the bill!" Many FBOs offer to carry out an annual inspection for a flat labor charge, with any extra labor and parts required for AD compliance, fixing things, etc., being extra.

Plane Profile 23: Cessna 152

Seats	2
Cruise speed, 65% power, 8,000 feet	100 knots
Range, 65% power, full optional fuel, 8,000 feet	580 nm
Maximum endurance	6.8 hours
Gross weight	1,675 pounds
Empty weight	1,112 pounds
Full optional fuel	225 pounds
	37.5 gallons
Useful load, full fuel	338 pounds
Fuel efficiency, 65% power	19.4 nmpg
Stall speed, flaps down	43 knots
Rate of climb, sea level	715 fpm
Minimum field length	1,340 feet
Engine type Lycoming O-235-L2C	110 hp
Engine TBO	2,000 hours
Remarks Trainer	

Preventive maintenance

The holder of a pilot certificate issued under FAR Part 61 may perform preventive maintenance on any aircraft owned or operated by him or her that is not used in air-carrier service (FAR 43.3h and FAR 43 Appendix A). All other maintenance, repairs, rebuilding, or alterations must be performed by persons authorized to do so by the FAA.

Except for items authorized under preventive maintenance, all repairs are classified as either major or minor. Major repairs or alterations must be approved and returned to service by an appropriately rated certificated repair facility, an A&P mechanic holding an inspection authorization, or a representative of the FAA. Minor repairs and alterations may be returned to service by an appropriately rated certificated A&P mechanic or repair facility.

If you decide and are qualified to perform any of the preventive-maintenance items that are allowed, you *must* use methods, techniques, and practices that are acceptable to the FAA. You *must* use the tools, equipment, and test apparatus necessary to ensure completion of the work in accordance with accepted industry practices. If special equipment or test apparatus is recommended by the manufacturer involved, you *must* use that equipment or apparatus or its equivalent acceptable to the FAA. If you decide to perform any of the preventive-maintenance items allowed, you *must* do the work in such a manner and use materials of such a quality that the condition of the aircraft, airframe, engine, propeller, or appliance worked on will be at least equal to its original or properly altered condition.

As modern-day aircraft become more and more complex, preventive maintenance on some of the aircraft components may seem to be a simple matter when in fact it is an exacting job, even for the experienced aircraft mechanic. If in doubt, ask a mechanic to help.

Work of the following type is classed as preventive maintenance. This is the *only* work that a certificated pilot may perform, without supervision, on an aircraft that is owned or operated by that pilot:

1. Removal, installation, and repair of landing gear tires
2. Servicing landing-gear shock struts by adding air, oil, or both
3. Replacing defective safety wiring or cotter keys
4. Making simple fabric patches not requiring rib stitching or the removal of structural parts or control surfaces
5. Refinishing the decorative coating of fuselage, wings, tail-group surfaces (excluding balanced control surfaces), fairings, cowlings, landing gear, cabin, or cockpit interior when removal or disassembly of any primary structure or operating system is not required
6. Servicing landing-gear wheel bearings, such as cleaning or greasing
7. Lubrication not requiring disassembly other than removal of nonstructural items such as cover plates, cowlings, and fairings
8. Replenishing hydraulic fluid in the reservoir
9. Applying preservative or protective material to components where no disassembly of any primary structure or operating system is involved and where such coating is not prohibited or contrary to operating practices
10. Repairing upholstery and decorative furnishings of the cabin or cockpit interior when the repairing does not require disassembly of any primary structure or operating system, interfere with an operating system, or affect primary structure of the aircraft
11. Replacing safety belts
12. Troubleshooting and repairing broken circuits in landing-light wiring
13. Replacing bulbs, reflectors, and lenses of position and landing lights
14. Replacing elastic shock-absorber cords on landing gear
15. Replacing seats or seat parts with replacement parts approved for the aircraft not involving disassembly of any primary structure or operating system
16. Replacing wheels and skis where no weight-and-balance computation is involved
17. Replacing prefabricated fuel lines
18. Cleaning fuel and oil strainers
19. Replacing or cleaning spark plugs and setting of spark plug-gap clearance
20. Making simple repairs to fairings, nonstructural cover plates, cowlings, and small patches and reinforcements not changing the contour so as to interfere with proper airflow
21. Replacing side windows when that work does not interfere with the structure or any operating system such as controls or electrical equipment
22. Replacing any hose connection except hydraulic connections
23. Removing and installing glider wings and tail surfaces that are specifically designed for quick removal and installation when such removal and installation can be done by the pilot
24. Replacing batteries and checking fluid level and specific gravity

Note that none of these preventive maintenance items may be delegated by the pilot to a third party other than a certificated mechanic.

Preflight inspection

The FARs do not specifically require a pilot to carry out a preflight inspection. FAR 91.29 makes the following statement, however:

1. No person may operate a civil aircraft unless it is airworthy.

Fixing it

2. The pilot in command of a civil aircraft is responsible for determining whether that aircraft is in condition for safe flight. He shall discontinue the flight when unairworthy mechanical or structural conditions occur.

A careful pilot will always conduct a thorough preflight inspection before every flight to be satisfied that the aircraft is safe for flight.

When a repair or alteration has been made to your aircraft, the person authorized to return the aircraft to service should decide if a flight test is necessary. If the decision is affirmative, the aircraft must be flight-tested after repair or alteration *before* it may be used to carry passengers. The test pilot must hold at least a private pilot certificate with an appropriate aircraft rating. The test pilot must log the findings of the test flight in the aircraft log book or maintenance record (FAR 91.167).

Fuel-use tips

The buildup of cylinder deposits from lead and lead-scavenging compounds and the adverse effects of these deposits due to the use of 100-octane fuels in 80-octane engines can be minimized by the following actions.

1. Spark plugs. Clean the spark plugs more frequently or change the type to an alternate one recommended by the engine manufacturer. At more frequent intervals, such as when changing the oil, check the lower plugs for deposits. If globules appear in between normal plug-cleaning intervals, interchange the lower with the upper plugs. Interchanging plugs in other cylinders may help because of uneven distribution of lead to the cylinders.

2. Compression check. Make simple checks for obvious compression leaks through valves and rings or uneven compression. Do this by pulling the propeller through compression very slowly on each cylinder to check for a "wheeze" sound. If you detect this, have the compression checked properly and check the valves and rings.

3. More frequent oil changes. These will reduce the accumulation of lead in oil passages and other internal locations. Have the oil analyzed for lead content (see page 142).

4. Replace the valves. In some cases new valves made of improved material can be installed to help reduce the erosion caused by high-lead fuel. The valve-guide clearances may also be revised, or new guides can be installed made of improved material.

5. Consider using TCP. See page 177. Warning! Never use automotive gasoline in an airplane engine! Even if the auto gas has a similar octane rating, it is not a suitable substitute. Aircraft engines are certificated for operation only with aviation fuel.

Plane Profile 24: Piper Navajo C

Seats	6/8
Cruise speed, 65% power,	
8,000 feet	176 knots
18,000 feet	192 nm
Range, 65% power, full	
optional fuel, 18,000 feet	1,017 nm
Maximum endurance	6.3 hours
Gross weight	6,536 pounds
Empty weight	4,003 pounds
Full optional fuel	1,124 pounds
	187.3 gallons
Useful load, full fuel	1,409 pounds
Fuel efficiency, 65%	
power	6.7 nmpg
Stall speed, gear and	63 knots
flaps down	
Rate of climb, sea level	1,300 fpm
	245 fpm s/e
Minimum field length	3,250 feet
Engine type Lycoming	
TSIO-540-A2C	310 hp
Engine TBO	1,800 hours
Remarks Pressurized, turbocharged twin.	

Fixing it

The use of auto gas will at least void the engine warranty, but there are other reasons why you must not use it.

1. Auto fuels have a wider distillation range than aviation fuels, and this promotes poor distribution of the high antiknock compounds of the fuel. The octane ratings of auto and aircraft fuels are not comparable due to the different methods used to rate the two types of fuels. This results in an appreciable difference in actual knock rating for two fuels that have the same octane number. This difference could lead to destructive preignition and detonation.

2. Auto fuels are more volatile and have high vapor pressure that can lead to vapor lock. The low vapor pressure in aviation fuel is designed to eliminate vapor lock caused by altitude or heat. The greater volatility of auto fuel increases the fire hazard.

3. The lead in auto fuels may contain an excess of chlorine and bromine, while aviation fuel only has a minimum of bromine. The chlorine can be very corrosive and can lead to exhaust-valve failures. Even though some auto fuels contain no lead, the other objections still apply.

4. Auto fuels are less stable and can form gum deposits. Gum deposits can cause valve sticking and poor fuel distribution.

5. Auto fuels may have solvent characteristics not suitable for aircraft engines. Seals, gaskets, and flexible fuel lines are susceptible to attack.

6. Aircraft engines operate at higher power settings than auto engines—55 to 75 percent of power vs 20 to 40 percent for a car engine. The aircraft engine is also operating at higher temperatures and pressures, wider variation in climatic conditions, and more rapid changes in atmospheric temperature and pressure.

Warning! Never use aviation-jet fuel in a gasoline engine! Mistakes do happen, and once in a while a piston-engine aircraft will be refueled with jet fuel. Here's what to do if this happens to you.

1. If the engine was not operated subsequent to the refueling with jet fuel, drain the fuel tanks, lines, and system completely. Refill the tanks with the proper grade of aviation gasoline and run the engine for about five minutes.

2. If the engine was operated after refueling with jet fuel, investigate any abnormal engine-operating conditions such as those related to the fuel mixture and cylinder operating temperatures. In addition, carry out the following.

   a. Perform a compression test of all cylinders.

   b. Completely inspect the interior of the cylinders with a boroscope, giving special attention to the combustion chamber and the piston dome.

   c. Drain the engine oil and check the oil screens.

   d. If you find any unsatisfactory condition after performing the above three checks, correct it.

   e. Completely drain the fuel tanks and the entire fuel system, including the carburetor, if you have one.

   f. Flush the fuel system and carburetor with gasoline and check for leaks.

   g. Fill the fuel tanks with the proper grade of aviation gasoline.

   h. If the engine inspection was satisfactory, complete an engine run-up check.

It is the pilot's responsibility to see that the correct type of fuel is loaded on the aircraft.

Fuel contamination

Fuel is contaminated when it contains any material that was not provided under the fuel specification. This can include water, rust, sand, dust, microbial growth, and certain additives that are not compatible with the fuel, fuel-system materials, and engine.

1. *Water.* All aviation fuels absorb moisture from the air and contain water in both suspended-particle and liquid form. The amount of suspended particles varies with the tem-

The Champion Tri-Traveler is typical of airplanes facing a problem with the 80 octane fuel shortage

perature of the fuel. When the fuel temperature goes down, some of the suspended particles are drawn out of the solution and slowly fall to the bottom of the tank. When the fuel temperature rises, water is drawn from the atmosphere and stays in a saturated solution. Changes in fuel temperature therefore result in a continuous accumulation of water. During freezing temperatures this water may turn to ice, restricting or stopping fuel flow.

2. Rust. Pipelines, storage tanks, fuel trucks, and fuel drums tend to produce rust that can be carried in the fuel in small particles. A high degree of filtration is required to remove the liquid water and rust particles from the fuel.

3. Dust and sand. The fuel may be contaminated by dust and sand particles through openings in tanks and from the use of fuel-handling equipment that is not clean.

4. Microorganisms. Many types of microorganisms have been found in unleaded fuels, particularly jet fuels. The microbes, which may come from the atmosphere or storage tanks, live at the interface between the fuel and liquid water in the tank. These microorganisms of bacteria and fungi rapidly multiply, cause serious corrosion in tanks, and may clog filters, screens, and fuel-metering equipment. The growth and corrosion are particularly serious in the presence of other forms of contamination.

5. Additives. Certain oil companies, in developing products to cope with aircraft-fuel icing problems, found that their products also checked "bug" growth. These products, known as biocides, are usually called additives. Some additives may not be compatible with the fuel or the materials in the fuel system and may be harmful to other parts of the engine with which they come in contact. Additives that have not been approved by the engine manufacturer and the FAA should not be used.

Follow these steps to check for fuel contamination.

1. Refueling. Fuel with a cloudy appearance should be suspected of con-

tamination or deterioration and should not be used. Refueling from drums or cans is an undesirable operation and should be avoided whenever possible. All containers of this type should be regarded with suspicion and the contents carefully inspected, identified, and checked for water and other contamination. Use at least a 5-micron filtered portable pumping unit or the best filtering equipment available locally, or, as a last resort, a chamois-skin filter and filter funnel. If the aircraft fuel tanks have not been used for some time, drain their sumps *before* refilling. The agitation action of fresh fuel entering the tank may suspend or entrain liquid water or other contaminants, which may not resettle until after the aircraft is airborne.

2. Preflight action. Drain a generous sample of fuel—considerably more than just a trickle—from each of the fuel sumps and from the main fuel strainer or gascolator into a transparent container. In field tests three gallons of water were added to the half-full fuel tanks of a popular-make high-wing airplane. After several

minutes the fuel strainer was checked for water. It was necessary to drain *ten* liquid ounces of fuel before any water appeared. In another test one gallon of water was added to a half-full fuel tank. More than a quart of fuel had to be drained before any water appeared. In both these tests about nine ounces of water remained in the fuel tank after the belly drain and the fuel strainer had ceased to show any sign of water. This residual water could only be removed by draining the tank sumps. On certain aircraft with fuel tanks in both wings, positioning the fuel selector valve to the both-on position may not adequately drain the system. This is because the fuel tends to take the path of least resistance. In this case the fuel-selector valve should be positioned at each tank in turn. Examine the fuel samples for water and dirt contamination. If present, it will collect at the bottom of the container and should be easily detected. Continue to drain fuel from the contaminated sump until you are certain that the system is clear of all water and dirt.

The Piper Seminole has an easy fuel drain system

Fixing it

3. Postflight. A good way to keep condensation to a minimum is to completely fill the fuel tanks at the end of each day's flying. However, this may be an awkward procedure if you have to operate the next day with a reduced fuel load in order to stay under gross takeoff weight with a full load of passengers and baggage.

4. Routine maintenance. In addition to the preflight and postflight actions, certain precautionary or routine maintenance actions should be taken at regular intervals. These include inspecting and cleaning fuel-tank-outlet strainers and carburetor screens and flushing the carburetor bowl.

In-flight fuel siphoning is chiefly attributable to poor maintenance and service practices. With rare exception, siphoning problems begin when fuel filler caps are incorrectly installed and/or worn fuel filler caps and gaskets are not removed from use promptly. Always check the con-dition of the fuel filler caps for evidence of wear and/or deterioration. If you find that a tank is siphoning in flight, feed off that tank to reduce the amount of fuel in the tank. I sometimes get this problem in my right auxiliary tank in my Comanche. I simply feed off that tank as soon as possible after takeoff, and the siphoning stops within about two minutes. It is a good idea to check all fuel tanks visually after takeoff, if you can see them, to make sure that you're not siphoning.

The fuel tank must have a vent so that air can get in to replace the fuel as it is used. A blocked vent can cause an interruption in fuel flow and possible engine failure. Always check your fuel vents for stoppage, bends, kinks, or distortion before flight. Some vents are right in the fuel cap. If you replace such a cap, make sure that the replacement part is also vented and is approved for use on the specific type of aircraft.

Oil analysis

I recommend that you have your engine oil analyzed at each oil change. The purpose of the oil analysis is to detect metal particles in the oil and the extent to which they are present. In this way an early indication is given of possible wear over and above what would be considered normal for the type of engine. For example, if an analysis indicated a high chrome content and you have chrome cylinders, you would get the idea that the cylinders were getting high wear. The oil analysis can detect the presence of the following:

Substance	Wear Item
Aluminum	Pistons, bearings
Chromium	Rings, cylinders
Copper	Bearings
Iron	Cylinder rings, crankshaft, camshaft
Lead	(Gasoline additive)
Magnesium	Piston rings
Nickel	Piston rings, bearings
Silicon	Dirt (through air intake)
Silver	Bearings
Tin	Bearings

The elements are given in parts per million (PPM) by weight in the oil. Some labs also report the oil's viscosity, acidity, and sludge content.

To have your oil analyzed, you obtain a kit from one of the labs. The kit consists of a small bottle to put a couple of ccs of oil in and a form on which you must record the details about the engine, type of oil used, hours since last change, and so on. You take a sample of the oil, according to the instructions received with the kit, and mail it to the lab. Soon after you will receive a report and comment about the analysis. Some labs will telephone you if they find something drastically wrong.

The oil analysis is done in an emission spectrometer. By flash burning the oil and measuring the light frequencies emitted, the lab can detect the metallic content of the oil. The cost varies by lab between $6 and

With 108 gallons, the Navion Rangemaster offered a 1565 nm range in 1966

$15. Oil analysis must be done on a continuing basis in order to establish trends in metallic content. That's why I suggest you do it at every oil change—ask the FBO to save you a sample of oil when they do the change. The oil should be hot when collected.

Oil analysis is not a cure-all. However, it is a small price to pay for getting a better picture of your engine's wear patterns, and it can predict things such as worn piston rings, dirty air filters, or high wear in the bearings, which, if corrected soon enough, can prevent the engine from needing a premature overhaul. It is important to stay with one lab for consistency of measurement. Analyses from different labs will be pretty meaningless.

I have been satisfied with the service of Spectro, Inc. They send you the kit free and you return the kit with the oil sample and your check. When you receive the analysis report, they send you another kit for next time. Their address is:

Spectro, Inc.
Box 16526,
Fort Worth, Texas, 76133.

Buying spare parts

The biggest complaint of aircraft owners is the high cost of ownership and the biggest complaint about high costs is for parts. Aircraft parts can be frighteningly expensive. This can be dangerous—you may thus be tempted to use some other type of part in your aircraft because it seems to be the same and costs only 20 percent as much at the automotive store.

All parts used in an aircraft that holds an FAA type certificate must meet the standards specified for the issuance of that type certificate. To do otherwise invalidates the certificate of airworthiness, unless a supplemental type certificate (STC) has been issued to cover the nonstandard part (see page 164).

Parts that meet FAA requirements are manufactured by the original manufacturer and are certified by the FAA as a part of the original type certificate. Alternatively, the parts

may be made by someone else but guaranteed to be of the same quality as the original equipment. Such manufacturers have an FAA Parts Manufacturing Approval (PMA). Such parts are stamped or tagged to indicate that they comply with the FAA requirements. These may also be used in certificated aircraft.

Some parts do not meet FAA requirements but may be presented as if they do. You may see terms like "tagged," "inspected," "aircraft quality," and such. Make sure that the tags and inspections are referring to those that are FAA-approved, or you are not buying the real thing.

Parts come in two categories—those that are designed for the specific airplane, such as a windshield or an elevator for a Cessna 172, and those that are components, used in many types of airplanes, such as a starter, a navigation light, or an altimeter. You really don't have much choice when you need a specific airplane part. The line boys in my hangar crimped my left aileron when moving my Comanche recently. The new aileron came from Piper. But a new left tire can be bought anywhere.

All parts used in airplanes must be FAA-approved. To obtain FAA approval costs a lot of money and time. Aircraft parts are low-volume items when compared with other manufactured devices. One question that came through loud and clear in my survey of aircraft owners, carried out as research for this book (see page 2), was "why do airplane parts cost so much more than automobile parts?" One of the biggest points is that it costs much more to make 1,200 pieces than it does to make 1,200,000 on a per-piece basis. So specific airplane parts are going to cost a lot of money. General parts (the kind that can be used in many different types of airplane, such as nav lights) are still relatively low-volume items and must still be approved for each model of airplane (each type certificate). Now consider a part that is made by a subcontractor and sold to the factory. You can bet that the factory is not going to pass the part

Avoid hangar rash! A replacement elevator for a Bonanza costs about $750, excluding the trim tab and installation!

on to you at cost. They are going to factor in their overhead and profit. Then the part is going to go to a distributor, who will add on some markup, and finally to the FBO, who will also add on a markup. The secret is to find out where you can get the general parts other than from the airframe manufacturer. In this way you will cut out several middlemen and pay a more reasonable price. A good source is *Trade-a-Plane*. (Their address is: Trade-a-Plane, Crossville, Tenn. 38555). You will find tons of parts advertisements in every issue, but beware of buying bogus materials. You still want the legitimate stuff. Items such as tires, batteries, lights, sparkplugs, filters, hoses, and instruments can be bought in this way. Radios can also be bought through discount houses. However, your installation costs may exceed your discount savings, and you may get into warranty problems when buying avionics by mail order.

Costs can soar for parts for aircraft no longer in production. Most of the major manufacturers support their extinct aircraft with parts for several years, but the older the bird, the

worse the situation becomes. And if the manufacturer has gone out of business, you may have a real problem. Quite often, in the extinct-manufacturer area, a firm will buy the tooling from the bankruptcy trustees or such and will continue to offer parts. (Univair Aircraft Corporation, Route 3, Box 59, Aurora, Colo. 80011 specializes in Stinson parts, for example. They also offer parts for many other older aircraft.)

Another solution is available through the various owners' clubs. Many aircraft types have an owner's club related to them—for example, Bonanzas, Comanches, and Navions all have clubs (see page 224 for a list). I strongly recommend that you join the appropriate club for your aircraft if there is one. Members help each other locate parts or perhaps band together to get one elusive part built in a reasonable quantity.

Trade-a-Plane is, as always, a good source for old airplane parts. Either you run an ad saying what you want or you may find it being offered. Some people buy wrecks for parts recovery—you'll see ads such as "Dismantling two Aztecs. Two right

wings, two tail units, and many other parts available."

The last resort is simply to have the part made. This can be a problem, especially where the FAA is concerned. Talk to your mechanic or FBO about how to do this effectively.

When you buy a part for your airplane, it will most likely have a tag attached to it. The different colors of the tags tell a story.

Yellow tag—means an overhauled part. On the tag will be the date of the overhaul, who did it, and the signature of the inspector.

Green tag—means an "airworthy" part. A part that has perhaps been removed from an aircraft and was working perfectly when it was taken off but has not been overhauled.

Red tag—means a rejected or non-airworthy part.

Keep the tags in the airplane log books when you put in replacement parts.

Some parts have limited shelf lives. Anything with rubber in it will deteriorate over the years. Altimeters have to have been checked within two years for use in IFR (FAR 91.170). Make sure that the inspection date on the yellow tag respects this. A yellow tag on an instrument that was inspected in 1948 (such as on a mail-order DG) is worthless today.

Most airplanes use automotive generators and starters or alternators. But you can't just drop into your local Chevy dealer and pick up a Delco alternator for your airplane. The parts may look the same, but they are *not* the same. The airplane part will be stamped with the FAA-approved part number and will conform to the FAA specifications. That's what you must use. For example, Piper uses a Chrysler alternator in some airplanes. But don't replace it with one you buy at the garage. The airplane version rotates in the opposite direction to the automobile version! Parts for use in aircraft have heavier-duty components, and different materials are used in some cases.

A car battery will not do

144

Spark plugs

See page 147 for how spark plug examination can help in determining the condition of a high-time piston engine.

Spark plugs should be serviced (cleaned, regapped, or changed) as often as may be necessary to assure smooth engine operation. Bad plugs can cause preignition, misfiring, rough running, hard starting, or loss of power. The most prevalent cause of poor plug performance is fouling. The common causes of fouling are:

1. Oil fouling. Caused by oil getting by piston rings or intake-valve guides. This is often an indication of more serious trouble. Oil fouling is identified by a wet, oily coating on the electrodes or the ceramic insulator.

2. Lead fouling. Aviation fuels contain tetraethyl lead as an antiknock agent. When this lead has done its job, most of it is changed chemically and blown from the cylinder. The imperfection of normal combustion, however, permits a buildup of lead deposits in the plug shell cavity. Since some deposits will carry electricity, the spark gap is altered. If the insulator contains deposits, the current may flow from the center electrode to the ground. In this case the spark does not jump the gap, and you get a magneto drop and a rough engine. Make certain that you are using the plugs recommended by the engine manufacturer and have them checked regularly.

3. Carbon fouling. Lengthy ground idling, idle mixture too rich, or plug type too cold are generally the causes of carbon fouling, which leaves black, sooty deposits on the plug. Make sure that you are using the correct plug type and that the idle-mixture setting is correct.

4. Cigarette fouling. The "cigarette" is the white insulator that fits over the ignition lead wire running down to the contact button inside the top of a shielded spark plug. Any dirt or moisture on the "cigarette" exterior or damage to the plug terminal may short out the current before it jumps the gap in the form of a spark. Keep the "cigarettes," plug leads, and wells clean, dry and free of damage.

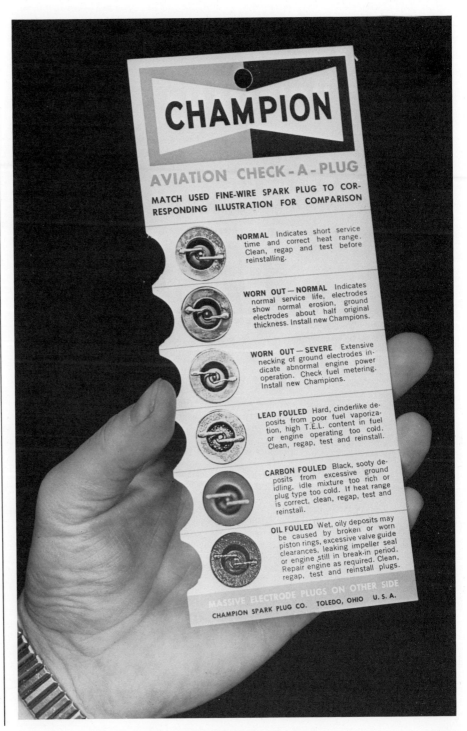

The compression check

The compression check is a method of evaluating the compression available in the individual cylinders of the engine. By checking each cylinder in turn it is possible to get an idea of the condition of the engine. It is thus a good idea to have one done on the engine(s) of an aircraft you're thinking of buying. It is analagous to having your blood pressure checked in a physical and is almost as easy!

The compression check is used as an engine-maintenance aid and is considered part of the 100-hour or annual inspection. Most experienced maintenance people use the compression check at regular intervals to chart a trend over a period of flight hours. However, the check can be made if a pilot notices loss of power in flight, finds high oil consumption, or observes soft spots when hand-pulling the prop. If you keep a run-ning chart of the compression checks, a gradual deterioration of charted compression taken during routine maintenance checks would be a sound basis for further investigation and possible cylinder removal. This would be a good example of preventive maintenance.

There are two basic systems in use, the *direct compression* (old automotive type) and the *differential*, using an input of 80 lbs of air. Of these two the differential is considered better in that it is a more precise method of locating specific areas of trouble, it is simpler to use, and it is more reliable in locating combustion-chamber problems in an early stage of their development.

Either method of compression check can be handled in such a way as to give almost any reading. This suggests that cylinders should not be pulled indiscriminately after one low reading. Here are some cross-checks that can be carried out if low readings are observed.

1. Consider using the direct com-pression check first and then following with the differential. The direct tends to blow out loose deposits, lubricates the piston rings, and serves as a general cross-check on the differential equipment and readings.

2. Spark plugs tell a story. Carefully check the spark plugs removed from any cylinder with a low reading.

3. Use at least a goose-neck light and preferably a boroscope and carefully check the top of the piston and cylinder walls.

4. Consider the history of the engine. Has it had a previous difficulty of this nature?

5. Have you noticed any loss of power in the engine during flight or run-up?

6. How has the engine been maintained and operated during its life? If the maintenance and care have been proper and consistent, there is less likelihood of trouble.

7. The chief mechanic should evaluate all these factors and make a recommendation.

Plane Profile 25: Cessna Corsair

Seats	6/8
Cruise speed, 26,000 feet	257 knots
Range, full optional fuel	
26,000 feet	1,053 nm
Gross weight	8,275 pounds
Empty weight	4,915 pounds
Full optional fuel	2,452 pounds
	366 gallons
Useful load, full fuel	908 pounds
Fuel efficiency, 75% power	4.3 nmpg
Stall speed, gear and flaps down	79 knots
Rate of climb, sea level	2,027 fpm
	434 fpm s/e
Minimum field length	3,116 feet
Engine type 2 Pratt & Whitney PT6A-112	450 shp
Engine TBO	3,500 hours
Remarks Turboprop version of Cessna Golden Eagle.	

Fixing it

Determining the condition of high-time piston engines

As an engine gets considerable time on it and approaches the manufacturer's recommended time for overhaul, the question arises concerning the decision to either continue flying, do a top overhaul or a major overhaul, or exchange engines. Here is a quick reference checklist to help make such a decision:

1. Oil consumption—any unusual increase?
2. Fuel consumption—has it been running lean at more than cruise power?
3. General engine history
4. Pilot and maintenance opinions of the engine
5. How has the engine been operated?
6. Maintenance—what kind has the engine received?
7. What does the oil filter tell (if no filter, have there been frequent oil changes?)
8. What has been the trend in the regular oil analysis?
9. What has been the trend in compression checks?
10. What do the spark plugs show?
11. Refer to the engine manufacturer's service bulletin for engine life and recommended overhaul periods

Following is a brief explanation of each point.

1. Oil consumption. The operator or maintenance people (one or the other) should know the general history of oil consumption during the life of the engine. A possible danger signal concerning engine health is a definite increase in oil consumption during the most recent 25 to 50 hours of flight time. The oil screens and filter should be carefully observed for signs of metal. Maintenance should also take a good differential-compression check at this time. They should also look in the cylinders with a gooseneck light or a boroscope to detect any unusual conditions in the combustion chamber. If you haven't looked at your air filter lately, it would be a good idea to carefully inspect it for wear and proper fit. This is all the more important when operating in dusty areas and could definitely be a cause of increased oil consumption.

2. Fuel consumption. If there has been any radical change in fuel consumption on the lean side of the manufacturer's predicted consumption, particularly at takeoff and climb, damage from detonation, which is not always easily detected, may have been done to the engine. A higher-time engine that has been in detonation might necessitate an engine overhaul or change. (Detonation occurs when the fuel-air mixture within the cylinder burns too rapidly after the spark plug fires. Engines are designed so that the mixture will burn at a certain controlled rate. The "pinging" that can be heard from some automobile engines under acceleration when using low-octane fuel is an example of detonation. However, it may not be heard in an aircraft engine, and continued detonation could cause engine damage and ultimate failure. It can be caused by too-low octane fuel, too much manifold pressure for the RPM setting, overheating from excessive use of carburetor heat, closed cowl flaps that should be open, or too lean a mixture.)

3. General engine history. If a powerplant has been basically healthy throughout its life, this would be a favorable factor in continuing to operate it as the engine approached high time. Alternatively, if it has required frequent repairs, the engine may not achieve its normal life expectancy. The engine log book should contain this accumulative record. Another important aspect of an engine's history is its calendar age. Although engine flight time is of primary importance, the calendar age could be equally important to the operator. Engines infrequently flown tend to age or deteriorate more quickly than those flown on a regular basis. It may be necessary to top- or major-overhaul an engine with 600 hours on it if it is ten years old, even if the TBO (time between overhauls) is slated as 1,200 hours, due to this calendar-age deterioration.

4. Pilot and maintenance opinions of the engine. Your opinion of the engine based on your experience in operating it is another important point in this checklist. You opinion should be based on whether the engine is reliable and dependable and whether or not you have confidence in it. A lack of confidence as the engine approaches its expected overhaul time could be a weighty factor in the decision to keep flying or to overhaul the engine. Consult with maintenance people for their evaluation of the powerplant.

5. Operation. The basic question here is how the engine has been operated for most of its life. Some engines operating continuously at high power or in dusty conditions (e.g., crop dusting) could have a reduced life. Likewise, if the pilot hasn't followed the manufacturer's recommendations on operation, it may cause engine problems and reduce the expected life. This becomes a more critical influence on a decision on single-engine aircraft and also for single- or twin-engine aircraft flown frequently at night or IFR.

6. Maintenance. Good maintenance should aid in achieving maximum engine life. Poor maintenance tends to reduce the expected life. Often smaller engines are run until something goes wrong and seem to receive less care and attention, according to Lycoming, commenting on engines coming into their shop for remanufacturing. The higher-powered engines have generally had better maintenance and show evidence that operators do not wait until something goes wrong but tend to observe the manufacturer's recommended overhaul time for change, Lycoming has found. The engine log books should properly reflect the kind of maintenance provided the engine or engines.

7. Oil-filter or oil-change history.

Fixing it

Clean oil has consistently been an important factor in aiding and extending engine life. A good full-flow oil filter has been a most desirable application here. When the filter is exchanged, the mechanic should open it and carefully examine for any foreign elements, just as is done at oil change when the engine-oil screen is also examined for the same purpose. Just as the spark plugs tell a story about what is going on in the engine, so the engine oil screen and the external oil filter tell a story about the health of an engine. If the engine has no oil filter, oil changes should have been carried out according to the manufacturer's recommendations and recorded in the engine log book, as should any oil change.

8. Oil analysis. The trend in regular oil analysis should be checked. See page 142.

9. Compression checks. What has been the trend in compression in at least the last two differential-compression checks? The differential-compression check is the more reliable and should be taken on a warm engine. If the differential check shows a 25-percent loss or more, trouble may be developing. See page 146.

10. Spark plugs. The spark plugs, when removed and carefully observed, tell the skilled mechanic what has been happening in the cylinders during flight and can be a helpful factor in deciding what to do with a high-time engine.

a. Copper runout and/or lead fouling mean excessive heat.

b. Black carbon and lead bromide indicate low temperatures and possibly excessive richness of fuel metering at idle.

c. Oil-fouled plugs may indicate that piston rings are failing to seat or that excessive wear is taking place.

d. The normal color of a spark plug deposit is generally brownish gray.

e. In high-compression and supercharged engines a cracked spark plug porcelain (nose ceramic) will cause or has been caused by preignition. (Preignition may be confused with detonation. It is also caused by carbon deposits on the cylinder head, which become hot and act as spark plugs, causing premature ignition of the fuel-air mixture. This can cause backfiring through the intake manifold. Damage from preignition can be quite severe.)

11. Engine manufacturer's recommended overhaul life. The engine manufacturers publish a service bulletin or service instruction that lists a factory-recommended overhaul time period for the specific engine as a reference. The amount of total time on an engine will be a basic factor in any decision to continue flying, change, top-, or major-overhaul the engine. Note that the hours of service life shown are recommendations for engines manufactured and delivered from the factory. These hours can normally be expected provided recommended operation, periodic inspections, frequent flights, and engine maintenance have been carried out in accordance with respective engine operator's manuals. If you desire to operate an engine *beyond* the recommended time and you are concerned about the cost of the eventual overhaul, bear in mind that it is possible that the overhaul cost will become higher with increased time. Engines may have received a top overhaul during their life. Does this extend the life of the engine? Officially, no. However, assuming the engine has been operated properly, you should be able to get at least the recommended TBO hours out of it. A top overhaul should not be carried out unless it is deemed necessary. If the engine is healthy and running satisfactorily, Lycoming suggests that it be left alone. However, there is no substitute or cheap route to safety in the proper maintenance or correct overhaul of an engine.

Apply *all* these basic points concerning your engine or engines and then make your decision as to whether you should top-overhaul, major-overhaul, exchange engines, or continue flying.

An engine overhauler overhauling an engine

Fixing it

Engine overhauls

Aircraft engines are given a suggested life span by their manufacturers, which is called "TBO"—time between overhauls. The TBO is a *recommended* number of operating hours based on the manufacturer's experience with the engine. A newly designed engine might have a relatively low TBO. As the years go by and operating experience increases, the TBO may be modified for the engine type. TBOs for the common light-aircraft reciprocating engines run between 1,000 and 2,000 hours. Turbine engines can go much higher to 3,000 or 3,500 hours and even more, reflecting their relative simplicity. The TBO is not a mandatory figure that must be complied with. It is the factory's recommendation. Well-maintained engines can go several hundred hours past the TBO provided they are properly inspected at frequent intervals (see page 147 for details). A poorly maintained engine that has been subjected to a lot of stress (such as one in a twin used for multi-engine instruction that has been shut down in flight many times) may not even make it halfway to the TBO. The factors affecting the ability of an engine to make it to its TBO and beyond are:

1. Operating conditions
2. Proper maintenance
3. Proper lubrication practices, including regular oil changes, a full-flow oil filter, and regular spectrometric oil analysis
4. Regular spark plug inspections and cleaning as required
5. Proper leaning techniques
6. Proper fuel usage
7. Smooth power adjustments
8. Proper cooling actions (use of cowl flaps, avoidance of lengthy low-power descents or lengthy high-power climbs)

As you start to omit parts of the above, the engine will develop more wear. Probably the worst thing that can happen to an engine is for it to be installed in a light twin used for multi-engine and instrument train-

ing. In almost 25 years of flying I have had two engine problems—a blown valve and a runaway prop. In both cases the aircraft was an Apache, used almost exclusively for training. The more you bash the engine around, the more likely it is to bite back at you.

The two broadest distinctions between engine overhauls are the major and the top overhaul. The term "TBO" refers to the time between *major* overhauls. A major overhaul consists of the complete disassembly of the engine. The engine parts are inspected, repaired as necessary, reassembled, tested, and approved for return to service within the fits and limits specified by the manufacturer's overhaul data. These could be either *new* fits and limits or *serviceable* limits. You should understand clearly what fits or limits are being used during an overhaul when you schedule it. You should also be aware of any parts that are replaced, regardless of condition, as a result of manufacturer's overhaul data, service bulletins, or an AD.

A *top overhaul* consists of the repair of parts outside the crankcase and can be done without completely disassembling the engine. It can include the removal of cylinders; inspection and repair of cylinders; inspection and repair of cylinder walls, pistons, valve-operating mechanisms, valve guides, and valve seats; and the replacement of pistons and piston rings. The engine of my Comanche (a Lycoming O-540 A1D5—250 hp) was topped at 800 hours just before I bought it. It got six new chrome cylinders, and the valves were replaced by larger half-inch ones. The larger valves enable the TBO to be extended from 1,200 hours to 2,000 hours on this model of engine. About 250 hours later the engine is running like a well-oiled sewing machine and using about one quart of oil every five hours.

It is important to note that a top overhaul does not replace the need for a major overhaul at the appropriate time. Yes, my top extended my TBO from 1,200 to 2,000 hours. This

is because there is a stipulation by the manufacturer that the change to the larger valves allows the TBO to be so extended, and that is what was done. But this does not mean that all tops extend TBOs. Each engine has its own situation. You might have a 1,500-hour-TBO engine that gets topped at 600 and again at 1,200 hours. Its TBO will still be 1,500 hours, and the engine should be inspected carefully to determine its needs at that time.

There are two kinds of limits observed during an engine overhaul. These limits are outlined in the engine overhaul manual as a table of limits or a table of dimensional limits. These tables, listing the parts of the engine that are subject to wear, contain minimum and maximum figures for the dimensions of those parts and the clearances between mating surfaces. Typical limits run to five thousandths of an inch (.005 inch). The lists specify two limits, as follows.

1. Manufacturer's minimum and maximum. These are also referred to by some manufacturers as new parts or new dimensions. These are the dimensions that all new parts meet during manufacture and are held to specific quality-control standards as required by the FARs in the issuance of an engine type certificate to the manufacturer. Note that the term "new dimensions" does not necessarily mean that new parts are installed in an engine—even one that is designated as a zero-time engine by the manufacturer in accordance with FAR 91.175. It does mean that used parts in the engine have been inspected and found to meet the manufacturer's new specifications.

2. Service limits. These are the dimensions that represent limits that must not be exceeded and are dimension limits for permissible wear. The manufacturer's new dimensions or limits are used as a guide for determining the amount of wear that has occurred during service. In an engine overhaul certain parts have to be replaced regardless of condition. If an engine is overhauled to serviceable

Fixing it

limits, the parts must conform to the fits-and-limits specifications so listed in the manufacturer's overhaul manuals and service bulletins. If a major overhaul is performed to serviceable limits or an engine is top-overhauled, the total time on the engine continues in the engine records.

The term "rebuilt" is defined in FAR 91.175. The definition allows the operator to use a new maintenance record without a previous operating history if the engine has been rebuilt by the manufacturer or an agency approved by the manufacturer. It is defined as "a used engine that has been completely disassembled, inspected, repaired as necessary, reassembled, tested, and approved in the same manner and to the same tolerances as a new engine with either new or used parts." All parts used must conform to the production drawing tolerances and limits for new parts or be of approved oversize dimensions for a new engine.

The term "remanufactured" has no specific meaning in the FARs. A new engine is a product that is manufactured from raw materials. These raw materials are made into parts and accessories that conform to specifications for the issuance of an engine type certificate. The term "remanufactured" implies that it would be necessary to return the part to its basic raw material and manufacture it again. "Remanufactured," as used by most engine manufacturers and overhaul facilities, means that an engine has been overhauled to the standards required to zero-time it in accordance with FAR 91.175. However, not all engine-overhaul facilities that advertise "remanufactured engines" overhaul engines to new dimensions. Some of these facilities do overhaul to new dimensions but may not be authorized to zero-time the engine records. FAR 91.175 allows only the manufacturer or an agency approved by the manufacturer to grant zero time to an engine.

Engine-overhaul facilities can include the manufacturer, a manufacturer's approved agency, FAA-certificated repair stations both large and small, engine shops that perform custom overhauls, and individual certificated powerplant mechanics. Regardless of the size or type of facility, all are required to comply with FAR 43.13 (a) and (b). It is the owner's responsibility to assure that proper entries are made in the engine log books (FAR 91.165 and 91.173). Engine-overhaul facilities are required by FAR 43.9 to make appropriate entries in the engine logs of maintenance that was performed on the engine. You should make sure that the overhauler shows the tolerances used (new or serviceable) to accomplish the engine overhaul.

Since engine overhauls can be accomplished to various standards, the facility selected to carry out an overhaul should be determined by the type of overhaul you want to have done. The most expensive way of replacing an engine is to simply buy a new one and trade in the old. Next comes the so-called "factory reman," which should be a factory or factory-agency engine rebuilt to new tolerances, with a zero-time log book. Next would be to have your own engine overhauled to new tolerances by an appropriate shop. Last and least would be to have your engine overhauled to within service limits. The last two types of overhaul do not give you a zero-time log book. You get your old log book back, with appropriate entries.

FAR 43.13 (a) requires that the person performing the overhaul shall use methods, techniques, and practices that are acceptable to the administrator. In most cases the standards that are outlined in the engine-manufacturer overhaul manuals are FAA-acceptable. These manuals clearly stipulate the work that must be done during engine overhauls and outline the limits and tolerances used during the inspections.

For a major overhaul the following steps take place.

1. Engine is disassembled and all accessories are removed.

2. All parts are inspected and cleaned. Certain parts are Zyglo-treated. This is a dye that penetrates any cracks. The parts are then inspected under ultraviolet light so that any cracks may be easily discerned. Zyglo treatment is applied to parts such as the crankcase and other magnesium and aluminum parts. Steel parts are magnafluxed. This calls for the part to be washed with a solution containing fine iron particles while it is electrically charged to make it highly magnetic. Again, inspection under ultraviolet light shows up any cracks. Parts are also measured with extremely accurate measuring devices to determine how much wear exists. Any damaged parts are discarded, while parts that fit acceptable limits are retained. Some parts are placed as a matter of course. It depends on the shop as to what their standards are. Most shops discard such items as valves, valve stems, bearings, bushings, pistons, fuel pumps, oil pumps, camshafts, seatings, and such. Some parts may be reground to bring them within acceptable limits.

3. The parts to be reused are repainted and logged into the engine.

4. The engine is reassembled and adjusted for correct fittings of all parts, such as pistons and cylinders, valves, and so on.

5. The engine is run in and tested. After final inspection it is certified by the inspector and is ready to be reinstalled in the aircraft.

Any ADs or factory-service bulletins outstanding on the engine are complied with during the overhaul.

Items such as magnetos, fuel pumps, starters, ignition harness, and such are usually overhauled at the same time, although they may be sent out to a specialty shop. Make sure that any quote you get for an overhaul covers the accessories.

Fixing it

The radio shop

Radio shops may be either independent operations, maybe renting space from the FBO, or be simply a part of the overall FBO's service. Many radio shops work like aircraft dealers, representing specific lines of avionics, such as King, Narco, Edo-Aire, Bendix, and so on. Most shops offer several lines. The biggest investment a radio shop makes is in its test equipment, which can run to many tens of thousands of dollars. Each piece of avionics in the airplane has a corresponding piece of test equipment in the radio shop. When you are selecting a radio shop, make sure that they have the equipment needed to test the types of radios you have or are buying. Some of the test equipment is for use on the bench, while some is portable for use in the airplane.

Whether buying or servicing your avionics, your best bet is to go to a factory-authorized dealer for the model you are involved with. Such a dealer will have all the factory service manuals and bulletins and will be in regular contact with the factory sales and service representatives. Make sure that the dealer is factory-authorized to do warranty work on the type of radio—not just the brand. A franchised dealer may not be authorized to do warranty work on all models of the line.

The FAA requires (FAR 43, Appendix A) that any major repairs to avionics equipment be carried out by an FAA-approved radio shop. The approvals are issued under FAR 145.31. There are three classes of radio shop:

Class 1: Communication equipment

Class 2: Navigation equipment

Class 3: Radar equipment (this includes pulsed-frequency devices such as DMEs and transponders)

FAA approvals may, however, be limited, under FAR 145.33, to radio equipment of a particular make and model.

When a new radio is installed and/or an old one is removed, an entry must be made in the aircraft log book, and the equipment list and

Your typical small avionics shop

weight and balance must be amended accordingly. The addition of new equipment requires that an electrical-load analysis be performed to make sure that no more than 80 percent of the generator or alternator output is being used. The load being checked is the nighttime load—i.e., with navigation lights, strobes, radios, pitot heat, and such all operating. It does not include the load when landing lights are on. If the load exceeds 80% of the output of the

generating system, a placard must be put on the panel stating that not all the equipment may be run at the same time.

An FAA Form 337 may need to be filed on a new installation, depending on the complexity and design approval status of the job. A simple job would only require a log-book entry. See page 134 for details about the 337 form.

The compass should be reswung after new radios have been installed.

Avionics maintenance

Avionics maintenance is a major area of concern among aircraft owners. It is often expensive and frequently unsatisfactory, either because the airplane gets tied up for too long or because the job isn't done right, and it is bewildering to the aircraft owner, because few owners understand what their problem is.

The airlines handle avionics maintenance the best way. They keep a supply of replacement units on hand at their various bases. If something goes wrong, they simply unplug the offending unit, plug in another one, and get on with the flying. Unfortunately, the private owner is not blessed with such a luxury. A step is being made in this direction by some manufacturers who have plug-in components in their avionics so that if something is found wrong, the technician whips out the old and snaps in a new one. This is fine if you have that type of radio and the technician has the right module. However, most of us are doomed to

fly around with what we've got, and if something goes wrong, we simply have to get it fixed.

The first step in getting good avionics maintenance is for you to understand precisely the characteristics of your equipment. Avionics technicians tell me that a lot of the problems that get handed to them are not avionics problems—it's simply that the pilot doesn't understand the equipment and thinks there is something wrong when there isn't. See the box for some examples of things that pilots commonly identify as problems.

All these problems can be attributed to the fact that the pilot does not know the equipment or the installation properly. There's really nothing wrong with the radios.

Narco DME 190 warranty is invalid if cooling kit not installed

How to communicate with the radio-shop technician

The more you tell the technician about your radio problem, the better it can be understood. Imagine you are going to be cross-examined by F. Lee Bailey when you walk in the door. Be ready to answer every question with the truth, the *whole* truth, and nothing but the truth. The accent here is on the word "whole." Let me give you an example of a good description of a problem—one that a technician can work from.

"I have two Narco Mark 12s, one driving a DGO-10 and the other driving a VOA-4. The aircraft has a generator, which was rebuilt last year. The battery was new last year. The ammeter reads a charge in cruising flight. The problem is that the #1 NAV is very weak. This is the one driving the DGO-10. The #2 NAV will give me a good signal at 8,000 feet up to about 100 miles, but the #1 is only good for about 15 miles, then I get the red flag. When I get the flag, I lose the ident signal. I can still hear the ident on the #2 very clearly. The #1 will not give a readable signal on the ground unless I have takeoff power, while the #2 works fine on the ground. Both VORs check out perfectly on VOR test signals. I notice that if I increase RPM in flight, I can get the #1 NAV to come back in, just after I have lost the signal, for a few more miles. Then it goes out again, even with the higher RPM. I have tried turning off all electrical equipment but the #1 NAV/COMM to see if the signal improves. It doesn't. I also only receive an ILS localizer signal within about five miles of the airport on #1, while I get a good signal a long way out on #2. The Narco Mark 12 is very old, while the DGO-10 was installed 15 months ago and has worked per-

Problem	Probable cause and solution
VHF receiver intermittent	Squelch knob set too low — turn it higher
Ground not receiving transmissions when taxiing	Not enough amperage available — increase engine RPMs until ammeter shows a charge
VOR goes off intermittently; red flag shows with full deflection of needle	On some units the red OFF flag shows when the TO/FROM flag is at the midpoint — rotate the OBS to see if a TO/FROM flag comes in at a different setting
VOR loses signal during VHF transmissions — red flag shows	This is a normal situation with many radio installations — the signal should return when the mike is unkeyed
DME ground speed decreases rapidly near the station	This is normal — that's because your ground speed *is* decreasing rapidly relative to the station
DME won't go to zero near station — it sticks at one mile	DME reads slant range — if you're 5,000 feet over the station, it will read one mile (your height above the ground)
DME ground speed only reads accurately when going to or from the station	This is normal — the DME is measuring the rate of change of your distance — if you are not going to or from the station, the rate of change will not be meaningful

Fixing it

fectly. I have not had any other recent service done on these units relevant to this problem, which has only shown up in the last few days. I installed the King KMA-20 audio panel last year, and the avionics were completely rewired at that time. Please fix the #1 so that I get a good signal on both VOR and ILS, at least as good as I get on the #2. One other thing: sometimes the #1 goes off the air completely—I get the red flag on the DGO-10 and no audio on the COMM side. Other times when I lose the VOR signal, I still get audio on the COMM side."

That's the kind of communication that a radio technician can do something with. The problems were found to be:

1. several weak tubes
2. poor connection between Mark 12 and airplane—one pin was misaligned
3. aircraft voltage regulator set low
4. Mark 12 input voltage regulator set too low

The technician was able to figure out the problem and fix it in a minimum of labor time. So when you have an avionics problem be ready to answer questions like those in the box.

I suggest that you use the questions as a guide to writing up a description of the problem next time you have one and give the written data to the radio shop. After they read it, find out if they have any further questions. Then check back a few hours after you think they've started to work on it to see how it is going and if they have any more questions.

Bear in mind that they may need to start the engine, so offer them the keys and give them the necessary authority to do this.

The technician may ask to fly with you after the problem has been fixed to see if it really has been licked. Too often the radio works perfectly on the bench and doesn't work in the airplane. If such is the case, try to install an identical radio in place of the faulty unit. If the new radio also doesn't work, the problem is most likely in the installation, wiring, or

antennas, not in the radio. If the new radio does work, the problem must be in the old radio.

Get to know the operating characteristics of your equipment, detect

problems as early as possible, and communicate these problems as clearly and in as much detail as you can, and you have half the avionics-maintenance jungle cleared.

Avionics Maintenance Questions

1. What is the nature of the problem?
2. Is this the first time this has happened?
3. Has it happened and been fixed before?
4. Does it happen all the time or intermittently?
5. How new is the equipment?
6. Has anything else ever failed on this equipment before?
7. Have you had any other avionics troubles that have been fixed recently?
8. When did you first notice the problem?
9. What was the airplane doing then? (e.g., climbing, cruising at 10,000 feet, on takeoff, after engine shutdown, etc.)
10. When this problem occurred, did everything else continue to work properly?
11. What happens when you turn other radios on or off?
12. If there is a second system (e.g., as in a dual NAV/COMM), does the other system display the same problem or what?
13. What happens if you turn the generator or alternator off?
14. What happens if you change the power setting?
15. Does the problem only occur at certain power settings or in certain configurations?
16. If the problem is audio-related, does it happen through both phones and speaker or one or the other only?
17. Have you checked all circuit breakers and fuses?
18. Is the battery fully charged?
19. Is the generator or alternator system working properly?
20. In spite of the problem, do you get any normal indications in the equipment? (e.g., if ATC says they are not receiving your transponder, does the interrogation light flash? Does it glow when you squawk ident?)
21. In what condition is your avionics wiring?
22. What other avionics problems have you had recently?

A masterpiece of solid state miniaturization. Inside the King KY 92 COMM transceiver

Troubleshooting guides

The following troubleshooting guides are not intended to replace the services of a certificated mechanic. Check the section on preventive maintenance (page 138) to see what you are entitled to do as the owner of an aircraft if you are not certificated as a mechanic.

These guides are given to help you isolate a problem so that you can speak more intelligently to your mechanic about it. They will be helpful in establishing a rough idea of what might be wrong. Some of the fixes you *can* do yourself. Those that are illegal without supervision are marked with an asterisk. Bear in mind that different aircraft have different systems, so the probable causes or remedies suggested here may not apply in the case of your particular aircraft. I have deliberately excluded items that are usually unique to a particular type of plane. The items in these guides are fairly general and appropriate for most general-aviation light aircraft.

When discussing a problem with your mechanic, be as specific and detailed as possible. If you are writing out the problem, write as if you were being paid $1 a word! Discuss all differences from normal and explain exactly what your were doing when you saw the problem first develop. Explain any situations where things seemed normal and where they changed. For example, when I discovered that I had a leaking fuel tank, the first indication was a fuel smell that occurred whenever I put the wheels down and only then. A subsequent visual inspection of the underside of the wing showed fuel stains and actual moist fuel. When I noticed that the MP gauge still read 30" as I throttled back to climb power on takeoff from Boston, I figured I had a broken MP line (true).

Here are the sort of questions you should be able to answer.

If you are writing out the discrepancy, leave your phone number or location in case the mechanic has a question for you. If you don't hear from the airport within a reasonable time, call or visit and see how things are going. It's amazing how some little remark you make can point the mechanic right at the trouble even after you very carefully wrote it all out.

If you currently don't have any problems, it is still a good idea to get to know your plane well enough so that you can isolate any irregularities quickly. If you don't have a feel for things, take a clipboard and a friend up and write down all the instrument readings for the various flight conditions. Keep them handy for reference when you think something is wrong.

Aircraft Maintenance Questions

1. What is the nature of the problem?
2. Under what conditions did this problem manifest itself?
3. What were the power settings when you saw the problem?
4. What fuel tank were you using?
5. What altitude were you at?
6. What was the outside-air temperature and weather situation?
7. Did the problem go away if you did anything; if so, what did you do? Did it come back? What did you do that made it come back?
8. When you were having the problem, what instruments read normally and what instruments read abnormally?
9. Were there any noises? What and from where?
10. Was there any vibration? Could you control it?
11. Were there any smells? What type?
12. Was there any smoke? What color? From where?
13. Were any controls loose or slack? Which?
14. Were any controls tight or binding? Which?
15. Was there any heat or cold? From where?
16. What do *you* think is the trouble?

Quick! Where's the vaccuum pump? Inside a Beech Debonair engine compartment.

Fixing it

Problem	Probable cause	Remedy
Starting Problems		
Engine fails to crank	1. Master switch off 2. Battery flat 3. Master switch defective 4. Defective starter switch or circuit 5. Starter lever does not activate switch 6. Defective starter	1. Turn on master switch 2. Use external power or recharge battery 3. *Check switch and circuit 4. *Check switch and circuit 5. *Check starter-lever adjustment 6. *Check starter and repair or replace
Starter motor runs but does not turn crankshaft	1. Starter lever activates switch but does not engage pinion with crankshaft gear 2. Defective overrunning clutch or drive 3. Damaged starter pinion gear or crank-shaft gear	1. *Check starter-lever adjustment and correct 2. *Remove starter and check starter drive and overrunning clutch 3. *Remove and check these items
Starter drags	1. Low battery 2. Starter switch or relay contacts burned or dirty 3. Defective starter 4. Dirty commutator	1. Use external power source or recharge battery 2. *Check contacts and replace if needed 3. *Check and repair or replace starter 4. *Clean, check, and adjust commutator
Starter excessively noisy	1. Worn starter pinion 2. Worn or broken teeth on crankshaft gears	1. *Remove and examine pinion, replace starter drive 2. *Remove starter and turn over by hand to check crankshaft gear, replace if needed
Engine fails to start	1. Pilot starting technique 2. Lack of fuel 3. Engine flooded or overpriming 4. Underpriming 5. Incorrect throttle setting 6. Mixture in idle cutoff 7. Magneto-impulse coupling not operating properly 8. Defective sparkplugs or ignition wire 9. Improper magneto operation 10. Inoperative or defective vibrator 11. Water in fuel lines or carburetor 12. Impulse coupling magnetized 13. Frozen sparkplug electrodes 14. Shorted ignition switch or loose ground	1. Refer to *Pilot's Operating Handbook* for correct technique 2. Check fuel selector on Check fuel quantity Check fuel system for leaks *Clean dirty lines, strainers, or fuel valves 3. Clear engine by opening throttle, putting mixture in idle cutoff, and turning over with starter 4. Use correct priming procedure 5. Set throttle correctly 6. Set mixture correctly 7. *Remove magneto and check for binding or other problems 8. *Inspect plugs, clean and replace as necessary; test leads 9. *Check magneto timing 10. *Check and replace vibrator if needed 11. *Drain carburetor and fuel lines 12. *Demagnetize coupling 13. Replace or dry out plugs 14. *Check and replace or repair
Engine backfires during starting	1. Insufficient prime	1. Increase amount of prime, make sure primer is not leaking

*May only be carried out by or under supervision of certificated mechanic.

Fixing it

Problem	Probable cause	Remedy
Idling Problems		
Engine does not idle properly	1. Mixture control set improperly 2. Open or leaking primer 3. Incorrect idle mixture 4. Incorrect carburetor idle-speed adjustment 5. Leak in induction system 6. Dirty air filter 7. Low cylinder compression 8. Faulty ignition system 9. Improper sparkplug setting for altitude	1. Set mixture control correctly 2. Lock or *repair primer 3. *Adjust mixture in engine 4. *Adjust throttle stop to obtain correct idle 5. *Tighten all connections in the induction system, replace any defective parts 6. *Clean or replace 7. *Check cylinder compression 8. *Check and repair ignition system 9. Check and regap sparkplug if needed
Run-up Problems		
Engine does not develop enough power and runs unevenly	1. Mixture too rich (sluggish engine operation, red exhaust flame, black smoke) 2. Mixture too lean (overheating or back-firing) 3. Improper grade of fuel 4. Defective sparkplugs 5. Leaks in the induction system 6. Magneto breaker points not working properly 7. Defective ignition wire 8. Defective sparkplug terminal connectors 9. Incorrect valve clearance 10. Restriction in exhaust system 11. Improper ignition timing	1. Adjust mixture, check primer, *re-adjust carburetor mixture control 2. Adjust mixture, check fuel supply, *check fuel lines for dirt or other restrictions 3. Drain and fill tank with correct grade 4. Clean or replace sparkplugs 5. *Tighten all connections, replace defective parts 6. *Clean points, check internal timing of magneto 7. *Test and replace any defective wires 8. *Replace connectors on sparkplug wire 9. *Adjust valve clearance 10. *Remove restriction 11. *Check magnetos for timing and synchronization
Engine fails to develop full power	1. Improper fuel 2. Throttle lever out of adjustment 3. Leak in induction system 4. Restriction in carburetor airscoop 5. Faulty ignition 6. Propeller governor out of adjustment	1. Drain tank and refill with correct fuel 2. *Adjust throttle lever 3. *Tighten all connections and replace defective parts 4. *Examine airscoop and remove restriction 5. *Tighten all connections, check ignition system, check timing 6. *Adjust governor
Other Engine Problems		
Rough-running engine	1. Primer unlocked 2. Mixture too rich or lean 3. Lead deposit on sparkplugs 4. Defective engine mounting bushings 5. Cracked engine mount 6. Unbalanced propeller	1. Lock primer 2. Adjust mixture 3. Lean out mixture to burn off deposit, clean or replace sparkplugs 4. Install new mounting bushings 5. *Repair or replace engine mount 6. *Remove propeller and check for balance

*May only be carried out by or under supervision of certificated mechanic.

Fixing it

Problem	Probable cause	Remedy
Low oil pressure	1. Insufficient oil	1. Check oil supply and add oil
	2. Wrong grade of oil	2. Replace with correct grade
	3. Defective pressure gauge	3. *Replace gauge
	4. Dirty oil strainers	4. *Remove and clean oil strainers
	5. Air lock or dirt in relief valve	5. *Remove and clean oil-pressure relief valve
	6. Leak in suction line or pressure line	6. *Check gasket between accessory housing crankcase
	7. Stoppage in oil-pump intake passage	7. Check line for obstruction, clean suction strainer
	8. Worn or scored bearings	8. *Overhaul engine
High oil temperature	1. Insufficient oil supply	1. Fill oil tank to proper level
	2. Wrong grade of oil	2. Replace with correct grade
	3. High ambient temperatures	3. Reduce power, climb to cooler altitude or land and allow to cool
	4. Insufficient air cooling	4. Check air inlet and outlet for deformation and obstruction
	5. Clogged oil lines or strainers	5. *Remove and clean oil lines or strainers
	6. Defective thermostats	6. *Replace thermostats
	7. Defective gauge	7. *Replace gauge
	8. Failing or failed bearings	8. *Examine sump for metal particles; if found, overhaul engine
	9. Excessive blow-by	9. *If caused by weak or stuck rings, overhaul engine
Excessive oil consumption	1. Worn or broken piston rings	1. *Install new rings
	2. Incorrectly installed piston rings	2. *Install new rings
	3. External oil leaks	3. *Check engine carefully for leaking gaskets or O rings
	4. Leakage through engine fuel-pump vent	4. *Replace fuelpump seal
	5. Engine breather or vacuum-pump breather	5. *Check engine, overhaul or replace vacuum pump
	6. Failing or failed bearing	6. *Check sump for metal particles; if found, overhaul engine
Poor idle cutoff	1. Vapor in fuel lines	1. Avoid prolonged operation at low RPM and idle, use fuel pump if necessary
	2. Improperly rigged mixture-control linkage	2. *Adjust rigging
	3. Dirt in air-bleed hole of nozzle	3. *Remove and clean
	4. Mixture valve stuck	4. *Clean valve seating
High cylinder head temperature	1. Climbing at too low an airspeed	1. Increase airspeed
	2. Cowl flaps closed	2. Open cowl flaps
	3. Mixture too lean	3. Enrich mixture
	4. Power setting too high for forward speed	4. Reduce power setting and/or increase speed
	5. Sparkplugs of improper heat rating installed in engine	5. Check and install correct plugs
	6. Cooling baffles missing or broken	6. *Check and repair cooling baffles
	7. Engine improperly timed	7. *Check and correct timing
	8. Mixture control improperly rigged	8. *Rerig mixture control
	9. Partially plugged fuel nozzles	9. *Clean nozzles
	10. Wrong fuel lines in use	10. *Check and replace incorrect fuel lines

*May only be carried out by or under supervision of certificated mechanic.

Fixing it

Problem	Probable cause	Remedy
High manifold pressure at idle	1. Broken manifold-pressure line (MP reads about 30) 2. Improperly adjusted fuel injector or carb 3. Air leak in induction system 4. Hydraulic lifters not operating properly	1. *Replace line 2. *Adjust idle mixture 3. *Repair leak 4. Replace lifters
Gyro Instrument Problems Artificial horizon, directional gyro, or turn-and-bank/turn coordinator read improperly	*Suction:* 1. Vacuum-pump failure (low suction-gauge reading) 2. Broken suction line 3. Instrument failure *Pressure:* 1. Pressure-pump failure 2. Broken pressure line 3. Instrument failure *Electric:* 1. Not receiving enough power 2. Instrument failure	 1. *Replace vacuum pump 2. *Repair line 3. *Replace instrument 1. *Replace pump 2. *Replace line 3. *Replace instrument 1. Check generator or alternator ON, check circuit breaker, reduce electrical load by turning other items OFF Check master switch Recharge or replace battery 2. *Replace instrument

Directional Gyro
 	
Excess drift in either direction
	1. Excessive vibration
	2. Insufficient vacuum:
	  a. Relief valve improperly adjusted
	  b. Incorrect vacuum-instrument reading
	  c. Vacuum-pump failure
	  d. Vacuum line kinked or leaking
	
	3. Defective instrument
		1. *Check shock mounts
		
		  a. *Adjust
		  b. *Recalibrate vacuum indicator
		  c. *Repair or replace
		  d. *Check and repair, check for collapsed inner wall of hose
		3. *Replace instrument

Dial spins continuously	1. Defective instrument	1. *Replace instrument
Artificial Horizon Bar fails to respond	1. Insufficient vacuum or pressure 2. Excessive vibration 3. Defective instrument	1. *Check pump and lines 2. *Check shock mounts 3. *Replace instrument
Bar oscillates or shimmies continuously	1. Excessive vibration 2. Vacuum or pressure too high 3. Defective instrument	1. *Check shock mounts 2. *Adjust valve 3. *Replace instrument
Turn and Bank Indicator Pointer fails to respond	1. Foreign matter lodged in instrument 2. No electric power (electrical model)	1. *Replace instrument 2. Check fuses or circuit breakers, *check for voltage at instrument

*May only be carried out by or under supervision of certificated mechanic.

Fixing it

Problem	Probable cause	Remedy
Incorrect sensitivity	1. Sensitivity spring out of adjustment	1. *Readjust spring or replace instrument
Pointer does not set on zero	1. Gimbal and rotor assembly out of balance 2. Pointer incorrectly set on its staff 3. Sensitivity adjustment pulls pointer off zero	1. *Replace instrument 2. *Replace instrument 3. *Replace instrument
Vibrating pointer	1. Gimbal and rotor assembly out of balance 2. Pitted or worn pivots or bearings	1. *Replace instrument 2. *Replace instrument
Pitot-Static System Problems		
Airspeed indicator reads low	1. Pitot tube icing 2. Pitot tube blocked 3. Airspeed indicator defective	1. Turn on pitot heat 2. Check pitot tube for dirt and bugs, *clean pitot lines 3. *Replace instrument
Airspeed indicator reads high, vertical speed indicator reads zero, altimeter does not move	1. Static line blocked	1. Select alternate static source; if unavailable, carefully break glass on vertical-speed indicator
Altimeter pointer oscillates	1. Defective mechanism	1. *Replace altimeter
Setting knob is hard to turn	1. Wrong lubrication or lack of it	1. *Replace altimeter
Needles fail to move when knob is rotated	1. Defective mechanism	2. *Replace altimeter
Setting-knob set screw loose or missing	1. Excessive vibration	1. Tighten screw if loose, replace altimeter if screw missing
Cracked or loose glass	1. Excessive vibration	1. Replace altimeter
Magnetic Compass Problems		
Excessive compass errors	1. Compass not properly compensated 2. External magnetic interference	1. *Swing compass and compensate instrument 2. Locate interference and eliminate or reswing compass
Excessive card oscillation	1. Improper mounting 2. Insufficient liquid	1. *Mount properly 2. *Replace compass
Card sluggish	1. Weak card magnet 2. Excessive pivot friction or broken jewel 3. Instrument too heavily compensated	1. *Replace compass 2. *Replace compass 3. *Remove excess compensation
Liquid leakage	1. Loose bezel screws 2. Broken cover glass 3. Defective sealing gaskets	1. *Replace compass 2. *Replace compass 3. *Replace compass
Defective light	1. Burned-out lamp or fuse, broken circuit	1. Check lamp, fuse, *wiring

*May only be carried out by or under supervision of certificated mechanic.

Fixing it

Problem	Probable cause	Remedy
Engine Instrument Problems		
Manifold Pressure Gauge		
Excessive error at existing barometric pressure	1. Pointer out of alignment	1. *Replace instrument
Excessive error when engine is running	1. Leak in line	1. *Tighten line connections, replace line if needed
Sluggish or jerky pointer movement	1. Improper damping adjustment	1. *Adjust damping screw
Broken or loose cover glass	1. Vibration or excessive pressure	1. *Replace glass and reseat case
Incorrect reading	1. Moisture or oil in line	1. *Disconnect lines and blow out
Tachometer		
No reading or intermittent reading on indicator	1. Broken shaft 2. Springs weak	1. *Replace instrument 2. *Replace instrument
Pointer oscillates excessively	1. Broken shaft 2. Excess friction in instrument	1. *Repair or replace 2. *Replace instrument
Oil Pressure Gauge		
Excessive error at zero	1. Pointer loose on shaft 2. Overpressure or seasoning of Bourdon tube	1. *Replace instrument 2. *Replace instrument
Excessive scale error	1. Improper calibration adjustment	1. *Replace instrument
Excessive pointer oscillation	1. Improper damping or rough engine-relief valve	1. *Disconnect line and drain, check for leaks, clean, and adjust relief valve
Sluggish operation or pointer or pressure fails to build up	1. Engine relief valve open	1. Check and clean
Oil Temperature Gauge		
Instrument fails to show any reading	1. Broken or damaged capillary 2. Wiring broken	1. *Check engine unit 2. *Check wiring
Excessive scale error	1. Improper calibration adjustment	1. *Repair or replace
Fuel Pressure Gauge		
No fuel pressure indication	1. Fuel valve stuck 2. No fuel in tanks 3. Defective fuel pump 4. Defective gauge	1. *Check valve 2. Check fuel, fill tanks 3. *Check pump for pressure buildup, check diaphragm and relief valves in engine pump, check for obstruction in electric pump, check bypass valve, check for air leak in intake lines 4. *Replace instrument

*May only be carried out by or under supervision of certificated mechanic.

Fixing it

Problem	Probable cause	Remedy
Low pressure or pressure surges	1. Obstruction in inlet side of pump 2. Faulty bypass valve 3. Faulty diaphragm 4. Surge dome on pump filled with fuel	1. *Trace lines and locate obstruction 2. *Replace valve 3. *Replace or rebuild pump 4. *Remove and empty
Battery Problems		
Discharged battery	1. Battery worn out 2. Charging rate not set right 3. Discharging rate too great 4. Standing too long 5. Master switch left on 6. Impurities in electrolyte 7. Short circuit in aircraft wiring 8. Broken battery cell partitions	1. Replace battery 2. *Reset 3. Reduce electrical load when generator or alternator is not charging, reduce use of starter on ground, use external ground power 4. Remove and recharge battery if left in unused aircraft 3 weeks or more 5. Remove and recharge battery 6. Replace battery 7. *Check wiring 8. Replace battery
Battery life is short	1. Overcharge due to level of electrolyte below top of plates 2. Heavy discharge 3. Sulfation due to disuse 4. Impurities in electrolyte 5. Low charging rate	1. Maintain electrolyte at proper level 2. Remove loads (turn off equipment) when generator or alternator is not charging 3. Replace battery 4. Replace battery 5. *Adjust voltage regulator
Cracked battery cell jars	1. Hold-down bracket loose 2. Battery frozen	1. Replace battery and tighten bracket 2. Replace battery
Compound on top of battery melts	1. Charging rate too high	1. *Adjust voltage regulator to reduce charging rate
Electrolyte runs out of vent plugs	1. Too much water added to battery and charging rate too high	1. Drain and keep at proper level, *adjust voltage regulator
Excessive corrosion inside container	1. Spillage from overfilling 2. Vent lines leaking or clogged 3. Charging rate too high	1. Be careful when adding water 2. *Repair or clean 3. *Adjust voltage regulator
Battery freezes	1. Battery discharged 2. Water added and battery not charged immediately	1. Replace battery 2. Battery should always be recharged for at least a half hour after addition of water in freezing weather
Leaking battery jar	1. Battery frozen	1. Replace battery
Battery polarity reversed	1. Connected backwards on airplane or charger	1. Battery should be slowly and completely discharged, then charged correctly and tested
Battery consumes excessive water	1. Charging rate too high (if in all cells) 2. Cracked battery jar (one cell only)	1. Correct charging rate 2. Replace battery

*May only be carried out by or under supervision of certificated mechanic.

Aircraft modifications

No sooner has one person done something, such as design and build an aircraft, than there's someone else coming along and saying, "I can do it better." Fortunately for us, they often go on to prove it and make their refinements available to all at a price. Almost every aircraft built in the general aviation fleet has some kind of modification available for various purposes. They can range from little things such as an extra window or an extra fuel tank through major conversions of the wings for STOL performance right on up to making a single-engine airplane into a twin. Let's look at some of the ideas and the specifics.

Aircraft mods can be divided into three broad groups: performance improvements, utility enhancements, and aesthetic improvements.

Performance improvements include changes such as:
1. Turbocharging
2. Fuel injection
3. More powerful engines
4. STOL kits
5. Longer wings
6. Aerodynamic cleanups
7. Twin engines from a single engine

Utility improvements include:
1. Tail-wheel to tri-gear
2. Floats or amphibious floats
3. Larger fuel tanks
4. Tip tanks
5. Pressurization
6. Metalizing fabric coverings
7. 80-octane engine to 100-octane engine
8. Dual brakes
9. Extra baggage space, such as wing lockers
10. Camera hatch for aerial-survey work
11. Ambulance conversions

Aesthetic improvements include:
1. One-piece windshield
2. Extra side windows
3. Redesigned wingtips
4. Single fin from twin fins
5. New instrument panels

(Note: Some mods can invalidate the aircraft or engine warranty. Ask about this before you decide—it won't matter if it is out of warranty, of course.)

Some mods are cost-effective and pay for themselves by improved efficiency or utility. Others are not worth it from a performance point of view but might enhance the appearance and value of the airplane. It's very hard to tell an old, highly modified Bonanza from a recent one at first glance. It's amazing what a third window and snazzy new paint will do to an old bird.

If you are going to make a lot of use of your aircraft after it is modified, go ahead and get it done. However, if you think your utilization may not justify the extra expense of a modification, maybe the best way to enjoy the mod is to buy an aircraft that has already been modified. You will probably not get the value of the modification out of the aircraft if you sell it soon after. Of course, money isn't everything. If you know your aircraft well and you want to upgrade it, go ahead. You just may not get your money's worth.

The Super-Vee Bonanza twin conversion

Below Regular Piper Comanche windshield

Below one-piece Comanche windshield conversion

Fixing it

Here are some examples of typical modifications offered on some general-aviation aircraft.

Modifications available for the Cessna 172:

1. STOL kits
2. Auxiliary fuel tank (adds 24 gallons in wingtip)
3. Convert existing engine to 160 hp (100 octane)
4. Convert existing engine to 180 hp and constant-speed propeller

Here are performance comparisons for the Cessna 172 conversion from 150 hp to 180 hp (this is the conversion offered by Mid America STOL Aircraft-MASA).

The cost of the conversion runs around $14,000, depending on the model of Cessna being converted, less an allowance for the old engine.

Now let's look at a STOL (short takeoff and landing) conversion on a Piper Arrow (PA-28R-200). This is the kit offered by Robertson Aircraft Corporation.

Here is what is done to convert the aircraft to STOL:

1. Drooped and sealed ailerons
2. Fuselage flap
3. Raked wingtips
4. Stall fences
5. Dorsal fin
6. Recontoured wing leading edge
7. Automatic stabilator trim system

The cost of the STOL conversion, including painting, is between $7 and $10,000, installed. It takes about ten days to install.

	Standard 172	180hp 172
Engine	Lycoming O-320	Lycoming O-360
HP	150 at 2700 RPM	180 at 2700 RPM
Prop	Fixed pitch	Constant speed
Top speed	120 knots	139 knots
75% power		
Cruise speed	114 knots	135 knots
Takeoff distance	780 feet	400 feet
Rate of climb	730 fpm	1100 fpm
Fuel consumption	9.2 gph	10.5 gph
Empty weight	1260 lbs	1299 lbs
Useful load	940 lbs	901 lbs
Fuel grade	80 octane	100 octane

The Robertson STOL conversion to the Piper Arrow

	Normal Arrow	STOL Arrow	
		Normal technique	STOL technique
Takeoff distance over 50 feet	1800 ft	1290 ft	1130 ft
Takeoff speed	61 kts	51 kts	47 kts
Approach speed	78 kts	61 kts	57 kts
Landing distance over 50 feet	1360 ft	1045 ft	930 ft

Fixing it

Finally, let's look at an Apache conversion—from tired old PA-23 to Geronimo. These are the components of a complete Geronimo conversion:

1. Dual alternators
2. Dual vacuum pumps
3. Strobe lights
4. Custom instrument panel with post lighting
5. 31" extended nose with baggage compartment
6. Hoerner wingtips
7. Totally enclosed wheel well doors
8. New tail assembly (dorsal fin, square tail, tail cone)
9. Three tinted side windows
10. One-piece tinted windshield
11. New dual rams-horn control wheels
12. Engine nacelle and wing-root fairings
13. Major airframe overhaul and inspection
14. Customized interior
15. Complete strip and repaint (epoxy)
16. Rear baggage compartment
17. Flush camlock fasteners
18. Super-soundproofing
19. Fiberglass split cowlings
20. Five individual adjustable seats
21. New Lycoming 180-hp O-360 engines

All this costs about $82,000 plus an old Apache, or about $100,000 plus avionics if you don't have an old Apache to rework. Here are the comparison figures.

	PA-23 Apache (1958 model)	Geronimo conversion (performance data at 3800-lb gross weight)
Engines	Lycoming O-320	Lycoming O-360
HP	160 hp	180 hp
Gross weight	3800 lbs	4000 lbs
Useful load	1570 lbs	1500 lbs
Rate of climb	1260 fpm	2000 fpm
Top speed	159 kts	173 kts
Cruise at 75% power	140 kts	168 kts
S/E rate of climb	180 fpm	750 fpm
Best rate-of-climb speed (Vy)	87 kts	87 kts
Best angle-of-climb speed (Vx)	66 kts	76 kts
Stall speed g/f down (Vso)	53 kts	47 kts
Service ceiling	17,000 ft	23,000 ft
S/E ceiling	5500 ft	12,000 ft

The Geronimo conversion offered by Seguin Aviation Inc., Box 2075, Hwy 46, Seguin, Texas 78155. Conversions take ten weeks.

Developing your own modifications

FAR 21.113 states that any person who alters a product by introducing a major change in type design not great enough to require a new application for a type certificate under FAR 21.19 must apply for a supplemental type certificate (STC). Minor changes can be handled by filing an FAA Form 337. I wanted to install a convex mirror on the left wingtip of my Comanche so that I could tell if all three wheels were down or not. I talked this over with the FAA, and they suggested that it would have to go through the STC process.

The FAA suggests that, prior to initiating a modification, the summary of STCs be examined to see if the desired change has been previously approved. The use of a previously approved modification could, of course, save a lot of time and money. You won't get detailed information about the STC in this summary, since the FAA regards the data as proprietary, so you would have to contact the holder of the STC for this. You can examine the STC summary at the local FAA GADO (General Aviation District Office).

If you want to go ahead with your own STC, you then apply using FAA Form 8110-12, accompanying this form with data (drawings, sketches, marked photographs, process specifications, etc.) that completely describe the modification to be made. If the procedures for welding, riveting, wiring, and so on are as described in FAA Advisory Circular AC 43.13-1, you so state and you don't have to describe those procedures in detail. If the procedures are different, you must describe them in detail. In addition, you must furnish installation instructions and substantiating data that show that the change complies with the applicable FARs.

The FAA reviews the application,

and any corrections or substantiating tests are made (these tests usually must be carried out before an FAA engineer). If the data is acceptable to FAA engineers, any required flight tests and conformity inspections are carried out. You make the initial tests, followed by tests made by the FAA. When everything has been satisfactorily carried out, the STC is issued.

There are two types of STC—individual and multiple approvals. An individual approval applies to one aircraft or component only, identified by serial number. Multiple approvals may be applied to all aircraft or components having the same type certificate.

Repainting your aircraft

Nothing dresses up a tired old airplane better than a smart new paint job. This was one of the first things I did after I bought my Comanche, with its 13-year-old enamel looking much the worse for wear. The results were very satisfactory—people would ask me if I was flying a new Comanche when I pulled up on the line. I used Dupont Imron, which is a modified polyurethane that gives the wet look—a very high-gloss finish. Eighteen months later, it still looks good.

There are basically four types of paint available for aircraft use—polyurethanes, modified polyurethanes, enamels, and lacquers. Probably the best types now available are the polyurethanes, which give that beautiful wet-look finish. Most aircraft paint shops use only these types of paint. In addition to the high-gloss finish, polyurethanes offer a harder surface and lower maintenance when compared to enamels and lacquers. Polyurethane paints must not be waxed or polished, whereas enamels and lacquers should be. However, the polyurethanes don't "breathe", and

thus filiform corrosion can spread under the paint without being seen. The other paints will crack or otherwise allow such corrosion to show through.

Piper uses acrylic lacquers on all its aircraft except the Cheyenne, although some models may have polyurethanes as an optional extra. Acrylic lacquers are probably the cheapest types of paint to have applied, since they are easy to spray on and dry quickly. They also touch up well.

Beechcraft uses acrylic enamels as standard finishes (except on the King Air), but polyurethane paint is available as an optional extra on any model and is standard on the King Air. Acrylic enamels are hard to touch up. They give a good gloss but not the wet look.

Bellanca uses acrylic enamels on the Champion and polyurethanes on the Viking.

Cessna uses polyurethanes exclusively—straight polyurethanes on

their twins and modified polyurethanes on their singles.

Grumman American, Mooney, and Rockwell use modified polyurethanes.

Anatomy of a paint job

There are two ways to repaint an airplane—the quick way and the proper way. In the quick way the aircraft is washed and sanded down, and the new paint is sprayed over the old. Some paints do not go on well over other paints, so this technique is not the most desirable. It will also not give a long-lasting finish and will add the weight of the new paint to the weight of the old—about 10 to 15 pounds on a typical single-engine airplane.

The first step in a new paint job is to get rid of the old and get down to the bare metal

Fixing it

Here is the proper way, as described by U.S. Paint for its Alumigrip brand of polyurethane.

1. Aircraft is stripped of all old paint (this is done chemically) and foreign matter.

2. The surface metal is cleaned, polished, and inspected.

3. The surface is thoroughly washed and rinsed.

4. Aluminum surfaces are treated with an acid etching solution. This is wiped or sprayed on and then washed off immediately.

5. A corrosion-resistant primer is applied.

6. A urethane primer is applied.

7. The final basic outer surface paint is applied.

8. Masking is put in place for striping and lettering.

9. Secondary colors are applied.

10. Masking is removed, and *voilà*!

Choosing a paint shop

As with everything else, in aircraft refinishing you get what you pay for. A proper paint job that will last for years and not start to "orange-peel," or crack quickly, takes time and a great deal of care and expertise to apply. The best way to choose a paint shop is to go by reputation. Ask around when you see a nicely painted older airplane. Find out what the customers think of the quality and service they received. A good paint shop should guarantee its work for at least a year.

You can expect your aircraft to be down for two to three weeks for repainting—and, with a good shop, you'll probably have to book well ahead to get in—maybe several months. Getting your aircraft repainted well is not something you can do fast. While you are waiting for your appointment, consider any work that has to be done on the aircraft that would be better done be-fore painting. I found I had to take all my fuel tanks out just after I repainted, so I got an instant aging of my sleek new finish. If I had planned more carefully, I could have fixed the tanks first, *then* repainted! This would be a good time to get a custom N number (see page 96). Allow yourself plenty of time to arrange this—at least 6 weeks.

Redoing the interior

Upholstering and fixing up the inside of the airplane are among the items classed as "Preventive maintenance" (see page 138) that can be performed by the owner. This is good, and some beautiful results of this enlightened rule can be seen in some aircraft.

The simplest way to accomplish a good-looking new interior is to buy what you need in prefabricated form and install it yourself. I redid my seats with the reupholstery sets offered by Airtex of Fallsington, Pennsylvania. You'll see their ads throughout the aviation press. I am very pleased with the results, and I recommend Airtex highly. For less than $200 I got a very attractive set of new upholstered seat covers, and I installed these myself in less than a day. I needed a mechanic to get the back seat in and out but otherwise had no problems. I plan to install the wall coverings next.

I got a quote on a new interior for the Comanche from one of the better shops around and they wanted almost $3,000 for the job. Of course, it would then be a very classy job. But I put the difference into a new HSI and some other radios instead!

The important thing to bear in mind in redoing the interior is that the materials used must comply with the fire-resistant requirements of FAR 23.853.

A lot of very attractive aircraft interiors are around, and when you ask the owner where it was done, he often replies, "I had our local auto-upholstery shop do it. They do beautiful work, don't they?" Yes, they do. But make sure that if you go to an auto shop to get your interior redone, they use materials that are flame-resistant to comply with FAR 23.853.

Recovering fabric-covered airplanes

Stock recover envelopes can be bought from suppliers such as Airtex of Fallsington, Pennsylvania. Recovering an aircraft constitutes a major repair, so any work you do yourself must be supervised by a certificated Airframe mechanic, who will be responsible for the work done, inspection of the airframe, supervision of the covering and doping operations, and signing of FAA Form 337.

Fresh recover envelopes are important. Airtex makes theirs to order (they also make all the envelopes for the new Piper Super Cubs and Pawnees). Fresh dope is also required. Old dope turns acid with age and will attack the fabric. Automotive thinners must not be used—they have a high acid content.

The best type of recover material is Ceconite. It is more resistant to sunlight, moisture, sulphur dioxide, and other chemicals than the alternative fabric, grade-A cotton. Ceconite is 87 percent stronger than Grade-A cotton. Ceconite is a woven Dacron-Polyester fabric. It has a life expectancy of about ten years and a tensile strength of 150 pounds, vs grade-A cotton's 80-pound strength and five-to-seven year service life.

Airtex offers a booklet called "Modern Aircraft Re-covering" for $2 which tells you all you need to know.

Airtex Products Inc.,
Lower Morrisville Road,
Fallsington, Pa. 19054
Telephone 215-295-4115

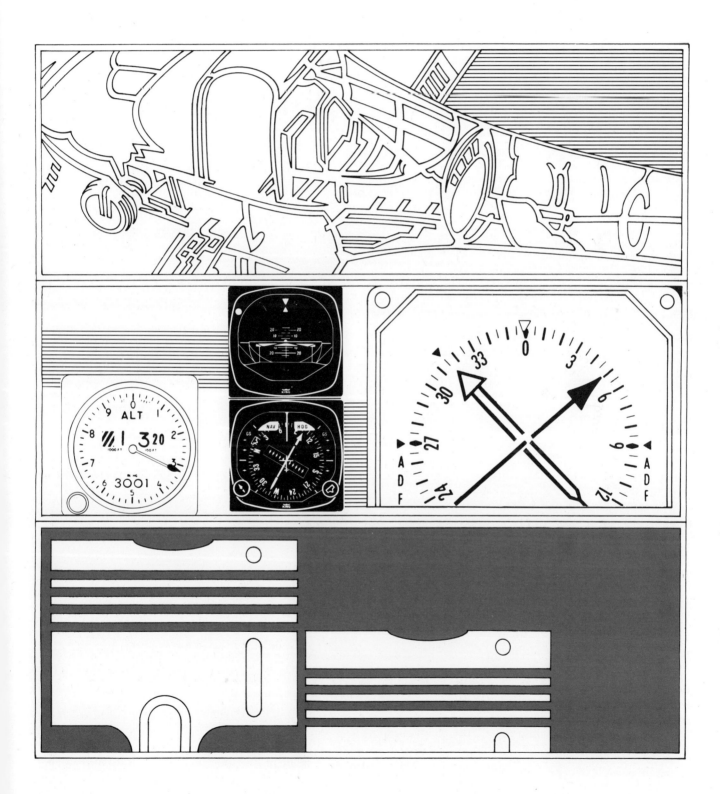

Aircraft structures

Most of today's light aircraft are all metal in construction, although some of the traditional types still use fabric covering over metal or metal and wood structures. By "traditional" I mean the oldies but goodies that are still being made, such as the Piper Super Cub, Bellanca Decathlon, Bellanca Viking, and the like.

The older designs employ a tubular-steel truss construction, which doesn't give a very aerodynamic shape. So around the framework are placed formers made of wood or metal, and to these are attached the skin. The Piper Aztec fuselage is built around a truss structure, although you probably wouldn't know it to look at it from the outside. Other typical aircraft using the truss method are the Piper Tri-Pacer, the Aeroncas, the Taylorcraft, the Piper Apache (forerunner of the Aztec), and the old biplanes, such as the Stearman.

Outer-skin material for these types of aircraft may be fabric (cotton, linen, or Dacron) or sheet aluminum. Some fabric-covered aircraft may be recovered in metal. Some aircraft use both coverings—the early Cessna 140s, for example, had a stressed-skin metal fuselage and fabric-covered wings. Other aircraft have a metal covering but fabric-covered control surfaces (e.g., the Douglas DC-3).

Modern aircraft use stressed-skin structures. In this type of construction the skin of the aircraft carries some of the loads. There are two basic types of stressed-skin design to be found in light aircraft—monocoque and semi-monocoque. Semi-monocoque is the most prevalent type. It employs skin riveted to formers and stringers. For example, in a wing the rib will provide the shape, and the stringers will add stiffness, while the skin will carry some of the load. There may be several spars in this type of wing, rather than the one or two spars to be found in a truss-type wing. In the less-used monocoque construction the skin carries much more of the load—like an eggshell. This type of skin will lose strength if it is dented, since much of the strength comes from the actual shape of the skin. A propeller spinner is an example of a monocoque structure. It may have no stiffeners inside, with the strength coming from its shape.

One form of construction finding increasing popularity among manufacturers is metal bonding. Grumman American uses this type of fabrication extensively in all of its light aircraft. Cessna is also making good use of it in some wing structures. In bonding, the metal is treated in several vats of chemicals to prepare it for the bonding process, then the pre-formed components are assembled in a jig and literally glued together under great pressure. Part of the bonding process involves heat treatment in large ovens. Bonding is slightly more expensive than conventional rivetting, but it results in a very strong structure with smooth contours. Take a look at the wings of one of the Grumman American aircraft to see for yourself.

Some components, notably parts of the fuselage, use a sheet metal-honeycomb metal-sheet metal sandwich which provides enormous strength with lightness. Bonding is a process which will be seen more and more in future aircraft as the technology becomes more widespread in the industry.

Structural materials are described below:

1. Metals. The most commonly used metals in aircraft construction are aluminum alloys, magnesium alloys, and steel alloys. An alloy is a combination of different metals for improved characteristics. Stainless steel is an alloy of steel, chrome, nickel, and other substances and does not rust. When normally soft aluminum is alloyed with copper, manganese, and magnesium, it becomes five times stronger. However, it becomes more susceptible to corrosion in its alloyed form. For this reason the metal is coated with a thin layer of pure aluminum for aircraft use. Pure aluminum oxidizes on the surface and retards further corrosion when exposed to air or moisture. Alumi-

This Rockwell Commander uses semi-monocoque construction, with some skin sections corrugated for extra strength

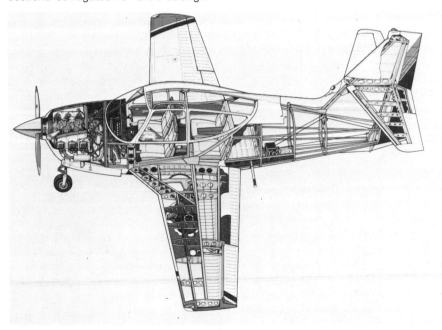

Knowing it

num alloys will be found in stressed-skin aircraft for both the skin and the stiffening parts, such as stringers, ribs, and formers. They can be easily formed, and their strength can be enhanced by heat treating. Magnesium alloys will be found in wheels and some control surfaces. Magnesium is lighter than aluminum. It also has a

tendency to corrode and it can crack, so magnesium parts need to be closely inspected for cracks at regular intervals. Steel alloys will be found in the tubular truss-type fuselages. The tubing is a chrome-molybdenum-steel alloy. Hardware, such as nuts and bolts, are made of nickel steel in most cases.

2. *Wood.* Very few wood components are used today. It is too expensive to manufacture and repair wooden structures. It is most commonly found in wing spars. The wood used is Sitka spruce. Laminated spars may be used instead of one piece of wood. Laminated wood is made of sections or sheets of wood glued together with the grains all running in the same direction. Propellers may also be made of laminated wood. Plywood is used in some structures, for example, in wooden stressed-skin constructions (confined almost exclusively to home-built aircraft), in which case it will be mahogany plywood. Birch plywood is used for reinforcements. Plywood is made up of wood veneers glued together with the grains at 45° and 90° to each other. It is very strong and can be formed and shaped. Probably one of the best examples of a wooden aircraft was the World War II De Havilland Mosquito bomber.

3. *Fabric.* Fabric is used for covering truss-type structures and some control surfaces. The fabric used may be cotton, linen, or Dacron. Dacron is a synthetic material that will resist mildew and lasts much longer than cotton or linen. Fabric-covered aircraft need to be recovered at regular intervals—every few years.

4. *Plastics.* There are two types of plastics to be found in aircraft—thermosetting and thermoplastic. "Thermosetting" means that the plastic will not change its shape when it gets hot. Typical items made out of this type of plastic (often reinforced with fiberglass) include wheel pants, radomes, wingtips, propeller spinners, and such. "Thermoplastic" means that the application of heat causes the material to soften. Cooling returns the material to its original hardness. Aircraft windshields and side windows are made of thermoplastic acrylic sheet in most cases. Another familiar thermoplastic device is the navigation computer. You can get a very good illustration of thermoplastic properties by leaving a plastic computer on top of the instrument panel under the windshield on a sunny day! The warped mess that

Above The 1946 Cessna 140 had an all-metal fuselage with a fabric covered wing
Below A brand new Cessna 150 about to receive its wing

will greet you when you return is an expensive lesson in the properties of plastics. The day of the all-plastic airplane is not yet with us. Several attempts have been made, with beautiful-looking results in some cases (the Windecker Eagle was a prime example), but the solution has so far evaded the demands of mass production. So plastic will continue to be found mostly in components rather than in primary structures.

Engine configurations

Light aircraft piston engines come in three shapes—flat (also called horizontally opposed), radial, and in-line. Flat and radial engines are always air-cooled. In-line engines may be air-cooled or liquid-cooled in the more powerful versions. The engine found in all U.S. light aircraft is the flat type, with four, six, or eight cylinders. Jacobs radial engines are still being made in the U.S. for agricultural aircraft by Page Industries of Oklahoma. The in-line engines are to be found in some European light aircraft. But the standard light-aircraft

engine throughout the world today is the horizontally opposed air-cooled model.

Various attempts have been made at installing automobile engines in airplanes—a Cessna 182 was flying a few years ago with an Oldsmobile engine. A lot of homebuilt aircraft use converted Volkswagen engines. However, it hasn't really happened and it doesn't seem that it will in any major way. This is a pity, because aircraft engines are far more expensive than car engines.

It is beyond the scope of this book to cover turbine engines, which are priced far beyond the reach of most owner-flown aircraft operators. Turbine engines are very efficient, light in weight, and troublefree. They just cost too much! They also use a lot of fuel at low altitudes, so they're not suitable for many operations.

They come in three basic types, pure jet, fan jet, and prop-jet (also known as turbo-prop). The pure jets are the biggest fuel users and make the most noise. Many bizjets are using fan jets, which are very quiet and use far less fuel. Turbo-props are the lightest users of fuel in the turbine group but are more complicated because they use propellers to deliver their power. They can be very noisy or very quiet, depending on the type (listen to an older MU-2 and a King Air to see the contrast!).

Engine components

These are the main components of a horizontally opposed aircraft engine.

1. Crankshaft. This is a heavy piece of forged steel that is connected to each piston by a connecting rod. Its function is to translate the back-and-forth motion of the pistons into the rotary motion needed to drive the propeller. It is usually hollow, with oil running through it. When you speak of engine RPM, it is the rotation of the crankshaft that is measured. Most engines are *direct-drive*, which means that the crankshaft is connected directly to the propeller. Some engines are *geared*, meaning that gears are used between the crankshaft and the propeller, allowing the engine to run at a higher speed than the propeller.

2. Crankcase. The crankcase is made out of aluminum alloy and ties the whole engine together. In it are mounted the crankshaft, on bearings, and the camshaft, on its own bearings. Attached to the crankcase by bolts are the cylinders as well as the various components such as the magnetos, carburetor, fuel pump, and so on. The engine is mounted onto the airframe by bolting the crankcase, usually through a shock-mount system, sometimes onto a rig of tubular steel, which is in turn attached to the airframe, otherwise directly to the firewall or some other main structural member.

3. Cylinders. These are made out of steel. The interiors may be *chrome-plated* when the engine is overhauled to provide better wear and rust resistance. Another treatment is called *nitriding*, in which the cylinder walls are treated with an ammonia substance. This hardens the walls. The *cylinder head* is made out of cast-aluminum alloy. This contains the ports for the intake and exhaust valves and the mountings for the two spark plugs. The entire cylinder exterior is covered with *cooling fins* to dissipate the heat generated when the engine

The Windecker Eagle. Sm-o-o-o-th.

is running.

4. Pistons. The pistons sit inside the cylinders and move back and forth, driven by the exploding fuel-air mixture. They are usually made out of forged-aluminum alloy. Mounted on the pistons are the *piston rings*, cast-iron seals between the piston and the cylinder wall. There are several rings on each piston. Some are used for sealing, others for controlling the amount of oil used to lubricate the cylinders.

5. Valves. Each cylinder has an intake and an exhaust valve. The fuel-air mixture enters the cylinder through the intake valve, which then closes for the compression stroke. The compressed mixture is ignited by the spark plugs and explodes, driving the piston away. The piston returns and the exhaust valve opens to release the burnt gas from the cylinder. Then the process repeats. Valves are usually made of nickel-alloy steel, riding in bronze valve guides. Some exhaust valves are hollow and contain metallic sodium for extra cooling. The intake and exhaust valves are actuated by connection to the *camshaft*, which in turn is driven by gears connected to the crankshaft. Between the camshaft and the valves is a linkage made up of a *rocker arm*, a *push rod*, and a *valve lifter*. The valve lifter is operated hydraulically, using engine oil in most modern engines.

6. Cooling baffles. The engine is tightly cowled and partly shrouded by cooling baffles, which are vanes of sheet metal used to direct ram air from the air intake around the cylinder fins and out. Some aircraft have *cowl flaps* to vary the amount of cooling air available. The cowl flaps are opened when extra cooling is required, as on takeoff and climb, and closed when less cooling is needed, as on descent.

The other accessories associated with the engine, such as fuel pumps, carburetors, magnetos, starters, generators or alternators, and so on are discussed in detail under the appropriate systems descriptions that follow.

The four-stroke cycle

Piston engines operate on a four-stroke cycle—i.e., the piston moves back and forth four times to complete one cycle, rotating the crankshaft twice in the process.

1. Intake. The piston moves from the top of the cylinder to the bottom, with the intake valve open. It sucks in the fuel-air mixture.

2. Compression. With both valves closed, the piston moves back up to the cylinder head, compressing the mixture.

3. Ignition. The spark plugs ignite the compressed mixture, causing rapid expansion, forcing the piston back down, and turning the crankshaft.

4. Exhaust. As the piston starts to move up, the exhaust valve opens and the burnt gases are expelled into the exhaust pipe. At the top of the stroke the exhaust valve closes again, the intake valve opens, and a new intake cycle begins.

The pistons are connected to the crankshaft in such a way that at least one piston is always on a power stroke for each half rotation of the shaft. In a six-cylinder engine, two pistons are driving the crankshaft at one point and one at another point. So the crankshaft keeps turning, being driven by the power strokes of each cylinder in turn. The more cylinders, the smoother the engine.

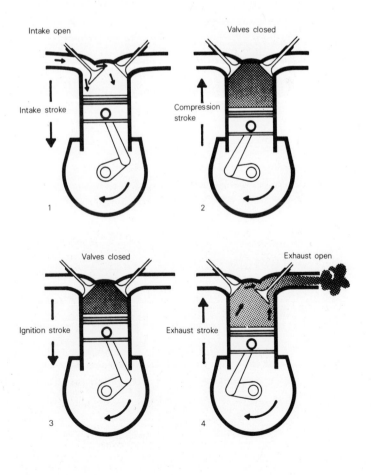

171

Understanding aero-engine nomenclature

Aircraft engines have a string of letters and numbers after the manufacturer's name to differentiate them from each other, for example, Continental GTSIO-520H, or Lycoming IO-540-C1B5. What do these mean? It's really quite simple. First comes the manufacturer. There are only a few light-aircraft piston engine manufacturers still around: Teledyne-Continental (mostly known simply as Continental) and Avco Lycoming (mostly known simply as Lycoming) are the most common. The Jacobs radial engines are now built by Page Industries of Oklahoma. Franklin engines are now being built in Poland. All others are long out of production or installed in larger aircraft beyond the scope of this book.

The letters that follow the manufacturer's name describe the basic configuration of the engine. Here is the key:

A = aerobatic—limited inverted-flight system
AE = aerobatic—full inverted-flight system
G = geared—the crankshaft rotates faster than the propeller
GS = gear supercharged—as opposed to turbosupercharged
H = horizontal—refers to horizontal mounting of a helicopter engine
I = injected—fuel injection
L = left-hand rotation—found in reference to the engine that counterrotates, as in a Piper Twin Comanche C/R, Seneca, etc.—this engine actually mounts on the *right* wing
O = opposed—refers to the arrangement of the cylinders—horizontally opposed, or "flat"
R = radial—radially arranged cylinders

T = turbocharged—Lycoming nomenclature
TS = turbosupercharged—Continental nomenclature
V = vertically mounted—refers to helicopter engines

The smallest, oldest Continental engines did not use this type of nomenclature. Types such as the A65-8F and C90-8F refer to the horsepower ratings of the engines (65 hp, 90 hp, etc.). The letters preceding the power were simply type designators in alphabetical order.

The three-digit number following the letter codes refers to the approximate engine displacement in cubic inches (e.g., 540, 320, etc.).

The numbers and digits following the displacement size are codes distinguishing various accessories, such as fuel pumps, magnetos, and so on, used on different engines of the same basic type installed in various specific aircraft models. Here are a couple of engines "decoded":

GTSIO-520-F = geared turbosupercharged injected opposed, 520 cubic inches

TIGO-541-E1A = turbocharged injected geared opposed, 541 cubic inches

The engine displacement is no direct giveaway to the horsepower nor to commonality of parts. Lycoming 540s, for example, run from 235 hp in the Piper Cherokee Pathfinder through 250 hp in the Piper Aztec, 290 hp in the Aerostar 600, 300 hp in the Cherokee Six, 310 hp in the Navajo, 325 hp in the Navajo C/R to 380 hp in the Beech Queen Air. Figure out the differences:

Type of engine	Horsepower
O-540-B4B5	235 hp
IO-540-C4B5	250 hp
IO-540-K1F5	290 hp
IO-540-K1G5	300 hp
TIO-540-A2C	310 hp
LTIO-540-F2BD	325 hp
TIO-540-J2BD	350 hp
IGSO-540-A1D	380 hp

Although they are all 540-series engines, they are in many cases different engines, with few common parts and little compatibility of parts.

Avco Lycoming IO-360

The horsepower differences are obtained by increasing the compression, increasing the RPM, turbocharging, and such. The lower-horsepower engines for a given displacement are sometimes called "derated" to denote that something has been done to hold the available power down, such as limiting the RPM output. This implies a rugged engine, since it is running at less than it is capable of all the time. Similarly, an engine at the top end of the horsepower scale needs more "babying," since it is running much closer to its limits. It is often a much stronger engine than its lower-powered brother, however.

The horsepower referred to in engine descriptions is the horsepower delivered by the engine at maximum takeoff power. Most engines are limited to very short operations at the maximum setting—sometimes only a few minutes at a time. A power reduction has to be made as soon as possible after takeoff. However, it puts an unnecessary strain on the engine to attempt to take off at less than full power. Most cruising flight is done at 75-percent power for high-speed cruise, 65-percent power for normal cruise, and 45- or 55-percent power for economy cruise. A nonturbocharged engine will not deliver much more than 65-percent power above about 7,000 feet in any event.

Understanding engine color codes

Look at an aircraft engine and you will probably see some colored paint on the cylinders. It might be orange, blue, green, yellow, or just gray. These colors have a definite meaning and provide valuable information about the engine.

In the past color coding of cylinders was confined to colored bands around the base of each cylinder. Today new methods of painting (enameling) engines and the need for quick, easy engine identification were instrumental in changing color-code location.

The factory color code, a large painted stripe, is now located on the cylinder head between the push rods from the spark plug boss to the bottom of the cylinder head. Additional color coding has been added to identify cylinders requiring long-reach spark plugs versus short-reach spark plugs. Location of spark plug identification-color coding is between the spark plug boss and rocker box.

Color-code engine-identification keys are described below.

Location—between push rods on cylinder head or band around base of cylinder barrel

Engine gray or unpainted—standard steel cylinder barrels

Orange stripe—chrome-plated cylinder barrels

Blue stripe—nitride-hardened cylinder barrels

Green stripe—steel cylinder 0.010 oversize (engines overhauled in the field, not rebuilt)

Yellow stripe—steel cylinder 0.020 oversize (engines overhauled in the field, not rebuilt)

Color-code spark plug-identification keys are listed below.

Location—fin area between spark plug and rocker box

Engine gray or unpainted—short-reach spark plugs

Yellow—long-reach spark plugs

Fuel systems

There are two types of fuel systems found in light aircraft, gravity-fed and pump-fed.

1. Gravity-fed fuel system. This is the simpler system and is found mostly in high-wing aircraft. The fuel tanks are installed in the wings, and the fuel feeds by gravity to the carburetor. Only engines with float-type carburetors can use gravity feed.

Above Tip-tank conversion for the Bonanza adds 30 gallons

Below This fuel-flow meter has a "gallons used" feature

2. Pump-fed fuel system. Low-wing aircraft and any aircraft with fuel injection or pressure-type carburetors must have a fuel pump to deliver the fuel from the tanks to the engine, even in a high-wing airplane. The main fuel pump is driven by the aircraft engine. An auxiliary electric fuel pump is needed to supply fuel in case the engine-driven pump fails.

Fuel tanks may be installed in the wings, wing tips (as in the Cessna 310), fuselage, or a combination of these. Some Cessna twins can also carry fuel in the wing lockers, which are installed in a part of the engine nacelle otherwise used as a baggage compartment. The tanks may be made of aluminum alloy, neoprene-impregnated cloth, or a part of the wing structure that has been sealed off (the "wet wing"). The wet-wing tanks are occasionally prone to leakage. I found a leak in my Comanche (which has the neoprene bladder-type tanks) soon after I bought it. I noticed a gas-fume smell whenever I put the wheels down. Close inspection showed actual moist fuel on the underside of the wing. The location of this indicated that it was the left auxiliary tank. I ordered a new tank and flew the leaking tank until it was empty, then left it empty until the part came in. It cost only a few dollars more to get a new tank vs having the existing one repaired. Then I sold my old tank through an ad in *Trade-a-Plane* to a firm that repairs them.

A fuel selector enables the pilot to feed fuel from each tank, as desired. Some fuel-selector systems are excellent, others are horrible. The ideal type, from an operational point of view, allows the pilot to feed off the two main tanks simultaneously. This type is found in aircraft such as the Cessna 150 and 172. The selector has either a simple FUEL ON/OFF position choice or a LEFT/RIGHT/BOTH/OFF function. However, fuel systems using a pump feed cannot have a BOTH position unless there is another "header" tank into which the two main tanks feed and from which the fuel is fed to the engine. Without this there would be a danger of emptying one tank and feeding only air, even if the other tank contained fuel.

Any gravity-fed fuel system with a BOTH selector must have common venting between the two tanks. So fuel selectors that can feed off two main tanks simultaneously are found mostly on high-wing airplanes. Low-wing airplanes have fuel selectors that allow you to use only one tank at a time. This, of course, refers to single-engine aircraft. An exception is the Rockwell International line of singles in the 112 and 114 series. Twins feed off two tanks at a time, one for each engine. Twins also feature an additional selection possibility—CROSSFEED. This is a linkage between the fuel tanks in the left wing and those in the right wing. This enables the pilot, in an emergency, to feed the left engine from the right-wing tanks, or vice versa. It might be necessary in the event of an engine failure to keep the good one running with fuel from the other side, for example.

Badly designed fuel-selector systems feature problems such as having to move the selector through OFF to change tanks, selector levers that can be misread so that, while you think you have selected RIGHT, you

have in fact selected OFF, and systems that require you to select not only the fuel-feed but also the fuel-quantity indicator. For example, you might have one fuel gauge with a selector switch, say, LEFT/RIGHT. So when you select the LEFT fuel tank on the fuel selector, you must also select the LEFT position on the fuel gauge. If you don't do this properly, you could have a situation where you are feeding off the left tank and reading your fuel quantity off the right tank. A well-designed system is found in the Comanche. I have four fuel tanks and one fuel gauge. The gauge simply reads the quantity of whatever tank I am using, and I can read the quantity in any other tank by pressing a selector button momentarily. The Grumman American singles and the new Piper Tomahawk have a good selector-indicator system. The fuel gauges are part of the selector. The selector points at the fuel gauge of the tank being used. You can't possibly misread it.

Most light-aircraft fuel gauges are notoriously inaccurate anyway. The best way to manage fuel is to time its use from a known quantity. I have four tanks—two containing 30 gallons each and two holding 15 each. Since the airplane burns just under 15 gallons per hour, it's a simple matter of running for one hour out of each auxiliary tank after starting climb (I have to take off on a main tank). Then I have about four hours left in the mains. Of course, you need to make sure of your quantity to start with, or this method doesn't work!

Each fuel tank must be vented to the outside air so that air will replace the fuel as it is used. The vents should be in a non-icing location, since an iced-up fuel vent is just like having no fuel vent, making it impossible to get all the fuel out of the tank. Some vents are built in to the filler caps.

Each fuel tank is equipped with a drain plug or feeds to a single drain point. It is important that these drains be checked before flight (see page 141).

The well-designed fuel selector in the Gulfstream American Tiger

Some fuel tanks contain "unusable fuel." This means that the tank feeds in such a way that you can't get all the fuel out (in level flight). Some aircraft can only be operated on takeoff or landing on the main tanks. Some aircraft can have a problem with fuel flow if a rapid turn is made onto the runway just before takeoff and the tank is not full. Accidents have been caused by the fuel temporarily sloshing away from the fuel outlets, causing an engine failure. Engine failures have also occurred briefly due to similar fuel-flow interruptions caused by yawing or slipping maneuvers in the air. Some fuel tanks must be used in a certain sequence. For example, in the Cessna 310 you must use up some of the main fuel first, because when you use the auxiliary fuel, some fuel is returned to the main tanks. If there is no room in the main tanks for the returning fuel to go, it will vent overboard and be lost. Each airplane has its own fuel-system idiosyncrasies that you must be familiar with for your own safe operation.

Using the fuel in the engine

From the fuel tanks the fuel is fed, by a pump or by gravity, through the fuel-tank selector to either the carburetor or the fuel-injection system. Pure liquid fuel won't burn on its own. It has to be mixed with air in a specific proportion—about 12 parts of air to 1 part of fuel. The fuel is also vaporized in this process. This mixture is what is compressed in the cylinders by the pistons and ignited by the spark plugs, causing the power stroke to be delivered. Two systems can be used to make this happen, the carburetor or the fuel-injection system.

Carburetors are found in the smaller light aircraft (usually less than 200 hp) and in older higher-powered aircraft. Nearly all newer high-powered aircraft (over 200 hp) have fuel injection. The carburetor mixes the fuel and air in the right proportions for the required operation. Within it are the throttle-butterfly valve (which moves when you move the throttle control) and the mixture-control valve (connected to the mixture control in the cockpit). The throttle and mixture are two of three pilot-activated controls within the carburetor. The other is the carburetor heat, described below. Other controls are activated automatically within the carburetor, depending on the settings of the throttle and mixture controls. For example, when you apply full throttle, as for takeoff, a device automatically enriches the fuel-air mixture (provides more fuel) to give extra cooling. If you should open the throttle suddenly from idle, an accelerator pump increases the amount of fuel going into the engine, thereby preventing any hesitation in power pickup. When you are idling the engine, another system takes care of the lower vaporization ability of the fuel at idle and makes it right.

The purpose of the mixture control is to provide the ability to lean the mixture as the aircraft climbs to altitude and to provide the proper fuel-air mixture at the selected cruising altitude. Leaning should be done by means of an exhaust-gas-temperature gauge (EGT), which will provide the best lean mixture for the selected altitude. The mixture control is also used to shut the engine down. Moving the control to full-lean brings in the idle cutoff, which in effect shuts off the fuel to the engine.

Associated most importantly with the carburetor is the carburetor heating system. Since the vaporization of fuel causes a drop in temperature, it is possible to drop the temperature within the carburetor venturi (where the air and the fuel meet) to below freezing, even if the outside air is well above. If there is any moisture in the air (and there *is*), this moisture can freeze into ice, causing an eventual blockage in the carburetor and thus engine failure. To solve this problem, carbureted engines have a carburetor heat control, which simply takes hot air from around the

Schematic of a float-type carburetor

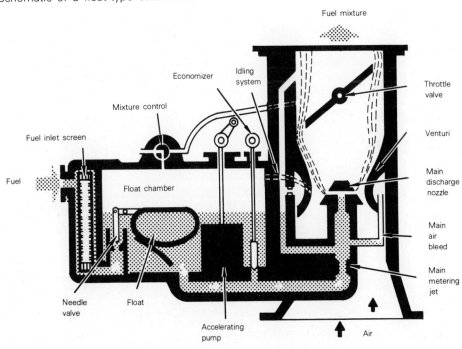

Above This twin-engine fuel flow meter is used for leaning with fuel injection

Left One way to beat the carb ice problem is to install a carb-ice detector

exhaust pipes and feeds it into the carburetor instead of the outside air. This can *prevent* carburetor icing much better than it can *eliminate* it. However, you shouldn't fly around with the heat on all the time unless carburetor icing is actually prevalent. A carburetor-temperature gauge is a good idea. If you do need to use heat for a lengthy period, you should lean the mixture somewhat, since the hot air enriches it. Try pulling on heat with climbing power at 6,000 feet and you'll see what I mean! The engine will run very rough (too rich a mixture), and you can eliminate the roughness by leaning or by going back to cold air in the carb.

It is also possible to *induce* carb icing with the application of carb heat. In very cold temperatures (below 0° F) putting the heat on might bring the temperature within the carb *up* to the freezing level, causing carb ice! This is why partial application of heat is a bad idea without a carb-temperature gauge. You want to make sure that the temperature within the carb is well above freezing.

The use of carb heat on the ground

should be avoided as much as possible, since the air going through the heater is unfiltered. Any dust, etc., you pick up in this way can ruin the engine fast.

Fuel injection supplies a more even flow of fuel to the cylinders than a carburetor, so it gives a smoother-running engine. It does not suffer from carb icing, since it works in a different way, and there is no point of induced temperature drop as there is in a carburetor.

In Continental engines the fuel is metered to the engine in direct relation to the flow of air through the throttle valve and to engine RPMs. Proper use of the mixture control is very important in this system, and a combination of a fuel-flow gauge and exhaust-gas-temperature gauge is used for leaning. Power adjustments require precise settings on the fuel-flow meter using the mixture control. Throttle adjustments are made to give required manifold-pressure readings, while RPMs are set with the propeller control, as with any system using a variable-pitch propeller.

Lycoming engines use a different

fuel-injection system—the Bendix system—than that used in Continentals. Its end results are the same in any event. In the Bendix system an airflow sensor in the throttle valve determines how much fuel is to be fed to the injection nozzles and thus to the cylinders. In this system, too, accurate use of the mixture control through interpretation of the fuel-flow meter is essential for proper power settings.

As I said, there is no carb-ice problem with fuel injection. Induction ice can form, which is ice forming on the air intake. But this type of ice would probably form only when you are experiencing airframe icing anyway—in other words, you can get it because of icing conditions, not because you reduce power. Fuel-injected engines have alternate air doors that open automatically if induction ice forms, and alternate air selector controls.

Before air enters the induction system, it passes through an air filter. This filter must be kept clean or replaced as necessary every 50 hours or less if you are operating in dusty environments.

Aviation fuels

Most nonturbine general-aviation aircraft use either 80- or 100-octane aviation gasoline. In recent years 80-octane fuel has become much scarcer, if not unavailable. It is used by the lower-powered airplanes, with 100-octane required for the higher-compression engines found on heavier and faster light aircraft. A recent addition to fuel types has been 100 LL, which is 100-octane fuel with a low lead content. This is better than regular 100-octane fuel for engines designed for 80-octane. Fuel types are color-coded as follows:

Red 80/87 octane (½ ml of lead per gallon)

Green 100/130 octane high lead (3 to 4 ml of lead per gallon)

Blue 100/130 octane low lead (100 LL) (2 ml of lead per gallon)

Purple 115/145 octane (4.6 ml of lead per gallon)—at military bases only

Clear aviation-jet fuel

The octane rating designates the antiknock qualities of the fuel. The higher the rating, the more compression the fuel can stand without detonation taking place. (Detonation occurs when the fuel-air mixture within the cylinder burns too rapidly after the spark plug fires. Engines are designed so that the mixture will burn at a certain controlled rate. The "pinging" that can be heard in certain automobile engines under acceleration is an example of detonation, which is also called "knocking.") The more compression the fuel can stand without detonation, the more power can be developed from it. The first of the two numbers in a fuel designation (e.g., 100/130) indicates the lean-mixture rating (such as during cruising flight), and the second the rich-mixture rating (such as during takeoff and climb).

It is not good for your engine to use fuel with an octane rating other than that recommended by the manufacturer. With the scarcity of 80-octane fuel, you should consider using an aircraft with an engine designed for 100-octane. Unfortunately, there are thousands of airplanes flying with engines designed for 80-octane. So what do you do? The most expensive solution is to convert the airplane to take a 100-octane type of engine. There are several conversions available. (See page 163 for an example.) The alternative is to use 100-octane fuel. Normal 100-octane fuel contains up to 4 ml of tetraethyl lead per gallon. 100 LL (low-lead) fuel contains 2 ml, while 80-octane has only .5 ml per gallon. Using the higher-lead-content fuel can cause these problems in a low-compression engine:

1. valve sticking
2. exhaust-valve stem and head erosion
3. intake-valve head burning
4. spark plug lead fouling and erosion
5. piston-ring sticking
6. detonation
7. preignition
8. lead deposits in the oil

The purpose of the lead content in the fuel is to increase its octane rating. The presence of lead in the fuel and the bromine used to help scavenge the lead from the cylinder will increase the number of deposits in the combustion chamber. Some engine manufacturers allow unrestricted use of 100 LL fuel in their engines that had been designed for 80 fuel. Certainly, prolonged use of the higher-lead 100-octane fuel must be avoided.

If you have to use high-lead 100-octane fuel in an 80-octane-type engine, you should avoid operating at too lean a mixture. Running very lean will raise the cylinder-head and exhaust-gas temperatures. The higher cylinder-head temperatures can cause hot spots and detonation. So lean on the rich side.

The FAA has approved the use of an additive, TCP (tricresyl phosphate) in non supercharged Continental and Lycoming engines. Embry-Riddle Aeronautical University recently completed a testing program to determine if TCP can substantially reduce spark plug fouling caused by 100 LL fuel. They found that TCP cut fouling as much as 68 percent in engines rated for 80 octane but run on 100 LL, and that it helps reduce valve sticking problems as well.

Embry-Riddle found that using TCP in its fleet of Cessna 172s equipped with the Lycoming 0-320 engine brought spark plug fouling problems down from about one per 100 hours of flight to about one per 600 hours. This contrasted with a drop to one problem every 200 hours or so produced by changing the oil every 25 hours, giving the engine a top overhaul at half TBO and observing strict leaning procedures. The TCP treatment was considerably cheaper. One quart of TCP (about $3) treats over 300 gallons of 100 LL. TCP is sold by:

Alcor, Inc.,
Box 32516,
San Antonio, Texas, 78284.

However, Lycoming, as of this writing, does not approve the use of TCP in its engines. They feel that there is no need for the additive, since most of the complaints about spark plug fouling have disappeared, according to the *Avco Lycoming Flyer* (December, 1977 issue). So there seems to be a difference of opinion between the FAA and Lycoming.

Oil and your engine

There are two basic types of FAA-approved aviation oil used in general-aviation-aircraft piston engines:

1. Straight mineral
2. Ashless dispersant (AD)

Most of these engines use straight mineral oil for break-in purposes with a new, remanufactured, or overhauled engine. Then the operators tend to switch over to AD. If you continue to use mineral oil after the break-in period and later switch to AD oil, you should carefully check the oil screens after each flight until clots of sludge no longer appear. Ac-

Knowing it

cording to Lycoming, modern FAA-approved oils do not need additional additives, and Lycoming does not approve oil additives for use in their engines.

Clean engine oil is essential to long engine life, and the full-flow oil filter is an added improvement over older methods of filtration. Generally, service experience has shown that the use of external oil filters can increase the time between oil changes, provided filter elements are changed at each oil change. The oil filter element should be replaced after each 50 hours of engine operation, and it should be cut open in order to examine the material trapped in the filter for evidence of internal engine damage. In new or recently overhauled engines some small particles of metallic shavings might be found, but these are not dangerous, according to Lycoming. The oil filter does not remove water, acids, or lead sludge from combustion from the oil.

The oil filter is even more important to the high-compression or higher-power engine. Some aircraft manufacturers have had good success in the small, lower-compression, four-cylinder engines without using a full-flow filter. Generally speaking, these engines are also able to achieve their expected overhaul life, as long as the oil is constantly changed and operation and maintenance are accomplished in accordance with the airframe and engine manufacturers' recommendations.

Pilots and mechanics should know what weight, type, and brand of oil is being used in the engine. At each oil change this specific information should be recorded in the engine log book. Except as a temporary measure in an emergency, different oils should not be mixed. Indiscriminate mixing of oil can cause a high oil-consumption problem or clogged oil-control rings and oil screens.

Oil consumption is a very important trend to monitor in an engine. The operator and maintenance people should know the general history of oil consumption during the life of the engine. It is typical of an engine during seating of new piston rings that oil consumption may be erratic or high. But after the rings are seated, generally within the first 25 to 50 hours, oil consumption should level off below the maximum limits established by the manufacturer. Later, during the life of the engine, if there is a noticeable increase in oil consumption within a 25-hour period, this could be a possible danger signal and call for an investigation. The oil screens and filter should be examined carefully for signs of metal. Maintenance personnel should take a compression check of the cylinders, using differential-pressure equipment, and should also look inside the cylinders with a boroscope or gooseneck light to detect any unusual conditions.

The primary purpose of a lubricant is to reduce friction between moving parts. Another responsibility of the oil is to help cool the engine. As it circulates through the engine, the oil absorbs heat from the parts. Pistons

Plane Profile 26: Beech Baron E 55

Seats	4/6
Cruise speed, 65% power, 8,000 feet	190 knots
Range, 65% power, full optional fuel, 8,000 feet	950 nm
Maximum endurance	6.0 hours
Gross weight	5,324 pounds
Empty weight	3,291 pounds
Full optional fuel	996 pounds / 166 gallons
Useful load, full fuel	1,037 pounds
Fuel efficiency, 65% power	7.1 nmpg
Stall speed, gear and flaps down	73 knots
Rate of climb, sea level	1,628 fpm / 388 fpm s/e
Minimum field length	2,202 feet
Engine type Continental IO-520-CB	285 hp
Engine TBO	1,700 hours

Remarks Also available in turbocharged versions, both pressurized and unpressurized.

and cylinder walls are especially dependent on the oil for cooling. In addition to reducing friction, the oil acts as a cushion between metal parts. The oil also aids in forming a seal between the piston and the cylinder wall to prevent leakage of gases from the combustion chamber. Oil helps reduce wear by picking up foreign particles and carrying them to a filter, where they are removed from circulation. An oil cooler is required for most engines so that the oil temperature may be kept within prescribed limits.

In addition to the two basic types of oil, straight mineral and ashless dispersant, there are three *weights* of oil, which are classified under an SAE (Society of Automotive Engineers) system, dividing the oils into groups as follows:

Commer-cial Aviation No.	Commer-cial SAE No.	Army and Navy Spec. No.	Viscosity
65	30	1065	Low
80	40	1080	Middle
100	50	1100	High

If you are looking for a can of 30-weight aviation oil and it has the number 65 on it, then it is also 30 and 1065 under the Army and Navy spec. If it has a W on the can, it means that it is ashless-dispersant oil. The three grades of oil refer to their *viscosity*. Viscosity of oil is *resistance to flow*.

An oil that flows *slowly* has a *high* viscosity. If oil flows *freely*, it has a *low* viscosity. Unfortunately, viscosity of oil is affected by high or low temperatures. At below-freezing temperatures some high-viscosity oils become virtually solid, which makes circulation and lubrication impossible. So the grade of oil is changed with the season. Low-viscosity oils are used in cold temperatures and changed to high-viscosity oils in warmer temperatures. The lower the oil-grade number, the lower the temperature. I use grade 65 oil (SAE 30) in the winter and grade 80 (SAE 40) as it gets warmer.

The wrong type of oil or insufficient oil supply may interfere with any or all of the basic oil functions—lubrication, sealing, cleaning, and cooling—and cause serious engine damage. Use only oil that has been recommended by the engine manufacturer. Never use any oil additive that has not been recommended by the engine manufacturer or authorized by the FAA.

Always make certain that the oil-filler cap and the oil dipstick are secure after adding oil or checking the oil level. If these are left off or not properly secured, oil loss may occur. I was once flying an old Cessna 210 that had two separate doors into the engine, one for the oil-filler cap and one for the dipstick. I had had the aircraft serviced and I checked the oil level, but I did not check the filler cap. The line boy had not put the cap on properly, and on the takeoff roll the windshield suddenly became covered in black oil and I had to abort the takeoff. I was lucky and I learned a lesson. You gotta check these things yourself! Remember, a proper oil supply and properly functioning oil system are extremely important items for safe aircraft operation. You cannot be too careful.

Turbocharging and supercharging

Aircraft operate more efficiently at high altitudes, where the air is thinner and there is less drag. Most normally aspirated (i.e., nonturbocharged or supercharged) engines deliver their best power up to about 7,000 feet. Above this altitude the air gets too thin for the engine to be able to deliver full cruise power. You notice this when climbing. As you climb, it is normal to keep adding power above that of the low-altitude climb setting. I climb my Comanche at 25 inches of MP and 2,500 RPM. Above about 2,000 feet I have to increase the power by opening the throttle to maintain the 25 inches of MP. By about 5,000 feet I am at full throttle, and from there on the MP drops steadily as I climb. At 10,000 feet full throttle gives me only about 20 inches of MP. Since a normal cruise setting at a lower altitude might be 23 inches, I can't get as good a cruise speed at 10,000 feet on 20 inches as I can at 7,000 feet at 23 inches. And I can't climb as well at 10,000 feet at 20 inches as I can at 4,000 feet at 25 inches. So the whole performance drops off with altitude.

If I could compress the air back to its low-altitude density, I would still be able to deliver the 23 or 25 inches at 10,000 feet or higher as I can at 5,000 feet or lower. And in the lower-drag air I would fly much faster.

There are two ways of compressing the air—turbocharging and supercharging. *Turbocharging* uses the exhaust gases to drive a turbine that is on the same shaft as a compressor. As the turbine rotates, so does the compressor. It compresses the induction air up to low-altitude density and enables the engine to deliver sea-level power at high altitudes. *Supercharging* uses a compressor driven by gears connected to the engine crankshaft. Supercharged engines are seldom found in owner-flown light aircraft, so I will deal only with turbocharging.

There are various types of turbocharger to be found. Some are manually controlled; others are automatic. The item that is being controlled in a turbocharger is the turbine speed. Varying the turbine speed varies the amount of air compression available and thus the amount of manifold pressure. The turbine speed is varied by means of a *wastegate* that is opened or closed. The wastegate simply directs exhaust gases over the turbine blades or not, as desired. When the wastegate is closed, all the exhaust gas passes over the turbine. As the wastegate is opened, less and less exhaust gas goes over the turbine, thus delivering less extra power. The wastegate may be manually controlled by sensors that adjust for temperature and pressure. Thus, in an automatic turbocharger all the pilot has to do is to operate the throttle normally.

"Normal" throttle activity in a turbocharged engine means *gentle* power adjustments. Any increase in power is always done by increasing RPMs first, then MP. Any decrease calls for reducing MP first, then RPMs. This is to avoid *overboosting*, which means delivering more air than the induction system can handle. It is very easy to overboost a turbocharged engine by ham-fisted power use. An overboost of 10 inches or more requires the engine to be overhauled and the crankshaft to be scrapped. An easy way to overboost is to open the throttle too quickly on takeoff. Another easy way is to forget to reduce MP on descent. And a full-power overshoot after a missed approach can make it happen if you don't make sure that the RPMs are increased before the throttles are opened.

Some turbocharging systems only operate at altitude. Others operate on the ground and deliver more than the ambient air pressure of 29 to 30 inches. An engine that can handle ground boosting will deliver MPs as high as 40 inches or more. This type of engine requires more than just a turbocharger to handle the extra power. It has to be much stronger to withstand the higher stresses it is subjected to. It will have valves capable of handling the higher exhaust temperatures and extra lubrication for greater cooling. It will also have a bigger, stronger crankshaft.

The compressed air produced by the turbocharger is hotter than the surrounding air. This can produce higher cylinder-head temperatures. It also usually requires that the mixture be left rich during climb for extra cooling. The airplane flight manual will give you the correct information about leaning a turbocharged engine. Some turbocharged airplanes are equipped with a *turbine-inlet temperature gauge*.

An additional benefit available from turbocharging is the ability to provide compressed air for the aircraft pressurization system. See the section on pressurization for more details (page 198).

Turbocharging is available as original equipment on some new aircraft or as a retrofit on some existing aircraft. The accompanying table shows how turbocharging improves performance.

Comparison of turbocharged and nonturbocharged aircraft (manufacturer's figures)						
	75% cruise-speed kts			Basic list price ($000)		
Type	Nonturbo	Turbo	% gain	Nonturbo	Turbo	% increase
Cessna Stationair	147	167	+14%	$ 45.4	$ 51.3	+13%
Cessna Skywagon 207	143	161	+8%	$ 48.7	$ 54.8	+13%
Rockwell 112	142	165	+16%	$ 44.9	$ 50.9	+13%
Bellanca Viking	165	193	+17%	$ 54.8	$ 64.8	+18%
Cessna Centurion	171	198	+16%	$ 60.0	$ 66.0	+10%
Piper Aztec F	175	200	+14%	$110.1	$123.5	+12%
Cessna 310	194	223	+15%	$114.6	$138.5	+21%
Beech Baron 58	200	241	+21%	$150.0	$170.8	+14%
Aerostar 600/601	217	247	+14%	$156.9	$174.9	+11%

Note: the 75%-power cruise speeds are at the appropriate optimum altitude — about 7,000 feet for nonturbocharged and about 20,000 feet for turbocharged aircraft.

1982 Piper Turbo Arrow IV

Propellers

The propeller provides the thrust necessary to move the aircraft through the air. It is in fact a miniature airfoil of varying cross section. The simplest form of propeller is *fixed-pitch*. This type of prop is probably made out of one piece of forged-aluminum alloy. Older props were made out of laminated wood. Some plastic props were made, but they are very uncommon. You can get a prop with a pitch angle best suited to the type of operation. Most light aircraft have a *cruise prop*, which will enable the engine to deliver its best performance in cruising flight. Such a prop does not do such a good job in the climb or on takeoff. For applications requiring good performance in these areas you can install a *climb prop*. This has a finer pitch, enabling the engine to deliver more RPMs for a given throttle setting.

However, it also acts as a bit of an air brake at high power settings. It can prevent you from using full power, because you can overrev the engine with high power settings. Thus, an aircraft equipped with a climb prop won't go as fast as one with a cruise prop. But it'll climb very well. I know because I once had to ferry a Cessna 172 from Winnipeg to Toronto (about 1,200 miles on the route I used). I was taking off and I noticed that the engine was really turning over at full power—the RPMs were over the red line. I quickly throttled back and suddenly got the significance of all the bracing tubes going back and forth across the windshield—I was in an ex-seaplane and I had a climb prop! I also realized I was doomed to a slow cruise for the next few hours—I never got over 90 knots and it took me 10:25 to make the trip.

To eliminate the problem of prop inefficiencies in climb or cruise, the *variable-pitch* propeller was de-veloped. The early ones had two positions, and you simply set the appropriate position for climb or cruise. Then came the *constant-speed* prop. This added a governor to a variable-pitch prop. The governor controls the blade angle to maintain the desired RPM level. For example, in a fixed-pitch-prop airplane, if you dive, the RPMs will increase even if you throttle back. With a constant-speed prop the governor automatically flattens the pitch to hold the RPMs at a constant level.

There are several terms in use to denote prop pitch angle. Here is a key:

Low RPM	High RPM
High pitch	Low pitch
Coarse pitch	Fine pitch
	Flat pitch
Cruise prop	Climb prop

All the *low-RPM* terms—high pitch, coarse pitch, and cruise prop-mean the same thing. And all the *high-RPM* terms—low pitch, fine pitch, flat

Plane Profile 27: Cessna Skylane

Seats	4
Cruise speed, 65% power, 8,000 feet	133 knots
Range, 65% power, full optional fuel, 8,000 feet	878 nm
Maximum endurance	7.6 hours
Gross weight	3,110 pounds
Empty weight	1,730 pounds
Full optional fuel	528 pounds
	88 gallons
Useful load, full fuel	852 lbs
Fuel efficiency, 75% power	11.9 nmpg
Stall speed, gear and flaps down	49 knots
Rate of climb, sea level	865 fpm
Minimum field length	1,350 feet
Engine type Continental O-470-U	230 hp
Engine TBO	1,500 hours

Remarks Also available turbocharged, and both turboed and non-turboed in a retract-able-gear version.

pitch, or climb prop—mean the same thing.

Multi-engine aircraft need to be able to reduce drag to the minimum on the prop in the event of an engine failure, so they are equipped with *feathering* props. When a prop is feathered, its pitch goes through high or coarse to a no-drag position in which the blade angle lines up with the direction of flight. Look at an aircraft with PT-6 turboprops, such as a King Air or a Twin Otter, when it is parked, and you will see props in the feathered position.

Finally, the ultimate luxury is the *reversible* prop, also known as the *beta* prop. Here the prop-pitch angle is rotated through the feathered position to a reverse angle. The continued rotation of the engine will now produce thrust forward instead of to the rear, providing a reversing capability. For some reason you can't get beta props on light aircraft except in special cases. One company sells a conversion for seaplane use. It is:

Aero Accessories/Parts Company,
360 North Rock Road,
Wichita, Kans. 67206,

The advantage of the beta prop is that it provides braking action on landings and in taxiing—a very useful feature if the surface is slippery and braking action is poor. And, of course, you can back up. This is particularly useful for seaplane operations.

Adjustable propellers are controlled by various methods. The first Bonanzas had an electric prop, originally with no governor (i.e., no constant-speed unit). Later, an electric governor was made available as an option. With the H35 model a hydraulically controlled prop was introduced. Hydraulic props are the most common in today's light aircraft. The hydraulically controlled prop works with engine oil. The centrifugal force of the spinning prop always tends to cause the prop blades to go into low pitch (high RPM). In the hub of the propeller is a hydraulic piston, driven by engine oil. The back-and-forth movement of the piston actuates the pitch change

of the blades. The oil used to move the piston is released from the engine through a pilot valve in the governor. The opening and closing of the pilot valve are actuated by changing the tension on a spring in the governor. That's what you move when you adjust the prop control in the cockpit.

A specific tension on the speeder spring will maintain the pilot valve in a position that will cause a certain oil pressure to be maintained in the prop hub piston. This holds the blades at the required angle. If the RPMs tend to increase, as in a dive, the governor flyweights open out and the pilot valve opens, changing the mount of oil in the prop hub piston. The blade angles change to a higher pitch, and the RPMs are held at the desired speed.

In a prop using counterweights, the counterweights provide a stronger centrifugal force than the natural tendency of the blades to go into low pitch. The counterweights tend to move the blades to high pitch. When the governor moves oil into the prop piston, it moves the blades to low pitch. When it takes oil

out, the blades naturally return to a higher pitch through the centrifugal force of the counterweights.

In a prop using a spring instead of counterweights, the engine oil action is reversed. The spring works in the same direction as the centrifugal force, tending to move the blades into low pitch. The engine oil is used to drive the piston, actuating the blades into high pitch. Taking oil out of the piston causes the blades to return to the lower pitch called for by the combination of centrifugal force and the spring.

Some twins are equipped with *unfeathering accumulators*. These may be needed to provide fast unfeathering, due to the way that the props feather in the first place. The way they feather is to drain all the oil from the hub piston back to the engine. The propeller is equipped with a feathering spring, which, as the oil drains out, moves the blades into the feathered position. Of course, the engine should already be shut down at this stage, either due to a practice stoppage or a genuine engine failure. To unfeather the prop, the prop con-

Beech Baron 58P panel. Note throttle and prop controls are reversed (this is true of all Barons).

Knowing it

trol is repositioned in the normal cruising RPM range and the engine is restarted. As the engine begins to turn over, the oil returns into the piston and the prop starts to unfeather. The windmilling action helps here.

The unfeathering accumulators are helpful if engines are hard to restart. The system consists of a spherical container (the accumulator) that takes the oil emitted by the piston when feathering is initiated. It is held, with air, under pressure, and is released back into the piston as soon as unfeathering is initiated, providing a very quick return to normal.

A safety feature of this type of feathering is that the blades will automatically feather if the oil pressure drops to zero in the governor system. Since the governor gets its oil from the engine, it follows that the engine running out of oil or having a significant drop in oil pressure due to a part failure will cause the prop to go into feather, which is what you would like it to do under such circumstances.

In a twin it is desirable to have the engines precisely synchronized—i.e., running at the same RPM. There are two easy ways of accomplishing this and one less easy way. The less easy way is to listen to the sound of the two engines and move one of the prop controls until the sound indicates the props are in synch. When they are out of synch, a definite repetitive beat can be heard between the two engines. This is unpleasant and very tiring to listen to for long. As they go into synch, the sound smooths out and appears as one engine. An easier method is to have a *fast-slow* indicator on the tachometer or instrument panel. This can be a little disc that rotates to indicate the relative speed of one prop to the other. By adjusting the prop control until the disc stops rotating, you can quickly synch the props. The most expensive method is to have automatic prop synchronizers. These detect the out-of-phase prop and automatically adjust the governor to bring the props into synch.

Most light aircraft have two-bladed props. Some of the higher-powered ones have three-bladers. The three-bladed props give a quieter, smoother ride, but they don't contribute much to performance. Three-bladed props also have a smaller disc than do two-bladers. This provides for extra ground clearance. Some of the highest-powered engines drive four or even five blades but not on light aircraft. And, of course, to delight the eccentrics, you can find the occasional one-bladed prop on a home-built.

Some twins are equipped with *contrarotating* props. These eliminate the critical-engine problem found in conventional twins. With both props going in the same direction in a twin, an engine failure on the left side is more critical than one on the right. This is because the airflow from the good engine is unfavorable to good control at low airspeeds when the left engine fails. With contrarotating props the direction of the airflow is favorable from either engine and thus there is no critical engine on a c/r twin. The critical engine is the one that, if it fails, causes the most severe controllability problems.

Obviously, with contrarotating props you must have engines with contrarotating crankshafts. The first light twin to have c/r props was the Piper Twin Comanche, which was having more than its share of fatal stall-spins accidents since it was used so much for training. That aircraft is no longer in production, but Piper has followed it with the c/r Navajo, Seneca, and the new Seminole. The Beech Duchess also has c/r props. The c/r props considerably improve the handling characteristics of light twins when flying on one engine.

Props are very susceptible to damage when operated over gravel. Nicks can occur from flying stones and can cause catastrophic damage if not attended to. Nicks must be filed out right away by a qualified mechanic. The prop should always be inspected before flight for such nicks. Cleaning up the leading edge of the blades is called "dressing the prop."

The Piper Seminole shows off its C/R props

Cooling system

Aircraft engines are great heat producers. They need to be properly cooled to avoid excessive temperatures and resultant engine failures. There are three reasons why you don't want too much heat around the engine. Too much heat:

1. Affects the behavior of the combustion of the fuel-air mixture

2. Weakens and shortens the life of the engine parts

3. Impairs lubrication

About a quarter of the heat produced in an aircraft engine is used as power. The other three-quarters must be dissipated so as not to be destructive to the engine. Typically, half the heat goes out with the exhaust, and the other half is taken up by the engine. Circulating oil picks up some of this heat. The rest must be taken care of by the cooling system.

Some aircraft engines are liquid-cooled, like most automobile engines. However, all general-aviation-production light aircraft have air-cooled engines. All over the cylinders are mounted fins, which are part of the cylinder structure. These fins greatly increase the area of the engine exposed to the flow of cooling air. Cowlings and baffles are designed to force air over these fins. The baffles direct the air close around the cylinders and prevent it from forming hot spots of stagnant air while the main streams of air rush by unused.

An engine can have an operating temperature that is too low. For the same reasons that an engine is warmed up before takeoff, it is kept warm during flight. Fuel evaporation and distribution and oil circulation depend on a warm engine. Keeping the engine warm can be done simply with appropriate power settings (for example, you'd never throttle right back to minimum for a descent from 10,000 feet—remember how you give the engine a burst of power every so often during forced landing practice?), or it can be controlled with cowl flaps.

Cowl flaps are opened and closed

Two parts of the cooling system. *Above* Bonanza cowl flap. *Right* Cylinder head temperature gauge.

by the pilot as needed—usually wide open for takeoff and climb, half open for cruise-climb, and closed for cruise and descent. They vary the amount of cooling air going through the engine by opening and closing the back door, as it were. They provide flow-through ventilation when they are open. Cowl flaps should normally be wide open on the ground.

Oil is used to cool the engine, so it is equipped with its own cooling system. On most light aircraft you can't control the oil cooler. Some aircraft have oil-cooling shutters, however.

For winter operations you can install plates over the air intakes of the engine and oil cooler to restrict the flow of air. These, of course, *must* be

removed in warm temperatures. If you live in the north and you are flying south in winter, don't forget to take the cooling plates off at an appropriate location on the way (and to put them back on when you're going home to the cold climes).

The instrument most useful to monitor engine cooling is the cylinder-head-temperature gauge. The oil-temperature gauge is also helpful. If the temperatures get too high and you can't open the cowl flaps any more or don't have any, increase speed to improve the airflow. This may mean that you have to climb at a slower rate, so you could have severely limited performance on a very hot day, since the airplane doesn't climb well in hot air anyway.

Electrical system

Two electrical systems are to be found in most light aircraft—14 volt or 28 volt. Most singles have 14-volt systems, while most twins have the 28-volt type. However, Cessna and others have now changed over to 28-volt systems in their new singles. The systems are DC.

Power sources are batteries and either generators or alternators. Virtually all new aircraft are equipped with alternators. Older models with generators can often be retrofitted with an alternator, and this is recommended. The advantage of an alternator over a generator is that it will deliver a charge even at low engine-power settings. This can be very important if you have to spend a lot of time at low settings with a lot of avionics on, such as when you are sitting at the end of the runway for 20 minutes waiting for an IFR clearance. The alternator is also simpler than a generator.

Safety circuits are provided by circuit-breakers in most modern aircraft, although a few still cling to fuses. A circuit-breaker can be simply pressed to reset, whereas a fuse needs to be changed if it blows.

The important instrument for measuring your electrical system is the ammeter. In addition, a low-high-voltage warning light or a voltmeter is helpful.

The ammeter measures the electrical current in a circuit, which is the number of electrons being moved through the wires at any time. The voltmeter measures the electrical force available to deliver the current. If you are using electrical power, an ammeter will measure that some electrical current is being taken. The more items you use, the higher will be the amperage taken. For example, a King KX-170 nav/comm uses 1.1 amps when it is receiving and 3.0 amps when it is transmitting. Add on an ADF, and you will draw another .16 amps (King KR 85 ADF). A King KN 65A DME will take another 2.8 amps. So you would be using a total

of 5.96 amps with all these items on at the same time. The more items you turn on, the more current you will use. Landing lights, pitot heat, and electric prop deicers are heavy users of electricity. With no electrical items turned on, you would be using 0 amps. In all cases, however, the power of your battery would be 12 volts (in a 14-volt system; it would be 24 volts in a 28-volt system).

The alternator or generator typically generates 50 to 70 amperes and might be connected to a 35-ampere-hour 12-volt battery in a typical light single. What this means is that, with a fully charged battery and the engine turned off, you could get about 35 amps out of the battery for maybe 5 hours before you'd run it flat. Or you could get 180 amps for about 5 minutes or 10 amps for a much longer time. With the engine on and the alternator or generator charging, you can use much more than 35 amps. The alternator or generator would supply the power needed, with any excess unused power being used to keep the battery

charged. Thus, if you had everything on full blast (e.g., pitot heat, all radios, all landing lights, strobes, prop de-ice, heated windshield, and so on), you might exceed the amperage available from the alternator and start going into the battery, and very soon you'd run the battery flat.

If you do run the battery low, say, in starting the engine, your battery would take a lot of the alternator or generator's output until it is recharged. It would be better to keep your electrical needs low until you have recharged the battery in such an event.

Have you ever wondered why a 14-volt system has a 12-volt battery and a 28-volt system has a 24-volt battery? It has to do with the charging capability. Take the lower voltage system. If you apply 14 volts to a 12-volt battery, you will charge it fully. If you apply less than 12 volts, the battery will try to send power back to the generator or alternator and won't charge. It takes time to charge up. You have to put back in the same number of ampere hours you took

This entire Bendix 2000 system draws less than 10 amps. It features dual 720 COMM, dual 200 NAV, transponder, DME and 10 waypoint RNAV.

out. The more run down the battery, the longer it takes to recharge it. The 14 volts is the limit that the voltage regulator allows the alternator or generator to deliver to the electrical system. The battery puts out 12 volts, and as its power runs down, this voltage drops.

The voltage regulator keeps the voltage coming from the generator or alternator at the correct level. It is a limiting device on the top end—in other words, it prevents the output from exceeding 14 volts. At the bottom end it acts as a sort of one-way barrier. If the generator was putting out substantially less voltage than the voltage in the battery, the battery would try to force electricity into the generator. The voltage regulator prevents this needless exchange. The regulator also contains a current limiter designed to prevent the generator from delivering more current than it should. (This is not needed with an alternator.) If more current is called for than is supposed to be, the limiter lowers the voltage and thus limits the current. This prevents the generator from being damaged by excessive demands.

If more voltage is created by the generating system than it is designed for, the battery can become overcharged, which can cause damage to it and even to surrounding sections of the airplane, due to the forcing out of acid from the battery. Overvoltage can also burn out bulbs, tubes, and other electrical parts.

There are two types of ammeters found in aircraft. One type is the zero-center type; the other is the zero-left type. The zero-center type is usually found in airplanes with generators, and the zero-left type is mostly found where alternators are installed.

The zero-center type will read just to the right of center when the battery is being charged. The more to the right it reads, the more of a charge the battery is taking. As you turn on electrical equipment, you will see a momentary flick of the needle, and then it should return to about the same position it was in just before. If you turn on a lot of

Above Cessna 150 instrument panel (1975 model). Electrical circuit protection is provided by fuses at the lower left side. Note center type ammeter at extreme right side of panel. Note also split alternator/battery switch at bottom left of panel.

Below Cessna 180 instrument panel. Circuit breakers are used here instead of fuses (lower left of panel).

equipment, the needle will go more to the right, indicating that your battery is taking a lot of charge. When you are running off just the battery—i.e., when the battery is not charging—the needle will read at zero or to the left of zero. You should not let this type of condition exist for very long, or you'll end up with a flat battery. In my airplane I have a couple of old Narco Mark 12s, which use a lot of juice. When I'm on the ground, I almost always have to open the

throttle up to about 1,500 RPM to get the ammeter to show a plus reading so that my transmissions will be heard. That's why I'm going to rip out my generator and put in an alternator as soon as I can. An alternator will provide a charge even at idle. Of course, newer radios, which use less power, would help, too!

The zero-left type of ammeter reads zero with everything turned off, and as you add electrical load (by turning things on), it increases its reading. The more you turn on, the higher it will read. And as you turn things off, it will read lower.

There are two types of batteries in use—the old lead-acid type and the new nickel-cadmium type. The latter is much more expensive, but it retains its voltage for a longer time as it discharges and works better in cold weather. Nickel-cadmium batteries are found mostly in turbine airplanes.

The lead-acid battery creates electricity by reaction of chemicals in its cells. It contains a mixture of water and sulfuric acid. As the battery discharges, the acid is converted to lead sulfate and the water is left over. You can measure the amount of water vs the amount of acid by checking the specific gravity of the liquid, which is done with a hydrometer. This will tell you if the battery needs recharging. The liquid in the battery is called electrolyte. Its level should be above the top of the lead plates in the cells, which you

check visually. If the level is low, you should add distilled water to bring it back. Don't add water in freezing temperatures unless you are about to use the battery. You should also be careful not to overfill the battery. Overfilling can cause the electrolyte to boil over and damage the battery and its surroundings.

As the battery is recharged, which should be done by removing it from the aircraft and connecting it to a charger, the lead sulfate is reconverted to sulfuric acid. When the battery is fully charged, it should be ready to deliver another 35 ampere hours or whatever it is rated for. In cold weather a battery will not deliver nearly as much power. For this reason it is wise to use an external power source for engine starting in winter. If your aircraft doesn't have an external source, consider having one installed. I put one in my Comanche, using a factory kit. It has already paid off. Without one, getting a jump start is a real pain, since the

battery is located behind the baggage compartment and it takes a lot of unwrapping and wrapping to get at it and make the connection. This can be a real problem in very cold weather, and after you get it going, someone has to stand in the icy slipstream and put it all together again. With the external source, it's simply a matter of plugging into a jack. The other end of the cable has standard battery clips on it so you can get a jump off a car or the like.

Nickel-cadmium batteries should *not* be checked for specific gravity. First of all, the specific gravity will not be an indication of the charge. Secondly, if you get some of the sulfuric acid from a lead-acid battery mixed up inside the nickel-cadmium one, you can ruin it.

One part of the aircraft's electrical system is not connected to the master switch. This is the ignition system, which operates completely independently of the generator/alternator battery circuits. The power to

Plane Profile 28: Piper PA Turbo Saratoga SP

Seats	6/7
Cruise speed, 65% power,	
8,000 feet	149 knots
18,000 feet	164 knots
Range, 65% power, full optional fuel, 18,000 feet	787 nm
Maximum endurance	5.8 hours
Gross weight	3,617 pounds
Empty weight	2,066 pounds
Full optional fuel	612 pounds
	102 gallons
Useful load, full fuel	939 pounds
Fuel efficiency, 65% power	9.6 nmpg
Stall speed, gear and flaps down	60 knots
Rate of climb, sea level	1,120 fpm
Minimum field length	1,420 feet
Engine type Lycoming TIO-540-S1AD	300 hp
Engine TBO	1,800 hours

Remarks Also offered without turbocharging—as the Saratoga SP—and with fixed gear, both turboed and non-turboed—as the Saratoga.

drive the sparkplugs is supplied by dual magnetos, which are like mini-generators and are driven by direct drive from the engine. Thus it is possible to operate the engine with the master switch off.

The starter motor is connected to the crankshaft through reduction gears and a clutch. When the motor is engaged, the starter solenoid closes and the starter cranks at high torque. After the engine reaches a predetermined speed, the clutch releases and the starter disengages. One or both magnetos may carry an impulse coupling, which is a device designed to produce a very hot, delayed spark to aid in starting. Another type of hot, late spark producer is the induction vibrator. This is connected to the left magneto and delivers the desired extra, slow spark for starting purposes.

Aircraft lighting consists of internal cabin lighting for reading the instruments and providing illumination inside; landing and taxi lights for landings, takeoffs, and ground maneuvering; and anticollision lighting (including navigation lights).

Many new aircraft are being delivered with *integral* instrument lights at last. This has been a long time coming and is the answer. The next best type of instrument lighting is *post lights*. These are small lights, about the size of the first section of your little finger, which mount just above each instrument. Next in efficiency comes *eyebrow* lighting. It is a leftover from World War II but works well. I installed some of these in my Comanche. I bought them surplus through Trade-A-Plane. The only problem with them is that they stick out a lot over the top of the instrument, making it hard to read the top numbers on some dials. The worst form of instrument lighting is *flood* lighting. This is usually delivered from one or two lamps mounted in the roof. It is dim, and when you lean forward, you block it out. I regard it as strictly a standby system. The most exciting lighting I've ever seen was in an old Cessna 182. The owner had had all the markings treated with luminous paint, and his lighting consisted of two ultraviolet

floods. The effect was brilliant and highly legible.

Landing and taxi lights are big users of amps. Some are attached to the landing gear or are retractable. Others are mounted in the wing leading edge or the nose. Most people leave their landing lights on while flying around airports or terminal areas for extra visibility. They also help to keep the birds away. Avoid using your landing lights for a long time on the ground. They can overheat very quickly.

The familiar red, green, and white navigation or position lights are mounted on the left, right, and rear extremities of the aircraft, respectively. They may be steady or flashing. Some aircraft use colored strobe lights as position lights.

Strobe lights are the best type of anticollision light. They may replace the familiar red rotating beacons or be installed with them. Strobes are mounted on the wingtips, tail, or fuselage. They are controlled by a timing circuit. They must be FAA-

approved for installation in an aircraft. There are many good strobe-light systems available. Some, for retrofit on the wingtips, use the existing position-light wiring and have minipower supplies mounted in the tip. This makes for a cheap installation, since you don't have to poke a wire down the inside of the wing. You have to rewire the switch, because you want to be able to have the position lights on whether the strobe lights are on or off or vice versa. These installations may only be carried out by or under the supervision of a certificated mechanic.

A new anticollision-light system finding favor is the so-called logo light. It was developed for the airlines so that people on the ground would see the brightly painted tail as the 707 roared off into the night. It quickly became popular as an extra anticollision light and is now available for many light aircraft. They are made by DeVore Aviation Corporation under the name Tel-Tail.

Above Combination wingtip strobe and position light on a Bonanza. Note glare shield.

Below Landing light extended, Cessna 310

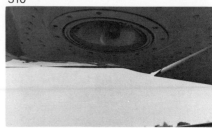

Below Landing light retracted, Cessna 310

Knowing it

Instrument systems

Effective instrumentation is essential in an airplane. Certain instruments are mandatory in all aircraft, and others are required for night and IFR flight. FAR 91.33 states the requirements as follows.

a. Day VFR:

1. Airspeed indicator
2. Altimeter
3. Magnetic direction indicator
4. Tachometer for each engine
5. Oil-pressure gauge for each engine
6. Temperature gauge for each liquid-cooled engine
7. Oil-temperature gauge for each air-cooled engine
8. Manifold-pressure gauge
9. Fuel gauge indicating the fuel quantity in each tank
10. Landing-gear-position indicator if the aircraft has retractable gear

b. Night VFR:

1. All the above
2. Approved position lights
3. An approved red or white anti-collision-light system
4. If operating for hire, one landing light
5. An adequate source of electrical energy for all installed electrical and radio equipment
6. A spare set of fuses or three spare fuses of each kind needed

c. IFR:

1. All the items required for day VFR, plus those required for night VFR if the flight is at night
2. Two-way-radio communications system and navigational equipment appropriate to the ground facilities to be used
3. Gyroscopic rate-of-turn indicator
4. Slip-skid indicator
5. Sensitive altimeter, adjustable for barometric pressure
6. A clock presenting hours, minutes, and seconds with a sweep second hand or a digital presentation
7. A generator or alternator of adequate capacity
8. Gyroscopic bank-and-pitch indicator (artificial horizon)
9. Gyroscopic direction indicator (directional gyro or equivalent)

Aircraft instruments work by a variety of means. Some are simply electrical meters; others have air-pressure or suction lines attached to them. Some are driven by gyroscopes; others have aneroid pressure-sensing devices inside. Here is a brief description of the major instruments.

1. Flight instruments.

The flight instruments consist of the airspeed indicator, altimeter, vertical-speed indicator, artificial horizon, turn indicator, directional gyro, and magnetic compass. The airspeed indicator, altimeter, and vertical-speed indicator are connected to the *pitot-static system*. The next three instruments are driven by gyroscopes.

a. Pitot-static-system instruments.

(1) Airspeed indicator. The airspeed indicator measures the difference between the ram air pressure caused by the forward motion of the aircraft (dynamic pressure) and the ambient air pressure surrounding the aircraft (static pressure). The faster the aircraft goes, the greater the dynamic pressure and the higher the indication of airspeed become. The dynamic pressure is obtained from the *pitot tube*, which is a tube whose opening faces the airflow, usually mounted on the wing, outside the prop blast. The static pressure comes from the static vents, which are holes either on each side of the fuselage or on the pitot tube itself, connected to an airtight line that is connected to the appropriate inlets on the airspeed indicator, altimeter, and vertical-speed indicator. In the airspeed indicator the two pressure lines come into each side of a capsule containing a diaphragm. The movement of this diaphragm is translated by geared linkages to a needle movement that indicates the airspeed. The reading on the airspeed indicator is *indicated airspeed* (IAS). Calibrated airspeed (CAS) is IAS corrected for installation and position error inherent within the particular instrument installed in the particular airplane. In most aircraft there is little difference between IAS and CAS. True airspeed (TAS) is the actual speed of the aircraft through the air and is calculated by taking into account the outside air temperature and the pressure altitude. Some airspeed indicators have an adjustable control so that you can set in the temperature and altitude to get a true airspeed reading right off the needle.

(2) Altimeter. Although FARs permit a nonsensitive altimeter in VFR aircraft, you will only see them in antiques these days. A sensitive altimeter has an adjustable knob for setting in the local barometric pressure. It consists of a series of aneroid capsules or bellows from which air has been evacuated. As the airplane climbs and descends, the difference in outside air pressure (taken from the static line) and the pressure within the bellows is translated by linkages to needle movements. For IFR flight the altimeter must be checked every 24 months for accuracy, and the static system must be checked for leaks (FAR 91.170). Many altimeters are now equipped with an altitude encoder. This hooks into the transponder and transmits the aircraft altitude to the ATC computer whenever the transponder is interrogated by ground radar. Altitude encoders are required for IFR and VFR flight within controlled airspace

above 12,500 feet (except the airspace at and below 2,500 feet above the ground) and in certain terminal control areas. Some encoders are "blind" encoders, which means that the encoder is a separate unit from the altimeter and operates independently of it.

(3) Vertical-speed indicator. The VSI measures the vertical speed of the aircraft in hundreds of feet per minute. It also contains an aneroid capsule that has a very fine metering vent to the inside of the instrument case. The case is connected to the static line, and any change in altitude causes a difference in pressure between the inside of the capsule and the inside of the case. This difference is slowly equalized through the vent.

As the aircraft continues to climb or descend, the difference in pressure remains and is read, through linkages, as a needle indication. When the aircraft levels off, the pressure difference equalizes through the vent and the needle returns to zero. Because of this slow bleeding of air the VSI lags a bit. It may take as much as 10 seconds to get a true reading after a change in vertical speed.

(4) Instantaneous vertical-speed indicator. To overcome the lag problem inherent in a normal VSI, the IVSI was developed. It is also known as the inertial-lead VSI. It is similar to a normal VSI, but it includes a couple of accelerometers. These are actually small pumps that generate pressure differences in the instrument's system whenever the aircraft experiences acceleration. They effectively cancel out the lag found in a normal VSI and deliver an almost instant readout of vertical speed. I have a Teledyne IVSI in my Comanche that is also hooked up to the glideslope receiver. A small bug comes into view whenever a glideslope signal is received, and it tells you where to put the IVSI needle to capture and track the glideslope. I am very pleased with this. It makes flying the glideslope a breeze.

(5) Alternate static source. Aircraft operating under Part 135 (carrying passengers IFR) must have an alternate source of static pressure for the airspeed indicator, altimeter, and VSI (FAR 135.155). It is a good idea to have an alternate static source, since if the static system becomes plugged, the VSI needle will read zero and the ASI and altimeter will read incorrectly. If you don't have an alternate static source and it becomes plugged, you should break the glass of the VSI. This will vent the static system into the cabin. It will give slightly erroneous readings on the three instruments, but it is satisfactory in an emergency. Most alternate static sources vent into the cabin in unpressurized airplanes.

b. Gyroscopic instruments.

A gyroscope tends to remain on a rigid axis in space. When a force is applied to the spinning gyro, it reacts as if the force were applied 90° away from where it was applied. It responds as though the force had been applied 90° around the rotor in the direction of rotation. This is called precession. All gyro instruments use the two properties of rigidity in space and precession. The gyro rotor may be driven by electricity, by suction, or by air pressure. It is usual to have both electric and vacuum or pressure gyros in an airplane so that if you have an electrical failure, you will still have the others and if you have a suction or pressure failure you will still have the electrical system. Pressure systems are usually found in aircraft fly-

Above Heated pitot tube
Below True airspeed indicator

Above Static air vents
Below The trusty altimeter

ing at high altitudes because the air pressure at such altitudes is so light that you can't get enough suction to drive the instruments properly. The suction or pressure system is driven off the engine. Some old airplanes supply vacuum suction through an externally mounted device called a *venturi tube*. This is a conical tube mounted on the side of the fuselage that causes a suction due to the forward motion of the airplane, thus driving the gyros. This system is not satisfactory for IFR flight. First, it does not become effective until flying speed is reached, and second, it is prone to icing.

(1) Artificial horizon. This is the most important instrument for IFR use. It tells the pilot the attitude of the aircraft relative to the horizon. A gyro mounted on gimbals maintains a rigid position in space, and as the aircraft banks and pitches, the gyro appears to move. These apparent movements are connected to the familiar horizon bar for pilot interpretation.

(2) Directional gyro. It employs a fully gimballed gyro mounted with its axis horizontal. It operates on the principal of rigidity in space. As the aircraft turns, the aircraft and the instrument case revolve around the gyro, thus depicting a change in heading. Some DGs are slaved to a magnetic compass and thus depict the correct magnetic heading as long as they are slaved. An unslaved gyro must be set to the heading by reference to the magnetic compass. It will drift off this relationship after a few minutes, so the DG has to be reset every 10 to 15 minutes for complete accuracy. Older DGs showed the heading through a window so that you could only see the current heading and a few degrees on either side. Modern DGs employ a vertical compass card that rotates, with the heading at the top. The heading reference point is called the *lubber line*. These types of DGs are musch easier to use. If you have a choice, go with the vertical-card type.

(3) Turn and bank. This instrument supplies roll and yaw information. The latest version is called the *turn coordinator*. Turn coordinators *look* a bit like an artificial horizon with a ball underneath. But they don't act like one—the little airplane banks to show a roll or yaw. Some turn coordinators are placarded "No pitch information" because they look like the artificial horizon. When an aircraft yaws, precession acts on the gyro and moves a needle or the little airplane symbol. When the yaw ceases, a spring returns the indication to neutral. The fluid-filled tube with a ball in it is used to indicate whether you need rudder trim. It denotes a slip or skid, depending on which side it moves to.

Above Venturi tubes

Below Directional gyro

This instrument, plus airspeed indicator, altimeter, clock, and compass, forms the basic instrument-flying panel (the old "needle, ball, and airspeed").

c. Magnetic compass.
The compass is probably the most basic and simplest instrument in the airplane. It suffers from errors when the aircraft is turning, accelerating, or decelerating and it tends to jump around a lot, but it is always there, pointing to magnetic north. Due to all the magnetic-influencing devices in the airplane, such as radios, electrical wiring, and so on, the compass must be *swung* after installation,

Above Turn-coordinator

Below Hamilton vertical card compass

Knowing it

which means that as many of the installation errors as possible are removed by making adjustments on the instrument, after which a *compass-deviation card* is mounted adjacent to the instrument to show how much off it is on various headings. Whenever new radios or other electronics are added to the panel, the compass should be reswung. Mine was 30° out after I installed an audio panel immediately beneath the compass. When aircraft are equipped with gyro-slaved compass systems, the magnetic detector (sometimes called a flux-gate compass) is installed in some remote part of the airplane, such as a wingtip or the tail. A regular magnetic compass will still be found up front—you even see them in 747s and the like. A new vertical-card magnetic compass has

been introduced. This looks like a miniature DG, but it is just a compass. It is easier to read, especially in turbulence.

2. Clocks and timers.

The FAA now allows a choice of either a regular clock with a sweep second hand or a digital clock. Some of the new digital clocks are electronic wonders. Not only do they tell the current time, but they also show elapsed time and have up-and-down counters. An up counter starts at zero and counts elapsed time until you stop it—just like a stopwatch. A down counter is set to the specific time to be measured—such as the time from the outer marker to the missed approach point on an ILS—is

activated at the appropriate moment, and starts ticking off the seconds, e.g., 4:32, 4:31, 4:30, etc. It shows the minutes and seconds *remaining* until you reach the point. When you get there, it beeps and flashes and starts counting *up* to show the time elapsed *since* you got there. I have a Davtron digital countdown timer in the Comanche. I use it not only for IFR approaches but for time to station, time to change tanks, time to start descent, and so on.

3. Engine instruments.

Engine instruments are available in either the usual round format or in vertical formats. The vertical formats are easy to read and take up less space. They are only to be found now in a few light aircraft but can be found in many military aircraft. I will discuss only the round-type gauges. Some gauges may have more than one instrument in the same dial—such as a cylinder-head-temperature gauge and an oil-pressure gauge. Others have dual needles or two gauges to give the readings for two engines.

a. Tachometer. This is also called the RPM indicator. It shows the engine revolutions per minute. (Note: some airplanes have *geared* engines, where the propeller runs at a slower RPM than the engine. In such a case the tachometer still shows the *engine* RPM, not the propeller speed.) The tachometer may be mechanical, electric, or electronic. The mechanical type is connected to the engine by an enclosed flexible shaft that actually rotates as the engine rotates. This rotation, through gears, is measured to show the engine RPM. The electric tachometer uses a small generator at the engine that produces electric current proportional to the engine RPM. The tachometer is connected to the generator by a wire, measures the amount of current produced, and reads this out as RPM. The electronic system works by electronically counting the impulses to one of the spark plugs and reading this as RPM. Most tachometers have an engine-

A vertical instrument package by Aircraft Instrument and Development, Inc. of Wichita installed in a Cessna 210 Centurion. The instruments are internally lighted and save about 50% in instrument panel space over conventional round instruments.

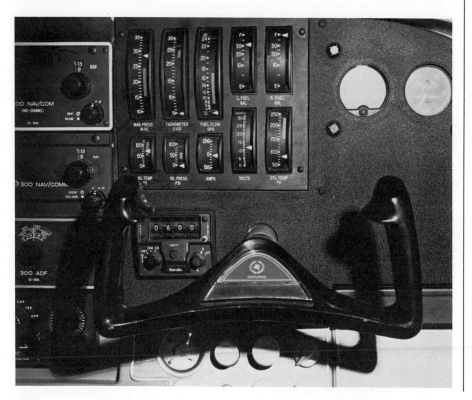

Knowing it

hour recording device. This shows the number of hours the engine has run. It reads in decimal hours down to 1/100 of an hour (36 seconds). Thus, if you change engines, you should change tachometers as well so that your recording of engine hours stays consistent. This did not happen in my airplane, with the result that I have to add a factor to the tachometer reading to get the true engine hour.

b. Manifold-pressure gauge. This instrument measures the air pressure within the intake manifold of the engine. A pressure line runs from the manifold to the instrument, where a set of bellows compares ambient and manifold pressure. The gauge is calibrated in inches of mercury. When the engine is not running, the MP gauge shows the ambient air pressure—about 29 inches, like an altimeter setting. When the engine is idling, MP readings will be low—about 15 inches. When the throttle is opened, the MP gauge reads higher. Without any form of supercharging

the gauge won't read any higher than the ambient pressure. With supercharging ·or some types of turbocharging you can get much higher readings, such as 45 inches. To better understand the function of the MP gauge, think of the throttle as a device for restricting the flow of air into the intake manifold. Without it the engine would run at maximum power. With the throttle open wide, reduce power. As you bring the throttle back, the restriction begins and the engine seeks more air. The more the throttle is retarded, the greater the air-pressure reduction, or tendency towards a vacuum, and the lower the MP reading. As the throttle is opened, the restriction opens, pressure within the manifold begins to rise, and the MP gauge gives a higher reading. The MP gauge reads the power you are *putting in* to the engine, while the tachometer reads the power you are *getting out* of the engine. Too high a manifold pressure with too low an RPM can cause *overboosting.* This means that the cylin-

der is getting more air than it should be and results in excessive pressure within the cylinder, which can cause detonation and engine damage. The normal way to make power settings is to increase power with the RPM (propeller control) first and the MP (throttle) second. To decrease power, first the manifold pressure is reduced with the throttle, then the RPMs are reduced with the prop control. For example, if you climb at 25 inches and 2,500 RPM and you cruise at 21 inches and 2,200 RPM, you would never want to get yourself in a situation where the readings were 25 inches and 2,200 RPM. First you bring back the MP to 21 inches, then you bring back the RPM to 2,200.

c. Oil-pressure gauge. This measures the pressure of the oil as it enters the engine from the pump. It can give warning of a possible engine failure caused by running out of oil, failure of the oil pump, burned-out bearings, or ruptured oil lines. Rest your eyes on it at frequent intervals! One type of oil-pressure gauge uses a Bourdon

Plane Profile 29: Piper PA 28-236 Dakota

Seats	4
Cruise speed, 65% power, 8,000 feet	137 knots
Range, 65% power, full optional fuel, 8,000 feet	726 nm
Maximum endurance	6.3 hours
Gross weight	3,000 pounds
Empty weight	1,608 pounds
Full optional fuel	432 pounds
	72 gallons
Useful load, full fuel	960 pounds
Fuel efficiency, 65% power	12.6 nmpg
Stall speed, flaps down	56 knots
Rate of climb, sea level	1,110 fpm
Minimum field length	1,530 feet
Engine type Lycoming O-540-J3A5D	235 hp
Engine TBO	2,000 hours
Remarks Was once also offered in a turbocharged version.	

tube. This is a curved, thin-wall metal tube mounted within the instrument that measures changes in pressure by trying to unbend or return to its natural curve. A linkage to the needle gives the pressure reading. An electrical oil-pressure gauge uses a small diaphragm mounted in an electrical transmitter assembly on the engine. The diaphragm is connected by a capillary tube to the inlet port of the transmitter, where the actual oil pressure is applied. The motion produced by the diaphragm's expansion and contraction is amplified through a lever-and-gear arrangement and transmitted electrically to the instrument, where it reads as a needle movement.

d. Oil-temperature gauge. This measures the temperature of the oil after it has passed through the oil cooler. In most cases the oil-temperature gauge is really a pressure gauge that measures the pressure of a vapor in an enclosed tube. A bulb containing a highly volatile liquid sits in the engine-oil system and is connected electrically to the instrument. As the engine-oil temperature increases, the vapor pressure increases within the bulb and the change in pressure is read on the instrument but is calibrated in degrees. Any malfunction of the oil-cooling system will be read by an abnormal reading on the oil-temperature gauge. Proper oil temperatures, as indicated in the *Pilot's Operating Handbook*, are required before takeoff. This is especially important in winter flying.

e. Cylinder-head-temperature gauge. This is an important instrument in the higher-performance engines. Cylinder-head temperatures are controlled by power setting, fuel mixture, and cowl flaps, either in combination or individually. Obviously, a higher power setting will give higher cylinder-head temperatures. So will too lean a mixture. Enriching the mixture can bring temperatures down, due to the cooling action of the extra fuel. Opening cowl flaps will provide extra cooling. The gauge is measuring very high temperatures in the 200°-to-500° F range. A thermocouple

is inserted in the cylinder head and is connected by wire to the gauge. A thermocouple consists of two different metals, which generate a voltage when they are heated. The gauge is simply an instrument that reads the current produced in degrees. Another type of instrument uses a bayonet probe that provides changes in electrical resistance caused by temperature changes, which are measured electrically in the gauge and read out as temperature indications.

f. Exhaust-gas-temperature gauge. This instrument is used for setting the proper fuel-air mixture. As the mixture is leaned, the temperature of the exhaust gas increases up to a peak and then decreases as leaning is continued. Mixture settings are usually made to a specific temperature point below peak—maybe 50° or 100° F. The EGT is the most accurate device for proper mixture leaning. I recommend it highly. Some EGTs measure the temperature only of the hottest exhaust outlet. Others have a knob by which you can select the reading for each cylinder. The EGT uses a

thermocouple and works like the cylinder-head-temperature gauge. The thermocouple is mounted right in the exhaust tube just as it comes out of the engine. Temperatures run between 1000° and 1600° F.

g. Carburetor-air-temperature gauge. If you have a carburetor, you should have one of these gauges. The temperature of the air in the carburetor venturi is measured. In carb-icing conditions the carb-air temperature should be kept above freezing by the use of carb heat. Without a gauge you just have to apply full heat. With one you can apply just the right amount of heat and no more, which is more efficient and better for the engine.

h. Fuel-pressure gauge. This is essential in an aircraft equipped with fuel injection. You should also have one in any low-wing airplane, since the fuel has to be pumped to the engine from the fuel tanks rather than feeding to it by gravity. It works by a Bourdon tube in the same way as the oil-pressure gauge. To check your

The instrument panel of the classic V35B Bonanza

Above Suction gauge
Below Exhaust gas temperature gauge. This model can read 4 cylinders

auxiliary fuel pumps, turn them on before you start the engine and note the fuel-pressure reading. After starting the engine turn them off to check the engine-driven pump.

i. Fuel-quantity gauge This is often the most inaccurate instrument in the airplane. Always check fuel quantity by actual inspection of the tanks. *Never* rely on the fuel-quantity gauge. There are basically two types of gauge in modern light aircraft. The *resistor* type works via a float sitting on top of the fuel in the tank. The movement of the float rotates an arm connected to a variable electric resistor. The change in resistance is read electrically and depicted in gallons or pounds of fuel. The *capacitance* type consists of a tubular probe

mounted in the fuel tank. The probe is an electrical capacitor that is connected to a bridge circuit and measures the electricial capacity of the probe. Variable fuel quantitics change the capacity of the probe and thus the reading on the gauge.

j. Suction gauge. This gauge is needed when you have vacuum-operated gyro instruments. If these gyros are operated by pressure, then you will have a pressure gauge. Some gauges have little red markers that pop into view in the event of the loss of suction or pressure. The gauges work like a manifold-pressure gauge. The purpose of the gauges is to indicate that the gyro instruments are getting the right type of pressure or vacuum for their operation. The gauge should be monitored regularly during instrument flight. Too low a reading indicates that the air-driven gyros willl read improperly, and you should transfer your attention to your electrically driven gyros.

Landing-gear systems

The landing gear receives constant heavy use and wear. It must support the airplane when at rest, when taxiing, and during takeoffs and landings. It must be light in weight, low in drag, and effective in operation. Its components consist of the following:

1. Suspension and shock-absorption system
2. Wheels
3. Brakes
4. Tires
5. Retracting mechanisms
6. Steering systems

The following is a description of each element.

1. Suspension and shock-absorption system. There are various types of suspension and shock-absorption systems to be found in light aircraft. Some systems absorb shocks; others take the shock and then give it back. The most common type of shock absorber is the *air-oil strut* (also known as the *oleopneumatic strut*). This consists of a cylinder and a piston. The wheel axle is attached to the piston, and the cylinder is attached to the

airplane. The piston is linked to the cylinder by a set of torsion links (scissors) that prevents the piston from twisting and from falling out of the cylinder. With the aircraft at rest, the weight of the aircraft compresses the piston into the cylinder. In the air, with no weight on the legs, the piston extends out from the cylinder. The cylinder is filled with hydraulic fluid when the strut is collapsed, and then it is inflated with compressed air or nitrogen until the piston is exposed to the desired amount. The cylinder contains two chambers one above the other. With the strut extended, as in flight, the oil is in the lower chamber. There is a very small hole between these chambers. When the aircraft lands, its weight forces the oil into the up-

Above Nose oleo on a Cessna 310
Below Trailing beam gear on Beech Sierra

Knowing it

per chamber through the hole, and the hydraulic fluid takes on the energy of the landing shock by getting hot. Additional loads are taken by compression of the air in the system. Another system finding increasing popularity is the *trailing-beam suspension*. The Cessna Crusader and Corsair have this type of gear. This uses an air-oil strut for shock absorption, but the wheel is mounted on an axle located to the rear of the shock piston on a beam. The front end of the beam is mounted ahead of the piston on a pivot. The effect is to give a softer landing than with conventional shock struts. Mooneys use a variation of trailing-beam suspension with blocks of rubber instead of shock struts to take the shocks. These rubber blocks simply compress as a load is applied. The system is thus easier to maintain and less expensive than one with oleos. Older light aircraft in the Piper Cub class use rubber cords in tension. These are called *bungee cords*. The Piper Tri-Pacer has the same system. It consists of a series of rubber cords wound around two parts of the landing-gear legs in such a way that when a load is imposed, the cords are stretched. Some aircraft use a hydraulic snubber to ease the spring-back tendency of the cords as they try to return the shock. Cessna uses a very simple system on their single-engine line. The earlier version consisted of a piece of spring steel that extended out from the fuselage, with the springing action of the leg taking the initial shock of a landing. Later Cessnas use a similar system but with a tubular-steel leg instead of a solid one. This takes loads torsionally (by twisting) as well as by bending. These are used for the main gear, with air-oil struts being used for the nose gear.

2. Wheels. Most airplanes use a split wheel, with bolts holding the two sides together. The wheels are made of aluminum or magnesium alloy. They can take either tubeless or tube-type tires. An O ring is used to seal the wheel halves when used with tubeless tires.

3. Brakes. Most aircraft use hy-

draulic brakes. Some earlier models use cable-actuated brakes. The brakes are of the disc type. Brake linings have to be replaced fairly regularly, as they get a lot of wear. The hydraulic system employs its own master cylinder and is not associated with other hydraulic systems in the aircraft (such as those used to operate the gear or flaps) in most cases. Some larger aircraft have very complex hydraulic systems with the brakes included as a part of the system. The brake master cylinder is usually located with the rudder pedals. Pushing in the top of the rudder pedal actuates the cylinder and moves the hydraulic fluid through flexible lines to the wheel cylinder, thus clamping the caliper onto the brake disc. Brake-fluid reservoirs may either be on the master cylinder or in another location, usually the firewall. Only proper hydraulic fluid (MIL-H-5606) should be used in brake systems. Parking brakes are simply mechanical locks that hold the hydraulic piston in place with the brakes on. Sponginess felt when applying the brakes indicates air in the lines and a possible leak. This should be looked into by a mechanic.

4. Tires. The performance of tires on landing and takeoff is a critical function of your aircraft. Proper inflation is the key to aircraft-tire maintenance. If you install a new tire, the nylon cord will stretch dur-

ing the first 24 hours, resulting in a 5- to 10-percent drop in tire pressure. It is not a good practice to place a new tire in service until it has been left to stand for at least 12 hours after being mounted and inflated to the proper operating pressure. The air pressure should then be adjusted to compensate for the stretching of the cord body. Follow the manufacturer's recommendations regarding proper tire inflation. Whenever your tires have been subjected to severe landing shock or other stresses, have them dismounted and inspected by a mechanic. Periodic inspections of the exterior tread and sidewall of the tire are a good idea. Pieces of glass, stones, nails, or other objects that might be embedded in the tread should be removed, and cuts or other injuries should be examined carefully. A dull screwdriver or a blunt awl makes a good examination tool. When tires show uneven wear, the cause should be determined and any necessary corrections made. Spotty, uneven wear may be caused by faulty brakes. Tires and tubes should be installed properly so that correct balance is maintained. Excessive use of brakes, fast taxiing and turning, and turning with a wheel locked all contribute to fast tire wear. Landing habits also have a decided influence on the life of your tires. Touching down "hot" often calls for heavy braking, which can produce flat spots

Piper J-3 Cub landing gear

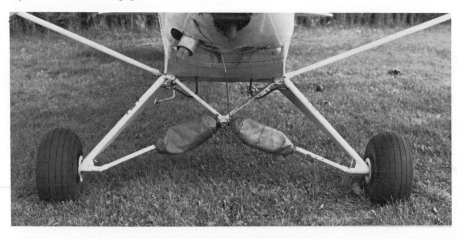

196

on the tires. If the brakes are applied when all the weight of the aircraft is not yet on the tires during the landing roll, the tires may skid and be damaged beyond further use. I make a practice of raising the flaps as soon as I have landed, which transfers more of the weight from the wings to the wheels of my Comanche. Some airplanes have their gear and flap controls close to each other. Thus you must be sure that you are raising the *flaps* and not the *gear* on rollout! Retreaded tires may be used on aircraft provided that the retreading has been carried out by an FAA-approved repair station. The name of the repair station, date of retread, and number of times the carcass has been used must be permanently displayed on the retreaded tire.

5. Retracting mechanisms. Landing gears may be retracted by hydraulic, electric, or manual means. *Hydraulic systems* may use an electric power pack that drives a hydraulic pump, or they may use an engine-driven hydraulic pump. The pump is reversible so that when the gear is selected up, it pumps the hydraulic fluid in one direction and when the gear is selected down, it pumps the other way. Hand-operated pumps are used in case of a power failure. Some gear systems hold the gear up by hydraulic pressure. If the pressure is lost, the gear free-falls down. Emergency extension is done by removing the hydraulic pressure. *Electric systems* simply have an electric motor that operates a screw jack that extends or raises the gear. When there is an electrical failure, the gear may be extended manually either by winding a handle a large number of times or by throwing a lever. A clutch has to be released first to disconnect the electric motor. *Manual systems* may consist of a large lever (as in the older Mooneys) that is deftly thrown from one position to the other or of a crank handle that is rotated several times. Some gear systems use a carbon-dioxide (CO_2) bottle to blow the gear down in the event of a failure. To prevent inadvertant retraction on the ground, a *squat switch* is usually installed on

one of the gear legs. As long as the aircraft's weight is on the gear, the switch cannot move and the gear cannot be raised. A gear warning horn is tied into the throttle. This blows anytime the throttle is closed beyond a certain level while the gear is up. Some aircraft have a warning-horn silencer switch so that you don't have to listen to the horn while practicing single-engine procedures. These are the aircraft in which a pilot often lands with the gear up later on! Some manufacturers offer either a standard or optional gear-extension device. It is standard on the Piper Arrow, for example. With this, anytime you do something that makes the device think you're going to land, it puts the gear down.

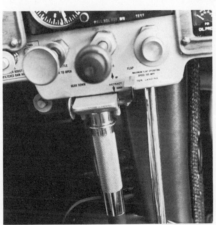

Above Manual gear lever on older Mooney

Below Cessna gear, older version

6. Steering systems. Nose and tail wheels are usually steerable, although some aircraft have castering wheels and steering is accomplished by differential braking. The Ted Smith Aerostar has electric power steering. Most other aircraft are steered through the rudder pedals. Very large aircraft have separate nosewheel steering wheels or tillers. The nosewheel steering is disconnected in flight so that the wheel will be lined up on landing, even if you have applied rudder pressure, as in a crosswind. Steering usually applies for a certain number of degrees and then the wheel casters a few more degrees beyond that. Thus a combination of steering, differential braking, and differential power (in a twin) can produce a very tight turning radius.

Above New Bonanza gear tucks up in 4½ seconds

Below Cessna 210 gear (it retracts)

Control systems

Control surfaces in general-aviation aircraft are moved by mechanical linkages consisting of either push rods or cables. The primary aero-dynamic controls are the ailerons, elevators, and rudder. Secondary surfaces include the flaps and trim tabs. The surfaces are usually made in the same way as the major items to which they attach—metal wings carrying metal flaps and ailerons, for example. Some aircraft may have fabric-covered control surfaces on an otherwise all-metal structure.

Variations in pitch control include the *stabilator*, as found in the Piper models, and the *V-tail*, as found in the Bonanza. The stabilator is one whole piece that moves to provide the desired effect instead of using separate tailplane and elevators. On the rear of the stabilator is mounted an *antiservo tab*, which helps prevent oversensitivity. Ahead of the stabilator is mounted a counterweight, which brings the center of gravity of the control surface forward and prevents flutter. The antiservo tab looks like a trim tab but moves in the same direction, as a trim tab would. The V-tail acts as both elevators and rudder. Its surfaces move like elevators (both up or both down) when acting as elevators and like ailerons (one up and one down) when acting like a rudder. An infinite variety of combination moves takes place as the pilot moves the control wheel back and forth and the rudder pedals from side to side.

Some aircraft have interconnected rudder and ailerons, designed to help make turning easier. You notice this when taxiing as the wheel moves whenever you push the rudder pedals.

All aircraft have some kind of elevator trim, which may be accomplished by movement of a trim tab, spring loading on the control wheel, or changing the angle of incidence of the tailplane. Many aircraft offer electric trim by means of a button control on the control wheel. This is a most attractive feature, and I recommend it if it is available as an option.

Rudder trim may be achieved by a trim tab or by spring loading on the rudder pedals. Some aircraft only have ground-adjustable tabs for rudder and aileron trim. Other aircraft have tabs on the ailerons. To adjust a ground adjustable aileron tab, you move it as follows: to correct right wing low, move tab on left aileron *down*. This will cause the left aileron to rise.

Some aircraft are equipped with *slots* in the leading edge of the wing (notably the Globe Swift). These serve to reduce the stalling speed of the outer wing and help to make the stall more gentle. Some aircraft have a *stall strip* attached to the front of the leading edge. These are designed to provide a more positive break to give a more definite stall. *Leading-edge slats* can be found in certain STOL aircraft. These pop out and in effect create, temporary slots to reduce the stalling speed. *Wing fences* are used in some aircraft to reduce the flow of air along the wing out toward the wingtip. *End-plates* can be found on some wingtips to cut down on wingtip vortices and improve lift. Wingtip fuel tanks provide this effect, too. You will occasionally see various *fillets* mounted at points where the wings join the fuselage. A *ventral fin* may be installed under the tail along the longitudinal axis, as on the later Cessna 310s. These are all designed to improve the aerodynamic characteristics of the aircraft.

Flaps come slotted, split, plain, or Fowler. Some flaps are settable only to certain positions. Others are infinietly adjustable. Flaps may be operated manually, electrically, or hydraulically.

Pressurization

Flight at high altitudes requires oxygen, and at very high altitudes pressurization is needed. In a pressurized airplane the cabin area is sealed, and the outside air is admitted only after it has been compressed to a level equivalent to that found at lower altitudes.

The pressure cabin must be as airtight, as possible, which means that doors, windows, and such must be very strong. In the larger pressurized aircraft the door acts as a plug and opens toward the inside. Thus the higher-pressure air within the cabin tends to push the door against its opening, keeping it closed. An airtight seal is mounted around the rim of the door. In some aircraft this seal inflates when pressurization is acti-

The Piper Comanche has a stabilator with an anti-servo tab

vated to further prevent leakage.

Pressurization is gradually creeping down into the smaller aircraft. Beechcraft offers the Duke and the Baron 58P. Cessna offers the 340, the Skymaster, and now the Centurion, their first pressurized single. Some years ago Mooney offered the Mustang, but this has since faded away and is no longer in production. Aerostar's 601P is also pressurized.

Pressurized air is taken from the compressor of the turbocharger in the engine. This, of course, steals some power from the engine. In turbine equipment (jets and turboprops) the pressurized air is taken from the compressor of the engine.

The lighter pressurized aircraft do not have a very great pressure-differential limit. For example, the Baron 58P's pressure differential is 3.7 psi (pounds per square inch). This can deliver a sea-level cabin altitude up to about 7,000 feet, after which the cabin altitude will start to climb as the airplane climbs. At about 21,000 feet the cabin altitude is 10,000 feet with 3.7 psi. By contrast, the Cessna Citation has a pressure-differential limit of 8.5 psi, which gives a cabin altitude of 8,000 feet at 41,000 feet.

The pressure differential is simply the difference in pressure between the air inside the pressure cabin and the air outside. Two factors determine the pressure differential for an aircraft. One is the strength of the cabin structure, which must be able to withstand the given differential. The other is the power of the pressurization system. The higher the differential, the greater must be the ability of the compressor to pressurize the air. Thus an engine failure or a significant power reduction may cause the actual pressure differential being *delivered* to drop. This would cause the cabin altitude to rise. A zero differential would bring the cabin altitude right up to the airplane altitude. Similarly, a leak in the pressure cabin would cause a drop in pressure differential and a rise in cabin altitude. If the leak is sudden, such as a breaking windshield, an *explosive decompression* can occur, with an immediate drop in cabin pressure and a rise in cabin altitude to the airplane altitude. At jet altitudes you remain conscious for about fifteen seconds in such circumstances. Thus the FAA requires at least one pilot to be *wearing* an oxygen mask above 41,000 feet at all times in most cases.

A typical pressurization system in light aircraft is that found in the Beech Baron 58P. The system consists of an altitude and rate controller, a test switch, a cabin-pressure switch, a door-seal switch, a cabin rate-of-climb indicator, a cabin-altitude indicator, and a cabin pressurized-air shutoff control for each engine.

Pressurized air for the cabin is taken from the turbocharger compressor of each engine and reduced to a controlled flow by a restrictor in

Plane Profile 30: Beech Baron 58P

Seats	6
Cruise speed, 65% power,	
8,000 feet	191 knots
18,000 feet	211 knots
Range, 65% power, full	
optional fuel, 18,000 feet	1,224 nm
Maximum endurance	5.8 hours
Gross weight	6,240 pounds
Empty weight	4,010 pounds
Full optional fuel	1,140 pounds
	190 gallons
Useful load, full fuel	1,090 pounds
Fuel efficiency, 65%	
power	6.7 nmpg
Stall speed, gear and	
flaps down	78 knots
Rate of climb, sea level	1,475 fpm
	270 fpm s/e
Minimum field length	2,498 feet
Engine type Continental	
TSIO-520-WB	325 hp
Engine TBO	1,600 hours

Remarks Also available in unpressurized versions, both turbocharged and non-turboed.

the line called a sonic nozzle. The air then passes through a firewall shutoff valve, through an intercooler, and into the cabin beneath the pilot and copilot floorboards. The intercooler reduces the heat acquired by the air during pressurization with a flow of ram air from a scoop at the top of each engine nacelle. After the air enters the pressure vessel, it is drawn into the conditioning plenums, where it is either heated or cooled, according to the selected system, and distributed throughout the cabin. Located on the aft-cabin bulkhead are two valves—the isobaric control and the safety valve. The controller pneumatically regulates the isobaric control valve to maintain the selected cabin altitude. The safety valve is connected to the cabin pressure switch and to the landing-gear safety switch. If either of these switches is closed, the safety valve will open and the cabin will depressurize. The cabin pressurized-air shutoff controls will stop the pressurized air to the cabin when placed in the full closed position.

The controller maintains a visual display of the selected altitude and includes an altitude selector and a rate control. The altitude outer scale on the indicator shows the selected cabin altitude, and the inner scale indicates the corresponding airplane altitude where the maximum differential pressure would occur. The rate control regulates the rate at which cabin pressure ascends or descends to the selected altitude.

Before takeoff the altitude may be set either to the desired cabin altitude (outer scale) or to the planned cruising altitude plus 500 feet (inner scale). Before descent or landing the outer scale should be set to the field elevation plus 500 feet. If the cabin differential pressure reaches the maximum and the aircraft is still climbing, the cabin altitude will climb with the aircraft altitude.

Pressurization is a boon to the high-altitude traveler. Oxygen masks are not particularly pleasant things to wear for extended periods of time. A pressurized aircraft enables the user to make maximum use of the efficiencies available at high altitudes in turbocharged and turbine equipment with no discomfort.

Oxygen systems

Oxygen may be available as a custom installation, with outlets by each seat, or as a portable setup, with a bottle and a number of masks plugging into it. I have a Scott Executive Mark I in my Comanche. This is a portable bottle with an 11-cubic-foot capacity. At full charge one person gets about three hours out of it. It is mounted on the back of the pilot's seat in a holder called a Papoose. Two masks can feed off it, cutting the endurance in half.

Oxygen requirements are given in FAR 91.32. For all aircraft, whether pressurized or nonpressurized, the requirements are as follows.

1. At cabin-pressure altitudes above 12,500 feet up to and including 14,000 feet the required minimum flight crew must have and use oxygen for that part of the flight at those altitudes that is of more than 30 minutes duration.

2. At cabin-pressure altitudes above 14,000 feet the required minimum flight crew must have and use oxygen during the entire flight at those altitudes.

3. At cabin-pressure altitudes above 15,000 feet all occupants of the aircraft must have oxygen.

Additional requirements for flight in pressurized aircraft above 25,000 feet are listed in the regulation.

There are four types of oxygen-delivery system:
1. continuous flow
2. demand flow
3. diluter demand
4. pressure demand
These are discussed below.

1. Continuous flow. In this system the regulator is designed to deliver a continuous flow of oxygen to the mask. The regulator may be automatic or manual. The mask is lightweight and covers the nose and mouth. It doesn't have to be individually fitted, so it is ideal for passenger use. The mask mixes the surrounding air with the incoming oxygen in a continuous supply to the user.

2. Demand flow. This system must be used with a demand-type mask, and it meters the oxygen to the user when the oxygen is demanded, or inhaled. The demand mask is designed to deliver oxygen to the user only when inhaled. It covers most of the user's face and creates an airtight seal. These masks are used mostly by aircrew members and have higher altitude capabilities than the continuous-flow masks.

3. Diluter demand. This system mixes oxygen from the cylinder with air so

Above Pressurized aircraft need a cabin altimeter, too
Below Scott Papoose carries oxygen on seat back

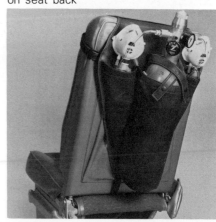

as to deliver a mixture of air and oxygen to the user. It automatically controls the ratio of oxygen and air mixture, giving more oxygen and less air at higher altitudes. This system must be used with a demand-type mask.

4. Pressure demand. The pressure-demand regulator incorporates an aneroid mechanism that automatically increases the flow of oxygen into the mask with positive pressure. This type of equipment is normally used at altitudes above 40,000 feet. The pressure-demand mask includes special pressure-compensating valves that provide for a buildup of oxygen pressure from the regulator and create an input of oxygen into the lungs.

If you are going to be using oxygen often, it might be worthwhile to consider getting your own mask with a microphone built in.

The biggest problem with oxygen is that of getting it refilled. It's not like getting fuel. It has to be handled by a qualified person. It must be aviator's breathing oxygen. You may find yourself paying one hour's labor for a refill, so try to schedule refills with other maintenance. By the way, it is a federal offense to refill an oxygen bottle that has not been pressure-tested within the last five years.

De-icing and anti-icing systems

Ice is one of the pilot's worst enemies. It can collect on the airframe and propellers, not only disrupting the airflow and spoiling lift but also adding substantially to the weight of the aircraft. Ice protection may be divided into two broad categories—deicing and anti-icing. Deicing refers to systems designed to remove ice after it has formed. Anti-icing refers to methods of preventing ice from forming in the first place.

Anti-icing is the most desirable way of protecting against ice. If it doesn't form, it won't disturb airflow or add weight. Anti-icing systems use either heat or a stream of alcohol to fend off ice. Typical installations include propellers and windshields. In the heat-prevention method usually an electrical element is turned on in anticipation of icing conditions, and its heat prevents ice from forming. These heaters should only be used in flight (windshields) or when the engine is running (props). Another method is to take hot air from the engine and feed it through channels into the component needing protection. Most large jets have "hot wings" and engine-air intakes. The Beech King Air has a hot-air brake de-icing system, which is designed to prevent the brakes from icing up in slush conditions, as an optional extra.

The alcohol-protection method of anti-icing calls for measured amounts of alcohol to be streamed over the surface to be protected—usually props and windshields. The old British DH Dove used porous wing leading edges for anti-icing-fluid distribution. The Beech Baron 58 offers a choice of alcohol or heated windshield. The alcohol version is not certificated for flight in known icing conditions, while the hot windshield is.

Deicing systems involve removing ice after it has started to accumulate. The most common method of doing this is the *deice boot*. This is an inflatable rubber boot cemented to the leading edges of the wings and tail. Ice must be allowed to build up (to about ¼-inch thickness), and then it is popped off by inflating the boot. If the boot is inflated prematurely, the ice will form over the inflated boot, thereby cancelling the deicing action. The air used to inflate the boots comes from an engine-driven pump. When the boots are not inflated, the same system provides a vacuum, which holds the boot surface snug to the aircraft skin.

Known icing conditions are defined as any conditions in which there is visible moisture and the air tempera-

ture is 5°C (41°F) or colder. Aircraft may not be flight-planned into such forecast conditions unless they are certificated for flight in known icing conditions. It is somewhat amusing to see an aircraft fitted out with boots and slingers (prop deice) and a placard on the panel stating "This airplane is not approved for flight in icing conditions." To be so certificated, the aircraft must comply with FAR 23.34.

Other aircraft parts that are protected by heat are such items as the pitot tube, the stall-warning vane, angle-of-attack vanes, fuel vents, and, of course, the carburetor or induction air system. In some aircraft the fuel vents may be installed in a nonicing area and so do not need further protection.

There are products available that

Above Windshield anti-ice on an Aztec
Below De-ice boots on an Aztec

can be applied to icing-prone surfaces before flight to retard ice formation. These are usually chemical sprays, which impart a very slippery surface, making it harder for ice to form. These may be applied to surfaces such as propellers, antennas, and such.

Not too many light aircraft have windshield wipers, although flight in rain cuts the visibility tremendously. Again, there are chemicals available that can be rubbed onto the windshield before flight to cut down the rate at which rain obscures the view.

For most light aircraft the best way to handle ice is to avoid it. Icing forecasts are pretty accurate. If you start getting ice and you have no protection, you should know how to handle it. In most cases a 180° turn is the best way out. The worst form of ice occurs in freezing rain. But freezing rain is caused by wet rain falling from warm temperatures aloft through subfreezing temperatures below. So a good way out of freezing rain is to climb. You won't get airframe ice flying in clear air.

Avionics

Data on selecting and buying avionics are given starting on page 66. The following gives a description of the various avionics components.

The Technical Standard Order (TSO)

The FAA has issued a set of specifications about environmental and performance capabilities for each type of radio equipment. The areas considered are:

1. Temperature and altitude
2. Humidity
3. Vibration
4. Audio-frequency susceptibility
5. Radio-frequency susceptibility
6. Spurious energy
7. Explosion
8. Electrical performance

For a piece of equipment to comply with the TSO, a sample must undergo certain tests, which set limits within which the equipment must operate. If it passes these tests, it may be allocated a TSO-compliance nameplate, which is to be found on the equipment.

The fact that a component has been TSO'd means that it should meet the limits set by the FAA for compliance. It doesn't necessarily mean that non-TSO'd equipment is worse than TSO'd. It just means that if it's TSO'd, it meets certain environmental and performance limits. Certain components, notably transponders, *must* be TSO'd.

Avionics cooling

Heat is the worst enemy of your avionics. And the way we stack radios on top of each other doesn't help. Especially with older radios containing tubes, good cooling is essential. Some radios *require* the installation of a cooling kit to make the warranty effective.

Mooney 231 with full avionics fit

The simplest form of cooling is to put a little scoop out there in the airflow and run a tube from the scoop to the radio stack. These cooling systems are very effective. Make sure that they are installed properly. There should be a drain hole in the bottom of the scoop so that water doesn't accumulate and get blown back into the radio stack.

Alternatively, small fans may be installed to take the hot air away from the radios. These will automatically go on when the radios are turned on.

See how hot your radios are to the touch—if they're too hot to leave your finger on, you should get a better cooling system installed.

I recommend that you use a set of internal heat shields under the windows when you park the airplane out of doors. The sun can build up the temperature within the cabin to way over 130° F while it is parked, which can cause damage to and poor performance of your radios. The shields keep the temperature at about the same as outdoors. It's more comfortable to get into, too!

Above Scoop for avionics cooling

Below and above right Heatshields produced by Thermacon.

Emergency locator transmitter (ELT)

Except for jets, airliners, single-seater airplanes, crop dusters, and airplanes undergoing test flights, the FAA requires (FAR 91.52) that all aircraft be equipped with an ELT. One other exception is aircraft used strictly for training operations within a 50-mile radius of base. So you will probably have to have one, and the airplane will doubtless already have one installed when you get it. ELTs come with their own batteries—they don't operate off the airplane's regular electrical system. They are designed to activate a signal on 121.5 mHz (the international distress frequency) in the event of a sudden deceleration, as would happen in a crash. The sound they generate is like a high-pitched siren. I make a habit of monitoring 121.5 on one of my radios and not long ago detected an ELT signal. I called the nearest flight service station and reported it, along with my position. They were not receiving it (I was at 8,500 feet) and said they would check it out. Later, on returning over the same route, the signal had gone. I never found out if it was real or a false alarm. It is a good practice to tune your radio to 121.5 just before shutting down after a flight to make sure that your ELT hasn't become activated (they sometimes go off on their own).

The ELT battery must be replaced or recharged either after one hour's continuous transmission or after half the useful life (or useful charge, if rechargeable) has expired. This period will be indicated by the manufacturer on the battery or unit. The expiration date must be marked on the outside of the ELT.

The FAA has recently amended the regulation which effectively grounded an aircraft if its ELT was not operating. It is now legal to fly if your ELT is out of the aircraft being fixed.

VHF COMM

For straight VFR you will need a minimum of 360 channels, which will enable you to communicate with control towers, flight service stations (FSS), Unicom, and the emergency frequency (121.5 mHz). A set with 360 channels gives you every 50-kHz frequency between 118.00 and 135.95—118.00, 118.05, 118.1, 118.15, 118.2, etc. You transmit and receive on the same frequency (this is referred to as *simplex* operation). When communicating with some FSS, they will receive you on a specified frequency (e.g., 122.7), and you will receive them on a nearby VOR navigational frequency (between 108.0 and 117.9 mHz). This can be a nuisance if your VOR receiver does not filter out the Morse-code identification signal sent on the same channel. All the newer VOR units have this type of filter, but the older ones don't. However, you can usually find a simplex frequency to carry the whole conversation. The advantage of the FSS transmitting on VOR is found with certain older radios that combine a VHF COMM and a VHF NAV but don't let you receive on the COMM frequency when you are navigating on the NAV unit. In other words, you lose your NAV signal if you want to receive on the COMM section. By receiving the FSS on the NAV frequency, you can communicate and navigate simultaneously. This is strictly a low-grade VFR-only operation, quite unsuitable for IFR.

For IFR, you will also need at least 360 VHF COMM channels, with which you will be able to talk to all IFR units—ATC centers, approach control departure control—and you will be able to receive the ATIS (airport-terminal information service), which is being increasingly found on a VHF COMM channel instead of the VOR NAV channel for the location. Many large airports also have a clearance-delivery frequency, which is often required even for VFR departures, on a channel that can only be received on a 360-channel radio. I recommend that your have a minimum of one 360-channel VHF COM radio.

For little extra money you can go to 720 channels—25 kHz spacing. This gives you everything from 118.000 to 135.975; 118.000, 118.025, 118.050, 118.075, 118.100, etc. You need 720 channels for IFR in the high-altitude spectrum in parts of the country. It makes sense to have at least one radio with 720 channels if you are putting in new radios.

Older radios had 90 channels or fewer. These are still of some value. Some 90-channel models, notably the Narco Mark 12, can be converted to 360 channels. I had this done. It's a simple job that only costs about $150 and is well worth the extra utility you get. I would not go out and buy a 90-channel radio today. It won't give you everything you need, even for VFR. A radio with 90 channels gives you every frequency in 100 kHz steps, from 118.0 to 126.9 (e.g., 118.0, 118.1, 118.2, etc.).

Above Collins VHF 251 COMM

Above Genave Alpha 200B NAV/COMM

Below Narco COM 120 720 COMM

Above The old standard—Narco Mark 12 NAV/COMM

Above Bendix BX 2000 CN 2013A NAV/COMM

VHF NAV (VOR and ILS)

The primary navigation system is based on VOR (VHF omnidirectional radio range). VOR operates in the VHF band between 108.0 and 117.95 mHz, just below the VHF COM band (which is 118.0 to 135.975). Most available VOR receivers have 100 channels—108.0, 108.1, 108.2, etc. More exotic models have 200 channels—108.00, 108.05, 108.10, etc. The instrument-landing-system (ILS) localizer frequency is in the same band as VOR but operates only on the odd tenth frequencies between 108.1 and 111.9. ILS glideslope frequencies are in the UHF band but are paired with localizer frequencies. Thus a separate ILS glideslope tuning head is not required. By selecting a localizer frequency you automatically select the correct paired glideslope channel.

Even though you have a tuner that operates in the VOR/ILS band, you also need to have a converter and an indicator to translate the radio signals received into readable navigation signals. The most common type of indicator in general-aviation aircraft is shown here. The pilot selects the desired radial to fly, and the left/right needle and to/from indicator show the aircraft's location relative

Below Collins IND-350 VOR/LOC indicator

Below Collins VIR-351 NAV receiver

Below Narco NAV 122 self-contained VOR/ILS

to the selected radial. Most general-aviation VOR indicators will also read out the ILS localizer (some older models don't, however). If there is a glideslope needle, there also has to be a glideslope *receiver* to make use of it. Some aircraft have a VOR/ILS indicator with a glideslope needle but there is no glideslope receiver installed, which makes the glideslope needle useless. Because there is no separate glideslope tuner, the only way to tell is to either look on the radio rack for the actual glideslope-receiver "black box" or tune in a good ILS signal and see if you get a reading on the glideslope needle.

The VOR converter is usually built in to either the VOR indicator or the VOR receiver. This will affect the price. You may see a VOR indicator selling for half the price of a similar-looking instrument. But you'll probably find that the cheap one doesn't have a converter, which would have to be a part of the receiver in that case.

A fairly recent development is the *digital VOR* indicator. It may be part of the tuning head (as in the Collins Micro Line), part of the VOR indicator (Bendix) or an independent system. This includes its own converter and may be installed parallel to your regular VOR indicator. It simply reads out, in lighted digits, the VOR radial or bearing to the station (a switch enables you to select which). This is a a very handy addition to the panel and I recommend it highly. Its cost is about $300—about half the cost of a regular VOR indicator. You use the DVOR for cross-checks. It will read your radial or bearing regardless of what you have your VOR

Below Davtron 902A VOR indicator

omnibearing selector (OBS) set to. You can have your standard VOR set to a specific airway radial that you want to fly on, and the DVOR will tell you what radial you are actually on all the time. Then, when you get on the airway, you fly the needle on the standard VOR. It is not easy to fly enroute strictly with the DVOR. The DVOR can be hooked into two separate NAV units, and a switch enables you to select which NAV you want to use. The DVOR is a very useful instrument. I have one in my Comanche.

With the rapid miniaturization taking place in the electronics industry, some remarkable developments are occurring. Narco, for instance, has a VOR indicator, tuner, converter, glideslope receiver, and marker-beacon receiver all in one 3-inch instrument. The only wires go to the antennas and the electrical system, and the weight is 3¼ pounds. Collins provides DVOR as an alternative to the frequency readout by throwing a switch—one way the tuner shows what frequency you are on; the other way shows the radial or bearing to the station. Bendix has a new totally solid-state indicator that does away with moving needles completely and depicts the aircraft's relationship to the radial by means of a light-deviation bar that is easy to interpret. The same indicator also shows the radial or bearing digitally.

Below Bendix electronic course deviation indicator

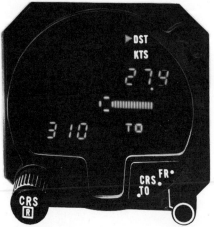

It can show the DME distance and groundspeed as well, if so equipped. You can also get frequency pre-select and storage features, which enable you to dial up your next frequency in advance or go back to the old one if the new one doesn't answer.

VHF frequency availabilities			
Number of channels	Spacing	MHz From	To
90 COMM	.1	118.0	126.9
360 COMM	.05	118.00	135.95
720 COMM	.025	118.000	135.975
100 NAV	.1	108.0	117.9
200 NAV	.05	108.00	117.95

Horizontal-situation indicator (HSI)

Once you've flown with an HSI, you'll never want to go back to the old way again. The HSI combines a vertical card-heading indicator with a VOR/ILS course-deviation indicator. Apart from saving you one valuable instrument hole (since you can replace a DG and a VOR indicator with one HSI), you will find the presentation of navigation information via HSI so simple and logical you'll

Below King KI 525A HSI

wonder why it was ever done any other way. All airliners and business jets use HSIs, usually as part of the flight-director system.

It used to be that all HSIs used a gyro-slaved magnetic compass to provide the heading information. This is the most desirable (and expensive) way. You're looking at a minimum of about $3,000 for this type of unit. But for about half that you can get an HSI that has a non-slaved DG to give heading information. I now have a NARCO HSI 100S slaved HSI and it does the job very well.

If you have a glideslope receiver, the HSI will present your glideslope information on the same instrument.

A heading bug is desirable on the HSI. This is simply a little indicator you can adjust to show the desired heading—useful for radar vectors, since you can quickly dial in the new assigned heading on the bug. The same bug can drive the heading command of an autopilot, if the systems are compatible, so that the aircraft will turn to whatever heading you select with the bug when you have the autopilot in the "heading" mode.

If you are installing an HSI in place of a DG, I suggest you keep the old DG and use it as a standby unit. The best way to have this is to have the HSI and the DG work on different systems. For example, my regular DG is vacuum-driven and the HSI is electric, so I have a fail-safe backup.

The gyro-slaved magnetic-compass-based HSI is the best type to get. This will give you constant, accurate, precession-free magnetic heading. It works off its own magnetic sensor,

1982 Piper Cheyenne I Turboprop

which is mounted remotely, usually in a wing tip. The sensor provides constant input to a directional gyro so that it is constantly correcting for precession and keeping the displayed heading accurate. The better HSIs provide a "bootstrap synchro" to drive the heading part of another instrument, such as a dual HSI or an RMI (radio-magnetic indicator).

The things to consider when buying an HSI are whether to go slaved (better and more expensive) or unslaved, electric or vacuum (I suggest you get the opposite of your standby DG—if the DG is electric, get a vacuum HSI and vice versa), heading-bug need and compatibility with existing or proposed autopilot installation, and compatibility with the NAV receiver and RNAV system if installed or planned.

I strongly recommend an HSI for your primary NAV display. It makes life much easier, especially when flying IFR. And ILS approaches seem to be almost automatic, compared to the old way of having to look at a DG and a separate ILS cross-pointer in some other location. Put the HSI high on your list.

Distance-measuring equipment (DME)

DME provides distance from a VORTAC station. A VORTAC is simply a VOR station with a colocated TACAN station. TACAN is a military navigational aid similar to VOR that operates in the UHF band. TACAN provides both *bearing* and *distance* information. VOR provides *only* bearing information. VORTAC provides *bearing* information to VOR- and TACAN-equipped aircraft and *distance* information to DME- and TACAN-equipped aircraft. So a DME receiver in an aircraft is getting its data from the TACAN component of a VORTAC. TACAN channels are paired with VOR channels, so if you are near a military base that has

only a TACAN station, you can use your DME to get your distance from the TACAN. TACAN frequencies are identified by channel numbers, and for each channel number there is an appropriate matching VOR frequency. For example, TACAN channel 112 is equivalent to VOR frequency 116.5.

DME is also available at some ILS locations. In such cases you simply tune the DME to the ILS localizer frequency to get your distance from the runway. There are also a few VOR-DME stations, which are simply VORs combined with the DME portion of TACAN but not including the bearing portion of TACAN.

The earlier DMEs installed in aircraft were heavy users of electricity. They would take a long time to lock on to a station and would quite often drift off. Readout was generally by a needle that would sweep back and forth when it was not giving a reading. Tuning was either via a tuning head that was a part of the DME or via automatic channeling off one of the NAV receivers. Some units would also read the groundspeed (if the aircraft was going directly to or from the station) at the flick of a switch.

Today's DMEs read out digitally, either with lit-up numbers or mechanical roll-over digits. Some give not only groundspeed but time to the station as well. Some have a "hold" feature that enables you to operate a single DME on two different VOR-

Collins DME-451

TACs, putting the first frequency into a memory while you tune the second, then enabling you to switch back to the earlier station. They can be channeled either by their own tuner or remotely through either of the NAV heads. They have low power needs, fast lock-on, and longer range, However, they are expensive. DME typically costs about twice as much as a NAV/COM from the same manufacturer—about $3000.

DME distance is *slant range* (line of sight). Thus, an aircraft flying over a VORTAC at 10,000 feet will show a DME range of 2 miles—straight down. DME is required (FAR 91.33) for all operations above 24,000 feet where VOR is required.

When considering a DME installation, the things you have to bear in mind concern the compatibility of the proposed DME with your NAV equipment. Do you want to channel the DME off your NAV tuner? If so, will this work? Not all NAV tuners can handle remote DME channeling, in which case the DME would have to have its own frequency selector. Do you want to have RNAV (area navigation)? Not all DMEs will drive all RNAVs, so you will need to consider the interface capacity of the proposed DME and RNAV units. Sometimes an incompatible DME and RNAV can be made to work with some black-box trickery, but this adds to the complication and the cost and may be more trouble than it's worth.

VORs are tuned by reference to the VHF frequency (in mHz). TACANs are tuned by channel numbers. All VOR frequencies are paired constantly with a matching TACAN channel number. It is not necessary to know which TACAN channel equals which frequency, because the VHF equivalent is shown in brackets next to the TACAN channel on TACAN-only stations on radio-navigation charts so that you can use these TAC-ANs for DME information if you want to.

Area navigation (area nav or RNAV)

Area nav takes information from your VOR and DME and enables you to create a VORTAC wherever you want one (within range of the VOR-TAC you are using to provide the input to your RNAV). You simply set in to the RNAV the radial and distance of the location you want for your phantom VORTAC and navigate to or from the phantom just as if it were a real one. The false VORTAC is called a *waypoint*. The equipment in the airplane consists of a computer and a selector head on which you set the desired radial and distance of your waypoint.

The more exotic RNAVs enable you to present more than one waypoint. Some units will accept two and others will take up to ten or more waypoints, so you can preprogram the flight before you take off.

Once your RNAV is set up for a route, you simply fly your regular VOR and DME indicators as you would normally. The only significant difference lies in how you interpret the course-deviation needle when it is not centered. In VOR the needle indicates how many *degrees* you are off track, and this, of course, widens the further away you are from the station. With RNAV the needle shows you how many *miles* you are off track, and this course width is constant all along the track.

A full deflection of the needle in RNAV mode would show that you are five miles off-track in one model, for example, regardless of your distance from the waypoint. This same model can be set to an "approach" mode, which reduces the track width so that a full deflection of the needle would indicate that you are 1¼ miles off-track instead of 5. This gives a much more sensitive needle for carrying out instrument approaches based on RNAV. Some RNAVs present bearing information digitally, as in a DVOR. They can be modified to drive a needle, which is preferable. In RNAV mode your DME and groundspeed readouts would be those relative to the selected waypoint, not to the basic VORTAC being used to make up the waypoint.

Jeppesen supplies special RNAV charts for VFR and IFR use. The use of IFR RNAV has been a long time coming, but the FAA seems to be accepting it more readily lately. RNAV for IFR must be an FAA-approved installation.

When considering RNAV, bear in mind that the proposed installation must be compatible with your DME and VOR units. Not all RNAVs will work off all VORs and DMEs. Some RNAVs require sepcial VOR deviation indicators, so you may have to exchange an existing unit for a special RNAV model. A good radio shop will be able to advise you in this area.

King KNS 81 provides 9-waypoint RNAV, plus VOR and GS

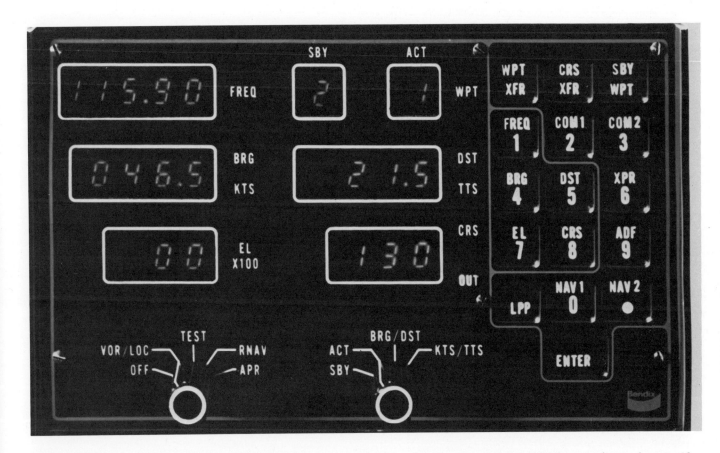

Above The Bendix BX 2000 system NCP 2040 computer programmer for inputting COMM, NAV frequencies and up to 10 waypoints or 20 courses for enroute navigation.

Vertical navigation guidance (VNAV)

VNAV can be found with the most exotic RNAV systems as an option. It puts the third dimension into navigation by giving you navigation information needed for you to get to some geographical point at some specific altitude. It is particularly useful for planning when to start a descent from high altitudes. If you're cruising at 200 kts at FL 200 and you want to let down and land at an airport with a field elevation of 690 ft, where do you start your descent? VNAV helps you decide.

VNAV uses extra computer components in the RNAV system. You have to input the appropriate altitudes and also the elevation of the VORTAC you are using. VNAV information comes to you either through a command needle, such as the vertical command bar on a flight director—so you fly the needle like a glideslope command—or through a digital altitude readout, which you must match with your actual altitude. In this system the VNAV tells you what altitude you should be at *now*, and you're supposed to be there.

Below King VNAV head

Automatic direction finder (ADF)

This navigation aid operates in the low-frequency (LF) band between 200 and 415 kHz. Your ADF receiver will also function on the commercial-broadcast band (550 to 1750 kHz). The ADF provides basic directional navigation over longer distances than VOR (except for some very low-powered ADF stations), since the LF signal is not "line of sight," as is the VOR signal.

The ground station providing the signal for an ADF is called a *non-directional beacon* (NDB). NDBs are used basically as approach aids in the U.S., but in Canada and elsewhere all over the world many airways are based on NDBs. Such airways are called *colored* airways, vs *victor* airways, the VOR-based system.

ADF is a useful backup to VOR in the airplane and is strongly recommended for IFR operations. Most ILS approaches have an NDB at the outer marker (these are called *compass locators*—the word "compass" referring to the old name for ADF, which was *radio compass*, not to your magnetic compass). An NDB at an outer marker is called an LOM (locator outer marker). One at a middle marker is called an LMM. Many IFR approaches throughout the world are based entirely on ADF.

ADFs are susceptible to interference from thunderstorms and are subject to certain errors at dusk and near coastlines.

The newer types of ADF have crystal-controlled tuning, just like VHF radios. This type is recommended. Alternatively, you can install on a tunable ADF a digital readout. This costs a couple of hundred dollars and shows you the actual frequency you are tuned to in lit-up numbers. I have a Davtron 701A hooked up to my old Motorola ADF T 12 and it works fine.

The presentation of the ADF navigation data is by a needle on a 360° azimuth. The newer ADF indicators have manually adjustable azimuth cards so that the present heading may be set under the lubber line at the top of the instrument. If you have a choice between a fixed-card ADF and an adjustable, pick the adjustable. It's much easier to read. You just have to remember to reset the card as your heading changes. Of course, the best way to get your ADF information is on an RMI (radio-magnetic indicator). This has an automatic rotatable azimuth card that is hooked up to the main compass system and thus constantly reads the heading under the lubber line. You don't have to keep setting it; it's done automatically. (See the following section on RMIs.)

An RMI can present either ADF or VOR imformation. It is most often slaved to the basic gyro-slaved magnetic-compass system in the aircraft. The basic compass has a "bootstrap synchro," which is a device that causes the RMI to read the same heading as the compass. Of course, not all aircraft are equipped with the gyro-slaved magnetic compass, making an RMI hard to install. However, Narco makes an RMI that can be driven off the heading information of its directional gyro-based (nonmagnetic) horizontal-situation indicator (see page 206).

When you are considering an ADF, you want to think about *digital tuning* (preferred), *rotatable azimuth card*, or compatibility or availability of an *RMI*, if desired (preferred).

Above Davtron 701A digital ADF tuning readout

Above Narco ADF indicator

Above King KNI 581 RMI

Below Narco ADF 141 tuning head

Radio-magnetic indicator (RMI)

The RMI puts an ADF and a compass on the same instrument. You can also have a needle that points to a VOR station (treating a VOR like a nondirectional beacon (NDB), giving an ADF-like presentation of VOR information).

The compass information on an RMI is supplied by another compass system in the aircraft, either a gyro-slaved magnetic compass or an HSI. The HSI will have to have a "bootstrap synchro" to get the heading data from the HSI to the RMI. Some DG-driven HSIs will not drive an RMI, but the Narco HSI-100 will.

One or two needles on the RMI will point to either an NDB or a VOR or a combination. The basic single-needle RMI just points to an NDB. King's dual-needle RMI has one needle pointing to an NDB (ADF data) and the other to a VOR. It will also point to an RNAV waypoint if everything is compatible. The best types of RMI have two needles and two switches. The pilot can then decide whether to have dual ADF, dual VOR, or one ADF and one VOR presented on the RMI, as required. The RMI will not point to an ILS.

Below King HSI with RMI needle. The RMI is showing 215°.

The things to consider when buying an RMI are whether you have a heading input available (from an HSI or gyro-slaved magnetic compass), whether to have one or two needles and what these needles should present—ADF, ADF and VOR, ADF or VOR, dual ADF and/or dual VOR and RNAV waypoint—and whether your existing or planned ADF and VOR receivers can drive an RMI needle (not all can do this).

Some HSIs incorporate an RMI needle in the presentation.

Transponder and encoding altimeter

The radar-beacon transponder is now required (FAR 91.24) for all operations within controlled airspace above 12,500 feet (except that portion within 2,500 feet from the ground) and in certain terminal-control areas. Included with the transponder, when a transponder is required, must be an encoding altimeter, which can send the aircraft's altitude to an interrogating ground radar in 100-foot increments. The transponder *must* be TSO'd (see page 202). Non-TSO'd transponders are illegal and may not be used, whether IFR *or* VFR.

An encoding altimeter is *not* required for IFR or VFR flight outside the airspace mentioned above. Nei-

Below Collins TDR-950 transponder

ther is a transponder. Each item costs about the same and, I strongly recommend that a minimum of a transponder be part of your avionics package. The encoder can be added later, as required. Some encoders are built into the altimeter (which means that you take out the old unit and install the new one in its place). If you do that, hang on to the old altimeter and reinstall it elsewhere in the panel as a standby unit). Others are called *blind* encoders and consist of a hidden black box that sends the information to ATC.

Note that, even though the transponder has a setting marked "ALT," it will not transmit your altitude unless you also have an encoding altimeter.

Transponders are so cheap now and so essential that many people install dual transponders. Serious and frequent IFR flying makes dual transponders a prime consideration.

Above encoding altimeter by Cessna

Audio-control panel and three-light marker beacon

An audio panel helps you sort out a variety of radios and put their sound where you want it—through the speaker, the headphones, or on standby. You can get cheap ones that are simply a switching center or better ones that include an amplifier. Many units also incorporate an integral marker-beacon receiver. Some include microphone selectors for intercom or a ramp hailer (a loudspeaker installed outside the airplane, usually in a wheel-well, for speaking to ground crew).

A three-light marker is essential for IFR work. This will enable you to receive the signals transmitted on 75 mHz at the outer and middle markers for ILS. Now markers are being added to certain nonprecision approaches (e.g., VOR or ADF approaches) to denote the *visual descent point* (VDP). A minimum requirement in any marker you install should be a high-low sensitivity switch. This enables you to receiver the beacon a little earlier in the high-sensitivity position and then get it very positively in the low position, a helpful feature. The three lights are blue (outer markers), amber (middle markers), and white (airway markers and inner markers on Category I ILS approaches).

Above Genave 3 light marker

Radar altimeter

Like many other pieces of avionics equipment, the radar altimeter is coming down in price to the range where it can be attractive to the single-engine and light-twin owner. These units still cost upwards of $3,000 in most models, but there is at least one available now for less than $1,000—the Bonzer Mini-Mark.

The radar altimeter will indicate your height above the terrain in feet. You can set a decision height on most models, and you will get a sig-

Above King KNI 415 radar altimeter

nal when the aircraft reaches that height. This, of course, can also be used as a ground-proximity warner.

The radar altimeter is an essential component for Category II IFR operations—basically, ILS approaches to 100-feet decision height. And it is a useful addition to the panel if you make a lot of IFR approaches to low limits—especially non-ILS approaches. The barometric altimeter only tells you your height above sea level. You must correlate that information with what you believe to be your position for terrain avoidance. The radar altimeter tells your your height above the ground no matter what. So if you set the wrong radial on your VOR or overshoot a fix and let down early, the radar altimeter can help protect you against hitting the ground.

Weather radar

Serious IFR flying demands weather radar, and it is at last available for some single-engine airplanes as well as light twins. Weather radar is used to detect precipitation, based on the fact that the worst turbulence is associated with the worst precipitation. Weather radar will not pick up clouds—just precipitation.

The type of radar available for light aircraft is almost exclusively digital now. Digital presentation means that the weather replies are processed through a mini-digital computer and stored in a grid pattern of memory cells. These memory cells are then scanned electronically to provide a TV-like presentation. It gives clean, bright, nonfading displays with good contrast for all lighting conditions. Because a computer is involved, it is possible to store a picture for a few seconds for easier viewing and interpretation. It also makes possible alphanumeric symbol display on the screen for such things as range arcs and bearing markers.

Soon radars will be offered with

Below King KMA-20 audio panel and marker receiver

complete alphanumeric readouts for interfacing with an airborne computer or memory bank. This will make possible the use of the radar screen to depict things such as checklists, emergency procedures, and even approach plates and enroute charts! Color radar is also here. This enables the pilot to see different intensities depicted on the screen by colored tones rather than variations of green. It costs about $24,000!

Ordinary radar costs somewhat less than $10,000 installed these days, and the price seems to be gradually creeping down. As the number of single-engine airplanes capable of taking radar increases, the price should drop some more.

An alternative to weather radar has been developed called the Ryan Stormscope. This is an ingenious device that detects lightning rather than precipitiation. It uses an ADF antenna and, in effect, is an ADF that uses a cathode-ray tube (CRT) instead of a needle. When lightning occurs, the relative location is depicted on the CRT as a bright dot (the equivalent of the ADF needle point-

ing). The dot stays there, and as each lightning strike occurs, more dots appear on the screen. When 128 dots have appeared, the oldest dots start to disappear as new dots come on. Otherwise, dots stay on the screen for five minutes. The CRT depicts a 360° azimuth around the airplane, as compared to weather radar, which only shows the picture straight ahead and about 30° on either side.

The dots stay in place regardless of how you turn the airplane. So if you did a 180° turn, the dots would still show as they did when you were flying in the other direction. To solve this problem, you have to cancel the picture and start building it up from scratch when you make a major heading change. The range shown is a function of the strength of the lightning strike. In other words, a very strong, far-away blast would show nearer than it is, and a nearby weak flash would show further than it really is. The control head is the size of a standard radio, and the CRT fits in a 3-inch instrument hole. The Stormscope costs somewhat less than weather radar and can fit in any radio-equipped aircraft. It ain't radar, but it is reported to be quite effective in showing thunderstorm locations, and is FAA-approved as a weather-avoidance system.

Above King KWX 50 weather radar

Below Beech Bonanza with Bendix weather radar

Below Ryan Stormscope indicator

Knowing it

Flight directors

Quite a few new single-engine aircraft are to be seen these days with complete flight-director systems, items that were only to be seen in business jets and airliners just a few years ago. The flight director may be just a device that tells *you* what to do after you have told it *what* you want to do, or it can hook into an autopilot and tell *it* what to do, in which case it's called an integrated flight control system (IFCS).

The typical flight director consists of a *director horizon* and an HSI. The director horizon combines raw artificial-horizon presentation with commands that tell you where to put the airplane to satisfy the objective you have programmed into it. The presentation of command can be by steering needles, rather similar to a rectilinear ILS cross-pointer, or by V-bars. With the steering-needle system, you simply fly the airplane in the direction the needles are pointing—e.g., fly up and to the right. When you have satisfied the command, the needles center, indicating that you are doing the right thing. When the director wants you to level off and stop turning, the needles indicate a pitch-down and roll-out maneuver, which you follow. Whenever the needles are correctly centered, you are, right now, doing the right thing, whether it be turning, flying straight and level, letting down, or whatever.

The V-bar presentation has two orange bars that look like an inverted V. The airplane is depicted by a triangular shape, with the apex at the top. Commands are given by movement of the V-bars to show a directional change. You fly the aircraft into the V-bars so that the bars line up with the aircraft symbol, and the command is satisfied.

The flight director can be programmed to handle virtually all flight maneuvers. It can be coupled to a nav instrument to give steering information for intercept and tracking of a

Collins FD 112C cross-pointer cuing flight director

radial or other navigational track, such as an RNAV track, localizer, or VLF/Omega track. It can be programmed to keep you on a heading and to hold you on an altitude. It can be coupled to a full ILS and give you commands to fly the ILS right down to minimums. And you can have it give you the correct go-around attitude if you decide to miss the approach. If your flight director has this type of input, you will have a go-around button either on the control wheel or the throttle. When you push it, the command bars will change from a "fly the ILS" mode to a "let's climb and get outta here" mode.

Superexotic director horizons have ILS glideslope, DME readouts, speed fast/slow readouts, and radar altitude readouts right on the same instrument. Flight directors start at about $10,000.

Collins FD 112V v-bar cuing flight director

Below Collins AP 105 controller

Autopilots

Autopilots range from simple single-axis wing levelers right up to complete three-axis systems, with autothrottle, altitude hold, navigation couplers, and such. Let's start at the low end of the scale and work up.

1. Single-axis autopilot. This in its most basic form is called a wing-leveler. Mooney used to offer it as standard equipment in some models—they called it PC (positive control). In the Mooney version it is on all the time. The pilot has an override switch on the control wheel for

214

making turns. The device works on the ailerons and receives sensing from one of the gyro instruments. I have the Piper Autocontrol II in my Comanche. This is a basic single-axis autopilot that must be turned on and off as needed. It provides heading select. You dial in the heading you want to fly on the DG, and it holds the heading for you. On earlier models you had to set the DG to 0°. This was a lousy system, since you lost your stabilized heading information and it was awkward to use when you wanted to make a turn to a new heading. A turn knob is provided to enable the pilot to turn the aircraft using the autopilot. The most exotic version of the single-axis autopilot also provides navigational couplers. You can select whether you want to couple to the VOR, ILS, ILS back-course, or just the heading mode. The autopilot will intercept and track the appropriate aid, as selected. Many VOR stations deliver less than straight radials (it's called scalloping). A VOR coupler in such cases is undesirable, since it will cause the airplane to chase all over the sky looking for the elusive radial. Flying the autopilot on heading mode makes for a smoother flight. You must then make any necessary corrections in selected heading to stay on the radial, using judgment to determine if the airplane is really off-track or if the radial is shifting around.

2. Two-axis autopilot. This model adds pitch control to the wing-leveling and turn-control capability of the single-axis system. In some models the autopilot will act as its own trim and simply hold the aircraft in the selected attitude by its own servos. With this type you have to be careful when you turn it off, since the aircraft may be out of trim and go into a fairly violent pitch up or down, depending on how you have the elevator trim set. Better models have an automatic trim feature that keeps the trim set properly as you adjust the autopilot pitch control. You usually get an altitude-hold feature in the two-axis autopilot. In most models there is simply a button marked

Above Cessna 200A autopilot

altitude hold, which you push when you are at your desired altitude. The autopilot then takes over and keeps your altitude where you want it. Piper has a model called Altimatic on which you dial in the desired altitude in advance and the autopilot takes you there and levels off!

3. Three-axis autopilot. Now the rudder control is added and the airplane should be completely controllable. A *yaw-damper* is not uncommon with this type of system. This senses and eliminates the fishtailing tendency of some of the short-coupled aircraft.

4. Couplers. In addition to the navigation couplers mentioned, a two- or three-axis system can be had that gives glideslope coupling. With this type the aircraft can be made to intercept the localizer and then fly it and the glideslope to minimums. Superexotic systems have auto throttles that make the necessary power adjustments for you.

Microphones and headsets

You'll doubtless find a mike in your airplane, whether you buy it new or used. Whatever you've got, I recommend that you install a boom mike with a control-wheel button. There is no reason at all why you should have to juggle with a hand-held mike when you are flying the airplane. I use a Plantronics boom mike, with a noise-cancelling device called a background-noise suppressor (BNS) and

a Rynearson custom-molded earphone—a plastic earphone that plugs into the headset and is molded to my own ear channel.

Listen around when you are flying and notice the terrible background noise in some transmissions. This is due to a lousy mike. The best type of mike to get is a dynamic model. Carbon mikes are not as satisfactory. A noise-cancelling mike is preferable to an ordinary unit.

Since the Plantronics only fits in one ear, I use an E.A.R. foam earplug in the other one. This combination suits me best. The Plantronics mike clips onto my glasses and gives a good, solid mount. If you don't wear glasses, the ear mold can hold the mike in place, or you can wear a headband. If you prefer, you can get a big headset-mike combination, such as the David Clark model. This will cut down on the noise you hear while giving excellent mike performance.

Below Plantronics headset. No self-respecting vase should be without one!

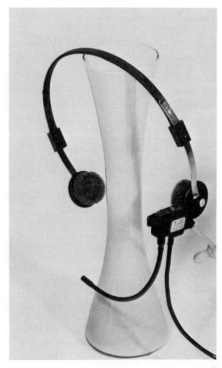

Airborne telephones

You can have a telephone in your plane that can be used to talk to any telephone in the world. There are 12 channels allocated to airborne telephones, with three usually being available in any area. There are about 50 ground stations in the United States. To make a call from the airplane, you find an open channel by depressing the channel-selector buttons until you get one that gives a dial tone. Then you signal the ground operator by pushing another button. The operator comes on the line and you give the number you want, either charging it to a telephone credit card or having it billed to you through your airborne phone number. The operator connects you and you are all set.

To call an airborne phone from the ground, you call the appropriate ground station (either through the operatory or by direct-dialing the number if you know it). The appropriate ground station is the one near where the airplane is flying. Range at 5,000 feet is about 100 miles, going up to 200 miles at 20,000 feet. The operator then dials the aircraft (you have to give the operator the aircraft phone number), and the airborne phone rings.

Antennas

A good avionics setup can be ruined by a lousy antenna array. Each type of radio has its own type of antenna. Selection and location of these antennas is an important part of designing your avionics package. Some antennas need to be located on the underside of the aircraft—e.g., DME, transponder, radar altimeter, and marker-beacon antennas. Others should be on top—either on the fuselage or the tail—e.g., VOR and VHF COMM units.

The cable connecting the antenna to the radio must also be of the proper type. Some radios come with antenna cable. Otherwise, 50-ohm coaxial cable should be used in most applications.

Antennas must not only perform their electronic function, but they must be strong enough to withstand the loads imposed in flight. These include simple air flow and also the ability to carry ice without damage. Next time you're up, look at the shadow of your roof antennas on the wing if you fly a low-wing plane. If it is the whip type, you'll be amazed at how much it flexes in the wind.

The location of the antenna must be made carefully so that you don't get interference. For example, putting a blade antenna (such as for a transponder or DME) directly behind the nosewheel would cause problems due to the shielding effect of the gear. Strobe lights should not be too close to antennas, because they can cause interference. And certain antennas should not be mounted too near certain other antennas, because they can electronically interfere with each other.

Static-discharge wicks

Flight through precipitation can build up a charge of static electricity in the airplane. This can cause severe interference with the radios. I suggest that you install static-discharge wicks if you expect to fly through precipitation often. These bleed off the static charge instead of letting it mess up your radio system. These wicks are small, taperlike devices that mount on the trailing edge of the wings and tail surfaces—I have ten on my Comanche. They are about eight inches long and flexible.

Left The King airborne telephone

Below A plethora of antennae beneath a Cessna 310

Selling it

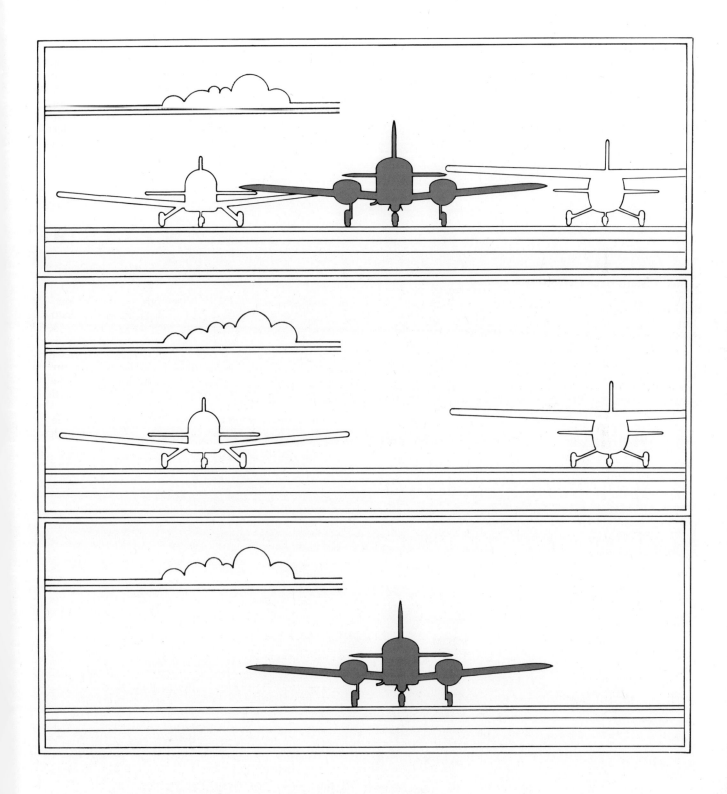

Selling it

You have two different situations when you are selling—one if you are selling and replacing and another if you are selling and not replacing. Obviously you want to get as much for your aircraft as you can. What can you expect to sell it for? Should you try to sell it through an ad,

through a broker, to a dealer, or what? It depends on what you've got and its condition. The people who advertise "certified cash on your ramp for your plane!" and so on are usually buying for inventory, so the price you could expect to get would be about the wholesale value, probably less an allowance in the dealer's mind for maybe a month or two's floorplan money. So selling your plane this way is fast but will proba-

bly bring you the lowest return. If you need to get out of the situation right away or you need cash now, this is one way to go. The more exotic your bird, the less of a good deal you'll get. A Cessna 172 is a lot easier to sell than a Waco Sirius this way.

Selling it yourself through an advertisement is the most time-consuming way but may bring you the highest price. You should take into consideration the value of your time

What your dealer uses to study the marketplace

Selling it

in showing the airplane and the possible liability you may have if you sell it and it turns out to be not quite right as soon as the buyer gets it home. You can have a lot of anguish dealing with an upset buyer who thinks you sold him a bill of goods, even if you didn't. The rule, of course, is "let the buyer beware," but that doesn't prevent you from being sued if the buyer is unhappy. Don't expect to sell the aircraft quickly, especially if you are holding out for a high price. Expect to show it to several people, which means that you will spend demonstrating time and expense for fuel and operating costs when letting other people try it out. Bear in mind that you may get into financing puzzles, too. Does the airplane now have a lien on it? Is the prospective buyer going to finance it? How will you be paid? How will you satisfy your lien? For all these reasons it probably makes best sense to have an aircraft dealer act as your broker in selling it. The dealer will

want a commission of 5 to 7 percent of the selling price, excluding taxes. Another way to handle this is to let the dealer sell it for any price, so long as you get a certain amount. Then the dealer keeps the change. The dealer will be responsible for advertising it and showing it. You need to work out when the airplane is available for showing. You should also check your insurance company to make sure that you are properly covered while other people are trying it out, especially if you aren't on board.

Getting quotes

You need to get a feel for the current value of the airplane. Ask your banker or insurance company to tell you what the approximate wholesale-price-guide value is for the airplane,

making the appropriate adjustments up or down to take into account such things as recent paint, recent major, high-time engine, and so on.

Look in the used-plane press. If you are a registered owner, you are undoubtedly receiving various publications such as *Aero*, *Runway*, *Air List-Ads*, and so on. Check *Trade-a-Plane* for the prices your kind of airplane is being offered at. Then contact a dealer and ask what they would offer for the airplane. Give very precise details about its equipment, time, and so on.

When you are asking dealers to make you an offer on the plane, ask them if they would be interested in acting as your broker and selling it for you. Find out what they think they can get and ask what kind of a fee they want. If you decide to take this route, it is a good idea to draw up an agreement. A standard real-estate agreement can give you the format. Few people do this, but it does serve to protect you when it

Plane Profile 31: Cessna 340A

Seats	6
Cruise speed, 65% power,	
8,000 feet	182 knots
18,000 feet	196 knots
Range, 65% power, full	
optional fuel, 18,000 feet	1,078 nm
Maximum endurance	6.5 hours
Gross weight	6,025 pounds
Empty weight	3,948 pounds
Full optional fuel	1,218 pounds
	203 gallons
Useful load, full fuel	859 pounds
Fuel efficiency, 65%	
power	6.5 nmpg
Stall speed, gear and	
flaps down	71 knots
Rate of climb, sea level	1,650 fpm
	315 fpm s/e
Minimum field length	2,175 feet
Engine type Continental	
TSIO-520-NB	310 hp
Engine TBO	1,400 hours
Remarks Pressurized, turbocharged twin.	

gets down to the nitty gritty.

If you are trading to buy another airplane, your dealer may take your old one in trade, especially if it is a popular type. If the dealer has a customer lined up for yours, you should get more for it than if he is just buying it for stock.

Should you fix it to sell it?

Depending on how doggy-looking your airplane is when you decide to sell, you should consider what to do to it to make it more attractive. Even though it may not look great, it probably is not worthwhile to paint it or redo the interior just to sell it. It is unlikely that you'll get your money out of such a renovation. Besides, the new owner can get it painted in a preferred color scheme—maybe put on a custom N number. And, assuming your bird is free of corrosion, it's easier to point this out on an old paint job than on a brand-new one. You can generally expect to get back 50 to 75 percent of the value of extras in the airplane. If you just spent $8,000 to put a turbocharger in, expect to get maybe $6,000 for it. If the airplane is *over*equipped, you'll probably only get 50 percent or even less for the extras. For example, a DME, RNAV-equipped Cherokee 140 will not sell for much more than one with just a simple nav/comm. If you have super radios that work very well and cost a lot of money, consider taking them out to put in your new airplane. But then you'll be selling an airplane with a bunch of holes in it, so you won't get quite so much as with a fairly standard avionics package. You're probably better off just leaving the avionics in the bird.

If you are wondering whether to fix it up to sell it, you could try getting two prices from two dealers. Tell one that you have what you've got— needs paint, needs interior work or new glass, or whatever. Then tell another one that you've got a real cream-puff. New paint, fresh annual, new glass, and so on. Compare the two prices and find the difference. Let's say the difference is $2,000. Can you bring it from dog to cream-puff status for less than $2,000? If you can, it might be worth doing so. If you can't, forget it. Needless to say, however, the aircraft should be as clean and shiny as you can make it.

Recapture Problems

As has been suggested in the *Funding It* section, one consequence of selling your aircraft can be a rather unpleasant and sudden increase in your taxable income. This is brought about if you have been depreciating the aircraft like mad every year on your tax return, while the aircraft has quietly been ignoring this procedure and staying quite valuable.

Let's look at an example. Suppose you paid $100,000 for an aircraft six years ago, and you have depreciated it on the double-declining balance method. Using the old tax laws, which would have applied at the time, you could have taken a bonus depreciation of 20 percent of the first $10,000 of its cost. If you filed a joint return, you could have taken $4,000. This left a cost basis of $96,000. Depreciating the aircraft over six years, here's how the ending value would have looked each year:

Year	Starting Value	Depreciation	Ending Value
1	$96,000	$32,000	$64,000
2	64,000	21,333	42,667
3	42,667	14,222	28,445
4	28,445	9,482	18,963
5	18,963	6,321	12,642
6	12,642	4,214	8,428

All over the country you'll see airplanes with "For Sale" signs on them. You can even buy special banners to put on your prop that say "For Sale."

So you have a book value of $8,428. If you sell the aircraft for that amount, you're in great shape. However, it would be un-American to sell it for less than what it is worth, and, inflation and replacement costs being what they are (see table on page 31), the cost of a new aircraft of the same type is probably now $250,000, and you can no doubt get $82,000 for your six-year-old airplane—assuming it hasn't had a sudden rash of ADs or nasty accidents to give it a bad name.

If you sell an airplane for $82,000 that is on the books at $8,428, you must add the difference to your income as a long-term capital gain—a chunk of $73,572—even though you actually lost $18,000 from what you paid for the airplane.

This disaster can be averted if you simply put the proceeds into another airplane. But at the same time, you have to change the cost basis of the new airplane to reflect this move. Say you bought a $250,000 airplane, using the $82,000 as a down payment. Your adjusted cost basis for the new airplane must be reduced by the "unrecovered recapture"—meaning that you can only show the new airplane on the books as being worth $176,428 up front. This is the "adjusted cost basis" for the new airplane, and it is on this that you must calculate your new depreciation schedule. Meanwhile, you can take the full investment tax credit on the $250,000.

This process neatly defers tax liability, and will do so indefinitely, as long as you keep rolling one airplane over into another one. And if you still own an airplane when you leave this earthly pale, disposition of the aircraft after death is not a taxable event.

A possible other alternative to disposing of the airplane and avoiding tax liability is to donate it to a worthy cause. Ask your tax advisor how much you should deduct for this charitable act—it's too complicated for me to figure out!

The bad news

There are several Damoclean swords that hang over all airplane owners. One is the unexpected-engine-overhaul sword. This particularly sharp jab, aimed directly at your wallet, can appear without warning. There you are, happy with your craft, flying through the air with the greatest of ease—and suddenly it coughs. You don't like the sound of it and put it down at the earliest opportunity.

Close inspection indicates a new engine is needed—or at least a rebuild. And you thought you still had 600 hours to TBO! This event has a tendency to depreciate the value of your investment without warning, a risk we all must take.

Another sword—and this one can be even sharper and more unpleasant—is the unexpected-AD model. How would you like to be the proud owner

Plane profile 32: Mooney 201 M20J

Seats	4
Cruise speed, 65% power, 8,000 feet	157 knots
Range, 65% power, full optional fuel, 8,000 feet	879 nm
Maximum endurance	6.6 hours
Gross weight	2,740 pounds
Empty weight	1,671 pounds
Full optional fuel	384 pounds
	64 gallons
Useful load, full fuel	658 pounds
Fuel efficiency, 65% power, 18,000 feet	16.8 nmpg
Stall speed, gear and flaps down	55 knots
Rate of climb, sea level	1,030 fpm
Minimum field length	1,610 feet
Engine type Lycoming IO-360-A3B6D	200 hp
Engine TBO	1,800 hours

of an airplane, and suddenly find that, before every flight, you must remove the cowlings and check for fuel leaks? Or that every ten hours you must remove the wing fillets and inspect for cracks on the spar? Or that *before further flight* you must change the propeller? Or that, within the next 100 hours, you must install a spar-reinforcing strap that costs $2,500 and forty hours of labor to do? These kinds of events, which appear without warning, can serve to reduce the value of your airplane instantly. CBS' *60 Minutes* runs a story suggesting the V-tail Bonanza breaks up very often, compared to the straight-tail model—and bang! There goes $15,000 or more off your value.

Rumors have a tendency to cut airplane values to pieces. The Twin Comanche got a reputation as a killer because people kept spinning them into the ground during training flights. In fact, the problem was related to exercises that the FAA used to require for multi-engine training (you would never encounter them outside of training) and a lot of good pilots were written off. The need for the exercises was eliminated (they demonstrated single-engine handling at speeds close to the stall), placards were placed in the airplane prohibiting the very thing that had been called for, and the airplane became safe again.

Remember the early days of the Boeing 727—now the most popular airliner, and probably the finest, in the world? There was an early rash of 727 drop-in accidents. The problem was that the airplane developed an enormous sink rate if certain flap and power settings were used. Procedures were changed—and suddenly no

more accidents of this type. Yet for a while many people refused to fly in a 727!

The TBO excuse

Many people sell their airplanes because the engine needs overhauling. As you know by now, the engine *time between overhauls* (TBO) is a suggested figure which you may or may not exceed, depending on how the engine behaves at compression-check and oil-analysis time. But one day, even though you have changed the oil religiously, and babied the engine always, it just won't cut it at check-up time, and a decision has to be made—to "re" or not to "re." These days, it costs a ton of money to overhaul an engine—anywhere from $5,000 to $20,000 or more, depending on its size and number of cylinders. A factory-rebuilt engine to zero-time specs can cost about 75 percent of the price of a new engine. Majoring it can cost about 50 percent. And if you decide to have *your* engine rebuilt, the airplane can be down for a month or more while the job is done.

If the airplane was beginning to grate on your nerves a bit, and the radios were getting scratchy, coming up to the TBO can be a good excuse for trading your bird. Needless to say, a high-time engine will seriously affect the price you can get. *Aircraft Price Digest* suggests the dealer use half the engine-overhaul cost to either increase or reduce the airplane's value when appraising it. For example, a 1977 Cessna Skylane's worth averages about $34,000 right now. It might cost $12,500 to replace its engine with a

new one, or $7,000 with a rebuilt one, or $5,500 to simply rebuild. Let's say your airplane is reduced to $31,000 because of its high-time engine. One with a low-time engine might cost you $37,000. Which is better—to replace your own engine, rebuild, or buy another airplane? You need to evaluate all the alternatives, factoring in time and convenience, possible ITC-recaptures, your awareness and comfort-level with your own airplane, as well as the relative costs of replacing the engine or the airplane.

What to do in a soft market

Suppose you no longer need your airplane, it is costing you too much to own, store, insure and maintain, you want to get rid of it, and the market is shot to hell—nobody's buying. What can you do?

If you can afford it, and the airplane is sound, one solution is to put it in dead storage for a while. You can get space in a hanger at an off-the-beaten-track airport for peanuts—about $30 a month. You can work a deal with your insurance company to protect your investment against ground perils, but eliminate any flying risks. You put the airplane into long-term storage, the sort of thing the air force does at Davis Monthan Air Base in Arizona. Ask a mechanic for advice on what to do to protect your airplane against the elements. Maybe, soon, things will turn up, and you'll be glad you hung in there!

Appendix

Addresses the aircraft owner needs

Government agencies

Civil Aeronautics Board,
1825 Connecticut Avenue NW,
Washington, D.C. 20428

Department of Commerce,
Commerce Building,
Washington, D.C. 20230

Department of Defense,
The Pentagon,
Washington, D.C. 20301

Department of Transportation,
400 Seventh Ave. SW,
Washington, D.C. 20590

Environmental Protection Agency,
401 M St. SW,
Washington, D.C. 20460

Federal Aviation Administration (DOT)
800 Independence Avenue SW,
Washington, D.C. 20591

FAA Aeronautical Center,
Box 25082,
Oklahoma City, Okla. 73125

Federal Communication Commission,
1919 M Street NW,
Washington, D.C. 20554

Federal Communications Commission,
Box 1030 (aircraft radio-station licenses).
Box 1050 (aircraft radio operators' licenses),
Gettysburg, Pa., 17325

Government Printing Office,
Superintendent of Documents,
Washington, D.C. 20401

National Aeronautics and Space Administration,
Fourth and Maryland Avenue SW,
Washington, D.C. 20546

National Air and Space Museum,
Smithsonian Institution,
Washington, D.C. 20560

National Ocean Survey,
NOAA,
Riverdale, Maryland, 20840

National Transportation Safety Board,
800 Independence Ave. SW,
Washington, D.C. 20594

National Weather Service,
NOAA, Gramax Building,
8060 13th St.,
Silver Spring, Md. 20910

U.S. Customs Service,
1301 Constitution Avenue NW,
Washington, D.C. 20229

State aviation agencies

Alabama Dept. of Aeronautics,
Room 627, State Highway Building,
11 S. Union St.,
Montgomery, Ala. 36130

Alaska Division of Aviation,
Dept. of Public Works,
4111 Aviation Avenue, Pouch 6900,
Anchorage, Alaska 99502

Arizona Dept. of Transportation,
Aeronautics Div.,
205 S 17th Ave.,
Phoenix, Ariz. 85007

Arkansas Division of Aeronautics,
Adams Field, Old Terminal Building,
Little Rock, Ark. 72202

California Division of Aeronautics,
1120 N Street,
Sacramento, Calif. 95814

[Colorado does not have an aviation agency]

Connecticut Bureau of Aeronautics,
DOT,
Drawer A,
Wethersfield, Conn. 06109

Delaware Div. of Transportation,
Aeronautics Section,
Box 778, Dover, Del. 19901

Florida Aviation Bureau, DOT,
605 Suwanee St.
Tallahassee, Fla. 32304

Georgia Bureau of Aeronautics, DOT,
5025 New Peachtree Rd. NE,
Chamblee, GA 30341

Hawaii State Dept. of Transportation,
Honolulu International Airport,
Honolulu, Hawaii 97819

Idaho Division of Aeronautics,
3483 Rickenbacker St.,
Boise, Idaho 83705

Illinois Division of Aeronautics,
Capital Airport,
Springfield, Ill. 62706

Indiana Aeronautics Commission,
100 N. Senate Ave.,
Indianapolis, Ind. 46204

Iowa Aeronautics Division, DOT
State House,
Des Moines, Iowa 50319

Kansas Aviation Division, DOT,
State Office Building
Topeka, Kansas 66612

Kentucky Division of Aeronautics,
DOT,
419 Ann Street,
Frankfort, Ky. 40601

Louisiana State Aviation Division,
DPW,
Box 44245, Capital Station,
Baton Rouge, La. 70804

Maine Bureau of Aeronautics, DOT,
State Office Building
Augusta, Me. 04330

Appendix

Maryland State Aviation Administration, DOT,
Box 8766,
Baltimore, Md. 21240

Massachusetts Aeronautics Commission,
Boston-Logan Airport,
East Boston, Mass. 02128

Michigan Aeronautics Commission,
Capital City Airport,
Lansing, Mich. 48906

Minnesota Department of Aeronautics,
Box 417,
St. Paul, Minn. 55155

Mississippi Aeronautics Commission,
Box 5,
Jackson, Miss. 39205

Missouri Dept. of Transportation,
Aviation Section,
Box 1250,
Jefferson City, Mo. 65101

Montana Board of Aeronautics,
Box 5178,
Helena, Mont. 59601

Nebraska Dept. of Aeronautics,
Box 82088,
Lincoln, Neb. 68501

[Nevada does not have an aviation agency]

New Hampshire Aeronautics Commission,
Municipal Airport,
Concord, N.H. 03301

New Jersey Division of Aeronautics, DOT,
1035 Parkway Avenue,
Trenton, N.J. 08625

New Mexico Aviation Department,
Box 579
Santa Fe, N.M. 87503

New York State, DOT,
1220 Washington Avenue,
Albany, N.Y. 12232

North Carolina Division of Aeronautics, DOT,
Box 25201,
Raleigh, N.C. 27611

North Dakota Aeronautics Commission,
Box U, Municipal Airport,
Bismarck, N.D. 58501

Ohio Division of Aviation, DOT,
2829 West Granville Road,
Worthington, Ohio 43085

Oklahoma Aeronautics Commission,
424 United Founders Tower Building;
Okahoma City, Okla. 73112

Oregon Aeronautics Division, State DOT,
3040 25th St. SE,
Salem, Oregon 97310

Pennsylvania Bureau of Aviation, DOT,
Capital City Airport,
New Cumberland, Pa. 17070

Puerto Rico Ports Authority, Aviation Dept.,
Box 2829,
San Juan, P.R. 00936

Rhode Island DOT, Airports Division,
T. F. Green State Airport,
Warwick, R.I. 02886

South Carolina Aeronautics Commission,
Box 1769,
Columbia, S.C. 29202

South Dakota Division of Aeronautics, DOT,
Pierre, S.D. 57501

Tennessee Bureau of Aeronautics, DOT,
Box 17326,
Nashville, Tenn. 37217

Texas Aeronautics Commission,
Box 12607,
Austin, Texas 78711

Utah Division of Aeronautical Operations, DOT,
135 N. 2400 W,
Salt Lake City, Utah 84116

Vermont Department of Aeronautics,
133 State Street,
Montpelier, Vt. 05602

Virginia Division of Aeronautics,
Box 7716,
Richmond, Va. 23231

Washington State Aeronautics Commisson,
8600 Perimeter Road,
Boeing Field,
Seattle, Wash. 98108

West Virginia State Aeronautics Commission,
Kanawha Airport,
Charleston, W.V. 25311

Wisconsin Division of Aeronautics, DOT,
Box 7914,
Madison, Wis. 53707

Wyoming Aeronautics Commission,
Cheyenne, Wyo. 82002

Aircraft manufacturers

Beech Aircraft Corp.,
9709 East Central,
Wichita, Kansas 67201

Cessna Aircraft Co.,
Box 1521,
Wichita,Kansas, 67201

Great Lakes Aircraft, Inc.,
Box 3526,
Enid, Oklahoma 73701

Gulfstream American Aviation, Corp.,
Box 2206,

Lake Aircraft,
Box 399,
Tomball, Texas 77375

Maule Aircraft Corp.,
Spence Air Base,
Moultrie, Georgia 31768

Mooney Aircraft Corp.,
Box 72,
Kerrville, Texas 78028

Piper Aircraft Corp.,
Lock Haven, Pa. 17745

Pitts Aviation Enterprises, Inc.,
Box 548,
Homestead, Fla. 33030

Taylorcraft Aviation Corp.,
Box 243,
Alliance, Ohio 44601

Wing Aircraft Co.,
2925 Columbia Street,
Torrance, CA 90503

Avionics manufacturers

Bendix Avionics Division,
Box 9414,
Fort Lauderdale, Fla. 33310

Bonzer, Inc.,
90th & Cody,
Overland Park,
Kansas 66214

Cessna Aircraft Co.,
Aircraft Radio and Control Division,
Rockaway Valley Road,
Boonton, N.J. 07005

Collins Avionics Division,
Rockwell International,
Cedar Rapids, Iowa 52406

Davtron, Inc.,
427 Hillcrest Way,
Redwood City, CA. 94062

Edo-Aire.
Box 610,
Mineral Wells, TX 76067

Foster Airdata Systems, Inc.,
7020 Huntley Road,
Columbus, Ohio 43229

General Aviation Electronics, Inc.,
4141 Kingman Drive,
Indianapolis, Ind. 46226

King Radio Corp.,
400 North Rogers Road,
Olathe, Kansas 66061

Narco Avionics,
Commerce Drive,
Fort Washington, Pa. 19034

PanTronics Corp.,
Box 22430,
Fort Lauderdale, Fla. 33316

Radair Division,
Dynair Electronics, Inc.,
6360 Federal Blvd.,
San Diego, Ca. 92114

RCA Avionics Systems,
8500 Balboa Blvd.,
Van Nuys, Ca. 01409

Ryan Stormscope,
4800 Evanswood Drive,
Columbus, Ohio 43229

Sunair Electronics,
3101 SW 3rd Avenue,
Fort Lauderdale, Fla. 33315

Wulfsberg Electronics, Inc.,
11300 West 89th Street,
Overland Park, Kansas 66214

Engine manufacturers

Avco Lycoming Engine Group,
652 Oliver Street,
Williamsport, Pa. 17701

Page Industries of Okla. Inc.,
Box 191,
Yukon, Okla. 73099

Teledyne Continental Motors,
Box 90,
Mobile, Ala. 36601

Aviation organizations

Aerobatic Club of America,
Box 401,
Roanoke, Texas, 76262

Aircraft Owners and Pilots Association,
421 Aviation Way
Frederick, MD 21701

American Aviation Historical Society,
Box 99,
Garden Grove, CA. 92642

American Bonanza Society,
Box 3749,
Reading Municipal Airport,
Reading, PA 19605

American Navion Society,
Box 1175,
Municipal Airport,
Banning, Ca. 92220

Antique Airplane Association,
Box 172, Route 2,
Ottumwa, IA 52501

Canadian Owners & Pilots Association,
Box 734,
Station B,
Ottawa, Ont. K1P 5S4, Canada

Cessna Skyhawk Association
Box 779,
Delray Beach, Fla. 33444

Cessna Skylane Association
Box 779,
Delray Beach, Fla. 33444

Cessna 120-140 Association,
Box 92,
Richardson, TX 75080

Cessna 150/152 Club,
Box 15388
Durham, NC 27704

Cessna 190-195 Owners Association,
Box 952,
Sioux Falls, ND 57101

Cherokee Pilots Association
Box 7636,
Tampa, FL 33673

Civil Air Patrol,
Maxwell Air Force Base,
Ala. 36112

The Continental Luscombe Association,
5736 Esmar Road,
Ceres, Calif. 95307

Appendix

Experimental Aircraft Association,
Box 229, Hales Corners, Wis. 53130

Flight Safety Foundation, Inc.,
1800 North Kent Street,
Arlington, Va. 22209

Flying Architects Association,
203 St. Paul Federal Building,
8th and Cedar St.,
St. Paul, Minn. 55101

Flying Chiropractors Association,
215 Belmont Street,
Johnstown, Pa. 15904

Flying Dentists Association,
5410 Wilshire Blvd.,
Los Angeles, Ca. 90036

Flying Engineers International,
Box 387,
Winnebago, Ill. 61088

Flying Funeral Directors of America,
10980 Reading Road,
Sharonville, Ohio 45241

Flying Funeral Directors of America,
811 Grant Street,
Akron, Ohio, 44311

Flying Veterinarians Association,
10519 Reading Road,
Cincinnati, Ohio 45241

General Aviation Manufacturers Association (GAMA),
Suite 517,
1025 Connecticut Avenue, NW,
Washington, D.C. 20036

International Aerobatic Club (div of EAA),
Box 229,
Hales Corners, Wis. 53130

International Aviation Theft Bureau,
7315 Wisconsin Avenue,
Bethesda, Md. 20014

International Cessna 170 Association,
Montezuma Airport,
Box 460,
Camp Verde, AZ 86322

International Comanche Society, Inc.,
Box 468,
Lyons, KS 67554

International Flying Bankers Association,
Box 11187,
Columbia, S.C. 29211

International Flying Farmers,
Mid Continent Airport,
Box 9124,
Wichita, Kans. 67277

International Swift Association,
Box 644,
Athens, Tenn. 37303

Lawyer-Pilots Bar Association,
Box 427,
Alhambra, Ca. 91802

National Aeronautic Association,
Suite 610, 806 15th Street NW,
Washington, D.C. 20005

National Association of Flight Instructors,
Ohio State University Airport,
Box 20204,
Columbus, Ohio 43220

National Association of Priest Pilots,
5157 South California Avenue,
Chicago, Ill. 60632

National Business Aircraft Association,
One Farragut Sq. South,
Washington, D.C. 20006

National Intercollegiate Flying Association,
Parks College, St. Louis University,
Cahokia, Ill. 62206

National Police Pilots Association,
Box 45,
Shenorock, N.Y. 10587

National Real Estate Fliers Association,
Box 6200 E,
Norfolk, Va. 23502

The Ninety-Nines Inc.,
Box 59965,
Will Rogers World Airport,
Oklahoma City, Okla. 73159

Pilots International Association,
Suite 500, 400 S. County Rd. 18,
Minneapolis, Minn. 55426

Professional Aviation Maintenance Association,
Box 12449,
Greater Pittsburgh International Airport,
Pittsburgh, Pa. 15231

Real Estate Aviation Council,
Box 6200 E,
Virginia Beach, Va. 23462

Seaplane Pilots Association,
Box 30091,
Washington, D.C. 20014

The Soaring Society of America, Inc.,
Box 66071,
Los Angeles, Calif. 90066

Taildragger Pilots Association,
Box 161079,
Memphis, Tenn. 38116

TriPacer Owners Club
353 Nassau Street,
Princeton, NJ 08540

Index

Index

Index

B

Note: **bold face** page numbers denote illustrations

Index

C

Note: **bold face** page numbers denote illustrations

Index

D

Note: **bold face** page numbers denote illustrations

Index

Note: **bold face** page numbers denote illustrations

Index

F

Note: **bold face** page numbers denote illustrations

Index

Index

Index

Note: **bold face** page numbers denote illustrations

Index

J

Note: **bold face** page numbers denote illustrations

Index

Note: **bold face** page numbers denote
illustrations

Index

Index

Index

Note: **bold face** page numbers denote illustrations

Index

O

Note: **bold face** page numbers denote illustrations

Index

Index

Note: **bold face** page numbers denote
illustrations

Index

Note: **bold face** page numbers denote illustrations

S

Note: **bold face** page numbers denote illustrations

Index

T

Note: **bold face** page numbers denote illustrations

Index

U

UHF equipment, 207
U.S. Code, Title 18, 44
U.S. Paint Co., Alumigrip, 166
U.S. Seaplane Pilot's Assn., 26
Unicom, 204
Univair Aircraft Corp., 144
Used aircraft
    Advertisements, 81
    Buying checklist, 83-84
    Price guide, 79-80
    Purchasing, 37, 38
    Sources, 80-81
    Trade-in, 75
Used Aircraft Price Guide, 79
Utah Dept. of Aeronautical
    Operations, address, 224
Utility use of aircraft, 30, 162
Utilization factors, 8, 11, 30
    Basic Annual Utilization Chart, 55
    Insurance, affect on, 101
    Repetitive trips, 50-51
    Total Annual Utilization Chart, 56

V

Index

Note: **bold face** page numbers denote illustrations